READINGS IN
INTRODUCTORY ECONOMICS

READINGS IN INTRODUCTORY ECONOMICS

JOHN R. McKEAN
RONALD A. WYKSTRA
Colorado State University

HARPER & ROW, PUBLISHERS
New York, Evanston, San Francisco, London

READINGS IN INTRODUCTORY ECONOMICS

For information address Harper & Row, Publishers, Inc., 49 East 33rd Street, New York, N.Y. 10016.

Standard Book Number: 06-044382-0

Library of Congress Catalog Card Number: 73-154881

Preface

Economics is a lively subject which is the product of both intellectual curiosity and a search for practical answers to some of the more perplexing issues encountered by mankind. Far too often students are given ample information about economic analysis, but they never fully comprehend the historical development, the problem orientation, or the policy implications of the subject. This collection of readings is designed to enrich the student's understanding of economic principles and to enliven the real-world importance of economic problems and policies.

As a subject, economics is rich in controversy and political and social viewpoints. Because it is impossible to present the full flavor and range of contrasting ideas in any basic textbook, a book of readings rounds out the necessarily condensed presentation of principles, problems, and policies discussed in a principles of economics textbook. By collecting and condensing articles and essays illustrative of the broad spectrum of economic topics, it is possible to reinforce the learning experience provided by economic analysis, as well as to emphasize the importance of economic policies.

The essays selected for this volume are organized around *Introductory Economics.* All of the readings are coordinated with the five basic parts of that book:

1. Fundamentals of Economic Systems
2. Macroeconomics: Employment, Prices, and Economic Stability
3. Microeconomics: Prices and the Allocation of Resources
4. Domestic Economic Issues
5. The International Economy

The readings begin with a biographical sketch of the author and an introduction to the selection. In addition, Guideposts for Thought While Reading are included to give the student an idea of what he might look for in each selection.

The papers presented in this collection are chosen to enlarge the student's understanding of economic principles and to emphasize current problems and policy issues. Also included are a few selected papers of classical importance which merit consideration. The topics covered are varied and sometimes controversial, and in many instances include materials which present conflicting views on issues. Although in some instances it was necessary to edit original articles, care has been taken to avoid distortion and to preserve the personality and original meaning of each selection.

Our acknowledgments to others are many; we are indebted to the authors and publishers who have graciously allowed their material to be reprinted. Special thanks are due the editorial staff of Harper & Row, and to Mrs. Sharon Allen who was meticulous in her secretarial tasks. We are indebted to many of our colleagues who brought materials to our attention.

John R. McKean
Ronald A. Wykstra

Contents

PART 3 Microeconomics: Prices and the Allocation of Resources

PART 4 Domestic Economic Issues

PART 5 The International Economy

Readings Listed by Author

PART 1
Fundamentals of Economic Systems

READING 1
The Methodology of Positive Economics
Milton Friedman

This reading by University of Chicago professor, Milton Friedman, a distinguished supporter of "conventional" price theory, is the classic statement on economic theorizing which has led to a continuing discussion among economists and scholars from other disciplines. For Friedman, the test of a theory is how well it predicts. Hence, a theory is judged on the basis of its implications rather than on its assumptions. This basic methodological tenet, if accepted, provides a crushing blow to propositions put forth by certain well-known economists. In particular, it refutes many attacks made against the neoclassical model of price theory.

Guideposts for Thought While Reading
Note carefully the logical argument which Friedman makes for discarding realism as a criterion by which to judge a theory. Why is the ability to predict purported to be a satisfactory basis for choosing among competing theories?

In his admirable book on *The Scope and Method of Political Economy* John Neville Keynes distinguishes among "a *positive science* . . . [,] a body of systematized knowledge concerning what is; a *normative* or *regulative science* . . . [,] a body of systematized knowledge discussing criteria of what ought to be . . . ; an *art* . . . [,] a system of rules for the attainment of a given end"; comments that "confusion between them is common and has been the source of many mischievous errors"; and urges the importance of "recognizing a distinct positive science of political economy."

This paper is concerned primarily with certain methodological problems that arise in constructing the "distinct positive science" Keynes called for—in particular, the problem how to decide whether a suggested hypothesis or theory should be tentatively accepted as part of the "body of systematized knowledge concerning what is." But the confusion Keynes laments is still so

Reprinted by permission of the publisher, abstracted from Milton Friedman, "The Methodology of Positive Economics," *Essays in Positive Economics*, The University of Chicago Press, Chicago, 1953, pp. 3–43.

rife and so much of a hindrance to the recognition that economics can be, and in part is, a positive science that it seems well to preface the main body of the paper with a few remarks about the relation between positive and normative economics.

I. THE RELATION BETWEEN POSITIVE AND NORMATIVE ECONOMICS

Confusion between positive and normative economics is to some extent inevitable. The subject matter of economics is regarded by almost everyone as vitally important to himself and within the range of his own experience and competence; it is the source of continuous and extensive controversy and the occasion for frequent legislation. Self-proclaimed "experts" speak with many voices and can hardly all be regarded as disinterested; in any event, on questions that matter so much, "expert" opinion could hardly be accepted solely on faith even if the "experts" were nearly unanimous and clearly disinterested. The conclusions of positive economics seem to be, and are, immediately relevant to important normative problems, to questions of what ought to be done and how any given goal can be attained. Laymen and experts alike are inevitably tempted to shape positive conclusions to fit strongly held normative preconceptions and to reject positive conclusions if their normative implications—or what are said to be their normative implications—are unpalatable.

Positive economics is in principle independent of any particular ethical position or normative judgments. As Keynes says, it deals with "what is," not with "what ought to be." Its task is to provide a system of generalizations that can be used to make correct predictions about the consequences of any change in circumstances. Its performance is to be judged by the precision, scope, and conformity with experience of the predictions it yields. In short, positive economics is, or can be, an "objective" science, in precisely the same sense as any of the physical sciences. Of course, the fact that economics deals with the interrelations of human beings, and that the investigator is himself part of the subject matter being investigated in a more intimate sense than in the physical sciences, raises special difficulties in achieving objectivity at the same time that it provides the social scientist with a class of data not available to the physical scientist. But neither the one nor the other is, in my view, a fundamental distinction between the two groups of sciences.

Normative economics and the art of economics, on the other hand, cannot be independent of positive economics. Any policy conclusion necessarily rests on a prediction about the consequences of doing one thing rather than another, a prediction that must be based—implicitly or explicitly—on positive economics. There is not, of course, a one-to-one relation between policy conclusions and the conclusions of positive economics; if there were, there would be no separate normative science. Two individuals may agree on the consequences of a particular piece of legislation. One may regard them as desirable on balance and so favor the legislation; the other, as undesirable and so oppose the legislation.

I venture the judgment, however, that currently in the Western world, and especially in the United States, differences about economic policy among disinterested citizens derive predominantly from different predictions about the economic consequences of taking action—differences that in principle can be eliminated by the progress of positive economics—rather than from fundamental differences in basic values, differences about which men can ultimately only fight. An obvious and not unimportant example is minimum-wage legislation. Underneath the welter of arguments offered for and against such legislation there is an underlying consensus on the objective of achieving a "living wage" for all, to use the ambiguous phrase so common in such discussions. The difference of opinion is largely grounded on an implicit or explicit difference in predictions about the efficacy of this particular means in furthering the agreed-on end. Proponents believe (predict) that legal minimum wages diminish poverty by raising the wages of those receiving less than the minimum wage as well as of some receiving more than the minimum wage without any counterbalancing increase in the number of people entirely unemployed or employed less advantageously than they otherwise would be. Opponents believe (predict) that legal minimum wages increase poverty by increasing the number of people who are unemployed or employed less advantageously and that this more than offsets any favorable effect on the wages of those who remain employed. Agreement about the economic consequences of the legislation might not produce complete agreement about its desirability, for differences might still remain about its political or social consequences; but, given agreement on objectives, it would certainly go a long way toward producing consensus.

Closely related differences in positive analysis underlie divergent views about the appropriate role and place of trade-unions and the desirability of direct price and wage controls and of tariffs. Different predictions about the importance of so-called "economies of scale" account very largely for divergent views about the desirability or necessity of detailed government regulation of industry and even of socialism rather than private enterprise. And this list could be extended indefinitely. Of course, my judgment that the major differences about economic policy in the Western world are of this kind is itself a "positive" statement to be accepted or rejected on the basis of empirical evidence.

If this judgment is valid, it means that a consensus on "correct" economic policy depends much less on the progress of normative economics proper than on the progress of a positive economics yielding conclusions that are, and deserve to be, widely accepted. It means also that a major reason for distinguishing positive economics sharply from normative economics is precisely the contribution that can thereby be made to agreement about policy.

II. POSITIVE ECONOMICS

The ultimate goal of a positive science is the development of a "theory" or "hypothesis" that yields valid and meaningful (i.e., not truistic) predictions about phenomena not yet observed. Such a theory is, in general, a complex intermixture of two elements. In part, it is a "language" designed to promote "systematic and organized methods of reasoning." In part, it is a body of substantive hypotheses designed to abstract essential features of complex reality.

Viewed as a language, theory has no substantive content; it is a set of tautologies. Its function is to serve as a filing system for organizing empirical material and facilitating our understanding of it; and the criteria by which it is to be judged are those appropriate to a filing system. Are the categories clearly and precisely defined? Are they exhaustive? Do we know where to file each individual item, or is there considerable ambiguity? Is the system of headings and subheadings so designed that we can quickly find an item we want, or must we hunt from place to place? Are the items we shall want to consider jointly filed together? Does the filing system avoid elaborate cross-references?

The answers to these questions depend partly on logical, partly on factual, considerations. The canons of formal logic alone can show whether a particular language is complete and consistent, that is, whether propositions in the language are "right" or "wrong." Factual evidence alone can show whether the categories of the "analytical filing system" have a meaningful empirical counterpart, that is, whether they are useful in analyzing a particular class of concrete problems. The simple example of "supply" and "demand" illustrates both this point and the preceding list of analogical questions. Viewed as elements of the language of economic theory, these are the two major categories into which factors affecting the relative prices of products or factors of production are classified. The usefulness of the dichotomy depends on the "empirical generalization that an enumeration of the forces affecting demand in any problem and of the forces affecting supply will yield two lists that contain few items in common." Now this generalization is valid for markets like the final market for a consumer good. In such a market there is a clear and sharp distinction between the economic units that can be regarded as demanding the product and those that can be regarded as supplying it. There is seldom much doubt whether a particular factor should be classified as affecting supply, on the one hand, or demand, on the other; and there is seldom much necessity for considering cross-effects (cross-references) between the two categories. In these cases the simple and even obvious step of filing the relevant factors under the headings of "supply" and "demand" effects a great simplification of the problem and is an effective safeguard against fallacies that otherwise tend to occur. But the generalization is not always valid. For example, it is not valid for the day-to-day fluctuations of prices in a primarily speculative market. Is a rumor of an increased excess-profits tax, for example, to be regarded as a factor operating primarily on today's supply of corporate equities in the stock market or on today's demand for them? In similar fashion, almost every factor can with about as much justification be classified under the heading "supply" as under the heading "demand." These concepts can still be used and may not be entirely pointless; they are still "right" but clearly less useful than in the first example because they have no meaningful empirical counterpart.

Viewed as a body of substantive hypotheses, theory is to be judged by its predictive power for the class of phenomena which it is intended to "explain." Only factual evidence can show whether it is "right" or "wrong" or, better, tentatively "accepted" as valid or "rejected." As I shall argue at greater length below, the only relevant test of the *validity* of a hypothesis is comparison of its predictions with experience. The hypothesis is rejected if its predictions are contradicted ("frequently" or more often than predictions from an alternative hypothesis); it is accepted if its predictions are not contradicted; great confidence is attached to it if it has survived many opportunities for contradiction. Factual evidence can never "prove" a hypothesis; it can only fail to disprove it, which is what we generally mean when we say, somewhat inexactly, that the hypothesis has been "confirmed" by experience.

To avoid confusion, it should perhaps be noted explicitly that the "predictions" by which the validity of a hypothesis is tested need not be about phenomena that have not yet occurred, that is, need not be forecasts of future events; they may be about phenomena that have occurred but observations on which have not yet been made or are not known to the person making the prediction. For example, a hypothesis may imply that such and such must have happened in 1906, given some other known circumstances. If a search of the records reveals that such and such did happen, the prediction is confirmed; if it reveals that such and such did not happen, the prediction is contradicted.

The validity of a hypothesis in this sense is not by itself a sufficient criterion for choosing among alternative hypotheses. Observed facts are necessarily finite in number; possible hypotheses, infinite. If there is one hypothesis that is consistent with the available evidence, there are always an infinite number that are. For example, suppose a specific excise tax on a particular commodity produces a rise in price equal to the amount of the tax. This is consistent with competitive conditions, a stable demand curve, and a horizontal and stable supply curve. But it is also consistent with competitive conditions and a positively or negatively sloping supply curve with the required compensating shift in the demand curve or the supply curve; with monopolistic conditions, constant marginal costs, and stable demand curve, of the particular shape required to produce this result; and so on indefinitely. Additional evidence with which the hypothesis is to be consistent may rule out some of these possibilities; it can never reduce them to a single possibility alone capable of being consistent with the finite evidence. The choice among alternative hypotheses equally consistent with the available evidence must to some extent be arbitrary, though there is general agreement that relevant considerations are suggested by the criteria "simplicity" and "fruitfulness," themselves notions that defy completely objective specification. A theory is "simpler" the less the initial knowledge needed to make a prediction within a given field of phenomena; it is more "fruitful" the more precise the resulting prediction, the wider the area within which the theory yields predictions, and the more additional lines for further research it suggests. Logical completeness and consistency are relevant but play a subsidiary role; their function is to assure that the hypothesis says what it is intended to say and does so alike for all users—they play the same role here as checks for arithmetical accuracy do in statistical computations.

Unfortunately, we can seldom test particular predictions in the social sciences by experiments explicitly designed to eliminate what are judged to be the most important disturbing influences. Generally, we must rely on evidence cast up by the "experiments" that happen to occur. The inability to conduct so-called "controlled experiments" does not, in my view, reflect a basic difference between the social and physical sciences both because it is not peculiar to the social sciences—witness astronomy—and because the distinction between a controlled experiment and uncontrolled experience is at best one of degree. No experiment can be completely controlled, and every experience is partly controlled, in the sense that some disturbing influences are relatively constant in the course of it.

Evidence cast up by experience is abundant and frequently as conclusive as that from contrived experiments; thus the inability to conduct experiments is not a fundamental obstacle to testing hypotheses by the success of their predictions. But such evidence is far more difficult to interpret. It is frequently complex and always indirect and incomplete. Its collection is often arduous, and its interpretation generally requires subtle analysis and involved chains of reasoning, which seldom carry real conviction. The denial to economics of the dramatic and direct evidence of the "crucial" experiment does hinder the adequate testing of hypotheses; but this is much less significant than the difficulty it places in the way of achieving a reasonably prompt and wide consensus on the conclusions justified by the available evidence. It renders the weeding-out of unsuccessful hypotheses slow and difficult. They are seldom downed for good and are always cropping up again.

One effect of the difficulty of testing substantive economic hypotheses has been to foster a retreat into purely formal or tautological analysis. As already noted, tautologies have an extremely important place in economics and other sciences as a specialized language or "analytical filing system." Beyond this, formal logic and mathematics, which are both tautologies, are essential aids in checking the correctness of reasoning, discovering the implications of hypotheses, and determining whether supposedly different hypotheses may not really be equivalent or wherein the differences lie.

But economic theory must be more than a structure of tautologies if it is to be able to predict and not merely describe the consequences of action; if it is to be something different from disguised mathematics. And the usefulness of the tautologies themselves ultimately depends, as noted above, on the acceptability of the substantive hypotheses that suggest the particular categories into which they organize the refractory empirical phenomena.

A more serious effect of the difficulty of testing economic hypotheses by their predictions is to foster misunderstanding of the role of empirical evidence in theoretical work. Empirical evidence is vital at two different, though closely related, stages: in constructing hypotheses and in testing their validity. Full and comprehensive evidence on the phenomena to be generalized or "explained" by a hypothesis, besides its obvious value in suggesting new hypotheses, is needed to assure that a hypothesis explains what it sets out to explain—that its implications for such phenomena are not contradicted in advance by experience that has already been observed. Given that the hypothesis is consistent with the evidence at hand, its further testing involves deducing from it new facts capable of being observed but not previously known and checking these deduced facts against additional empirical evidence. For this test to be relevant, the deduced facts must be about the class of phenomena the hypothesis is designed to explain; and they must be well enough defined so that observation can show them to be wrong.

The two stages of constructing hypotheses and testing their validity are related in two different respects. In the first place, the particular facts that enter at each stage are partly an accident of the collection of data and the knowledge of the particular investigator. The facts that serve as a test of the implications of a hypothesis might equally well have been among the raw material used to construct it, and conversely. In the second place, the process never begins from scratch; the so-called "initial stage" itself always involves comparison of the implications of an earlier set of hypotheses with observation; the contradiction of these implications is the stimulus to the construction of new hypotheses or revision of old ones. So the two methodologically distinct stages are always proceeding jointly.

Misunderstanding about this apparently straightforward process centers on the phrase "the class of phenomena the hypothesis is designed to explain." The difficulty in the social sciences of getting new evidence for this class of phenomena and of judging its conformity with the implications of the hypothesis makes it tempting to suppose that other, more readily available, evidence is equally relevant to the validity of the hypothesis—to suppose that hypotheses have not only "implications" but also "assumptions" and that the conformity of these "assumptions" to "reality" is a test of the validity of the hypothesis *different from* or *additional to* the test by implications. This widely held view is fundamentally wrong and productive of much mischief. Far from providing an easier means for sifting valid from invalid hypotheses, it only confuses the issue, promotes misunderstanding about the significance of empirical evidence for economic theory, produces a misdirection of much intellectual effort devoted to the development of positive economics, and impedes the attainment of consensus on tentative hypotheses in positive economics.

In so far as a theory can be said to have "assumptions" at all, and in so far as their "realism" can be judged independently of the validity of predictions, the relation between the significance of a theory and the "realism" of its "assumptions" is almost the opposite of that suggested by the view under criticism. Truly important and significant hypotheses will be found to have "assumptions" that are wildly inaccurate descriptive representations of reality, and, in general, the more significant the theory, the more unrealistic the assumptions (in this sense). The reason is simple. A hypothesis is important if it "explains" much by little, that is, if it abstracts the common and crucial elements from the mass of complex and detailed circumstances surrounding the phenomena to be explained and permits valid predictions on the basis of them alone. To be important, therefore, a hypothesis must be descriptively false in its assumptions; it takes account of, and accounts for, none of the many other attendant circumstances, since its very success shows them to be irrelevant for the phenomena to be explained.

To put this point less paradoxically, the relevant question to ask about the "assumptions" of a theory is not whether they are descriptively "realistic," for they never are, but whether they are sufficiently good approximations for the purpose in hand. And this question can be answered only by seeing whether the theory works, which means whether it yields sufficiently accurate predictions. The two supposedly independent tests thus reduce to one test.

The lengthy discussion on marginal analysis in the *American Economic Review* some years ago is an example. The articles on both sides of the controversy largely neglect what seems to me clearly the main issue—the conformity to experience of the implications of the marginal analysis—and concentrate on the largely irrelevant question whether businessmen do or do not in fact reach their decisions by consulting schedules, or curves, or multivariable functions showing marginal cost and marginal revenue.

III. THE SIGNIFICANCE AND ROLE OF THE "ASSUMPTIONS" OF A THEORY

Up to this point our conclusions about the significance of the "assumptions" of a theory have been almost entirely negative: we have seen that a theory cannot be tested by the "realism" of its "assumptions" and that the very concept of the "assumptions" of a theory is surrounded with ambiguity. But, if this were all there is to it, it would be hard to explain the extensive use of the concept and the strong tendency that we all have to speak of the assumptions of a theory and to compare the assumptions of alternative theories. There is too much smoke for there to be no fire.

In methodology, as in positive science, negative statements can generally be made with greater confidence than positive statements, so I have less confidence in the following remarks on the significance and role of "assumptions" than in the preceding remarks. So far as I can see, the "assumptions of a theory" play three different, though related, positive roles: (*a*) they are often an economical mode of describing or presenting a theory; (*b*) they sometimes facilitate an indirect test of the hypothesis by its implications; and (*c*), they are sometimes a convenient means of specifying the conditions under which the theory is expected to be valid.

IV. SOME IMPLICATIONS FOR ECONOMIC ISSUES

The abstract methodological issues we have been discussing have a direct bearing on the perennial criticism of "orthodox" economic theory as "unrealistic" as well as on the attempts that have been made to reformulate theory to meet this charge. Economics is a "dismal" science because it assumes man to be selfish and money-grubbing, "a lightning calculator of pleasures and pains, who oscillates like a homogeneous globule of desire of happiness under the impulse of stimuli that shift him about the area, but leave him intact"; it rests on outmoded psychology and must be reconstructed in line with each new development in psychology; it assumes men, or at least businessmen, to be "in a continuous state of 'alert,' ready to change prices and/or pricing rules whenever their sensitive intuitions . . . detect a change in demand and supply conditions," it assumes markets to be perfect, competition to be pure, and commodities, labor, and capital to be homogeneous.

As we have seen, criticism of this type is largely beside the point unless supplemented by evidence that a hypothesis differing in one or another of these respects from the theory being criticized yields better predictions for as wide a range of phenomena. Yet most such criticism is not so supplemented; it is based almost entirely on supposedly directly perceived discrepancies between the "assumptions" and the "real world." A particularly clear example is furnished by the recent criticisms of the maximization-of-returns hypothesis on the grounds that businessmen do not and indeed cannot behave as the theory "assumes" they do. The evidence cited to support this assertion is generally taken either from the answers given by businessmen to questions about the factors affecting their decisions—a procedure for testing economic theories that is about on a par with testing theories of longevity by asking octogenarians how they account for their long life—or from descriptive studies of the decision-making activities of individual firms. Little if any evidence is ever cited on the conformity of businessmen's actual market behavior—what they do rather than what they say they do—with the implications of the hypothesis being criticized, on the one hand, and of an alternative hypothesis, on the other.

A theory or its "assumptions" cannot possibly be thoroughly "realistic" in the immediate descriptive sense so often assigned to this term. A completely "realistic" theory of the wheat market would have to include not only the conditions directly underlying the supply and demand for wheat but also the kind of coins or credit instruments used to make exchanges; the personal characteristics of wheat-traders such as the color of each trader's hair and eyes, his antecedents and education, the number of members of his family, their characteristics, antecedents, and education, etc.; the kind of soil on which the wheat was grown, its physical and chemical characteristics, the weather prevailing during the growing season; the personal characteristics of the farmers growing the wheat and of the consumers who will ultimately use it; and so on indefinitely. Any attempt to move very far in achieving this kind of "realism" is certain to render a theory utterly useless.

Of course, the notion of a completely realistic theory is in part a straw man. No critic of a theory would accept this logical extreme as his objective; he would say that the "assumptions" of the theory being criticized were "too" unrealistic and that his objective was a set of assumptions that were "more" realistic though still not completely and slavishly so. But so long as the test of "realism" is the directly perceived descriptive accuracy of the "assumptions"—for example, the observation that "businessmen do not appear to be either as avaricious or as dynamic or as logical as marginal theory portrays them" or that "it would be utterly impractical under present conditions for the manager of a multi-process plant to attempt . . . to work out and equate marginal costs and marginal revenues for each productive factor"—there is no basis for making such a distinction, that is, for stopping short of the straw man depicted in the preceding paragraph. What is the criterion by which to judge whether a particular departure from realism is or is not acceptable? Why is it more "unrealistic" in analyzing business behavior to neglect the magnitude of businessmen's costs than the color of their eyes? The obvious answer is because the first makes more difference to business behavior than the second; but there is no way of knowing that this is so simply by observing that businessmen do have costs of different magnitudes and eyes of different color. Clearly it can only be known by comparing the effect on the discrepancy between actual and predicted behavior of taking the one factor or the other into account. Even the most extreme proponents of realistic assumptions are thus necessarily driven to reject their own criterion and to accept the test by prediction when they classify alternative assumptions as more or less realistic.

The basic confusion between descriptive accuracy and analytical relevance that underlies most criticisms of economic theory on the grounds that its assumptions are unrealistic as well as the plausibility of the views that lead to this confusion are both strikingly illustrated by a seemingly innocuous remark in an article on business-cycle theory that "economic phenomena are varied and complex, so any comprehensive theory of the business cycle that can apply closely to reality must be very complicated." A fundamental hypothesis of science is that appearances are deceptive and that there is a way of looking at or interpreting or organizing the evidence that will reveal superficially disconnected and diverse phenomena to be manifestations of a more fundamental and relatively simple structure. And the test of this hypothesis, as of any other, is its fruits—a test that science has so far met with dramatic success. If a class of "economic phenomena" appears varied and complex, it is, we must suppose, because we have no adequate theory to explain them. Known facts cannot be set on one side; a theory to apply "closely to reality," on the other. A theory is the way we perceive "facts," and we cannot perceive "facts" without a theory. Any assertion that economic phenomena *are* varied and complex denies the tentative state of knowledge that alone makes scientific activity meaningful; it is in a class with John Stuart Mill's justly ridiculed statement that "happily, there is nothing in the laws of value which remains [1848] for the present or any future writer to clear up; the theory of the subject is complete."

The confusion between descriptive accuracy and analytical relevance has led not only to criticisms of economic theory on largely irrelevant grounds but also to misunderstanding of economic theory and misdirection of efforts to repair supposed defects. "Ideal types" in the abstract model developed by economic theorists have been regarded as strictly descriptive categories intended to correspond directly and fully to entities in the real world independently of the purpose for which the model is being used. The obvious discrepancies have led to necessarily unsuccessful attempts to construct theories on the basis of categories intended to be fully descriptive.

This tendency is perhaps most clearly illustrated by the interpretation given to the concepts of "perfect competition" and "monopoly" and the development of the theory of "monopolistic" or "imperfect competition." Marshall, it is said, assumed "perfect competition"; perhaps there once was such a thing. But clearly there is no longer, and we must therefore discard his theories. The reader will search long and hard—and I predict unsuccessfully—to find in Marshall any explicit assumption about perfect competition or any assertion that in a descriptive sense the world is composed of atomistic firms engaged in perfect competition. Rather, he will find Marshall saying: "At one extreme are world markets in which competition acts directly from all parts of the globe; and at the other those secluded markets in which all direct competition from afar is shut out, though indirect and transmitted competition may make itself felt even in these; and about midway between these extremes lie the great majority of the markets which the economist and the business man have to study." Marshall took the world as it is; he sought to construct an "engine" to analyze it, not a photographic reproduction of it.

V. CONCLUSION

Economics as a positive science is a body of tentatively accepted generalizations about economic phenomena that can be used to predict the consequences of changes in circumstances. Progress in expanding this body of generalizations, strengthening our confidence in their validity, and improving the accuracy of the predictions they yield is hindered not only by the limitations of human ability that impede all search for knowledge but also by obstacles that are especially important for the social sciences in general and economics in particular, though by no means peculiar to them. Familiarity with the subject matter of economics breeds contempt for special knowledge about it. The importance of its subject matter to everyday life and to major issues of public policy impedes objectivity and promotes confusion between scientific analysis and normative judgment. The necessity of relying on uncontrolled experience rather than on controlled experiment makes it difficult to produce dramatic and clear-cut evidence to justify the acceptance of tentative hypotheses. Reliance on uncontrolled experience does not affect the fundamental methodological principle that a hypothesis can be tested only by the conformity of its implications or predictions with observable phenomena; but it does render the task of testing hypotheses more difficult and gives greater scope for confusion about the methodological principles involved. More than other scientists, social scientists need to be self-conscious about their methodology.

One confusion that has been particularly rife and has done much damage is confusion about the role of "assumptions" in economic analysis. A meaningful scientific hypothesis or theory typically asserts that certain forces are, and other forces are not, important in understanding a particular class of phenomena. It is frequently convenient to present such a hypothesis by stating that the phenomena it is desired to predict behave in the world of observation *as if* they occurred in a hypothetical and highly simplified world containing only the forces that the hypothesis asserts to be important. In general, there is more than one way to formulate such a description—more than one set of "assumptions" in terms of which the theory can be presented. The choice among such alternative assumptions is made on the grounds of the resulting economy, clarity, and precision in presenting the hypothesis; their capacity to bring indirect evidence to bear on the validity of the hypothesis by suggesting some of its implications that can be readily checked with observation or by bringing out its connection with other hypotheses dealing with related phenomena; and similar considerations.

Such a theory cannot be tested by comparing its "assumptions" directly with "reality." Indeed, there is no meaningful way in which this can be done. Complete "realism" is clearly unattainable, and the question whether a theory is realistic "enough" can be settled only by seeing whether it yields predictions that are good enough for the purpose in hand or that are better than predictions from alternative theories. Yet the belief that a theory can be tested by the realism of its assumptions independently of the accuracy of its predictions is widespread and the source of much of the perennial criticism of economic theory as unrealistic. Such criticism is largely irrelevant, and, in consequence, most attempts to reform economic theory that it has stimulated have been unsuccessful.

The irrelevance of so much criticism of economic theory does not of course imply that existing economic theory deserves any high degree of confidence. These criticisms may miss the target, yet there may be a target for criticism. In a trivial sense, of course, there obviously is. Any theory is necessarily provisional and subject to change with the advance of knowledge. To go beyond this platitude, it is necessary to be more specific about the content of "existing economic theory" and to distinguish among its different branches; some parts of economic theory clearly deserve more confidence than others. A comprehensive evaluation of the present state of positive economics, summary of the evidence bearing on its validity, and assessment of the relative confidence that each part deserves is clearly a task for a treatise or a set of treatises, if it be possible at all, not for a brief paper on methodology.

About all that is possible here is the cursory expression of a personal view. Existing relative price theory, which is designed to explain the allocation of resources among alternative ends and the division of the product among the co-operating resources and which reached almost its present form in Marshall's *Principles of Economics,* seems to me both extremely fruitful and deserving of much confidence for the kind of economic system that characterizes Western nations. Despite the appearance of considerable controversy, this is true equally of existing static monetary theory, which is designed to explain the structural or secular level of absolute prices, aggregate output, and other variables for the economy as a whole and which has had a form of the quantity theory of money as its basic core in all of its major variants from David Hume to the Cambridge School to Irving Fisher to John Maynard Keynes. The weakest and least satisfactory part of current economic theory seems to me to be in the field of monetary dynamics, which is concerned with the process of adaptation of the economy as a whole to changes in conditions and so with short-period fluctuations in aggregate activity. In this field we do not even have a theory that can appropriately be called "the" existing theory of monetary dynamics.

Of course, even in relative price and static monetary theory there is enormous room for extending the scope and improving the accuracy of existing theory. In particular, undue emphasis on the descriptive realism of "assumptions" has contributed to neglect of the critical problem of determining the limits of validity of the various hypotheses that together constitute the existing economic theory in these areas. The abstract models corresponding to these hypotheses have been elaborated in considerable detail and greatly improved in rigor and precision. Descriptive material on the characteristics of our economic system and its operations have been amassed on an unprecedented scale. This is all to the good. But, if we are to use effectively these abstract models and this descriptive material, we must have a comparable exploration of the criteria for determining what abstract model it is best to use for particular kinds of problems, what entities in the abstract model are to be identified with what observable entities, and what features of the problem or of the circumstances have the greatest effect on the accuracy of the predictions yielded by a particular model or theory.

Progress in positive economics will require not only the testing and elaboration of existing hypotheses but also the construction of new hypotheses. On this problem there is little to say on a formal level. The construction of hypotheses is a creative act of inspiration, intuition, invention; its essence is the vision of something new in familiar material. The process must be discussed in psychological, not logical, categories; studied in autobiographies and biographies, not treatises on scientific method; and promoted by maxim and example, not syllogism or theorem.

READING 2
The Substance of Economics
Alfred Marshall

The discipline of economics is hard to define, partly because many occupations require some economic knowledge and partly because economists can be found in almost every industry, as well as in government. Alfred Marshall, famous for his lucid explanation of markets through supply-demand analysis, provides a definition of economics in terms of the types of phenomena which economists study.

Guideposts for Thought While Reading

How does Marshall's definition of economics narrow the scope of the field so that not every participant in a market economy is classed as an economist?

Economics is a study of men as they live and move and think in the ordinary business of life. But it concerns itself chiefly with those motives which affect, most powerfully and most steadily, man's conduct in the business part of his life. Everyone who is worth anything carries his higher nature with him into business; and, there as elsewhere, he is influenced by his personal affections, by his conceptions of duty and his reverence for high ideals. And it is true that the best energies of the ablest inventors and organizers of improved methods and appliances are stimulated by a noble emulation more than by any love of wealth for its own sake. But, for all that, the steadiest motive to ordinary business work is the desire for the pay which is the material reward of work. The pay may be on its way to be spent selfishly or unselfishly, for noble or base ends; and here the variety of human nature comes into play. But the motive is supplied by a definite amount of money: and it is this definite and exact money measurement of the steadiest motives in business life, which has enabled economics far to outrun every other branch of the study of man.

Reprinted with permission of The Macmillan Company from *Principles of Economics* by Alfred Marshall. Published by The Macmillan Company, 1948. Permission by Macmillan and Co. Ltd.

The advantage which economics has over other branches of social science appears then to arise from the fact that its special field of work gives rather larger opportunities for exact methods than any other branch. It concerns itself chiefly with those desires, aspirations and other affections of human nature, the outward manifestations of which appear as incentives to action in such a form that the force or quantity of the incentives can be estimated and measured with some approach to accuracy; and which therefore are in some degree amenable to treatment by scientific machinery. An opening is made for the methods and the tests of science as soon as the force of a person's motives—*not* the motives themselves—can be approximately measured by the sum of money, which he will just give up in order to secure a desired satisfaction; or again by the sum which is just required to induce him to undergo a certain fatigue.

Economists study the actions of individuals, but study them in relation to social rather than individual life; and therefore concern themselves but little with personal peculiarities of temper and character. They watch carefully the conduct of a whole class of people, sometimes the whole of a nation, sometimes only those living in a certain district, more often those engaged in some particular trade at some time and place: and by the aid of statistics, or in other ways, they ascertain how much money on the average the members of the particular group, they are watching, are just willing to pay as the price of a certain thing which they desire, or how much must be offered to them to induce them to undergo a certain effort or abstinence that they dislike. The measurement of motive thus obtained is not indeed perfectly accurate; for if it were, economics would rank with the most advanced of the physical sciences; and not, as it actually does, with the least advanced.

But yet the measurement is accurate enough to enable experienced persons to forecast fairly well the extent of the results that will follow from changes in which motives of this kind are chiefly concerned. Thus, for instance, they can estimate very closely the payment that will be required to produce an adequate supply of labour of any grade, from the lowest to the highest, for a new trade which it is proposed to start in any place. When they visit a factory of a kind that they have never seen before, they can tell within a shilling or two a week what any particular worker is earning, by merely observing how far his is a skilled occupation and what strain it involves on his physical, mental and moral faculties. And they can predict with tolerable certainty what rise of price will result from a given diminution of the supply of a certain thing, and how that increased price will react on the supply.

And, starting from simple considerations of this kind, economists go on to analyse the cause which govern the local distribution of different kinds of industry, the terms on which people living in distant places exchange their goods with one another, and so on: and they can explain and predict the ways in which fluctuations of credit will affect foreign trade; or again the extent to which the burden of a tax will be shifted from those on whom it is levied, on to those for whose wants they cater; and so on.

READING 3
What Is Capital?
Eugen von Böhm-Bawerk

This excerpt from the *Positive Theory of Capital* by the Austrian economist Eugen von Böhm-Bawerk provides a classic definition and some examples of a capital resource. The economic definition of capital differs from the popular use of the word. Capital is used in economics to describe only those goods which are produced for use in production. Thus capital is an "intermediate" rather than a "final" good.

Guideposts for Thought While Reading
What is the essential distinction between consumer goods and capital goods? Why cannot economic reasoning show a priori that roundabout methods of production can be more efficient?

THE NATURE OF CAPITAL

The end and aim of all production is the making of things with which to satisfy our wants; that is to say, the making of goods for immediate consumption, or Consumption Goods. We combine our own natural powers and natural powers of the external world in such a way that, under natural law, the desired material

From Eugen von Böhm-Bawerk, *Positive Theory of Capital*, 1891.

good must come into existence. But this is a very general description indeed of the matter, and looking at it closer there comes in sight an important distinction which we have not as yet considered. It has reference to the distance which lies between the expenditure of human labour in the combined production and the appearance of the desired good. We either put forth our labour just before the goal is reached, or we, intentionally, take a roundabout way. That is to say, we may put forth our labour in such a way that it at once completes the circle of conditions necessary for the emergence of the desired good, and thus the existence of the good *immediately* follows the expenditure of the labour; or we may associate our labour first with the more remote causes of the good, with the object of obtaining, not the desired good itself, but a proximate cause of the good; which cause, again, must be associated with other suitable materials and powers, till, finally,—perhaps through a considerable number of intermediate members,—the finished good, the instrument of human satisfaction, is obtained.

SOME EXAMPLES

The nature and importance of this distinction will be best seen from a few examples; and, as these will, to a considerable extent, form a demonstration of what is really one of the most fundamental propositions in our theory, I must risk being tedious.

A peasant requires drinking water. The spring is some distance from his house. There are various ways in which he may supply his daily wants. First, he may go to the spring each time he is thirsty, and drink out of his hollowed hand. This is the most direct way; satisfaction follows immediately on exertion. But it is an inconvenient way, for our peasant has to take his way to the well as often as he is thirsty. And it is an insufficient way, for he can never collect and store any great quantity such as he requires for various other purposes. Second, he may take a log of wood, hollow it out into a kind of pail, and carry his day's supply from the spring to his cottage. The advantage is obvious, but it necessitates a roundabout way of considerable length. The man must spend, perhaps, a day in cutting out the pail; before doing so he must have felled a tree in the forest; to do this, again, he must have made an axe, and so on. But there is still a third way; instead of felling one tree he fells a number of trees, splits and hollows them, lays them end for end, and so constructs a runnel or rhone which brings a full head of water to his cottage. Here, obviously, between the expenditure of the labour and the obtaining of the water we have a very roundabout way, but, then, the result is ever so much greater. Our peasant needs no longer take his weary way from house to well with the heavy pail on his shoulder, and yet he has a constant and full supply of the freshest water at his very door.

Another example. I require stone for building a house. There is a rich vein of excellent sandstone in a neighbouring hill. How is it to be got out? First, I may work the loose stones back and forward with my bare fingers, and break off what can be broken off. This is the most direct, but also the least productive way. Second, I may take a piece of iron, make a hammer and chisel out of it, and use them on the hard stone—a roundabout way, which, of course, leads to a very much better result than the former. Third method—having a hammer and chisel I use them to drill a hole in the rock; next I turn my attention to procuring charcoal, sulphur, and nitre, and mixing them in a powder, then I pour the powder into the hole, and the explosion that follows splits the stone into convenient pieces—still more of a roundabout way, but one which, as experience shows, is as much superior to the second way in result as the second was to the first.

INDIRECT METHODS INCREASE PRODUCTIVITY

The lesson to be drawn from all these examples alike is obvious. It is that a greater result is obtained by producing goods in roundabout ways than by producing them directly. Where a good can be produced in either way, we have the fact that, by the indirect way, a greater product can be got with equal labour, or the same product with less labour. But, beyond this, the superiority of the indirect way manifests itself in being the only way in which certain goods can be obtained; if I might say so, it is so much the better that it is often the only way!

That roundabout methods lead to greater results than direct methods is one of the most important and fundamental propositions in the whole theory of production. It must be emphatically stated that the only basis of the proposition is the experience of practical life. Economic theory does not and cannot show *a priori* that it must be so; but the unanimous experience of all the technique of production says that it is so. And this is sufficient; all the more that the facts of experience which tell us this are commonplace and familiar to everybody. But *why* is it so? The economist might quite well decline to answer this question. For the fact that a greater product is obtained by methods of production that begin far back is essentially a purely technical fact, and to explain questions of technique does not fall within the economist's sphere. For instance, that tropical lands are more fruitful than the polar zone; that the alloy of which coins are made stands more wear and tear than pure metal; that a railroad is better for transport than an ordinary turnpike road;—all these are matters of fact with which the economist reckons, but which his science does not call on him to explain. But this is exactly one of those cases where, in the economist's own interest—the interest he has in limiting and defining his own task—it is exceedingly desirable to go beyond the specific economic sphere. If the sober physical truth is once made clear, political economy cannot indulge in any fancies or fictions about it; and, in such questions, political economy has never been behind in the desire and the attempt to substitute its own imaginings! Although, then, this law is already sufficiently accredited by experience, I attach particular value to explaining its cause, and, after what has been said as to the nature of production, this should not be very difficult.

In the last resort all our productive efforts amount to shiftings and combinations of matter. We must know how to bring together the right forms of matter at the right moment, in order that from those associated forces the desired result, the product wanted, may follow. But, as we saw, the natural forms of matter are often so infinitely large, often so infinitely fine, that human hands are too weak or too coarse to control them. We are as powerless to overcome the cohesion of the wall of rock when we want building stone as we are, from carbon, nitrogen, hydrogen, oxygen, phosphor, potash, etc., to put together a single grain of wheat. But there are other powers which can easily do what is denied to us, and these are the powers of nature. There are natural powers which far exceed the possibilities of human power in greatness, and there are other natural powers in the microscopic world which can make combinations that put our clumsy fingers to shame. If we can succeed in making those forces our allies in the work of production, the limits of human possibility will be infinitely extended. And this we have done.

INTERMEDIATE STEPS AS A TECHNICAL NECESSITY

The condition of our success is, that we are able to control the materials on which the power that helps us depends, more easily than the materials which are to be transformed into the desired good. Happily this condition can be very often complied with. Our weak yielding hand cannot overcome the cohesion of the rock, but the hard wedge of iron can; the wedge and the hammer to drive it we can happily master with little trouble. We cannot gather the atoms of phosphorus and potash out of the ground, and the atoms of carbon and oxygen out of the atmospheric air, and put them together in the shape of the corn of wheat; but the organic chemical powers of the seed can put this magical process in motion, while we on our part can very easily bury the seed in the place of its secret working, the bosom of the earth. Often, of course, we are not able directly to master the form of matter on which the friendly power depends, but in the same way as we would like it to help us, do we help ourselves against it; we try to secure the alliance of a second natural power which brings the form of matter that bears the first power under our control. We wish to bring the well water into the house. Wooden rhones would force it to obey our will, and take the path we prescribe, but our hands have not the power to make the forest trees into rhones. We have not far to look, however, for an expedient. We ask the help of a second ally in the axe and the gouge; their assistance gives us the rhones; then the rhones bring us the water. And what in this illustration is done through the mediation of two or three members may be done, with equal or greater result, through five, ten, or twenty members. Just as we control and guide the immediate matter of which the good is composed by one friendly power, and that power by a second, so can we control and guide the second by a third, the third by a fourth, this, again, by a fifth, and so on,—always going back to more remote causes of the final result—till in the series we come at last to one cause which we can control conveniently by our own natural powers. This is the true importance which attaches to our entering on roundabout ways of production, and this is the reason of the result associated with them: every roundabout way means the enlisting in our service of a power which is stronger or more cunning than the human hand; every extension of the roundabout way means an addition to the powers which enter into the service of man, and the shifting of some portion of the burden of production from the scarce and costly labour of human beings to the prodigal powers of nature.

And now we may put into words an idea which has long waited for expression, and must certainly have occurred to the reader; the kind of production which works in these wise circuitous methods is nothing else than what economists call Capitalist Production, as opposed to that production which goes directly at its object, as the Germans say, *"mit der nackten Faust."* And Capital is nothing but the complex of intermediate products which appear on the several stages of the roundabout journey.

READING 4
Incentives and Economic Growth: Changing Roles and Public Policies
William H. Meckling and Armen A. Alchian

The interaction of economic goals and political behavior depends partly upon the amount of freedom allowed to the individual. In the United States, where individual freedom is stressed, there is the ever-present danger that the checks and balances provided by the Constitution may be insufficient to prevent political power groups from changing the rules of the game to their advantage. In this reading, Professors Meckling and Alchian discuss the expanding role of government and the changing cost-reward relationships governing individual behavior in the United States. Although Meckling is currently professor and dean of the college of business at the University of Rochester and Alchian is professor of economics at U.C.L.A., their long association with the RAND Corporation, the so called "think-tank," might well have led them into the study of economic-political interaction in the United States.

Guideposts for Thought While Reading
Are mans' goals changing or is it the institutional framework of costs and rewards which change his behavior? What remedial steps might

Reprinted by permission of the publisher from William H. Meckling and Armen A. Alchian, "Incentives and Economic Growth: Changing Roles and Public Policies, Incentives in the United States," *The American Economic Review,* May 1960, pp. 55–61.

be taken to overcome the increasing tendency for the allocation of resources by power blocs in the United States?

Incentives are the prizes in the game of life—the goals individuals seek—the carrots. Through the ages of Tutankhamen, Alexander, Caesar, Louis XIV, and the Atom, they have remained the same. Men want, and have always wanted, exorbitant wealth, tyrannical power, idolatrous prestige, lavish consumption, and undisciplined leisure. And the men of Kharkov and Karachi are not different from the men of Kalamazoo. The specific objects of wealth or power may differ between Kalamazoo and Kharkov. But if Kalamazoo teems with thieves and brigands while Karachi is serenely industrious, the explanation lies not in differences in goals. Differences in goals will not explain differences in the way individuals pursue their goals.

What does explain the disparities? Differences in the relations between costs and goals. It is trite, but nonetheless important, that there is not enough wealth, power, prestige, etc., to go around. As all economists are aware, this scarcity becomes evident as costs. In seeking prizes, individuals must make sacrifices; for example, they must forego leisure or forego consumption. The existence of costs is universal—once again whether it be Kharkov, Karachi, or Kalamazoo. But the specific relations between costs and goals differ from place to place and from era to era. An hour of foregone leisure will not yield the same reward in Karachi as in Kharkov or Kalamazoo. There are two reasons for this. First, the technological circumstances—the resources and knowledge—are different. Second, the rules of the game—the mores and laws—that condition the hunt are different. The observed relation between cost and rewards—the relation that the contestants see—is a product of these two sets of factors. The technological circumstances imply a basic relation which in turn is conditioned by the rules of the game.

Observed cost-reward relationships are important because they govern individual behavior. Contestants perceive the schedules of prizes and costs and adapt accordingly. If the road to riches is dishonesty and deception, dishonesty and deception will flourish. If the state levies taxes on incomes, people will take more leisure. If the tax is limited to money incomes, the do-it-yourself club will flourish. It the tax exempts income from owner-occupied housing, the ranks of proud homeowners will swell. If corporate risk sharing is more efficient, the corporate organization will flourish.

But in trying to improve their lot individuals do more than merely adapt to given cost-reward relationships. They try to alter the schedule of prizes and costs to their own advantage. How? By changing the rules, especially through government. By pressing for advantageous legislative, administrative, or judicial action, individuals can and do use the power of government for personal gain. Thus economists describe the effects of reduced demand for an industry's product in terms of a new equilibrium with lower prices and lower output. But in a society where government can be summoned to the aid of distressed suppliers, that description is incomplete. For the industry may induce government to artificially maintain demand or subsidize losses.

Constitutional government is an attempt to limit this prerogative; but constitutional limitations are not and cannot be immutable. Even if legislative amendments were prohibited, experience suggests that *de facto* limitations are at the mercy of the courts which themselves adapt to social pressures. Of course, to get favorable changes in rules, individuals must incur costs. And the extent to which people attempt to change rules depends on the relation between the costs of changing rules and the potential rewards.

CHANGING COST-REWARDS IN THE U.S.

During the twentieth century a number of developments in the U.S., such as the growth of corporations, technical progress, and urbanization, have had important effects on cost-rewards relationships, including the costs of changing the rules. But to us the one that overshadows all others in significance is the growth of government activity.

During the past sixty years, a dramatic metamorphosis has taken place in the role of government in the United States. By any standard, there has been an astonishing expansion, not only of the federal government, but of all governments during the twentieth century. To quote Solomon Fabricant, in *Trend of Government Activity Since 1900* "In 1900 one out of 24 workers was on a government payroll, in 1920 one out of 15, and in 1940 one out of 11. The current ratio . . . is one out of 8. The trend is sharp and clear." "Today government holds 20 per cent of the nation's capital assets (exclusive of roads and streets and most military and naval equipment) not 7 per cent as in 1900." "The sixfold rise in government employment between 1900 and

1949, and the similar increase in capital assets, great as they are, understate the rise in total volume of resources used in producing government services. . . . The physical volume of goods and services purchased by government from private industry went up more than a thousand per cent between 1903 and 1949."

The facts disclosed by Fabricant, striking as they are, tell only part of the whole story. Transfer payments are not included. These were about 12 billion dollars in 1949, or 6 per cent of individual income compared to less than 1 per cent in 1900. Furthermore, Fabricant's data do not reflect the growth in government during the last ten years. Expenditures of government have doubled since 1949, the year on which his statements were based. Today they are about 30 per cent of gross national product.

National defense accounts for a significant part, but by no means all, of this increase. In 1903 defense expenditures were 10 per cent of total government expenditures. Today they are on the order of 35 percent. In 1900 there was no Old Age and Survivors Insurance, no Old Age Assistance program, no unemployment compensation, no Commodity Credit Corporation, no Federal Housing Administration, no urban renewal program, and no Reclamation Bureau.

Growth in expenditures is only one facet of the expansion of government. Important transformations have also occurred in regulation and control. The twentieth century has witnessed the birth and growth of the Securities and Exchange Commission, the Federal Communications Commission, the Federal Aviation Agency, the Federal Reserve Board, the Federal Deposit Insurance Corporation, the National Labor Relations Board, and minimum wage and hours laws. At state and local levels, planning and zoning commissions, building codes, public health regulations, and licensing have proliferated.

The fact of large government growth or change itself does not justify our concentration on this change. If the increased importance of the corporate structure or of urbanization or of complexity of modern technology were even more spectacular, we would still emphasize government activity. Increased corporate activity, greater urbanization, and increased complexity do not reduce the role of the market place or private property as institutions through which individual wealth, prestige, consumption, or leisure are determined. But the growth in government that has taken place does have that effect. Government as a taxer, a spender, an employer, and a regulator supplants the market place and private property, thereby changing patterns of individual behavior. Standards of behavior required in the market place lose viability with the expanded role of government.

PUBLIC FINANCE AND INCENTIVES

The wherewithal to support governments in the U.S. comes mostly from taxes on individual income, corporate income, sales, and property, and from miscellaneous excise taxes. All of these have important effects on cost-reward relationships. Even if tax laws were in a sense ideal, taxes would alter basic cost-reward relationships. Individual income taxes inevitably alter the rewards for foregone leisure. Corporate income taxes increase the cost of doing business as a corporation vis-à-vis alternative organizational forms. Sales taxes increase consumption costs relative to holding wealth. And so on!

But in practice the laws are not ideal. As we have noted, most home produced income, to the delight of farmers, is not taxed as individual income. Income from owner-occupied dwellings is largely exempted. Income spent on interest, charity, medical services, and employment fringe benefits is largely exempt. Co-operatives and so-called "nonprofit corporations" are exempted from corporate income taxes. Depletion provisions make the rate on extractive industries less than on other industries. Income taken in the course of conducting business—private airplanes, private cars, pretty secretaries, and thick rugs—is exempt from individual and corporate taxes. Certain forms of consumption, e.g., eating at home, are often exempt from sales taxes. The property tax turns out to be largely a tax on land and buildings.

In 1900, when government was small, such tax provisions would have been of little consequence. Government being what it is today, however, the effects are by no means trivial. Cost-reward relationships are effectively rewritten, and the contestants must revamp their style of play accordingly.

Government expenditures also affect basic cost-reward relationships. Farm price supports, various "low-cost" lending schemes, water, power, and reclamation projects, and postal subsidies to publishers and advertisers are some obvious examples. Unemployment insurance alters the rewards in seasonal industries. Old Age and Survivors Insurance penalizes employment after age sixty-five.

To economists these kinds of individual adaptation to taxes

and expenditures are a familiar subject, and we need not dwell on them further.

INCENTIVES WITHIN GOVERNMENT

When government employs a significant fraction of the wealth and of the labor force and buys an even greater share of the output, cost-reward relationships within government deserve attention. The prizes for various forms of behavior in government are markedly different from private markets. Private firms buy inputs and sell outputs, and the test of survival is the relation between the value of the two. Government buys inputs, but the inputs are paid for by levying taxes, while output is given away. The problem is identical with the familiar problem of divergence between private and social costs. Once tax receipts reach the Treasury, they are owned by no one. To the individuals entrusted with their expenditure, the cost of using these funds is not equal to their value. They are not required as a condition of survival to see that value of output exceeds the value of inputs.

Specific cost-reward relationships in government employment reflect these circumstances. The bulk of government employees fall into three categories: employees under civil service or merit systems; teachers; and military personnel. In all of these cases, seniority is the key to success and a premium is placed on job security. These systems owe their origin and survival to the fact that private and social costs diverge in government. Civil service and merit systems originated as answers to the spoils system. Why should government be marked with the spoils system? Why should politicians hire and promote unqualified people? Because the cost to them of doing so is not equal to the social cost (which, incidentally, is not to say that civil service is any improvement). Elaborate procedures to ensure competitive bidding are another device conceived as an answer to the same problem.

INCENTIVES AND GOVERNMENT REGULATION

Regulation is still another government activity affecting rewards and associated costs. The spectrum of government regulation runs from national minimum wage and hour laws to licensing itinerant fruit dealers. Frequently regulation confers valuable privileges on selected groups of individuals. Licensing of banks, insurance companies, security dealers, radio and television stations, airlines, taxicabs, and doctors are examples. Sometimes the valuable privilege consists of nothing more than the right to operate a monopoly, as is in the case of medicine and taxicabs. Other times a scarce resource is given away, as in the case of radio, television, and airlines. Frequently, a government agency is interposed between the consumer and the producer with the power to decide which producers are acceptable. An applicant producer must not only show that customers demand the service he proposes to offer, but must also satisfy whatever other criteria the regulatory agency adopts; e.g., that he is of good character. In technical terms, the money price of licenses is raised to infinity by legal prohibition of purchase; consequently, other kinds of activity that lead to obtaining a license become more rewarding. The reward for favorable personal impressions on the regulatory agency has increased. Statesmanship, conformity, sociability, prestige, political influence, civic-mindedness, and the like replace money as means to rewards. Where a monopoly is granted, as in medicine, constant vigilance is required against interlopers. Both the public and the politicians must be convinced in perpetuity that the monopoly is in their interest. Again statesmanship, conformity, sociability, prestige, political influence, etc., take on added importance.

Where valuable privileges are conferred, profit regulations are often imposed. Public utilities and nonprofit corporations are privately owned but profit restricted. Since the restriction takes the form of some percentage of investment (zero in the case of nonprofit firms), the firms actually operate on a cost-plus basis. What is restricted is only the money profits that can be taken out of the business. Potential profits can be turned to personal gain, however, by disguising them as costs. The cost of rewards taken in the form of business-connected purchases has gone down. Thick rugs, pleasant offices and colleagues, and even such seemingly mysterious activities as community affairs participation by officials, support of charity, and extensive fringe benefits become sensible.

INCENTIVES TO POLITICAL ACTION

A striking change in public attitudes toward the role of government has attended government expansion in the twentieth century, as Solomon Fabricant notes:

President Cleveland had vetoed an appropriation of $25,000 to buy seed corn for Texas farmers ruined by a drought. Even a democratic President, vetoing the appropriation . . . could state "I can find no warrant for such an appropriation in the Constitution, and I do not believe that the power and duty of the general government ought to be extended to the relief of individual suffering which is in no manner related to the public service or benefit. A prevalent tendency to disregard the limited mission of this power and duty should, I think, be steadfastly resisted, to the end that the lesson should be constantly enforced that, though the people support the government, the government should not support the people."

That the above statement, which was made in his first term, was not "political suicide" is about as eloquent a testimonial to the change in attitude as one could find. The change is not a change in the ends for which men strive; i.e., wealth, power, and prestige. It is a change in the relation between costs and rewards for political action. Nineteenth-century attitudes severely proscribed the use of the state as a means to individual ends. The twentieth century has seen this proscription eroded away. Behavior which society formerly held to be unacceptable has become standard practice.

The change in attitude toward the role of government has increased rewards for exerting organized political pressure—not only to recognized types of union and industry groups, but to doctors, teachers, fishermen, golfers, senior citizens, parents, *et al.* The services of professional lobbyists, public relations experts, and lawyers are more rewarding. Mass communication media—radio, television, newspapers, and magazines—are more earnestly courted because of their influence and power. Contributions of time and money to political campaigns have larger pay-offs. These are kinds of behavior that are efficient in bringing about changes in the rules of the game.

If it appears that we are pointing a fickle finger at government, the impression is correct. If it appears that this is also a condemnation, that impression, too, is correct. But the condemnation does not derive from the economic analysis. For the analysis merely identifies the changes in cost-reward relationships over the last half-century, and develops the implications for individual behavior. It is an ethical judgment that leads us to condemn the kinds of behavior that this has induced. And it is on the basis of an empirical judgment that we assert that cost-reward relationships have changed, not goals or incentives.

PART 2

Macroeconomics: Employment, Prices, and Economic Stability

READING 5
The Big Bull Market
Frederick Lewis Allen

Frederick Lewis Allen served in an editorial capacity with *The Atlantic Monthly, The Century Magazine*, and *Harper's Magazine*, becoming editor-in-chief, director, and vice-president of Harper and Brothers publishing company. The "Big Bull Market" is an excerpt from his book *Only Yesterday*, which is one of four books concerning American history and biography written by Allen. This article shows vividly the speculative psychology which existed prior to the Great Depression and offers some behind-the-scenes glimpses of the dealings by some stock manipulators and the failure of the Federal Reserve to cope with the problems of the speculative boom.

Guideposts for Thought While Reading
How did the acceleration of scientific discovery and development help stimulate speculative psychology? What is the meaning of the statement that the market was discounting not only the future, but the hereafter? What was the dilemma faced by the Federal Reserve, what solution did they try, and why was it unsuccessful? What was pyramiding of capital? Why did it occur?

The newspaper advertisements of investment services testified to the uncomfortable temper of Wall Street with headlines like "Will You 'Overstay' This Bull Market?" and "Is the Process of Deflation Under Way?" The air was fogged with uncertainty.

Anybody who had chosen this moment to predict that the bull market was on the verge of a wild advance which would make all that had gone before seem trifling would have been quite mad—or else inspired with a genius for mass psychology. The banker who advised caution was quite right about financial conditions, and so were the forecasters. But they had not taken account of the boundless commercial romanticism of the American people, inflamed by year after plentiful year of Coolidge Prosperity. For on March 3, 1928—the very day when the Harvard prophets were talking about intermediate declines and the *Times* was talking about hesitation—the stock market entered upon its sensational phase. . . .

General Motors stock, opening at 139¾ on the previous morning, had skyrocketed in two short hours to 144¼, with a gain of more than five points since the Friday closing. The trading for the day had amounted to not much more than 1,200,000 shares, but nearly a third of it had been in Motors. The speculative spring fever of 1928 had set in. . . .

On Monday General Motors gained 2¼ points more, on Tuesday 3½; there was great excitement as the stock "crossed 150." Other stocks were beginning to be affected by the contagion as day after day the market "made the front page": Steel and Radio and Montgomery Ward were climbing, too. After a pause on Wednesday and Thursday, General Motors astounded everybody on Friday by pushing ahead a cool 9¼ points as the announcement was made that its Managers Securities Company had bought 200,000 shares in the open market for its executives at around 150. And then on Saturday the common stock of the Radio Corporation of America threw General Motors completely into the shade by leaping upward for a net gain of 12¾ points, closing at 120½.

THE MANIPULATORS

What on earth was happening? Wasn't business bad, and credit inflated, and the stock-price level dangerously high? Was the market going crazy? Suppose all these madmen who insisted on buying stocks at advancing prices tried to sell at the same moment! Canny investors, reading of the wild advance in Radio, felt much as did the forecasters of Moody's Investors Service a few days later: the practical question, they said, was "how long the opportunity to sell at the top will remain."

What was actually happening was that a group of powerful speculators with fortunes made in the automobile business and in the grain markets and in the earlier days of the bull market in stocks—men like W. C. Durant and Arthur Cutten and the Fisher Brothers and John J. Raskob—were buying in unparalleled volume. They thought that business was due to come out of its doldrums. They knew that with Ford production delayed, the General Motors Corporation was likely to have a big year. They knew that the Radio Corporation had been consolidating its position and was now ready to make more money than it had ever made before, and that as scientific discovery followed discovery, the future possibilities of the biggest radio company were exciting. Automobiles and radios—these were the two most characteristic products of the decade of confident mass production, the brightest flowers of Coolidge Prosperity: they held a ready-made appeal to the speculative imagination. The big bull operators knew, too, that thousands of speculators had been selling stocks short in the expectation of a collapse in the market, would continue to sell short, and could be forced to repurchase if prices were driven relentlessly up. And finally, they knew their American public. It could not resist the appeal of a surging market. It had an altogether normal desire to get rich quick, and it was ready to believe anything about the golden future of American business. If stocks started upward the public would buy, no matter what the forecasters said, no matter how obscure was the business prospect.

THE SUCKERS

They were right. The public bought.

Monday the 12th of March put the stock market on the front page once more. Radio opened at 120½—and closed at 138½. Other stocks made imposing gains, the volume of trading broke every known record by totaling 3,875,910 shares, the ticker fell six minutes behind the market, and visitors to the gallery of the Stock Exchange reported that red-haired Michael Meehan, the specialist in Radio, was the center of what appeared to be a five-hour scrimmage on the floor. "It looked like a street fight," said one observer.

Tuesday the 13th was enough to give anybody chills and fever. Radio opened at 160, a full 21½ points above the closing price the night before—a staggering advance. Then came an announcement that the Stock Exchange officials were beginning an investigation to find out whether a technical corner in the stock existed, and the price cascaded to 140. It jumped again that same day to 155 and closed at 146, 7½ points above Monday's closing, to the accompaniment of rumors that one big short trader had been wiped out. This time the ticker was twelve minutes late.

And so it went on, day after day and week after week. On March 16th the ticker was thirty-three minutes late and one began to hear people saying that some day there might occur a five-million share day—which seemed almost incredible. On the 20th, Radio jumped 18 points and General Motors 5. On March 26th the record for total volume of trading was smashed again. The new mark lasted just twenty-four hours, for on the 27th—a terrifying day when a storm of unexplained selling struck the market and General Motors dropped abruptly, only to recover on enormous buying—there were 4,790,000 shares traded. The speculative fever was infecting the whole country. Stories of fortunes made overnight were on everybody's lips. One financial commentator reported that his doctor found patients talking about the market to the exclusion of everything else and that his barber was punctuating with the hot towel more than one account of the prospects of Montgomery Ward. Wives were asking their husbands why they were so slow, why they weren't getting in on all this, only to hear that their husbands had bought a hundred shares of American Linseed that very morning. Broker's branch offices were jammed with crowds of men and women watching the shining transparency on which the moving message of the ticker tape was written; whether or not one held so much as a share of stock, there was a thrill in seeing the news of that abrupt break and recovery in General Motors on March 27th run across the field of vision in a long string of quotations. . . .

THE IMPOTENT FEDERAL RESERVE

The Reserve authorities were disturbed. They had raised the rediscount rate in February from 3½ to 4 per cent, hoping that if a lowering of the rate in 1927 had encouraged speculation, a corresponding increase would discourage it—and instead they had witnessed a common-stock mania which ran counter to all logic and all economic theory. They raised the rate again in May to 4½ per cent, but after a brief shudder the market went boiling on. They sold the Government bonds they had accumulated during 1927, and the principal result of their efforts was that the Government-bond market became demoralized. Who would ever have thought the situation would thus get out of hand?

In the latter part of May, 1928, the pace of the bull market slackened. Prices fell off, gained, fell off again. The reckoning, so long expected, appeared at last to be at hand.

It came in June, after several days of declining prices. The Giannini stocks, the speculative favorites of the Pacific coast, suddenly toppled for gigantic losses. On the San Francisco Stock Exchange the shares of the Bank of Italy fell 100 points in a single day (June 11th), Bancitaly fell 86 points, Bank of America 120, and United Security 80. That same day, on the New York Curb Exchange, Bancitaly dove perpendicularly from 200 to 110, dragging with it to ruin a horde of small speculators who, despite urgent warnings from A. P. Giannini himself that the stock was overvalued, had naïvely believed that is was "going to a thousand."

The next day, June 12th, this Western tornado struck Wall Street in full force. As selling orders poured in, the prophecy that the Exchange would some day see a five-million share day was quickly fulfilled. The ticker slipped almost two hours behind in recording prices on the floor. Radio, which had marched well beyond the 200 mark in May, lost 23½ points. The day's losses for the general run of securities were not, to be sure, very large by subsequent standards; the *New York Times* averages for fifty leading stocks dropped only a little over three points. But after the losses of the preceding days, it seemed to many observers as if the end had come at last, and one of the most conservative New York papers began its front-page account of the break with the unqualified sentence, "Wall Street's bull market collapsed yesterday with a detonation heard round the world."...

But had the bull market collapsed? On June 13th it appeared to have regained its balance. On June 14th, the day of Hoover's nomination, it extended its recovery. The promised reckoning had been only partial. Prices still stood well above their February levels. A few thousand traders had been shaken out, a few big fortunes had been lost, a great many pretty paper profits had vanished; but the Big Bull Market was still young. . . .

RECURRENT SPECULATION

During that "Hoover bull market" of November, 1928, the records made earlier in the year were smashed to flinders. Had brokers once spoken with awe of the possibility of five-million-share days? Five-million-share days were now occurring with monotonous regularity; on November 23rd the volume of trading almost reached seven millions. Had they been amazed at the rising prices of seats on the Stock Exchange? In November a new mark of $580,000 was set. Had they been disturbed that Radio should sell at such an exorbitant price as 150? Late in November it was bringing 400. Ten-point gains and new highs for all time were commonplaces now. Montgomery Ward, which the previous spring had been climbing toward 200, touched 439⅞ on November 30. The copper stocks were skyrocketing; Packard climbed to 145; Wright Aeronautical flew as high as 263. Brokers' loans? Of course they were higher than ever; but this, one was confidently told, was merely a sign of prosperity—a sign that the American people were buying on the part-payment plan a partnership in the future progress of the country. Call money rates? They ranged around 8 and 9 per cent; a little high, perhaps, admitted the bulls, but what was the harm if people chose to pay them? Business was not suffering from high money rates; business was doing better than ever. The new era had arrived, and the abolition of poverty was just around the corner.

In December the market broke again, and more sharply than in June. There was one fearful day—Saturday, December 7th—when the weary ticker, dragging far behind the trading on the floor, hammered out the story of a 72-point decline in Radio. Horrified tape-watchers in the brokers' offices saw the stock open at 361, struggle weakly up to 363, and then take the bumps, point by point, all the way down to 296—which at that moment seemed like a fire-sale figure. (The earnings of the Radio Corporation during the first nine months of 1928 had been $7.54 per share, which on the time-honored basis of "ten times earnings" would have suggested the appropriateness of a price of not much over 100; but the ten-times-earnings basis for prices had long since been discarded. The market, as Max Winkler said, was discounting not only the future but the hereafter.) Montgomery Ward lost 29 points that same nerve-racking Saturday morning, and International Harvester slipped from 368½ to 307. But just as in June, the market righted itself at the moment when demoralization seemed to be setting in. A few uneasy weeks of ragged prices went by, and then the advance began once more.

THE FEDERAL RESERVE'S DILEMMA

The Federal Reserve authorities found themselves in an unhappy predicament. Speculation was clearly absorbing more and more of the surplus funds of the country. The inflation of credit was becoming more and more dangerous. The normal course for the Reserve banks at such a juncture would have been to raise the rediscount rate, thus forcing up the price of money for speculative purposes, rendering speculation less attractive, liquidating speculative loans, and reducing the volume of credit outstanding. But the Reserve banks had already raised the rate (in July) to 5 per cent, and speculation had been affected only momentarily. Apparently speculators were ready to pay any amount for money if only prices kept on climbing. The Reserve authorities had waited patiently for the speculative fever to cure itself and it had only become more violent. Things had now come to such a pass that if they raised the rate still further, they not only ran the risk of bringing about a terrific smash in the market—and of appearing to do so deliberately and wantonly—but also of seriously handicapping business by forcing it to pay a high rate for funds. Furthermore, they feared the further accumulation of gold in the United States and the effect which this might have upon world trade. And the Treasury had a final special concern about interest rates—it had its own financing to do, and Secretary Mellon was naturally not enthusiastic about forcing the Government to pay a fancy rate for money for its own current use. It almost seemed as if there were no way to deflation except through disaster.

The Reserve Board finally met the dilemma by thinking up a new and ingenious scheme. They tried to prevent the reloaning of Reserve funds to brokers without raising the rediscount rate.

On February 2, 1929, they issued a statement in which they said: "The Federal Reserve Act does not, in the opinion of the Federal Reserve Board, contemplate the use of the resources of the Federal Reserve Banks for the creation or extension of speculative credit. A member bank is not within its reasonable claims for rediscount facilities at its Federal Reserve Bank when it borrows either for the purpose of making speculative loans or for the purpose of maintaining speculative loans." A little less than a fortnight later the Board wrote to the various Reserve Banks asking them to "prevent as far as possible the diversion of Federal Reserve funds for the purpose of carrying loans based on securities." Meanwhile the Reserve Banks drastically reduced their holdings of securities purchased in the open market. But no increases in rediscount rates were permitted. Again and again, from February on, the directors of the New York Reserve Bank asked Washington for permission to lift the New York rate, and each time the permission was denied. The Board preferred to rely on their new policy.

The immediate result of the statement of February 2, 1929, was a brief overnight collapse in stock prices. The subsequent result, as the Reserve Banks proceeded to bring pressure on their member banks to borrow only for what were termed legitimate business purposes, was naturally a further increase in call-money rates. Late in March—after Herbert Hoover had entered the White House and the previous patron saint of prosperity had retired to Northampton to explore the delights of autobiography—the pinch in money came to a sudden and alarming climax. Stock prices had been falling for several days when on

March 26th the rate for call money jumped from 12 per cent to 15, and then to 17, and finally to 20 per cent—the highest rate since the dismal days of 1921. Another dizzy drop in prices took place. The turnover in stocks on the Exchange broke the November record, reaching 8,246,740 shares. Once again thousands of requests for more margin found their way into speculators' mail-boxes, and thousands of participators in the future prosperity of the country were sold out with the loss of everything they owned. Once again the Big Bull Market appeared to be on its last legs.

THE FEDERAL RESERVE LOSES AGAIN

That afternoon several of the New York banks decided to come to the rescue. Whatever they thought of the new policy of the Federal Reserve Board, they saw a possible panic brewing—and anything, they decided, was better than a panic. The next day Charles E. Mitchell, president of the National City Bank, announced that his bank was prepared to lend twenty million dollars on call, of which five million would be available at 15 per cent, five million more at 16 per cent, and so on up to 20 per cent. Mr. Mitchell's action—which was described by Senator Carter Glass as a slap in the face of the Reserve Board—served to peg the call money rate at 15 per cent and the threatened panic was averted.

Whereupon stocks not only ceased their precipitous fall, but cheerfully recovered!

The lesson was plain: the public simply would not be shaken out of the market by anything short of a major disaster.

During the next month or two stocks rose and fell uncertainly, sinking dismally for a time in May, and the level of brokers' loans dipped a little, but no general liquidation took place. Gradually money began to find its way more plentifully into speculative use despite the barriers raised by the Federal Reserve Board. A corporation could easily find plenty of ways to put its surplus cash out on call at 8 or 9 per cent without doing it through a member bank of the Federal Reserve System; corporations were eager to put their funds to such remunerative use, as the increase in loans "for others" showed; and the member banks themselves, realizing this, were showing signs of restiveness. When June came, the advance in prices began once more, almost as if nothing had happened. The Reserve authorities were beaten.

BOOM AND BUST PSYCHOLOGY

By the summer of 1929, prices had soared far above the stormy levels of the preceding winter into the blue and cloudless empyrean. All the old markers by which the price of a promising common stock could be measured had long since been passed; if a stock once valued at 100 went to 300, what on earth was to prevent it from sailing on to 400? And why not ride with it for fifty or a hundred points, with Easy Street at the end of the journey?

By every rule of logic the situation had now become more perilous than ever. If inflation had been serious in 1927, it was far more serious in 1929, as the total of brokers' loans climbed toward six billions (it had been only three and a half billions at the end of 1927). If the price level had been extravagant in 1927 it was preposterous now; and in economics, as in physics, there is no gainsaying the ancient principle that the higher they go, the harder they fall. But the speculative memory is short. As people in the summer of 1929 looked back for precedents, they were comforted by the recollection that every crash of the past few years had been followed by a recovery, and that every recovery had ultimately brought prices to a new high point. Two steps up, one step down, two steps up again—that was how the market went. If you sold, you had only to wait for the next crash (they came every few months) and buy in again. . . .

THE SCHEMERS

For many years rival capitalistic interests, imitating the brilliant methods of Sidney Z. Mitchell, had sought to secure control of local electric light and power and gas companies and water companies and weld them into chains; and as the future possibilities of the utilities seized upon the speculative imagination, the battle between these groups led to an amazing proliferation of utility holding companies. By the summer of 1929 the competing systems had become so elaborate, and their interrelations had become so complicated, that it was difficult to arrive at even the vaguest idea of the actual worth of their soaring stocks. Even the professional analyst of financial properties was sometimes bewildered when he found Company A holding a 20-percent interest in Company B, and B an interest in C, while C in turn invested in A, and D held shares in each of the others. But few investors seemed to care about actual worth. Utilities had a future and prices were going up—that was enough.

Meanwhile investment trusts multiplied like locusts. There were now said to be nearly five hundred of them, with a total paid-in capital of some three billions and with holdings of stocks —many of them purchased at the current high prices—amounting to something like two billions. These trusts ranged all the way from honestly and intelligently managed companies to wildly speculative concerns launched by ignorant or venal promoters. Some of them, it has been said, were so capitalized that they could not even pay their preferred dividends out of the income from the securities which they held, but must rely almost completely upon the hope of profits. Other investment trusts, it must be admitted, served from time to time the convenient purpose of absorbing securities which the bankers who controlled them might have difficulty in selling in the open market. Reprehensible, you say? Of course; but it was so easy! One could indulge in all manner of dubious financial practices with an unruffled conscience so long as prices rose. The Big Bull Market covered a multitude of sins. It was a golden day for the promoter, and his name was legion.

Gradually the huge pyramid of capital rose. While supersalesmen of automobiles and radios and a hundred other gadgets were loading the ultimate consumer with new and shining wares, supersalesmen of securities were selling him shares of investment trusts which held stock in holding companies which owned the stock of banks which had affiliates which in turn controlled holding companies—and so on *ad infinitum.* Though the shelves of manufacturing companies and jobbers and retailers were not overloaded, the shelves of the ultimate consumer and the shelves of the distributors of securities were groaning. Trouble was brewing—not the same sort of trouble which had visited the country in 1921, but trouble none the less. Still, however, the cloud in the summer sky looked no bigger than a man's hand.

How many Americans actually held stock on margin during the fabulous summer of 1929 there seems to be no way of computing, but it is probably safe to put the figure at more than a million. (George Buchan Robinson estimated that three hundred million shares of stock were being carried on margin.) The additional number of those who held common stock outright and followed the daily quotations with an interest nearly as absorbed as that of the margin trader was, of course, considerably larger. As one walked up the aisle of the 5:27 local, or found one's seat in the trolley car, two out of three newspapers that one saw were open to the page of stock-market quotations. Branch offices of the big Wall Street houses blossomed in every city and in numerous suburban villages. In 1919 there had been five hundred such offices; by October, 1928, there were 1,192; and throughout most of 1929 they appeared in increasing numbers. The broker found himself regarded with a new wonder and esteem. Ordinary people, less intimate with the mysteries of Wall Street than he was supposed to be, hung upon his every word. Let him but drop a hint of a possible split-up in General Industries Associates and his neighbor was off hot-foot the next morning to place a buying order. . . .

THE TOP

Stop for a moment to glance at a few of the prices recorded on the overworked ticker on September 3, 1929, the day when the Dow-Jones averages reached their high point for the year; and compare them with the opening prices of March 3, 1928, when, as you may recall, it had seemed as if the bull market had already climbed to a perilous altitude. Here they are, side by side —first the figures for March, 1928; then the figures for September, 1929, translated into 1928 terms—or in other words revised to make allowance for intervening split-ups and issues of rights. (Only thus can you properly judge the extent of the advance during those eighteen confident months.)

One thing more: as you look at the high prices recorded on

	Opening price March 3 1928	Adjusted high price Sept. 3 1929
American Can	77	181⅞
American Telephone & Telegraph	179½	335⅝
Anaconda Copper	54½	162
General Electric	128¾	396¼
General Motors	139¾	181⅞
Montgomery Ward	132¾	466½
New York Central	160½	256⅜
Radio	94½	505
Union Carbide & Carbon	145	413⅝
United States Steel	138⅛	279⅛
Westinghouse E. & M.	91⅝	313
Woolworth	180¾	251
Electric Bond & Share	89¾	203⅝

September 3, 1929, remember that on that day few people imagined that the peak had actually been reached. The enormous majority fully expected the Big Bull Market to go on and on.

For the blood of the pioneers still ran in American veins; and if there was no longer something lost behind the ranges, still the habit of seeing visions persisted. What if bright hopes had been wrecked by the sordid disappointments of 1919, the collapse of Wilsonian idealism, the spread of political cynicism, the slow decay of religious certainty, and the debunking of love? In the Big Bull Market there was compensation. Still the American could spin wonderful dreams—of a romantic day when he would sell his Westinghouse common at a fabulous price and live in a great house and have a fleet of shining cars and loll at ease on the sands of Palm Beach. And when he looked toward the future of his country, he could vision an America set free—not from graft, nor from crime, nor from war, nor from control by Wall Street, nor from irreligion, nor from lust, for the utopias of an earlier day left him for the most part skeptical or indifferent; he visioned an America set free from poverty and toil. He saw a magical order built on the new science and the new prosperity: roads swarming with millions upon millions of automobiles, airplanes darkening the skies, lines of high-tension wire carrying from hilltop to hilltop the power to give life to a thousand labor-saving machines, skyscrapers thrusting above one-time villages, vast cities rising in great geometrical masses of stone and concrete and roaring with perfectly mechanized traffic—and smartly dressed men and women spending, spending, spending with the money they had won by being far-sighted enough to foresee, way back in 1929, what was going to happen.

READING 6
The Fable of the Cat
George E. Cruikshank

Mr. Cruikshank, vice-president of Morgan Guaranty Trust, has spun a delightful fable, a town meeting in Mouseville, in which he gently pokes fun at the foibles of economic policy-makers, forecasters, and politicians. The cat, symbolizing a recession, was thought to be moving in the neighborhood. Identification of the cat, however, was far from certain. The mice of Mouseville represent such personages as Arthur Burns, Federal Reserve Board chairman, Paul McCracken, head of President Nixon's Council of Economic Advisers, and Professor Milton Friedman of the University of Chicago. The author also pointedly ribs the prestigious National Bureau of Economic Research, ". . . as a matter of general practice the institute does not announce that there is a cat until the cat has left the neighborhood."

Guideposts for Thought While Reading
How are the differences of opinion among the citizens of Mouseville related to their special positions or interests? Are any of the mice offering an unbiased prediction concerning the cat? How many viewpoints can you identify?

The meeting in Mouseville was uncommonly well attended. Every seat in the hall was taken. In the crowd were a sizable number of mice who were alarmed by recent events. Others at the meeting were quite calm, not at all concerned. And the rest—the vast majority—seemed bewildered. They simply wanted to be told what *really* was happening in their community.

The chairman, a no-nonsense type, quickly set forth the reason for the meeting. An old problem, it seemed, had returned to make life difficult for Mouseville and its inhabitants. After nine years of peace and quiet a cat was reported to be moving into the neighborhood.

When the squeaks of dismay died down, the chairman hastened to explain that reports of a cat were no more than that.

Reprinted by permission of the Morgan Guaranty Trust Company from George E. Cruikshank, "The Fable of the Cat," *Morgan Guaranty Survey*, March 1970.

No positive identification had yet been made. And there was considerable difference of opinion among knowledgeable members of the community as to whether such a cat even existed.

"I say there is too much loose talk about a cat," spoke up one member of the group who, owing to his position, could exert a powerful influence over the entire community.

"I heartily agree," was the comment uttered by another respected leader, who ranged high in the councils of government. He went on to say: "Even if something were to threaten us for two consecutive quarters I still would not jump to the conclusion that it was a cat, necessarily." An even more reassuring statement was made by a mouse who the audience knew held learned degrees in political economy—even though his statements sometimes lacked a sense of total commitment to proper English usage. With his cigar stabbing the air for emphasis, he stated: "There ain't gonna be no cat!" The flat prediction brought a chorus of approval and much pawclapping from a small group of mice who concerned themselves with Mouseville's political process. Their leader spoke out: "It is absolutely unacceptable to have a cat—especially in an election year."

SQUEAKERS OF GLOOM

Despite such attempts to allay the community's fears, not all the members seemed convinced. Some of the mice suspected that there might be a cat in the neighborhood. There *was* a certain smell in the air. Others were certain of it. The latter group, one by one, stood up to speak out against complacency:

From a builder of snug three and four bedroom nests: "I know a cat when I see one. This is a huge cat that is threatening my very life."

The gunslinging manager of the Trap-Free Growth Fund complained: "There is no doubt of it. It's a cat in bear's clothing."

Said the plump proprietor of Honest Sam's Auto Emporium, concerned about slumping sales of the new compact Rodent: "Consumers are not buying. They're worried about the cat."

There was no doubt in the mind of a workmouse, recently let go from his job: "To me it's a whole family of cats—a real disaster."

The tide of concern in the meeting clearly was rising. There seemed no end to those who were jumping to their feet to warn of impending danger. Even those mice who were merely visiting Mouseville felt constrained to speak up. One of these, a variety of Friedmouse hailing from the midwest, said: "We are bound to have a ferocious cat because the cheese supply has been flat for nine months."

A big-city mousebanker, worried about sinking prestige, credit-card backlash, and depreciated bond accounts, added: "Maybe we can now hope that our lords and masters will parcel out a slightly bigger ration of cheese. An extra sliver a day could keep the cat away."

A short, gnome-like mouse—obviously a foreign visitor—applauded that comment and advised: "You U.S. mice must do something about the cat. Every time you get a cat we have a lion in Europe." That comment led the mouse seated nearby, sad of face with whiskers that drooped forlornly, to warn in lugubrious tones: "The cat is the least of our worries. Pollution is going to kill us all."

Up to that point in the meeting the issue had been rather clean-cut. Some thought that there was no cat to worry about; others thought to the contrary. Then things began to get fuzzy.

One mouse insisted that what he had seen was a tiny kitten, not a cat. He called it a "mini-cat"—and drew some delighted squeaks from the audience for his originality. Another member of the community, an industry economouse cautious by nature although not always really careful, allowed that he had detected something but that he needed more time to decide what it was he had seen. "Maybe if I had a little longer to analyze the reports I have been getting I could be more certain," he added, a bit lamely.

By this time the audience was getting restive. A meeting called to eliminate confusion was merely adding to it.

"Words, words, figures, figures," cried one mouse, his tail twitching with impatience. "I hear descriptions, none of which is on the same base, that vary from a small furry animal, of unspecified origin, to a huge alley cat that will turn out to be worse than anything we have had to face since the Great Cat of the early 1930's. Is there a cat or isn't there?" The comment brought a chorus of agreement, much stamping of feet and lashing of tails. The meeting was threatening to get out of hand.

DEFINING A FELINE

Then the chairman displayed his storied wisdom. *The Institute*, staffed by economice with formidable powers of analysis, would decide whether there was a cat or not. Who would dispute the findings of *The Institute*? After all, was it not *The Institute* that had always made the determination? It could be counted on to make a calm, scholarly, dispassionate judgment, going in great depth into the size of the cat, when it arrived, and how long it had been around.

It was a masterstroke. The audience was delighted. Now they would know whether they should worry about a cat or go on munching their cheese free of worry.

Alas, one mouse was not quite satisfied. He raised his paw for attention—a timid gesture, almost as if he hoped the chairman would not notice. But the chairman did notice. The question came tumbling out: "When can we expect to get the news—whether there is a cat or not?"

The chairman had hoped no one would ask. But now the query had been made. He replied, as briskly as possible: "The last time *The Institute* was called upon to make a judgment about a cat was in 1960-61. It took the better part of a year to decide that there had been a cat. But, as a matter of general practice, *The Institute* does not announce that there is a cat until the cat has left the neighborhood."

As the chairman had feared, his reply led inevitably to further comments and queries. "That's a long time to wait to find out about the cat," shouted one mouse. Another asked: "What shall we do in the meantime?"

The chairman huffed and puffed but no answer came to mind. To his immense relief he saw the venerable elder of the community slowly rise from his chair and beckon for attention. The chairman was happy to oblige. All eyes shifted to the slightly stooped figure with white whiskers. He spoke:

"Fellow citizens, do not be excessively concerned about the various descriptions of the cat that you have been hearing. The mini-cat, the two-quarter cat, and so on. You can get caught in semantic quicksand.

"If there is a cat it will not be long now before we will all know. Any cat worthy of the name will not stay hidden indefinitely, I promise you. Meantime, do not panic and take rash action over a cat that may or may not materialize."

The quiet, measured tones of the oldtimer calmed the assembled mice. They liked his pragmatic approach—of crossing *that* bridge when they came to it. Besides, it put off to another day the dreary and difficult business of deciding what to do about a cat, if in fact there was one.

The mice filed out of the hall. The chairman silently congratulated himself on his adroit handling of the meeting. But in truth it must be said that the amount of bewilderment in Mouseville had not been reduced by as much as a cat's whisker.

READING 7
Inflation: Gainers and Losers
W. Lee Hoskins

This article by W. Lee Hoskins shows the effects of an inflation on the earnings of lenders and the real cost of borrowing to debtors. The costs of inflation are discussed in terms of equity for fixed-income groups and efficiency in the allocation of resources.

Guideposts for Thought While Reading
What is "inflationary psychology"? How does the form of asset-holding affect the outcome of an unexpected inflation? What sectors of the economy have been hurt by recent inflation?

How much is inflation costing you? When the cash register rings, the Pavlovian response of most Americans is "plenty." This reaction, reinforced by news media, civic leaders, and street-corner philosophers, may not be wholly warranted, for the burden of rising prices, like almost everything else, is not distributed equally among us. In fact, a sizeable number of Americans may actually gain from inflation.

EXPECTED VS. UNEXPECTED INFLATION

What people believe about the course of future events influences their present actions. Expectations about future inflation are no exception. If people, looking ahead, expect inflation, they may be able to adjust their *present* earning, purchasing, lending, and borrowing activities. By doing so, they may overcome the expected depreciation in the value of money. This process, recently dubbed "inflationary psychology," continues until people have reason to foresee or expect a stable price level.

One example of inflationary psychology in operation would be that of a lender who includes in his loan charges the expected or anticipated rate of price inflation. His reason for doing so is obvious. Suppose you loan $1,000 to a friend for one year, and

Reprinted by permission of the publisher from W. Lee Hoskins, "Inflation: Gainers and Losers," *Business Review*, Federal Reserve Bank of Philadelphia, February 1970, pp. 23–30.

you expect the price level to rise by 10 per cent during that period. What rate of interest would be appropriate if you wanted to earn a real return (in terms of constant purchasing power) of 5 per cent? Answer: about 15 per cent. This monetary return would allow you a *real return* of 5 per cent, and you would avoid a loss of wealth, but perhaps not of a friend. If, however, in making the loan, you underestimated the rise in prices, the return you would receive would be insufficient to compensate fully for the reduced purchasing power of the repaid loan plus interest, and you would have joined ranks with inflation losers. Your failure to foresee accurately the rate of inflation would result in a redistribution of your wealth from you to your friend. Your friend would be an inflation gainer because he does not repay as much in terms of purchasing power as he borrowed.

Not all people are equally able to make the necessary adjustments in their earning, purchasing, lending, and borrowing activities to compensate for inflation they see on the horizon. Even if they were, that would not be the end of the story, for it is because inflation is incorrectly foreseen that gains and losses are often incurred. All people do not have equal ability or luck at predicting future events or doing something about it. Consequently, inflations in the United States have not been *fully* anticipated by all, and wealth redistribution has occurred. One key to this redistribution is the relationship between debtors and creditors.

THE ADVANTAGE OF DEBT

The reason wealth is taken from some and bestowed on others by unforeseen inflation stems from the fact that there are two kinds of assets, monetary and real, linking debtors and creditors. Monetary assets include bonds, certificates of deposit, promissory notes, accounts receivable, and other legal contracts that promise a *fixed number of dollars*. Of course, for every monetary asset there is a monetary liability. For instance, to the landlord a lease represents a monetary asset, while to the tenant it is a monetary liability—a promise to pay a fixed number of dollars. In return for this promise to pay, the tenant receives a real asset —living space. People may issue monetary liabilities in order to finance purchases of real assets (cars, houses, inventories, and factories) or for consumption.

The crucial difference between the two is that a real asset is a claim to a *fixed amount of goods or services* whose money value is tied to inflation, while a monetary asset represents a claim to a *fixed number of dollars* regardless of inflation.[1] During an unexpected inflation, the dollar value of a real asset increases as prices rise, leaving its *real* value in terms of purchasing power unchanged; while the amount of dollars in a monetary asset (savings certificate) remains constant, and its real value falls. An investor holding a monetary asset loses purchasing power or wealth. The person who holds a monetary liability (in other words, who is in debt) during an unexpected inflation gains unexpectedly because he repays his debt in dollars that are worth less in terms of purchasing power.

Most families have real assets, monetary assets, and debts (monetary liabilities). The relative holdings of these items during periods of unanticipated increases in the price level determine whether or not a given family gains or loses from inflation. If a family holds more monetary liabilities than monetary assets, it gains. Conversely, if monetary assets exceed debts, the family loses. So, being in debt can have advantages during periods of unexpected inflation. This statement does *not* mean that saving makes no sense. Savings held in nonmonetary form do not lose value. Moreover, savings held in monetary form may lose value only when inflation is unanticipated. If inflation were accurately anticipated, adjustments could be made so that savings held in monetary asset form (except cash) would make sense as well.

CALCULATING GAINS AND LOSSES

The redistribution of wealth accompanying an unanticipated inflation can be better understood by tracing through some rela-

[1] The market value of the asset may vary but the number of dollars it promises to return remains fixed. Corporate and Government bonds are good examples of this type of monetary asset. A share of common stock represents ownership in an equity composed of both real and monetary assets. The extent to which the share price changes as a result of an unanticipated inflation depends on the relative holdings of these assets. Suppose a hypothetical firm has $200 million of monetary assets consisting of cash on hand, loans to other firms, Government securities, and accounts receivable. It also has $800 million in monetary liabilities (bonds, loans, and accounts payable). The firm is a net monetary debtor to the tune of $600 million. If 30 million shares of stock were outstanding, each would bear a debt of $20. Suppose the stock sold for $40. Then each share would represent a claim for real goods of $60 (the $40 received for the share plus $20 borrowed by the firm) and a 10 per cent rise in the price level would increase the equity of a shareholder by 15 per cent (10 per cent of $60 represents a 15 per cent rise in a $40 equity), unless other people anticipated the inflation and previously bid up the share price of the stock.

tively simple examples. Suppose a hypothetical balance sheet for an individual before an unanticipated inflation is:

Balance sheet—Inflation gainer

Market value *before* unanticipated inflation

Assets		**Equity + Liabilities**	
Cash	$ 500	Mortgage	$40,000
House	40,000	Equity	500
	$40,500		$40,500

If a particularly severe inflation occurs and the price level doubles, this individual would be in an enviable position indeed! Let's look at his new balance sheet:

Balance sheet—Inflation gainer

Market value *after* unanticipated inflation

Assets		**Equity + Liabilities**	
Cash	$ 500	Mortgage	$40,000
House	80,000	Equity	40,500
	$80,500		$80,500

The dollar value of his house rises with the price level, since it is a real asset. (The extent of the rise may vary depending on how the inflation is introduced into the economy and on other factors affecting the housing market). His $40,000 debt, a monetary liability incurred in purchasing the house, remains an obligation to repay $40,000. Equity has increased from $500 to $40,500 which, in terms of pre-inflation dollars, is a $19,750 increase in wealth. The increase in wealth is found by dividing the post-inflation equity, $40,500, by the new price level, which in this case is 2 (the old price level, taken as 1, plus the percentage increase in the price level), and subtracting from the result the original equity of $500.

Where did the gain come from? It came from the wealth of the creditor who lent $40,000 to finance the purchase of the house, but who failed to foresee that the price level would double. Some $20,000 was gained at the expense of the creditor; however, the value of the $500 cash dropped $250, leaving a net wealth gain in terms of constant purchasing power of $19,-750. If the lender had foreseen the inflation, he would have made adjustments in the amount to be repaid or in the interest charge upon granting the loan.

Losses result from holding more monetary assets than monetary liabilities. Let's suppose this is the balance sheet of the lender who loaned the money for the house before the unanticipated inflation:

Balance sheet—inflation loser

Market value *before* unanticipated inflation			
Assets		**Equity + Liabilities**	
Cash	$ 500	Debt	. . .
Mortgage Held	40,000	Equity	$40,500
	$40,500		$40,500

Now, if the price level were to double, the balance sheet would be unchanged.

Balance sheet—inflation loser

Market value *after* unanticipated inflation			
Assets		**Equity + Liabilities**	
Cash	$ 500	Debt	. . .
Mortgage Held	40,000	Equity	$40,500
	$40,500		$40,500

Since no real assets were held, equity did not increase. But, because of the higher price level, the $40,500 equity will not purchase as much in goods and services as it would have before the inflation. The loss in wealth is $20,250 in pre-inflation dollars or $\left(\frac{\$40{,}500}{2}\right) - \$40{,}500$. The lender lost $20,000 to the borrower, plus $250 as a result of holding $500 in cash.

TAKING ACCOUNT OF INCOME

A family's status as a net monetary debtor or creditor is not all that determines whether inflation robs it or blesses it. Income also fits into the picture. Let's focus first on income from certain pension plans, insurance policies, and other types of programs which promise to pay a *fixed number of dollars per year*. These promises to pay are monetary assets to the pensioner, and the *amount* they pay is unaffected by a rise in the price level.[2] People holding such assets are said to be on "fixed incomes;" hence, they suffer a loss from an anticipated inflation. However, the person on a "fixed income" may hold other monetary assets and liabilities as well. And it is the relative holdings of all of these that determine whether or not a person's wealth expands, shrinks, or is unaffected when the price level climbs unexpectedly.

REDISTRIBUTION ON WHAT BASIS?

The household sector of the economy has been, by far, the leading net monetary creditor since World War II, while the Federal Government has been in the enviable position of the number one net monetary debtor. The nonfinancial corporate sector also has been a net monetary debtor but to a much smaller degree than the Federal Government. To the extent that the household sector holds monetary debts and liabilities of the Federal Government, unanticipated inflation results in a gain for the Government and a loss to the household sector. This transfer of wealth is often called an inflation tax. But this does not end the process, because the Government (which belongs to all of us) passes its gain along to someone. The gain in the corporate sector goes only to net debtor firms. And since people own business firms, they ultimately realize most of the fruits, be they bitter or sweet, that corporations receive from an unexpected rise in the price level.

More importantly, however, both the business and household sectors are composed of monetary creditor and debtor units, and it is the unexpected price level increases which cause redistribution of wealth and income within these groups that many people find objectionable about inflation. Redistribution of wealth and income on some criterion which is in accordance with our con-

[2] Social Security payments do not appear to fall in this category. As prices climbed during the 1960's, Congress periodically raised the allowable monthly payments.

cept of fairness or equity is commonplace—witness the numerous subsidy and aid programs, not to mention that allegedly great equalizer, the progressive income tax. When inflation redistributes wealth, however, no consideration is given to individual circumstances, such as poverty, health, or number of dependents. Unanticipated inflation, unlike Robin Hood, takes from some and gives to others, be they poor, rich, young, or old. As a consequence, redistribution may not be on the basis of social goals or objectives.

Aside from its lack of social conscience, inflation has another trait which is reason for further concern. Use of money as a medium of exchange is an integral part of a high-output, specialized, and complex economy. Money makes possible the efficient flow of goods and services by eliminating the costly barter system. However, inflation makes the use of money more costly, and if severe enough, may cause a reduction in the real output of goods and services. People and business firms, in attempting to economize on the use of money, may resort to practices which tend to reduce specialization. They may spend time and effort searching out exchanges of goods and avoiding organized markets (for example, business firms integrating vertically to bypass supplier's and distributor's markets). Such actions would slash productivity in the economy. In a sense, society would be a loser.

ANTICIPATING INFLATION—HOW MUCH, FOR HOW LONG, AND AT WHAT COST

While there is little evidence that today's economy is coming apart at the seams, there are unmistakable signs that people, after experiencing four years of soaring prices, have come to expect future price increases. In order to protect themselves against the wealth-robbing effects of inflation, many people have acted upon their expectations. Consequently, we have high interest rates, built-in wage increases in some industries, reduced holdings of money balances by corporations and individuals, and wealth losses by those of us unfortunate enough to have had more money owed to us than we owed during these years.

Two considerable problems face the prospective anticipator of inflation. First, he must be able to estimate not only the amount or degree of inflation, but also its duration. That estimation is tough to make because the range of possible combinations of amounts and duration is infinite. For example, will prices rise 4 per cent for the next 20 years and then stabilize, or will they rise 6 per cent next year and then fall for several years? Even the best guru has trouble here. A correct answer would require an accurate forecast of future Government monetary and fiscal decisions in addition to any major event or disaster that would affect the physical stock of goods and services available. Instead of making crystal-ball estimates, many people simply negotiate contracts with escalator clauses tied to the cost of living or acquire assets with an equity "kicker" (such as convertible bonds). Increased use of such clauses and kickers in recent years is a rough gauge of how uncertain people are about the degree of expected inflation.

But an accurate estimate of expected changes in the price level is only the first obstacle to be overcome in anticipating inflation. The second and perhaps even more difficult problem centers on the ability of an individual to alter his asset and liability holdings to avoid being hurt by the coming inflation. For example, a person may not be able to reduce his holdings of monetary assets if they are of the nonnegotiable type, such as certain pension plans and insurance policies. Furthermore, he may not be able to contract enough debt to offset his holdings of monetary assets. In either case, even though the individual foresees the inflation, he is unable to forestall a loss in the purchasing power of his wealth when inflation occurs. Closely associated with this problem is that of the cost entailed in altering the form in which wealth is held. The cost of altering asset holdings depends upon the types of assets held; consequently, the cost of anticipating inflation differs among individuals holding different sets of assets.

Anticipating inflation for fun or profit is no easy matter. In addition, it is an expensive game to play because of the time and energy spent in calculating likely pricc level changes and attempting to alter the form in which wealth is held. If the costs and uncertainties entailed in anticipating inflation are added to those inefficiencies and inequities associated with inflation itself, it is easy to understand the merit of a stable price level. Price stability insures that gainers and losers will be determined on traditional values of thrift, hard work, and enterprise, rather than on the ability to anticipate and respond to price level changes.

READING 8
A Powerful Idea

"Keynesians need not apply" is a phrase that was once a common condition for employment of economists in many business and academic positions. John Maynard Keynes and his disciples, who were once regarded as left-wing socialists, are now legally institutionalized into the American establishment. Originally believed an enemy of the free-market system, Keynes is recognized to have been the chief instigator of far-reaching theoretical ideas that led directly to government intervention in a limited way to save the free-enterprise system from possible self-destruction. This article introduces us to Keynes and "The General Theory of Employment, Interest and Money," and shows how Keynesianism has spread from a few economists to the populace, eventually reaching the top levels of government.

Guideposts for Thought While Reading
What new concepts did Keynes develop about our economy? How has Keynesianism been implemented in America? How might Keynes have saved the free-enterprise system for Americans?

The Ideas of economists and political philosophers, both when they are right and when they are wrong, are more powerful than is commonly understood. Indeed the world is ruled by little else. Practical men, who believe themselves to be quite exempt from any intellectual influences, are usually the slaves of some defunct economist.

—*The General Theory of Employment, Interest and Money*

Concluding his most important book with those words in 1935, John Maynard Keynes was confident that he had laid down a philosophy that would move and change men's affairs. Today, some 20 years after his death, his theories are a prime influence on the world's free economies, especially on America's, the richest and most expansionist. In Washington the men who formulate the nation's economic policies have used Keynesian principles not only to avoid the violent cycles of prewar days but to produce a phenomenal economic growth and to achieve remarkably stable prices. . . .

Basically, Washington's economic managers scaled these heights by their adherence to Keynes's central theme: the modern capitalist economy does not automatically work at top efficiency, but can be raised to that level by the intervention and influence of the government. Keynes was the first to demonstrate convincingly that government has not only the ability but the responsibility to use its powers to increase production, incomes and jobs. Moreover, he argued that government can do this without violating freedom or restraining competition. It can, he said, achieve calculated prosperity by manipulating three main tools: tax policy, credit policy and budget policy. Their use would have the effect of strengthening private spending, investment and production.

FROM MISCHIEF TO ORTHODOXY

When Keynes first propagated his theories, many people considered them to be bizarre or slightly subversive, and Keynes himself to be little but a left-wing mischief maker. Now Keynes and his ideas, though they still make some people nervous, have been so widely accepted that they constitute both the new orthodoxy in the universities and the touchstone of economic management in Washington. They have led to a greater degree of government involvement in the nation's economy than ever before in time of general peace. . . .

WHY THEY WORK

By and large, Keynesian public policies are working well because the private sector of the economy is making them work. Government gave business the incentive to expand, but it was private businessmen who made the decisions as to whether, when and where to do it. Washington gave consumers a stimulus to spend, but millions of ordinary Americans made the decisions —so vital to the economy—as to how and how much to spend. For all that it has profited from the ideas of Lord Keynes, the U.S. economy is still the world's most private and most free-enterprising. Were he alive, Keynes would certainly like it to stay that way.

The recent successes of Keynes's theories have given a new stature and luster to the men who practice what Carlyle called "the dismal science." Economists have descended in force from their ivory towers and now sit confidently at the elbow of almost every important leader in Government and business, where they are increasingly called upon to forecast, plan and decide. In Washington the ideas of Keynes have been carried into the White House by such activist economists as Gardner Ackley, Arthur Okun, Otto Eckstein, Walter Heller, M.I.T.'s Paul Samuelson, Yale's James Tobin and Seymour Harris of the University of California at San Diego.

First the U.S. economists embraced Keynesianism, then the public accepted its tenets. Now even businessmen, traditionally hostile to Government's role in the economy, have been won over. They have begun to take for granted that Government will intervene to head off recession or choke off inflation, no longer think that deficit spending is immoral. Nor, in perhaps the greatest change of all, do they believe that Government will ever fully pay off its debt, any more than General Motors or IBM find it advisable to pay off their long-term obligations; instead of demanding payment, creditors would rather continue collecting interest.

TO A NEW STAGE

Though Keynes is the figure who looms largest in these recent changes, modern-day economists have naturally expanded and added to his theories, giving birth to a form of neo-Keynesianism. Because he was a creature of his times, Keynes was primarily interested in pulling a Depression-ridden world up to some form of prosperity and stability; today's economists are more concerned about making an already prospering economy grow still further. As Keynes might have put it: Keynesianism + the theory of growth = The New Economics. Says Gardner Ackley: "The new economics is based on Keynes. The fiscal revolution stems from him." Adds the University of Chicago's Milton Friedman, the nation's leading conservative economist, who was Presidential Candidate Barry Goldwater's adviser on economics: "We are all Keynesians now."...

Far from being a socialist left-winger, Keynes (pronounced canes) was a high-caste Establishment leader who disdained what he called "the boorish proletariat" and said: "For better or worse, I am a bourgeois economist." Keynes was suspicious of the power of unions, inveighed against the perils of inflation, praised the virtue of profits. "The engine which drives Enterprise," he wrote, "is not Thrift but Profit." He condemned the

Marxists as being "illogical and so dull" and saw himself as a doctor of capitalism, which he was convinced could lead mankind to universal plenty within a century. Communists, Marxists and the British Labor Party's radical fringe damned Keynes because he sought to strengthen a system that they wanted to overthrow.

TRUTH AND CONSEQUENCES

Keynes was born the year Marx died (1883) and died in the first full year of capitalism's lengthy postwar boom (1946). The son of a noted Cambridge political economist, he whizzed through Eton and Cambridge, then entered the civil service. He got his lowest mark in economics. "The examiners," he later remarked, "presumably knew less than I did." He entered the India Office, soon after became a Cambridge don. Later, he was the British Treasury's representative to the Versailles Conference, and saw that it settled nothing but the inevitability of another disaster. He resigned in protest and wrote a book, *The Economic Consequences of the Peace,* that stirred an international sensation by clearly foretelling the crisis to come.

He went back to teaching at Cambridge, but at the same time operated with skill and dash in business. The National Mutual Life Assurance Society named him its chairman, and whenever he gave his annual reports to stockholders, the London Money Market suspended trading to hear his forecasts for interest rates in the year ahead. He was also editor of the erudite British *Economic Journal,* chairman of the *New Statesman and Nation* and a director of the Bank of England.

Keynes began each day propped up in bed, poring for half an hour over reports of the world's gyrating currency and commodity markets; by speculating in them, he earned a fortune of more than $2,000,000. Money, he said, should be valued not as a possession but "as a means to the enjoyments and realities of life." He took pleasure in assembling the world's finest collection of Newton's manuscripts and in organizing London's Camargo Ballet and Cambridge's Arts Theater. Later, the government tapped him to head Britain's Arts Council, and in 1942 King George VI made him a lord.

Part dilettante and part Renaissance man, Keynes moved easily in Britain's eclectic world of arts and letters. Though he remarked that economists should be humble, like dentists, he enjoyed trouncing countesses at bridge and Prime Ministers at lunch-table debates. He became a leader of the Bloomsbury set of avant-garde writers and painters, including Virginia and Leonard Woolf, Lytton Strachey and E. M. Forster. At a party at the Sitwells, he met Lydia Lopokova, a ballerina of the Diaghilev Russian ballet. She was blonde and buxom; he was frail and stoop-shouldered, with watery blue eyes. She chucked her career to marry him. His only regret in life, said Keynes shortly before his death of a heart attack, was that he had not drunk more champagne.

THE WHOLE ECONOMY

The thrust of Keynes's personality, however strong, was vastly less important than the force of his ideas. Those ideas were so original and persuasive that Keynes now ranks with Adam Smith and Karl Marx as one of history's most significant economists. Today his theses are the basis of economic policies in Britain, Canada, Australia and part of Continental Europe, as well as in the U.S.

Economics is a young science, a mere 200 years old. Addressing its problems in the second half of its second century, Keynes was more successful than his predecessors in seeing it whole. Great theorists before him had tried to take a wide view of economic forces, but they lacked the 20th century statistical tools to do the job, and they tended to concentrate on certain specialties. Adam Smith focused on the marketplace, Malthus on population, Ricardo on rent and land, Marx on labor and wages. Modern economists call those specializations "microeconomics"; Keynes was the precursor of what is now known as "macroeconomics"—from the Greek *makros,* for large or extended. He decided that the way to look at the economy was to measure all the myriad forces tugging and pulling at it—production, prices, profits, incomes, interest rates, government policies.

For most of his life, Keynes wrote, wrote, wrote. He was so prolific that a compendium of his books, tracts and essays fills 22 pages. In succession he wrote books about mathematical probability (1921), the gold standard and monetary reform (1923), and the causes of business cycles (1930); each of his works further developed his economic thinking. Then he bundled his major theories into his magnum opus, *The General Theory,* published in 1936. It is an uneven and ill-organized book, as difficult as *Deuteronomy* and open to almost as many interpretations. Yet for all its faults, it had more influence in a shorter time than any other book ever written on economics, including Smith's *The Wealth of Nations* and Marx's *Das Kapital.*

PERMANENT QUASI-BOOM

Keynes perceived that the prime goal of any economy was to achieve "full employment." By that, he meant full employment of materials and machines as well as of men. Before Keynes, classical economists had presumed that the economy was naturally regulated by what Adam Smith had called the "invisible hand," which brought all forces into balance and used them fully. Smith argued, for example, that if wages rose too fast, employers would lay off so many workers that wages would fall until they reached the point at which employers would start rehiring. French economist Jean Baptiste Say embroidered that idea by theorizing that production always creates just enough income to consume whatever it produces, thus permitting any excesses of demand to correct themselves quickly.

Keynes showed that the hard facts of history contradicted these unrealistic assumptions. For centuries, he pointed out, the economic cycle had gyrated from giddy boom to violent bust; periods of inflated prosperity induced a speculative rise, which then disrupted commerce and led inexorably to impoverished deflation. The climax came during the depression of the 1930s. Wages plummeted and unemployment rocketed, but neither the *laissez-faire* classicists nor the sullen and angry Communists adequately diagnosed the disease or offered any reasonable remedies.

By applying both logic and historical example to economic cycles, Keynes showed that the automatic stabilizers that economists had long banked on could actually aggravate rather than prevent a depression. If employers responded to a fall-off in demand by slicing wages and dumping workers, said Keynes, that would only reduce incomes and demand, and plunge production still deeper. If bankers responded to a fall-off in savings by raising interest rates, that would not tempt penniless people to save more—but it would move hardpressed industrialists to borrow less for capital investment. Yet Keynes did not despair of capitalism as so many other economists did. Said he: "The right remedy for the trade cycle is not to be found in abolishing booms and keeping us permanently in a semi-slump; but in abolishing slumps and thus keeping us permanently in a quasi-boom."

MANAGEMENT OF DEMAND

The key to achieving that, Keynes perceived, is to maintain constantly a high level of what he called "aggregate demand." To him, that meant the total of all demand in the economy—demand for consumption and for investment, for both private and public purposes. His inescapable conclusion was that, if private demand should flag and falter, then it had to be revived and stimulated by the only force strong enough to lift consumption: the government.

The pre-Keynesian "classical" economists had thought of the government too. But almost all of them had contended that, in times of depression, the government should raise taxes and reduce spending in order to balance the budget. In the early 1930s, Keynes cried out that the only way to revive aggregate demand was for the government to cut taxes, reduce interest rates, spend heavily—and deficits be damned. Said Keynes: "The State will have to exercise a guiding influence on the propensity to consume partly through its scheme of taxation, partly by fixing the rates of interest, and partly, perhaps, in other ways."

A few other economists of Keynes's time had called for more or less the same thing. Yet Keynes was the only one with enough influence and stature to get governments to sit up and pay attention. He was the right man at the right time, and his career and fame derived largely from the fact that when his theories appeared the world was racked by history's worst depression and governments were desperately searching for a way out.

Contrary to the Marxists and the socialists, Keynes opposed government ownership of industry and fought those centralists who would plan everything ("They wish to serve not God but the devil"). While he called for conscious and calculated state intervention, he argued just as passionately that the government had no right to tamper with individual freedoms to choose or change jobs, to buy or sell goods, or to earn respectable profits. He had tremendous faith that private men could change, improve and expand capitalism.

PERHAPS IMMORAL

Like any genius, Keynes had plenty of faults and shortcomings. Even his admirers admit that he could be maddeningly abstruse and confusing. M.I.T.'s Paul Samuelson, for example, thinks that Keynes downplayed the importance of monetary policy. His few outright critics feel that, while he knew how to buoy a depression-stricken industrial economy, he offered little in the way of practical information about how to keep a prosperous modern economy fat and secure. Keynesian theories are certainly unworkable in the underdeveloped nations, where the problem is not too little demand but insufficient supply, and where the object is not to stimulate consumption but to spur savings, form capital and raise production.

Such critics as former U.S. Budget Director Maurice Stans still worry that Keynes makes spenders seem virtuous and savers wicked, and thus subtly threatens the nation's moral fiber. Other doubters contend that earlier obscure economists originated some of the ideas that Keynes popularized, and that all he did was wrap them up in a general theory. But even his severest detractors bow to his brilliance, use the macroeconomic terms and framework that he devised, and concede that his main theories have largely worked out in practice.

WHAT DID HE SAY?

Though Keynes's gospel has only recently come to full flower, a school of fervid apostles has been preaching it in the U.S. for more than a generation. Harvard's Alvin Hansen, the first great Keynesian teacher, taught it to hundreds of economists, many of them now in high positions. Hansen's brightest student was Paul Samuelson, who later wrote a Keynesian-angled college textbook on economics that has gone to 2,000,000 copies and influenced the thinking of countless teachers and students.

Franklin Roosevelt was at first no fan of Keynes—"I didn't understand one word that man was saying," he sniffed after being lectured by Keynes at the White House in 1934—but some of his economists gradually began to lean on Keynesian language and logic to rationalize huge deficits. In World War II, Washington planners used Keynesian ideas to formulate their policies of deficit spending.

Congress adopted the Keynesian course in 1946, when it passed the Employment Act, establishing Government responsibility to achieve "maximum employment, production and purchasing power." The act also created the Council of Economic Advisers, which for the first time brought professional economic thinking into close and constant touch with the President. Surprisingly it was Dwight Eisenhower's not-notably-Keynesian economists who most effectively demonstrated the efficacy of Keynes's antirecession prescriptions; to fight the slumps of

1953-54 and 1957-58, they turned to prodigious spending and huge deficits.

J.M.K. & L.B.J.

Still, Keynesianism made its biggest breakthrough under John Kennedy, who, as Arthur Schlesinger reports in *A Thousand Days*, "was unquestionably the first Keynesian President." Kennedy's economists, led by Chief Economic Adviser Walter Heller, presided over the birth of the New Economics as a practical policy and set out to add a new dimension to Keynesianism. They began to use Keynes's theories as a basis not only for correcting the 1960 recession, which prematurely arrived only two years after the 1957-58 recession, but also to spur an expanding economy to still faster growth. Kennedy was intrigued by the "growth gap" theory, first put across to him by Yale Economist Arthur Okun (now a member of the Council of Economic Advisers), who argued that even though the U.S. was prosperous, it was producing $51 billion a year less than it really could. Under the prodding and guidance of Heller, Kennedy thereupon opened the door to activist, imaginative economics.

He particularly called for tax reductions—a step that Keynes had advocated as early as 1933. The Kennedy Administration stimulated capital investment by giving businessmen a 7% tax kickback on their purchases of new equipment and by liberalizing depreciation allowances. Kennedy also campaigned for an overall reduction in the oppressive income-tax rates in order to increase further both investment and personal consumption. That idea, he remarked, was "straight Keynes and Heller."

Lyndon Johnson came into the presidency worrying about the wisdom of large deficits and questioning the need for a tax cut, but he was convinced by the Keynesian economists around him, and hurried the measure through Congress.

READING 9
Research on Household Behavior
Robert Ferber

Dr. Ferber is research professor of economics, Bureau of Economics and Business Research, and professor of economics in the Department of Economics, University of Illinois. In this paper, Dr. Ferber surveys the main empirical research of recent years on household behavior showing both empirical work and the underlying theoretical development of consumer spending and saving.

Guideposts for Thought While Reading
What is the "Pigou real-balance effect"? What are the three theories of spending or saving presented by Ferber in this excerpt? What conclusion does Ferber reach regarding the adequacy and the contribution to the development of economic thought provided by each of the theories?

I. GENERAL THEORIES OF SPENDING OR SAVING BEHAVIOR

Three general theories currently exist on the determinants of total consumer spending: the *absolute income hypothesis,* the *relative income hypothesis,* and the *permanent income hypothesis.* Though radically different in interpretation, they nevertheless possess certain properties in common. One such property is their purported generality. Each has been used on time series as well as on cross-section data and to derive macro- as well as micro-relationships. Each was advanced originally in terms of individual behavior and then generalized to aggregate behavior, sometimes with explicit recognition of the aggregation problem, and at other times largely ignoring it on the apparent presumption that nonlinearities or distributional effects are relatively unimportant.

Each hypothesis postulates a relationship between consump-

Reprinted by permission of the publisher from Robert Ferber, "Research on Household Behavior," *American Economic Review,* March 1962, pp. 20–32.

tion and income, though the concepts underlying these terms may vary substantially. In other words, the primary concern is to isolate the influence of income, and occasionally of wealth, on consumer spending, holding constant the effect of other possibly relevant, less important variables—age, family composition, location of residence, education, etc. Each is the subject of wide controversy, receiving support from some empirical studies but not from others. Finally, each when first presented appears deceptively simple, at least in theory, but when it comes to implementation, proponents of the same hypothesis often disagree with each other on appropriate definitions and approaches. This will become clear from a consideration of each hypothesis in turn.

A. Absolute Income Hypothesis

". . . men are disposed, as a rule and on the average, to increase their consumption as their income increases, but not by as much as the increase in their income." Whether or not this is the original statement of the absolute income hypothesis, there is no doubt that this statement by Keynes stimulated much empirical work to test this hypothesis and to derive "the consumption function." Many of these studies were carried out on time series, the general practice being to correlate aggregate consumption expenditures over time with aggregate disposable income and various other variables. They need not concern us here except to note that invariably they "corroborated" the hypothesis, producing very high goodness of fit (adjusted correlation coefficients of .98 or more), with current income accounting for the bulk of the variation in consumption, the average and marginal propensities being less than unity, and with the marginal propensity less than the average propensity.

One early modification of the absolute income hypothesis was brought about by a theoretical controversy regarding the existence of any automatic force to assure full-employment equilibrium. Keynes took a negative position, but others showed that a full-employment equilibrium position could exist if consumption expenditures depended on wealth as well as on income, the "Pigou real balance effect." It was only in the postwar period that data became available to test the relevance of a wealth variable. Such tests as were made did tend to show that aggregate consumption was influenced by this variable, though nowhere to the extent of the influence of current income. It is pertinent to note, however, that the early postwar years were characterized by high asset-income ratios, low stocks of durables, and relatively little debt.

At the micro level, many studies had been carried out prior to the advent of *The General Theory* but their focus invariably was on ascertaining budget relations for different groups of families or deriving Engel curves for particular components of expenditure. In retrospect, such of these studies as were applicable appeared to corroborate the absolute income hypothesis. Indeed, it was this hypothesis that served as the basis for the derivation of estimates of aggregate expenditures for different population groups in 1935-36, namely, by "blowing up" average consumption observed at each income level in the 1935-36 Consumer Purchases Study. The absolute income hypothesis also served as a basis for the derivation of aggregate forecasts of postwar consumption patterns, particularly the consumption patterns that might be expected under full employment.

In its empirical applications the absolute income hypothesis has generally followed one of two forms. One form has been to express the level of saving, or of consumption expenditures, as a function of income and of other variables, i.e.:

$$S = a + bY + cZ + u \tag{1}$$

where S represents saving, Y is income, Z is a conglomeration of other variables, u is a stochastic term, and the other letters represent parameters.

Questions about the adequacy of the absolute income hypothesis arose because of its apparent inability to reconcile budget data on saving with observed long-run trends. Estimates of national saving and other aggregates derived by Kuznets and later by Goldsmith indicated that the aggregate saving ratio had remained virtually constant since the 1870's. Yet budget studies showed that the saving ratio rose substantially with income level. Since incomes have risen tremendously since the 1870's by almost any standard, this would suggest, according to the absolute income hypothesis, that the aggregate saving ratio should have moved up noticeably over time.

B. Relative Income Hypothesis

An answer to this apparent inconsistency is provided by the relative income hypothesis, which seems to have been first propounded by Dorothy Brady and Rose Friedman. Its underlying assumption is that the saving rate depends not on the level of income but on the relative position of the individual on the income scale, i.e.:

$$\frac{s}{y} = a + b\,\frac{y}{\bar{y}} \tag{2}$$

where s and y represent individual saving and income, respectively, and $\bar{y}$ represents average income.

Much additional theoretical and empirical support of this hypothesis was provided by the work of Modigliani and of Duesenberry, carried out at about the same time. On a theoretical level, Duesenberry supplied psychological support for this hypothesis, noting that a strong tendency exists in our social system for people to emulate their neighbors and, at the same time, to strive constantly toward a higher standard of living. Hence, once a new, higher standard of living is obtained, as at a cyclical peak, people are reluctant to return to a lower level when incomes go down. In other words, people seek to maintain at least the highest standard of living attained in the past.

On the basis of this reasoning, Duesenberry inferred that from an aggregate time-series point of view the relative income hypothesis could be transformed into one expressing the saving rate as a function of the ratio of current income to the highest level previously reached, i.e.:

$$\frac{S}{Y} = a + b\,\frac{Y}{Y_0} \tag{3}$$

where Y_0 represents the highest level of income previously attained (after deflation for changes in prices and population).

The implication of this hypothesis is that the saving ratio in the long run is constant, independent of the absolute level of income, although in the short run (from one cycle to another) the rate depends on the ratio of current income to previous peak income.

One variation of this approach has been the suggestion by Davis: that previous peak consumption be substituted for previous peak income. The rationale for this suggestion is that people become adjusted to a certain standard of *consumption*, rather than to a certain level of income, so that it is past spending that influences current consumption rather than past income. An additional argument for the substitution of consumption for income is that current income, referring to a period of one year or less, is likely to be less stable and less representative of a family's living standard than is current consumption.

The empirical support for the relative income hypothesis has proceeded along two lines. One consisted of showing that the aggregate relations of a form similar to (3) provide at least as good explanations and statistical "fits" to fluctuations in national personal saving over time as the various forms of the absolute income hypothesis. Noteworthy in this respect was the finding of an independent evaluation that these functions yielded greater predictive accuracy outside of the period of observation than did various forms of the absolute income hypothesis. In addition, of course, there was the constancy of the aggregate saving ratio over time which fitted in with the relative income hypothesis.

Second, a number of instances were demonstrated in which the relative income hypothesis was, and the absolute income hypothesis was not, able to explain differences in saving or consumption patterns observed in budget data. Thus, Brady and Friedman by this approach were able to reconcile the higher saving rates of village than city families at the same levels of income in 1935-36, and again in 1941; the similarly higher saving rates of farm families than nonfarm families in 1935-36, and also in 1941; and various geographical differences in saving rates in 1935-36. Duesenberry used this hypothesis to reconcile the fact that dissaving at a given level of income was less frequent in 1941 than in 1935-36, that Negro families saved more than white families in 1935-36 at the same level of income, as well as to explain geographic differences in saving rates. Brady showed that family saving varied not only with family income but also with the income level of the community in which it resided.

Findings such as these do not necessarily serve to rule out the absolute income hypothesis, and it is still very much of an open question whether the facts do indeed conflict with the absolute income hypothesis or whether the hypothesis has been misinterpreted. A basic tenet of the hypothesis is the *ceteris paribus* assumption for all variables other than (current) income. Yet, data availability in empirical studies has been too restricted to allow other principal relevant variables to be held constant; and if such variables are indeed not constant, failure of saving, or the saving rate, to fluctuate with income may represent simply the effects of these omitted variables. Thus, Tobin shows that the apparent failure of the absolute income hypothesis to explain Negro-white saving differentials at the same level of income can be reconciled if allowance is made for the smaller financial resources available to Negro families than to white families. Because of this difference in wealth, Negro families are unable to dissave as frequently or as much as white families at the same income level, and therefore require extra financial reserves to tide them over emergencies.

In a similar manner Tobin shows that wealth differentials may explain geographic differences in saving rates, and even the historical constancy of the saving ratio. The latter is based on the presumption that the substantial growth in asset holdings over time may have reduced the need for saving out of current income and contributed to raising the propensity to consume as real income increased. Admittedly, the evidence is rather sketchy, as is noted by Tobin and is stressed by Milton Friedman. However, if a variable such as wealth could be shown to have influenced the secular propensity to consume, the absolute income hypothesis could be vindicated.

C. The Permanent Income Hypothesis

This most recent hypothesis on consumer behavior grew out of the rising concern regarding the adequacy of current income as the most appropriate determinant of consumption expenditures. Particularly among nonwage-earner families income receipts vary substantially from period to period, while consumption outlays exhibit much greater stability. This led to the belief that people geared their expenditures to average actual and anticipated income over a number of periods rather than only to income received in the current period. The central idea is as follows:

> Consider a large number of men all earning $100 a week and spending $100 a week on current consumption. Let them receive their pay once a week, the pay days being staggered, so that one-seventh are paid on Sunday, one-seventh on Monday, and so on. Suppose we collected budget data for a sample of these men for one day chosen at random, defined income as cash receipts on that day, and defined consumption as cash expenditures. One-seventh of the men would be recorded as having an income of $100, six-sevenths as having an income of zero. It may well be that the men would spend more on pay day than on other days but they would also make expenditures on other days, so we would record the one-seventh with an income of $100 as having positive savings, the other six-sevenths as having negative savings. Consumption might appear to rise with income, but, if so, not as much as income, so that the fraction of income saved would rise with income. These results tell us nothing meaningful about consumption behavior; they simply reflect the use of inappropriate concepts of income and consumption. Men do not adapt their cash expenditures on consumption to their cash receipts, and

their cash expenditures on consumption may not be a good index of the value of services consumed—in our simple example, consumption expenditures might well be zero on Sunday.

As is often the case with developments of this sort, a theoretical foundation for this hypothesis was developed more or less independently by two different people: by Milton Friedman and by Franco Modigliani, the latter with the collaboration of R. E. Brumberg and Albert Ando. The two versions are similar in principle, though different in certain respects.

In the Friedman version a consumer unit is assumed to determine its standard of living on the basis of expected returns from its resources over its lifetime. These returns are expected to be constant from year to year, though in actual practice some fluctuation would result over time with changes in the anticipated amount of capital resources. The expenditures of the consumer unit are set as a constant proportion (k) of this permanent level of income, the value of k varying for consumer units of different types and of different tastes. Actual consumption and actual income deviate from these planned, or permanent, levels to the extent that transitory factors enter in, e.g., a crop failure in the case of farm family income or unexpected medical bills in the case of spending. However, these transitory factors are essentially random and independent of each other, with the primary result of serving to obscure the true underlying relationship between the permanent components of income and of consumption.

The Modigliani-Brumberg-Ando (MBA) formulation is essentially a "permanent wealth" hypothesis rather than a "permanent income" hypothesis, though in practice the two approaches converge. In its most recent formulation, the household or consumer unit is assumed to determine "the amount available for consumption over life, which is the sum of the household's net worth at the beginning of the period . . . plus the present value of its non-property income . . . minus present value of planned bequests." The amount allocated to consumption is a certain proportion of these resources. Actual consumption, however, differs from this allocated amount by transitory expenditures and by certain stochastic factors (v).

Thus, this relationship is essentially the same as that derived by Friedman.

In either formulation the central tenet is the assumption that the proportion of permanent income saved by a consumer unit in a given period is independent of its income (or its resources) during that period, and furthermore that transitory incomes may have no (Friedman) or little (MBA) effect on current consumption.

Clearly, from an empirical point of view, this is a very difficult hypothesis to test, because of the difficulty of measuring permanent income and permanent consumption. Nevertheless, the permanent income hypothesis is analytically a very rich one and lends itself to a number of significant inferences regarding individual and aggregate behavior.

Despite some seemingly impressive arguments, the permanent income hypothesis is by no means established. Indeed, the evidence to the contrary seems at least as impressive. This opposing evidence, like the arguments for the theory, covers both theoretical and empirical considerations. On a theoretical plane, question is raised regarding the validity of the two central tenets of the theory, namely, the independence of k of the level of income, and the lack of correlation between transitory consumption and transitory income. Thus, Friend and Kravis note that the permanent income hypothesis implies "that low-income families will have no greater preference for purchase of future goods than will high-income families" while Duesenberry makes a similar criticism. Such a concept they find to be seriously deficient on purely deductive grounds because of the very different kinds of pressures and motivations acting on families at different income levels.

In a similar fashion, the assumption of a zero marginal propensity to consume out of transitory income is questioned, partly on the basis that low-income families are under strong pressures to spend any unexpected income to meet current needs, and partly because of the very unequal distribution of wealth which mitigates against dissaving by low-income families to maintain consumption in the face of temporary declines in income.

Criticism of the permanent income hypothesis on empirical grounds has followed two lines. One line has been to note that much of the evidence advanced is either inconclusive or is not inconsistent with other principal hypotheses. Thus, under the absolute income hypothesis one would also expect the marginal propensity to consume to be less than the average propensity. Furthermore, the interpretation given by Friedman to many of his test results is not the only possible interpretation and is at times subject to considerable doubt, though some of the evidence can apparently be interpreted only in terms of it.

To test the zero propensity to consume out of transitory income, Bodkin analyzed by correlation methods the extent to which consumption expenditures were made out of unexpected dividends paid in early 1950 out of National Service Life Insurance. This study yielded not only a statistically significant propensity but a propensity to consume out of these dividends much higher than out of regular income. On the other hand, Kreinin obtained a low marginal propensity to consume out of restitution payments made by Germany to former citizens in Israel. However, these payments could hardly have been unexpected.

Admittedly, these negative findings are themselves subject to question. For example, the reliability and representativeness of budget data collected in a partial wartime period such as 1950 is a matter of doubt. In any event, the permanent income hypothesis is far from proven. However, whether or not the permanent income hypothesis turns out to be valid, there is little doubt that, to quote Tobin, "This is one of those rare contributions of which it can be said that research and thought in its field will not be the same henceforth." Most of all, it has led to widespread recognition of the possible effects of variability in income on consumption patterns and has provided a theoretical basis for measuring these effects as a springboard for a more realistic theory of consumer behavior.

READING 10
What Is Inflation?

Martin Bronfenbrenner and
Franklyn D. Holzman

Dr. Bronfenbrenner, professor of economics at Carnegie-Mellon University, and Dr. Holzman, who is professor of economics at Tufts University, delineate the fundamental types of inflation which have been identified in our economy. This reading, which is an excerpt from a survey paper on inflation gives an analytical supply-demand

Reprinted by permission of the publisher from Martin Bronfenbrenner and Franklyn D. Holzman, "Survey of Inflation Theory," *American Economic Review*, September 1963, pp. 594–602.

approach to the inflation phenomena. The reader should be careful to note the special nature of the aggregate supply and demand curves as derived in this paper.

Guideposts for Thought While Reading

Why is it important from a policy standpoint to know whether inflation is caused by excess demand or by cost push? As outlined in this paper, what are the four possible ways in which inflation might occur?

Since 1945 the geographical extent and temporal stubbornness of *The Great Inflation* have shaken many economists' faith in the orthodoxies of preceding generations. Neo-orthodoxies, including restatements, are only dimly in evidence. Our survey is accordingly more of a guide through chaos than a history of received doctrine or a systematic critique of a few rival positions.

I. SOURCES AND DEFINITIONS OF INFLATION

Sources of Inflation

One key issue is the identification of the fundamental source or sources of inflationary pressure. Does inflation arise from the demand side of the goods, factor, and asset markets, from the supply side, or from some combination of the two—the so-called mixed inflation? Does the answer differ in the short and the long run, in developed and underdeveloped economies, with differences in countries' economic structures, in creeping, trotting, or galloping inflations, in the 1950's and the 1940's?

Answers to such questions are not only academic, but have important policy implications. Thus, if an inflation is due to excess demand, it is generally considered controllable by demand-reducing fiscal and monetary policies. If it is due largely to forces of cost and supply, it may not yield to such easy therapy. Fiscal and monetary policies, that is to say, may cure a cost inflation only at the price of unemployment and slower growth, either temporary or permanent. Many cost-inflation theorists therefore propose mitigation rather than elimination of inflation. Others rely on voluntary restraints in pricing and bargaining. Still others propose disequilibrium systems of direct control (wage- and price-fixing, rationing, allocations) if high levels of employment and growth are to be reconciled with price stability.

The four diagrams of Figure 1 illustrate different types of inflationary positions in a closed economy. The horizontal axes all represent real national income or GNP; the vertical axes represent "the" price level with no direct controls. Aggregate demand curves *D* are drawn sloping downward. This slope illustrates Patinkin real-balance effects with a constant nominal money supply and static price expectations. In some circumstances inflation-engendered redistribution of income and wealth also leads to a downward slope of *D*. Aggregate supply curves *S* are drawn sloping upward—in some full-employment cases, as vertical lines. Shifts in aggregate supply functions result from

FIGURE 1

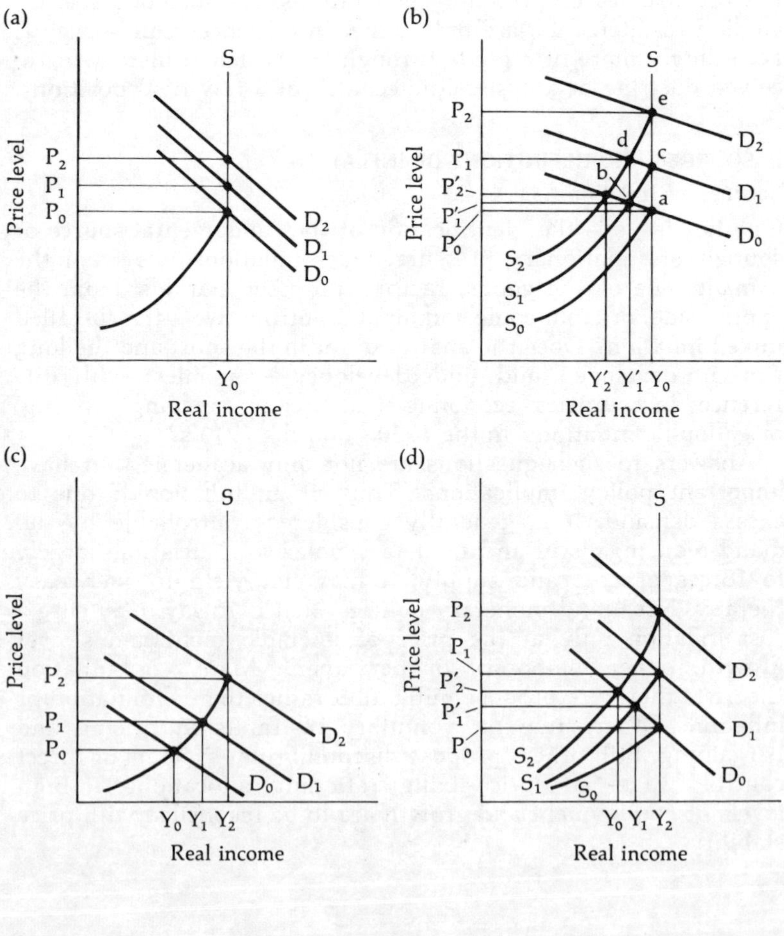

changes in money-profit margins and money-wage rates. Interdependence between D and S functions may exist; it is considered explicitly in Figure 1d.

Pure-demand-inflation theorists tend to assume that at some income level Y_0 (Figure 1a), corresponding to full employment, the aggregate supply function becomes completely inelastic, as drawn. No income level lower than Y_0 is a full-employment one, and increases in demand beyond D_0, as to D_1 and D_2, raise the price level from P_0 to P_1 and P_2.

Pure-supply-inflation theorists, on the other hand, maintain that, in societies of oligopolies, unions, and other pressure groups, the aggregate supply curve moves upward, as from S_0 to S_1 and S_2 in Figure 1b, whatever happens to aggregate demand. The full-employment real-income level Y_0 is then maintainable only at rising price levels (P_0, P_1, P_2). Unemployment is the cost of holding prices closer to P_0 or to any previously achieved level. If aggregate demand, for example, is held at D_0, real income falls to Y_1 and Y_2. Even so, the price level rises from P_0 to P_1' to P_2'. If the government is committed to full employment, the path of temporary equilibrium points will be something like *a-b-c-d-e*.

One variety of mixed-inflation theory denies for several reasons, one of them money illusion, that aggregate supply is price-inelastic at full employment. In Figure 1c, (Y_0, P_0), (Y_1, P_1), and (Y_2, P_2) are all full-employment positions in that no involuntary unemployment exists. The first corresponds to A. P. Lerner's "low full employment" with substantial voluntary unemployment, and the last to his "high full employment" with little or none. The region between low and high full employment was called by Keynes "semi-inflation" in contrast to the true or full inflation of Figure 1a. Mixed-inflation theorists usually think society prefers the couple (Y_2, P_2) to the other alternatives, even when all three are full-employment positions. In this type of mixed-inflation theory, inflation does not continue after (Y_2, P_2) is reached. In this respect, the solution is related more closely to demand than to cost inflation. This model is mainly relevant to the possible growth-inducing effects of inflation.

Another mixed theory is illustrated in Figure 1d, where interrelated shifts in S and D induce unemployment inflation. This differs from the pure cost inflation of Figure 1b in that the extent of the shift in supply increases as unemployment declines. Whether demand rises from D_0 to D_1 and D_2 or remains at D_0, supply moves from S_0 to S_1 and S_2; the shift is larger, the closer the economy approaches full employment at Y_2. In this version full employment is a more unstable position, and more difficult to achieve by rapid inflation than under pure cost-push, because the induced supply shifts are larger at low levels of unemployment. On the other hand, price stability may be possible at the cost of less unemployment in this model than in the one represented in Figure 1b. The model represented in Figure 1d may also be more realistic than that of Figure 1b; casual empiricism suggests that cost-push is often moderated by the level of demand.

Definition of Inflation

In the preceding diagrams and discussion, inflation has meant a rise in "the" price level, i.e., a depreciation of the monetary unit. This is the most obvious, but by no means the only, definition. Indeed, disagreement over the definition of the term is symptomatic of the confusion in inflation theory. We list some issues slurred over by definitions in terms of "the" price level. (No such list can be exhaustive.)

1. Which of an infinity of possible price levels is meant? An implicit national income or GNP deflator has recently come into favor. Such deflators were largely unknown before 1939, and reliance was usually placed on wholesale price indexes. In many cases price indexes will show widely differing rates of change, and the differences may become a political issue.

2. What allowance should be made for new products, quality changes, shifts in consumption habits, and other factors considered in the utility analysis of price index numbers? In the United States, an AFL-CIO task force relied on these factors during World War II in alleging that the official indexes understated the magnitude of wartime inflation. This was the Meany-Thomas Report. In the late 1950's, a National Bureau of Economic Research task force, headed by Stigler, suggested on similar grounds that the indexes have overstated the magnitude of U.S. inflation subsequent to the Korean War.

3. When price controls are in effect, should the indexes be based on black market as well as official prices? Even in the absence of organized black markets, what allowances, if any, should be made for lessened availability of goods under control? The terms "repressed" and "suppressed" inflation have been used to refer to these cases, as distinguished from "open" inflation when no anti-inflationary direct controls are in effect. Are "repressed" and "suppressed" inflation types of inflation or alternatives to inflation?

4. Assume that commodity taxes and subsidies are used

widely, as in contemporary France. Should prices be taken gross or net of such taxes and subsidies? Suppose also that, as in France before 1959, subsidies are used to hold individual prices down, with commodities in the official indexes being given larger subsidies (or lower taxes) than others. How reliable are price indexes under this sort of *a posteriori* sampling bias?

5. Assume that, following destruction and disruption due to war, flood, or earthquake, there is a sharp fall (i.e., shift to the left) in the aggregate supply curves of Figure 1. Is the result to be called inflationary when no increase in aggregate demand has occurred? Does it make any difference if the same destruction and disruption simultaneously create unemployment?

6. Consider Figure 1c, where a rise in the price level leads, at least in the short run, to an increase in real output and employment. Is this really inflationary, or should the term be limited to instances in which no significant increases in output or employment occur?

7. Suppose that, as probably happened in the 1920's, technical progress has brought about a widespread reduction in production costs with no corresponding reduction in prices. Were the resulting increases in money wages and gross profits inflationary?

8. Does it make a difference whether price increases have been anticipated correctly (so as to minimize their effects on the distribution of income), or whether they are unanticipated or anticipated incorrectly? As an extreme case of Lerner's "expectational" definition of inflation, suppose that prices fell by 5 per cent when a fall of 10 per cent was anticipated generally. Is this inflation?

9. Does it make a difference, as suggested by James, whether a price level change is or is not regarded as permanent and irreversible?

Our answers to these questions may be affected by extraneous issues such as whether or not we consider inflation, or tight money, or direct controls to be Good Things. If one considers inflation, for example, a Bad Thing, it is difficult to avoid a question-begging definition which will render Good Results somehow noninflationary, even when accompanied by price increases.

For those unwilling to accept the evidence of price indexes per se, a number of alternative definitions are available. By no means all of these are new, and, once again, the list is not intended to be exhaustive.

1. Inflation is a condition of generalized excess demand, in which "too much money chases too few goods."

2. Inflation is a rise of the money stock or money income, either total or per capita.

3. Inflation is a rise in price levels with additional characteristics or conditions: it is incompletely anticipated; it leads (via cost increases) to further rises; it does not increase employment and real output; it is faster than some "safe" rate; it arises "from the side of money"; it is measured by prices net of indirect taxes and subsidies; and/or it is irreversible.

4. Inflation is a fall in the external value of money as measured by foreign exchange rates, by the price of gold, or indicated by excess demand for gold or foreign exchange at official rates.

An unusually comprehensive definition (including cost-push in the factor markets and excess demand in output and factor markets) is Turvey's. He calls inflation "the process resulting from competition in attempting to maintain total real income, total real expenditure, and/or total output at a level which has become physically impossible, or attempting to increase any of them to a level which is physically impossible." In what follows, we avoid choice between alternative definitions in the hope that most of them will lead to similar qualitative results.

II. DEMAND INFLATION

Initial Orthodoxies

During World War II, Smithies maintained that: "The writer on inflation is fortunate in that his subject is generally well understood by economists." Nevertheless, two positions were rival claimants to the title of orthodoxy. The quantity theory of money, with centuries of tradition behind it, imputed price level changes to changes in the quantity of money (a stock). An increase in this stock generated excess supply of money at existing prices and interest rates, meaning excess demand for nonmonetary assets. The other position, following Keynes' *How to Pay for the War*, stressed the level of national expenditure (a flow) as the main determinant of the price level, with increasing expenditures opening an inflationary gap after full employment was attained.

Most pre-Keynesians used the quantity theory to assert long-run proportionality between the quantity of money and the price level, although neither was defined unequivocally. This theory fell into disrepute during the 1930's because of sharp changes in the velocity of circulation, which it had treated as nearly constant; in other words, money as a proportion of income and assets or of the volume of real income and transactions actually varied extensively. However, "under full employment" and "over the long run," the money supply was still considered the major single determinant of the price level. A restatement of the quantity theory for the short run was found in the work of Warburton, who showed that changes in the quantity of money led changes in velocity (interpreted as deviations from statistical trend lines). Warburton regarded changes in the quantity of money as the causal force in fluctuations of the price level, partly directly [$\Delta M \rightarrow (\Delta Y$ and $\Delta P)$], partly indirectly [$\Delta M \rightarrow \Delta V$, $\Delta V \rightarrow (\Delta Y$ and $\Delta P)$].

Keynesian inflation theory stressed income and expenditure flows rather than monetary stocks. The theory is presented in elementary form in a conventional "Keynesian cross" (Figure 2). Here, with standard notation, $C + I + G$ may be called an aggregate expenditure curve, while *OX* represents aggregate capacity at full employment in the prices of the beginning of the period, and *OF* is full-employment income in the same units. If desired expenditures at *OF* exceed aggregate capacity *OX*, the differential, *AB*, may be called an inflationary or expansionary gap (a deflationary or contractionary gap if *OX* exceeds *OF*). The gap *A′B′*, also shown in the diagram, can be proved equal to *AB* times the "standard" multiplier $1/(1-c)$, where c is the marginal propensity to spend on domestic goods. The degree of inflation is assumed, in simple formulations, to vary directly

FIGURE 2

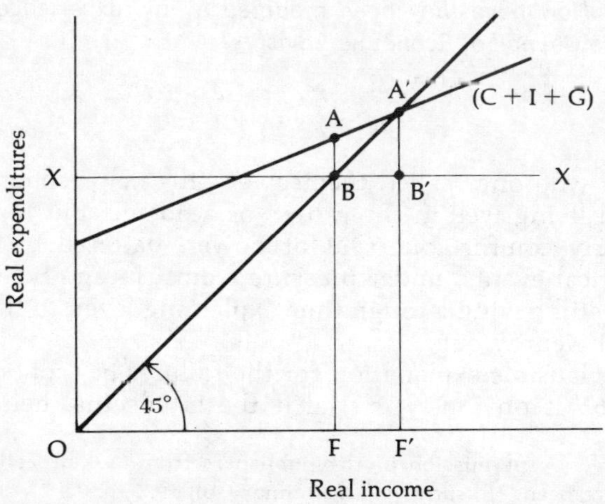

with AB/OF and $A'B'/OF'$. A cut of AB in aggregate expenditures through a reduction of G, an increase in taxes, or a decrease in the money supply presumably eliminates the inflationary pressure. The intersection of the expenditure curve with the aggregate capacity–full employment point (B on Figure 2) is sometimes called "full equilibrium," since the price level is stable at full employment.

READING 11
What Happened to Fine Tuning?

In his book *The Political Economy of Prosperity,* Arthur M. Okun comments on the inflationary record compiled during his tenure as chairman of the Council of Economic Advisers to the President during the Johnson Administration. This review of his book, taken from *Business Week,* suggests that Okun's recent experience may have led to a change in his belief in the responsiveness of the economy to fiscal fine tuning.

Guideposts for Thought While Reading
What were Okun's initial beliefs concerning fine tuning of the economy? How have they been modified by his experience as chairman of the Council of Economic Advisers?

The men who once called themselves "the new economists" are alive and living well in the groves of academe. But they are not particularly comfortable. Out of power, battered by economic and political events, under pressure from Chicago School rivals, they are still having a tough time explaining, even to themselves, just what went wrong.

Some plausible explanation for the failures of economic policy since 1965 is obviously crucial if the intellectual heirs of John

Reprinted by permission of the publishers from "Okun Tells It Like It Might Have Been," *Business Week,* January 10, 1970, p. 92.

Maynard Keynes are ever to regain their lost prestige. They came to power and influence in Washington because, like successful stock promoters, they had a convincing story to tell: The American economy consistently failed to live up to its potential on account of inappropriate fiscal policies. A comeback will be difficult, regardless of who wins elections, without an equally cogent analysis of what is behind the stubborn overexuberance that has afflicted the economy for the past five years.

TRANQUIL RECOLLECTION

Arthur M. Okun, who as chairman of the Council of Economic Advisers in the waning days of the Johnson Administration was the last of the new economists with the trappings of power, has now had a full year to recollect in enforced tranquillity. And, in *The Political Economy of Prosperity*, a book published this week by the Brookings Institution, he makes a strong pitch against drawing any permanent conclusions from the temporary embarrassment of the new economics.

"Vietnam plays the Danish prince in the *Hamlet* of recent economic history," Okun writes. The war so distorted the record that it is still impossible to answer the key questions "about how private demand and public policy would perform during an extended period of prosperity." Much of his book is a detailed account of how Vietnam spending was mishandled.

The war, along with President Johnson's decision in 1966 to reject his economists' tax-hike advice, is the easiest answer to charges that something is fundamentally wrong with the new economics. But Okun does not hold himself and his colleagues blameless.

"Enormous faith is occasionally displayed in the tax action that wasn't taken," Okun says. "No actual measure of economic policy has been nearly that effective."

One reason for this concession is that the tax hike, when it finally came in mid-1968, did not bring all of the benefits that Okun and his colleagues said it would. It is this failure of the economy to respond to a massive shift in fiscal policy that has struck at the roots of Keynesian theory.

"SOBERING"

The continuation of a boom that was supposed to be squelched by fiscal measures is, says Okun, "a sobering experience for many economic diagnosticians, forecasters, and policy planners."

He admits that he and economists at the Federal Reserve Board "misread some evidence provided by certain statistical indicators as signals of moderation in private demand." As a result, the Fed turned toward easier money soon after the tax surcharge was passed in mid-1968. This action has since delayed the slowdown and made monetary authorities gun-shy about easing credit again until they see unmistakable evidence that the economy has turned the corner and not just gone around the block.

Okun is still puzzled by the failure of businessmen and consumers to react to the tax hike in textbook fashion. He rejects the easy explanation of "inflationary psychology," but speculates that "perhaps expectations of long-term prosperity—rather than expectations of inflation—enhanced the appeal of investment. After four years in which expansion and investment had generally been profitable, businessmen may have been prepared to count on the long-run buoyancy of demand even when some current indicators pointed the other way."

As for consumers, Okun is now flirting with the "permanent income hypothesis," which says that they react mainly to changes in expectations. He also thinks that changes in household wealth, including events on Wall Street, may affect spending.

"SPEED LIMITS"

These possibilities call into question one of the key assumptions of the new economics: the notion that temporary changes in the tax rates could cool off an overheated economy. One of the premises of the early 1960s was that if the economy strayed toward inflation, fiscal policy could fairly easily bring it back. Okun now has a much more pessimistic view of the consequences of exceeding the economic "speed limits."

For the moment, Okun says with just about every other economist in the country, the economy must pay its fine in terms of slower growth and higher unemployment. Even in the long run he no longer has any illusions that attaining and sticking to a "middle road" of 4% unemployment and 2% inflation will be easy, but considers that combination the "best hope."

READING 12
Lessons of the 1960s
Paul A. Samuelson

In this article, renowned economist and recipient of the Nobel prize for distinction in economics Dr. Paul A. Samuelson of M.I.T. interprets the experience of the 1960s with regard to the goals of full employment, high rates of economic growth, and price stability. Professor Samuelson points out that some of the worries about coming developments in the U.S. economy raised by certain economists have proven more myth than fact.

Guideposts for Thought While Reading
Why does Samuelson feel that the macroeconomics practiced during the 1960s was successful? What errors does he admit were made by the economic authorities?

We are on the homestretch of the 1960s. What economic lessons has the decade taught us?

In answering such a question, I am torn two ways. On the one hand, to insist that I have learned nothing is to mark myself as an inflexible Bourbon. On the other hand, to admit that events of the 1960s have revolutionized our understanding of economic principles is to confess that economics is a soft and protean science.

Today I shall eschew the spurious sagacity resident in the golden mean. Objectivity obliges one, I think, to interpret economic experience of the 1960s as broadly confirmatory to the conventional wisdom—particularly to the avant-garde version of it that characterized the new economists on New Year's Eve 1959.

In one of the more quotable idiocies of history, Lincoln Steffens—after a few weeks' trip to Lenin's Russia—said, "I have seen the future. And it works!" Now that the data for the 1960s are virtually in, I can say, "I have seen the past. And it works."

Wisdom is easy after the fact. So let's recall some popular beliefs about economics, held by respectable authorities ten years ago, that have been proved false by history.

BEFORE AND AFTER

1. Arthur Burns, Herbert Stein, W. Allen Wallis and other economists close to Richard Nixon thought that the John F. Kennedy debate about stagnant American growth was all an elaborate numbers game. When such New Frontiersmen as Walter Heller, Arthur Okun and James Tobin calculated a quantitative "gap" of underemployed resources for the nation and projected growth of our real potential at 4-plus per cent a year, they were hooted at from both the right and left. (Leon Keyserling thought them pikers in their estimates.)

History has awarded the palm of victory to the new economists. Real growth has been pleasantly on target.

2. Charles Killingsworth, Norbert Wiener, Michael Harrington and other prophets of an automation revolution were sure ten years ago that "structural unemployment" was America's main problem. Robert Solow and other Kennedy advisers made econometric estimates to show that expansionary fiscal and monetary policies would melt the hard core of unemployment and that little of the excess unemployment that prevailed in 1961 was structural and new.

Again, events proved that macroeconomics can, black youths aside, achieve full employment.

3. In 1960, when I prepared for President-elect Kennedy a Report on the State of the American Economy, I had to express pessimism concerning the ability of any mixed economy to achieve *price stability along with full employment and free markets*. From 1960 to 1964, my fears were agreeably refuted by the moderation in wholesale and other prices.

After the 1965 Vietnam escalation, alas, one's worst fears concerning a "Phillips Curve" problem of creeping inflation were fulfilled. Presidential wage-price guideposts proved no substitute for adequate macroeconomic limitations on demand.

THE SOMETHING NEW

Before leaving the confrontation of expectation with fact, I must call attention to the surprising vitality of mixed economies all over the world in the 1960s. When I was preparing the 1961 edition of my textbook, the growth race with Russia and China was the popular theme of the day. Partly through the bad luck of unfavorable harvests, but mostly through the effectiveness of that new thing under the sun—the mixed economy—the advanced nations of the Western world have gained on the Soviet Union and mainland China during the 1960s, both absolutely and relatively.

Perhaps we are already jaded with the Japanese and Common Market miracles. But who would have thought that countries like Austria and Greece, Thailand and Formosa, to say nothing of such "old" economies as Canada and the U.S., would as a group average higher rates of real growth than the Eastern Europe centrally planned bloc? And who could have prophesied the disastrous effects of Maoist ideology on Chinese growth?

Have economists no errors to confess? Plenty. Econometric estimates of GNP have generally been in error on the low side. Few multiplier-and-accelerator models known to me predicted the exuberance of the 1969 investment boom. And still to be argued out within the guild is the proper quantitative potency of monetary versus fiscal policies.

Nonetheless, it's been a good decade. May the next be as good!

READING 13
We Must Stand Firm Against Inflation
Milton Friedman

There is mounting evidence that fine tuning of the economy to produce the level of aggregate demand required for full employment with low rates of inflation requires greater monetary and fiscal finesse than was shown by the government in the late 1960s. In this reading Professor Milton Friedman of the University of Chicago suggests a policy of moderation to prevent a recurrence of the destabilizing over-reactions characterizing previous monetary and fiscal policy.

Guideposts for Thought While Reading

What special interest groups are pressuring for an inflationary monetary and fiscal policy? Contrast the long-run implications of the Friedman policy prescription to the fine-tuning approach, assuming that Friedman is correct that recession is the only cure for an unwanted inflation.

Inflation is yesterday's problem, goes the current cry in Washington and Wall Street. After all, isn't the rate of price rises slowing? Until recently, prices were rising at the rate of seven percent and more a year; today they are still rising, but at a decidedly slower pace. Recession is today's concern, say politicians concerned about this fall's elections and financial analysts concerned about low stock prices. The government must spend more, they shout; the Federal Reserve Board must print more money to avoid a serious depression.

We, the public, must help the Nixon Administration to stand firm against this shortsighted view. Inflation remains the No. 1 economic problem. Shifting now to a policy of excessive monetary expansion would simply unleash once again the inflationary forces that have only been checked, not truly curbed. We must bear with some temporary difficulties if we are to get the economy back on a path of steady growth without inflation. Yet it will be impossible for the Administration to hold to its present moderate policy unless the country at large understands what is at stake and supports the long view.

WHERE ARE WE?

We are in an economic recession. Since last July industrial production (which includes those goods—automobiles, machines, and so on—whose production fluctuates most) has declined at about five percent a year—it had been rising six percent a year before that. There has been a moderate slowdown in industrial-plant expansion and in residential housing.

Unemployment has risen from about 3.4 percent of the working force a year ago to 4.4 percent this March. This is the figure that more than anything else has caught the public eye, producing near-hysterical pressure to shift Administration policy. But it is a misleading figure: of the four million unemployed, only some 200,000 are hard-core unemployed who have been out of work six months or more. To get a sense of perspective, one way to look at the increase in unemployment is that it now takes a person, on the average, five to six weeks to find a job instead of four to five weeks.

As a result of the economy's slowdown, interest rates have finally begun coming down from the eight- and nine-percent levels reached last December—levels unprecedented since the inflation of the Civil War over a century ago. Although stock prices have fallen drastically over the past year, the market now anticipates an upturn. Consumer prices are still rising, *but* not as fast as they were. This is the most encouraging sign of all. Those complaining that prices are still rising are like the man who believes he should be able to stop a speeding car on a dime—without going through the windshield.

HOW DID WE GET THERE?

The present recession is a direct outgrowth of the policies of the Johnson Administration and the independent Federal Reserve Board from 1964 to 1968. The Johnson Administration increased government spending at a rapid pace (for Vietnam and, more sharply, for domestic programs) and this in turn produced growing budget deficits. These deficits by themselves need not have led to inflation. If they had been financed by borrowing from the public, the government would have spent more and the lenders would have spent less. The one would largely have offset the other. To induce persons to lend the funds to government, however, this method of financing would have raised interest rates. This is where the Federal Reserve came in.

To try to keep interest rates down, the Federal Reserve Board partly financed the deficits by printing more money. This did temporarily hold interest rates down. But it also set off inflation, as a rapidly increasing quantity of money chased a slowly increasing quantity of goods—which in the end made interest rates higher, not lower.

In early 1966, disturbed by growing inflation, the Fed sharply reduced the rate of monetary growth. It moved in the right direction, but too far. Result: the credit-crunch of 1966 and signs of a recession. Frightened by its own handiwork, the Fed veered in the opposite direction—again too far, and at the cost of another burst of inflation.

To curb the renewed inflation, the ten-percent income surtax was enacted in mid-1968. The economists of the Johnson Administration expected the surtax to halt inflation promptly. Indeed, they were afraid that it would produce an overkill. The

Fed moved to prevent this possibility by again rapidly expanding the money supply.

The results were dramatic. Monetary expansion was far more potent than the tax increase. Instead of inflation being halted, it actually speeded up.

Finally, after Nixon's election, effective anti-inflation steps were taken: in December 1968 the Fed shifted to a slower rate of monetary growth. And the new Administration launched a determined campaign to stop the rapid rise in government spending. For a time, nothing seemed to happen. Prices not only continued to rise but rose faster. This is par for the course. It takes at least six months for a change in the quantity of money to affect the economy significantly.

Then the monetary slowdown started to bite. And its bite was reinforced when, in mid-1969, the Fed reduced money growth still further so that the quantity of money, which had grown more than seven percent a year in 1967 and 1968, grew at the rate of about four percent per year in the first half of 1969 and did not grow at all in the last half of 1969. We are only now feeling the full effects of this extremely tight—in my opinion, too tight—Federal Reserve policy.

The monetary restraint is the immediate cause of the present recession. But the underlying cause is the prior inflation. Once an inflation is started, it is impossible to stop it without an economic slowdown.

Where do we go from here? The Nixon Administration's aim to end the inflation *gradually* started out fine but miscarried somewhat when the Fed tightened up too severely in mid-1969. Since the beginning of 1970, and especially since Arthur Burns took over in February as chairman of the Federal Reserve System, the money supply has again been growing at a modest rate. But the change came too late; last year's mistake is *now* showing up in our deepening economic recession and growing unemployment.

Having made one mistake last year, we must try to avoid a second and far more serious one this year: over-reaction to the recession. That way would pull out *all* stops to offset unemployment, take off *all* restraints on government spending and money-supply expansion.

Time and again in the past the Fed and the Administration in power have gone from one extreme to the other: in 1957-59; 1959-61; 1966-67. Each time, too tight a monetary policy has been followed by too expansive a policy, buffeting the economy from one side to the other. Pressure for a similar over-reaction is clearly building up—reinforced by the coming elections in November.

It is already too late for measures taken now to affect substantially the political climate this fall. The main effect of pulling out all monetary and fiscal stops now would be a renewed surge of inflation in 1971, and thereafter price rises that might well reach ten percent and more per year. For a time, this would cut unemployment. But as workers came increasingly to recognize that high wages did not mean equally high purchasing power, they would try to protect themselves in advance—as they have been doing—by bargaining for high enough wages to more than cover the expected rise. Labor would thus become expensive, even compared to the rising prices of goods, and unemployment would rise again. The only way to keep it down would be by another explosive burst of still higher inflation.

All this would strengthen enormously the many misguided voices clamoring for compulsory wage and price controls. These controls will not work. They may for a time suppress the symptoms of inflation. But if prices are prevented by law from rising when there is pressure on them, there will be many buyers and few sellers. Result: black markets and distortion of production.

The alternative is to stick with the present policy: a moderate, steady growth of the money supply at, say, three to five percent per year; continued pressure to keep government spending and taxes down; continued avoidance of price and wage control. This would accept the recession as an unavoidable price of past mistakes.

This alternative is the right policy for the country. Its consequences: the recession will turn around toward year's end. Inflation, already tapering off, will fall to something like a three-percent rate by December and to less than a two-percent rate by mid-1971. Interest rates will continue falling. By 1972 at the latest, the economy will be expanding rapidly in real—not inflationary—terms, with prices nearly stable.

This policy of moderation will clearly serve the nation's interests far better than the policy of over-reaction. Yet it will take courage and farsightedness on the part of President Nixon to sacrifice immediate political advantage to a sound policy, to stick to the course of moderation that he has so far followed. It will take self-restraint and a regard for the true national interest for Congress to support this policy. And, above all, it will take the understanding and the sympathetic backing of the American people to make the wise policy a politically feasible policy.

READING 14
Why a Rising Federal Debt Is No Cause for Alarm
David B. McCalmont

The magnitude of the federal debt is of great concern to many citizens and political leaders in the United States. Many economists, however, seem less concerned with the growth of the federal debt, and some even suggest that debt and deficit spending by the federal government is a vital factor in looking after the welfare of future generations. This is in sharp contrast with the argument that federal debt represents a burden on taxpayers of the future. In this reading, Professor McCalmont, of Ohio State University, brings out an economic perspective on the relative costs and advantages of public debt and its current size in proportion to the growth of the economy.

Guideposts for Thought While Reading
When is debt a burden and when is it an advantage to society? How does the growth of public debt compare with our ability to pay or with the growth of private debt?

Editorials and public speeches frequently express the widely felt alarm regarding increases in the federal debt: "We are hopelessly burdening our grandchildren"—"A larger debt requires larger interest payments, and these will require higher tax rates"—"We've got to begin paying back sometime. We're only postponing the day of reckoning"—"If the national debt continues to rise, our nation will go bankrupt."

A large majority of economists and an increasing number of business and political leaders are finding such arguments unconvincing for reasons that will be set forth here. The weight and importance of any debt, it will be argued, depend upon its size in relation to the debtor's income and assets. A $100,000 debt, which would indeed be burdensome to a man with only $150,000 worth of assets and an income of $6,000 a year, would be of little importance to a man with assets of $15,000,000 and an income of $600,000. Similarly, the debt of a nation should be judged not by its absolute size but by its size relative to national income and wealth.

Debt always has two sides. If indebtedness increases, someone becomes the owner of a new claim against the debtor. To this owner, the new debt constitutes "wealth," and the interest paid on the debt is "income."

GROWTH OF THE PRIVATE DEBT

We take these things for granted when considering the debt incurred by nongovernmental corporations and by individuals. When we notice that the outstanding indebtedness of Columbia Gas System, Inc. increased more than 50 per cent between 1956 and 1963 we are not fearful for the safety of that enterprise, because we know that its assets and income also increased. Similarly, we need not be alarmed when we notice that total private debt in the United States rose by $672 billion between 1945 and 1963—an increase of 435 per cent.

Americans have not been alarmed by this enormous increase in private debt because they have been wise enough to realize that, even though it is huge, it is nevertheless smaller in proportion to total assets and incomes than in 1930.

GROWTH OF THE FEDERAL DEBT

A look at the growth of private debt in the United States provides a more realistic perspective from which to view the growth and level of the federal debt. In 1930 the federal debt was a mere $16 billion; even by 1940 it was still only $51 billion. The war effort against Hitler raised it to $279 billion, but from the end of World War II to 1963 it had risen only $31 billion, or 11 per cent. During this same period, private debt, as we have seen, rose by 435 per cent.

Growing private debts, it is often argued, are backed by the growing income-producing abilities and market values of the debtors' business assets, while federal debt is said to have no comparable "backing." This objection underestimates the power of the federal income tax. With this tax, the government can, if need be, reach all income and all income-producing property in the country. Thus all such income and property is, in a very real sense, backing for the public debt.

National Income and Wealth

Relating the federal debt to the gross national income (GNP) and to total wealth is, therefore, both realistic and legitimate. In relation to income, the federal debt in 1963 was less than half as important as it was in 1945, because national income had grown about 170 per cent during this period while the federal debt had grown about 11 per cent.

Similarly, the nation's wealth grew so rapidly after 1945 that in 1958 the federal debt was less than half as important, relative to national wealth, as it was in 1945. Yet in 1945 the United States showed no sign of being in danger of collapse because of the burden of its debt. Today far less danger exists.

In judging the significance of future increases in the federal debt, we must not compare it with present levels of GNP and wealth, for neither of these will remain frozen at its present level. If the annual rate of growth of GNP be 4 per cent, then the federal debt could be permitted to grow 4 per cent of the present debt annually without becoming a larger percentage of GNP.

Future Need for Deficits

Federal deficits of that magnitude or greater are likely to be needed if GNP is to keep growing fast enough to reduce unemployment to the much lower percentage levels found practical in recent years in Europe.

The wealthier a nation becomes, the more its people can satisfy their immediate needs without spending all their income, and the larger is the amount of disposable income that people try to save. However, since the savers amass surpluses and thus postpone some of their claims to current output, part of current output will remain unsold unless other spending units purchase extra goods or services equal in value to what the savers fail to purchase. When part of current output does remain unsold, firms naturally curtail their production, and GNP declines.

In other words, if GNP is to be kept from diminishing, the other spending units must spend on currently produced goods and services more than their own income entitles them to do; that is, they must "deficit spend." And if output is to rise, deficit spenders must spend an amount greater than the amount which savers are refraining from spending. Only in this way can the nation's total sales, production, and income become greater than in the previous period.

It is unreasonable to assume that the amount of investment in new buildings, machinery, or inventory which firms believe profitable in the light of prevailing market expectations will always be sufficient to enable their "deficit spending" to outweigh total saving enough to keep GNP moving upward at the right speed. Thus, reliance on the federal government to help supply the needed deficits may be expected to increase. After all, the federal government is a huge "firm" producing about 5 per cent of total U.S. production and, in addition, purchasing about 9 per cent of the output produced by private firms. There is no good reason why it should not help its fellow firms do the spending-in-excess-of-income (that is, run the deficits) needed to offset the huge and constantly growing surpluses piled up by the savers of an affluent country.

There is no sound basis, moreover, for a belief that the achievement of full employment will enable the federal budget to shift from deficit to surplus without harming the economy. One hears a good deal nowadays about the so-called full-employment surplus. But this is only an analytical tool to help us take account of the automatic changes in tax collections and transfer payments that occur when the national income changes. According to the full-employment surplus analysis, if tax rates and the rules regarding transfer payments remain unchanged, and if the GNP nevertheless rises to the full-employment level, tax collections would rise so much and transfer payments diminish so much that federal deficits would be converted into surpluses. But this purely hypothetical proposition says nothing at all as to whether the GNP *would* or *could* rise to the full-employment level under such circumstances. On the contrary, each increase in GNP enlarges the volume of saving and thus generates a need for a greater volume of private or governmental deficit spending if further increases in GNP are to be achieved.

These facts of economic life can be faced without any serious concern. Even if a continuing federal deficit of $25 billion a year were needed for the next ten years in order to keep GNP growing at 4 per cent a year, the effect on the national debt would not be at all alarming. At the end of the ten years, the debt would still be only 62 per cent of GNP, a little more than half the 123 per cent that the nation bore successfully in 1945.

Yet was 1945 the top limit? If World War II had continued for another year or two, the debt percentage would surely have risen far above 123 per cent. And there is no reason to think that the United States could not have borne this larger "burden" as successfully as that of 1945.

INFLATION AND THE DEBT

Wartime analogies inevitably raise the issue of the connection between the national debt and inflation. Because increases in the price level during the war and the immediate postwar period occurred simultaneously with increases in the federal debt, people are prone to reason that any increase in the debt is inflationary. The cause of the wartime and postwar inflationary pressure, however, was not the high level of the federal debt nor the fact that it was increasing, but only that the increase was too rapid in relation to the 1940–45 productive capacity. Deficits incurred to fight World War II were too large in relation to the slack then existing in the economy; the federal government ran deficits totaling $218 billion, an average deficit of $43 billion a year, at a time when GNP was rising from only $101 billion a year to $214 billion. The average annual deficit amounted to almost 24 per cent of the average GNP during that five-year period. Small wonder that total demand exceeded total capacity and that prices moved upward! Considering that GNP for the first quarter of 1964 was $609 billion, a comparable deficit at that time would have been $145 billion a year.

Most economists would agree that a federal deficit of $145 billion in fiscal 1965 would have been inflationary.

INTEREST PAYMENTS

After worries about inflation have been put aside, the problem of interest payments comes next. If the public debt grows, we are told, more tax money must be raised to pay interest, thus requiring higher tax rates.

In the first place, there is no ironclad necessity that all the money to pay interest on the federal debt be obtained by taxation. If the government has decided that a deficit is desirable for the stimulation of the economy, it could achieve that deficit simply by making some or all of its interest payments with borrowed money. If it did so, there would be less need of revenue from federal taxes, not more.

Yet even if taxes remain the only source of interest payments, persons who worry about the burden of the debt forget that unchanged tax rates can and do bring in increasing revenues in measure as the national income increases. To judge the significance of larger annual interest payments on a larger federal debt, therefore, such payments must be compared with the national income with which they are associated.

Computed annual interest payments on the public debt as of mid-1964 were a smaller percentage of the nation's gross income (1.8 per cent) than they were in 1946 (2.5 per cent), and also from 1955 to 1964, interest payments remained about the same percentage of the growing GNP. Actually, the amount paid out as interest would have become smaller in relation to GNP if the level of interest rates, on private as well as on public obligations, had not risen drastically after 1954.

Even if interest payments were to become an amount equal to a larger percentage of GNP than they are now, there would be no increased "burden" on the economy as a whole. Americans own 95 per cent of all federal securities. Accordingly, nearly all of the $7.5 billion in interest payments in 1963 was merely transferred to the personal and corporate incomes of American recipients. The larger these annual interest payments become, the greater will be this contribution to the financial well-being of the American families and businesses that receive them. Neither we nor our grandchildren, therefore, have anything to fear from the "burden" of growing interest charges on a growing federal debt.

ABOUT THOSE GRANDCHILDREN

Those who deplore the national debt worry unceasingly about the evil effect that they believe its enlargement will have on our grandchildren. Let us pause to examine the conditions of life of these unfortunate grandchildren who are to be so grievously burdened by our alleged "fiscal profligacy." Whether these unhappy grandchildren will be living ten, twenty, or forty years from now is not very clear; twenty years would be a reasonable compromise.

Thanks to the medical research paid for and executed mostly by previous generations, our grandchildren of 1984 will receive far superior medical service, will suffer less pain, and will have a longer life expectancy than the present generation. Technological advance and capital accumulation, also paid for and executed mostly by their predecessors, will enable them to enjoy a level of living that will make the present level look very modest by comparison.

Apart from all this, the argument that enlarging the federal debt will burden our grandchildren is based upon two false assumptions: (1) that the grandchildren will have to repay the debt, and (2) that their payments will have to be made to someone other than themselves. Neither assumption is valid.

As we have already seen, the private sector of our economy never pays off all its debt. Individual firms do pay off individual obligations. However, except at time of severest depression, new borrowing always exceeds repayments made on the old. Decade by decade, private debt *in toto* has continued to rise. Decade by decade it will continue to rise. Our grandchildren will not have to "pay it off" because it will never be "paid off."

There is no more reason why the governmental sector, as a whole, should pay off its debt. Individual government bond issues can and will be retired, but new borrowing will always exceed these repayments. This procedure is normal and proper for governmental units as well as for business firms in a growing economy.

However, assuming for the sake of argument that the federal debt were to be paid off twenty years from now, to whom would the repayments be made? Inasmuch as only 5 per cent of our national debt is owed to foreigners, practically all of the repayments would be received by our grandchildren. Grandchildren would pay; grandchildren would receive. In the case of individual grandchildren, the amounts paid and received might not balance, but for grandchildren as a group there would be no loss of income or wealth—unless higher tax rates were needed to accomplish the repayment and unless these rates impaired taxpayers' incentive to produce, thus diminishing the amount of human energy and risk capital devoted to production.

All of this, however, is academic because the debt can and will continue to grow and never need be paid off. Accordingly, we shall not involve ourselves here with the much debated issue of whether higher tax rates dull or sharpen the incentive to produce.

So far as the well-being of our grandchildren is concerned, then, the advocates of federal deficits have the stronger case. The level of living enjoyed by our descendants will depend upon their own productivity. This in turn will depend in no small measure upon the quantity and quality of the capital equipment —the roads, harbors, houses, and manufacturing plants—that we build and pass on to them and upon the amount of education and health service that we provide for them in their childhood. If this inheritance of capital goods, education, and health can be enlarged by incurring a larger federal debt, then a debt increase is a positive benefit to our grandchildren.

CAN A NATION GO BANKRUPT?

But neither we nor our grandchildren can be benefited, it is said, because the nation will go bankrupt. When a private debtor becomes bankrupt, a court frees it from any obligation to make any future payments to the creditors. A sovereign nation needs no discharge in bankruptcy in this sense, for no one can sue a sovereign state without its consent. What people mean when they talk about "national bankruptcy" is that they fear the federal government will be obliged to default on its debts.

No basis for such a fear exists with respect to the United States. When the U.S. Treasury markets a new issue of federal securities in order to raise money to pay off maturing issues, the question is always: "What rate of interest must the Treasury offer in order that the market will absorb the issue?" never: "*Will* the market absorb the issue?" Remember that the federal debt does not mature all in one lump.

The public possesses so much confidence in the worth of federal obligations that they are bought even though their yields are lower than those of private securities. This is because buyers take rational account of the fact that the taxing power and the power to control the banking system are more dependable guarantees of repayment than are the sales revenues of private firms.

ADVANTAGE OF A LARGER DEBT

Few critics of a growing federal debt stop to consider that federal securities play an extremely useful role in our economy quite apart from anything that the government may do with the borrowed money. If there were no federal debt, we could not feel wealthy and secure because of our possession of Treasury securities or because of the possession of such securities by our insurance companies or savings and loan associations. If the federal debt did not grow in tune with the growth of the nation, both private and institutional investors would have to venture their funds to a greater and greater degree upon the purchase of private indebtedness.

If our banks, insurance companies, and savings and loan associations were obliged to substitute private securities for federal, they would become either less safe as repositories of our savings or else greater risks to federal insuring agencies. On the other hand, if our financial institutions felt it necessary to compensate for the decreased safety of their investment holdings by becoming more conservative in their choice of private borrowers and by decreasing the percentage of loans in their total assets, they would be obliged to withdraw financial support from many a new and promising innovation or enterprise that otherwise would have become a reality. Viewed in this light, a growing federal debt is a positive benefit.

The federal debt, we must conclude, poses no menace to the American people. Viewed against the background of rapidly increasing national income and wealth, the debt is moderate in size and has been shrinking, relatively, ever since 1945. But whatever its size, it shows on both sides of the nation's balance sheet of assets and liabilities, so that its net burden is negligible. Our constantly growing income-tax base makes possible the payment of ever larger amounts of interest out of taxes, if so desired, without the need of increased tax rates and without the emergence of the transfer effects feared by some observers.

Clearly, worries regarding the growth of the national debt should no longer deter our government from incurring whatever future deficits may be required to cause the national income and output to grow at a rate consonant with the full potential of the American economy.

READING 15
First Steps in Banking

The idea of banking (lending money) for a profit is common to most market economies, and bank profits are often substantial due to governmental regulations to prevent excessive competition. If one has the misconception that a bank is literally a storehouse containing the savings of its depositors, this reading will surely destroy that misconception. Although the reading is a satire at the expense of the banking community, the basic principles of the business of banking are clearly shown.

Guideposts for Thought While Reading
Why is a bank willing to accept your deposit? What essential function

Reprinted by permission of the publisher from "First Steps in Banking," *Punch*, April 3, 1957, pp. 440–441. © *Punch*, London.

do banks serve with regard to the utilization of savings in a market economy?

Q. What are banks for?
A. To make money.
Q. For the customers?
A. For the banks.
Q. Why doesn't bank advertising mention this?
A. It would not be in good taste. But it is mentioned by implication in references to Reserves of £249,000,000 or thereabouts. That is the money they have made.
Q. Out of the customers?
A. I suppose so.
Q. They also mention Assets of £500,000,000 or thereabouts. Have they made that too?
A. Not exactly. That is the money they use to make money.
Q. I see. And they keep it in a safe somewhere?
A. Not at all. They lend it to customers.
Q. Then they haven't got it?
A. No.
Q. Then how is it Assets?
A. They maintain that it would be if they got it back.
Q. But they must have *some* money in a safe somewhere?
A. Yes, usually £500,000,000 or thereabouts. This is called Liabilities.
Q. But if they've got it, how can they be liable for it?
A. Because it isn't theirs.
Q. Then why do they have it?
A. It has been lent to them by customers.
Q. You mean customers lend banks money?
A. In effect. They put money into their accounts, so it is really lent to the banks.
Q. And what do the banks do with it?
A. Lend it to other customers.
Q. But you said that money they lent to other people was Assets?
A. Yes.
Q. Then Assets and Liabilities must be the same thing?
A. You can't really say that.
Q. But you've just said it. If I put £100 into my account the bank is liable to have to pay it back, so it's Liabilities. But they go and lend it to someone else, and he is liable to have to pay it back, so it's Assets. It's the same £100, isn't it?

A. Yes. But——

Q. Then it cancels out. It means, doesn't it, that banks haven't really any money at all?

A. Theoretically——

Q. Never mind theoretically. And if they haven't any money where do they get their Reserves of £249,000,000 or thereabouts?

A. I told you. That is the money they have made.

Q. How?

A. Well, when they lend your £100 to someone they charge him interest.

Q. How much?

A. It depends on the Bank Rate. Say five and a half per cent. That's their profit.

Q. Why isn't it my profit? Isn't it my money?

A. It's the theory of banking practice that——

Q. When I lend them my £100 why don't I charge *them* interest?

A. You do.

Q. You don't say. How much?

A. It depends on the Bank Rate. Say half a per cent.

Q. Grasping of me, rather?

A. But that's only if you're not going to draw the money out again.

Q. But of course I'm going to draw it out again. If I hadn't wanted to draw it out again I could have buried it in the garden, couldn't I?

A. They wouldn't like you to draw it out again.

Q. Why not? If I keep it there you say it's a Liability. Wouldn't they be glad if I reduced their Liabilities by removing it?

A. No. Because if you remove it they can't lend it to anyone else.

Q. But if I wanted to remove it they'd have to let me?

A. Certainly.

Q. But suppose they've already lent it to another customer?

A. Then they'll let you have someone else's money.

Q. But suppose he wants his too—and they've let me have it?

A. You're being purposely obtuse.

Q. I think I'm being acute. What if everyone wanted their money at once?

A. It's the theory of banking practice that they never would.

Q. So what banks bank on is not having to meet their commitments?

A. I wouldn't say that.

Q. Naturally. Well, if there's nothing else you think you can tell me . . . ?

A. Quite so. Now you can go off and open a banking account.

Q. Just one last question.

A. Of course.

Q. Wouldn't I do better to go off and open a bank?

READING 16
The German Nightmare
Donald B. Woodward and Marc A. Rose

The value of money, just as the value of goods and services traded in a free market, is subject to the laws of supply and demand. The German experience following World War I is an extreme example of the effects of governmental finance through the simple expedient of printing money. Donald Woodward, with a lifetime spent as an economic advisor and consultant with leading business and research firms, and the late Marc Rose, a former editor of *Business Week*, provide, in this reading, a vivid account of the ramifications of galloping inflation.

Guideposts for Thought While Reading

An extreme case often brings out more clearly some implications which might otherwise be overlooked. How many effects similar to the German inflation might we find in the economy of the United States during periods of rapid inflation such as occurred in the late 1960s? How does "galloping inflation" differ from "creeping inflation"?

The war put a severe strain on the German economy, but the depreciation of the mark was not beyond recovery; after the armistice, the mark was quoted at about 12 cents.

Reprinted by permission of the publisher from Donald B. Woodward and Marc A. Rose, "The German Nightmare," *Inflation*, McGraw-Hill, New York, 1935, pp. 56–61.

Then came the peace negotiations. When the full weight of the terms imposed under the Treaty of Versailles became apparent, the Germans felt their situation hopeless—and so did financiers in other countries. The new government's financial difficulties kept increasing. The nation's debt was heavy, and much of it was not funded.

MONETIZING THE DEBT

It was necessary to resort to the expedient of printing marks, mere fiat money, to pay the government's expenses. By early 1920, the mark was worth about 1 cent, gold. The decline was checked at that point, and there was even some improvement; but late in 1921, the mark began to sink again in terms of foreign exchange. Reparations had been fixed at 132,000,000,000 gold marks, or some $33,000,000,000. More and more, Germany was completely discouraged at the outlook; financial recovery looked impossible, and the occupation of the Ruhr in January, 1923, seemed to show that the harder the Germans tried to beat their way upward the more the demands that would be made upon them.

The Treasury proceeded to issue bills to the Reichsbank at an accelerating rate, discounting them for paper money. The printing presses ran more and more rapidly; pieces of currency were issued in denominations of millions of marks. Prices, of course, kept rising, which steadily increased the government's expenses and made it necessary to print more money. The spiral was started; nothing, it seemed, could break it. Under the conditions, there was little incentive to try.

The banks, which had participated very little at the outset, began to discount bills at the Reichsbank and to increase their loans and deposits. Ultimately, the municipalities began to issue money, also the railroads, and many other institutions. Metal coins previously used for small change disappeared into hoarding or were converted into paper, the bullion content being worth vastly more than the stamped value of the coins.

Before the war, the total money in circulation in Germany had averaged about 6,000,000,000 marks. At the end of 1923, the authorized circulation was 518,000,000,000,000,000,000—518 billions of billions. No estimate ever has been attempted of the amount of other currencies in circulation. Conditions were utterly chaotic.

In November, 1923, the situation was taken in hand. A new currency unit, the rentenmark, was established, its value put at

1,000,000,000,000—a million million—of the marks it was to supersede. The new rentenmark was fixed at parity with the prewar mark—that is, at 23 cents. Incidentally, it was pure fiat money, but its value was successfully controlled in terms of gold.

The Dawes plan was made effective in 1924, fixing Germany's obligations to the outside world at a point more nearly within reason. With that encouragement, the reichsmark was established on a gold basis, also at 23 cents.

THE CONSEQUENCES OF HYPERINFLATION

That was the end of inflation. Behind this bare story of the course of events are a million human comedies and tragedies. No one ever will record even a small part of them. But some of the most fantastic and absurd incidents are remembered.

As this one: the total German mortgage debt before the war was about 40,000,000,000 marks. At the peak of the inflation, 40,000,000,000 marks were worth less than a cent. All the mortgages in Germany could have been paid off for 1 cent, American. A box of matches sold for more than 6,000,000,000 marks, which it will be remembered was the total amount of money in circulation in Germany in prewar years.

Things happened as in a fever-ridden dream. Prices changed by the hour. Before the summit was reached, a ham sandwich was quoted at 14,000 marks one day and 24,000 marks the next. An article in a retail store priced at 5,000,000,000 marks in the morning had increased to 12,000,000,000 by afternoon. A sheet of writing paper cost 120 marks—$30 at prewar exchange—while yet the inflation was young. Interest rates rose to 900 per cent, and even then lenders at times were not protected, because by the time they were paid—even tenfold—the sum they received was worth less than the sum they lent.

What this meant in terms of human hardship can easily be imagined. Savings patiently built up by a lifetime of thrift might buy as much as a package of cigarettes. Life insurance policies matured—and the proceeds would not buy a handkerchief. It might be cheaper to light a cigar with a bond than to buy a match. The thrifty were penalized; the only wise folk were the spendthrifts. The nation became a spendthrift one, of course; everyone who received money rushed madly to convert it into goods. Things would be worth more tomorrow, perhaps this very afternoon. Money would be worth less. Debts were wiped out; farm mortgages were paid off with a sack of potatoes.

Translated into economic jargon, the creditor class was ruined; debtors were freed. People who had lived on investments were paupers.

The government tried to protect its citizens but could not do much. Prices of necessities were fixed from time to time to assure people of food and a roof over their heads, but fixing prices at a reasonable level one day did not solve the problem the next. Wages were moved up frequently—in the early stages, every month, then every ten days, but they always lagged behind the cost of living. The principle of fixing wages on a sliding scale geared to the cost of living was adopted, but it never was very popular with labor, because most workingmen did not understand its complexities, and those who did protested that the scale was inadequate. Labor troubles were widespread.

While great classes were being pauperized, other skillful manipulators were becoming fabulously wealthy. The speculators' method was to borrow money, buy goods or real estate or factories, then pay off the debt in worthless money. Then they could either keep the tangibles or sell them and repeat the operation.

Business of course boomed, for everyone was buying goods. A great boom developed in the stock market, from the scramble to buy shares in tangible properties.

Toward the close of the era, many localities began to quote prices in foreign currencies, usually dollars. Various institutions issued scrip redeemable in goods—rye, barley, coal, wood, and even kilowatt hours.

It was impossible, obviously, to plan ahead in terms of paper money. Construction and similar industries languished.

After monetary stabilization, there was a brief depression, but business did not for long stay inordinately dull, since there had been an accumulation of demands for goods and services that could not be supplied during the inflation—demands for new homes and improved factories, for example. So recovery progressed with reasonable rapidity.

But profound changes had been made in the social structure. There were new rich and new poor. The middle class, by and large, suffered most. The very poor had had little to lose; many of the wealthy had known how to protect themselves. Businesses emerged with most of their debts wiped out.

READING 17
The Myth of Fiscal Policy: The Monetarist View

Ira Kaminow

Although most economists are in basic agreement about the type of relationships underlying aggregate economic activity in a market economy, varying estimates about the precise nature of these relationships can result in vastly different policy interpretations. In this reading, Ira Kaminow of the Federal Reserve Bank of Philadelphia cogently explains the justification for the opposing viewpoints of the Keynesians and Monetarists. Using the same equations, but with differing estimates of some marginal propensities or slopes, Kaminow demonstrates how the Monetarists can argue for macro policy based primarily on changes in the money supply, while the Keynesians, using a similar model, strongly support the use of fiscal policy to stabilize the economy.

Guideposts for Thought While Reading
What is the essential difference in the macro models which accounts for the conflicting implications found by Monetarists and Keynesians? If the Keynesians are wrong, what changes should be made in the way our economy is currently monitored by the Federal Reserve Bank and the federal government?

Times are changing. What is obvious today was obviously wrong yesterday; this is as true of questions involving economic issues as any others. Many of us, for example, believe in the efficacy of fiscal policy—in the Government's power to influence the level of national income by its own spending and taxing policies. Indeed, the expenditure-income chain explanation of the operation of fiscal policy is part of today's conventional wisdom. The Government spends more or spurs private spending by taxing less, and so creates more jobs and higher profits.

Reprinted by permission of the publisher from Ira Kaminow, "The Myth of Fiscal Policy: The Monetarist View," *Business Review*, December 1969, pp. 10–18.

The new income so created generates additional demand and private spending, creating even more income.

All this is Keynesian economics—the so-called New Economics. But it wasn't long ago that the Keynesian Revolution was rejected by most laymen, and not long before that, that it was rejected by most economists. Today, with victory in hand, the New Economics is facing a counter-revolution which may again change the economic thinking of the nation. There is a small but highly vocal group of economists who are suspicious of Keynesian economics in general and of fiscal policy in particular. The members of the group are sometimes called Monetarists.

Monetarists view the controversy over economic theories as being like a law suit. As judges, they rule that the New Economists have presented no acceptable historical evidence in support of the income-expenditure theory. As litigants, they present the following case: (1) over the years, the major movements in national income have been associated with major movements in the money supply and *vice versa;* (2) no equally strong or systematic relation can be found to support the Keynesian view of the operation of fiscal policy; (3) therefore, monetary forces have played a much more important and/or more stable role in determining national income than fiscal forces. Monetarists do not claim that the income-expenditure chain is erroneous in principle—merely that history tells us it is too weak or unpredictable to be of much use for economic policy.

A SIMPLE EXPLANATION OF THE MONETARIST VIEW

How do the Monetarists reconcile their view of history with the apparently powerful logic of the income-expenditure chain? The heart of the Monetarist view is the supply of and demand for money—a dramatic shift from the usual emphasis. Because of the near total victory of the New Economics (at least in introductory textbooks on economics) in the fifties and sixties, the spotlight of popular policy discussions has been firmly set on the pivot point of Keynesian economics—the demand for goods.

A look at the economy from the perspective of the money side of things (or the goods side, for that matter) will reveal only a partial and perhaps slightly distorted picture of the economy. Nevertheless, anyone who has been to the circus knows how difficult it is to look at all three rings at once and that there is something to be gained from looking at only one at a time.

Although not all economists agree on the definition of money, we will not break too much with tradition if we use the term to mean all assets that are generally accepted as a means of payment. More concretely, we can define money as the sum of coins, paper currency, and checking account deposits.

An easy way to illustrate the Monetarist view is to suppose that a certain quantity of money is required to support any particular level of income. When national economic activity (as measured by income) rises, more money is required to carry on conveniently day-to-day transactions; when economic activity declines, households and businesses find that they engage in fewer transactions, and hence, need less money. More specifically, we can assume that the demand for money balances *relative* to the level of income (what economists call desired *relative* money balances) is fixed. By way of illustration, we can imagine that institutional arrangements—like the availability of credit cards and the length of the average pay period—lead the public to desire money balances equal in value to 10 per cent of national income. If annual national income is $800 billion, then desired balances would be $80 billion.

What happens if the economy has more money than it requires? Say, for the sake of argument, that the actual stock of money in the previous example is $90 billion, or $10 billion more than is required. Since money yields no pecuniary return, households and businesses will attempt to exchange money for other assets—assets that yield satisfaction directly (like television sets) and assets that yield a pecuniary return (like stocks and bonds). The increased demand for goods and services will stimulate greater output and perhaps will boost prices as markets respond to the new demand. At the same time, the increased demand for financial assets like stocks and bonds will drive interest rates down. The decline in interest rates will further encourage the demand for goods by making credit cheaper. This will induce still higher prices and output. The pace of economic activity will quicken. Economic activity will continue to increase until income is pushed up to a level consistent with the $90 billion money stock—that is, to $900 billion.

The rigid relationship between the demand for money and national income makes this environment inhospitable to fiscal policy. If the national goal is to raise income, it can be achieved only by raising the money stock. An increase in Government expenditures won't work except for a very short time. As soon as income rises a bit, the money stock will be inadequate. There will be a general scramble for money, and the private demand for goods will decline as businesses and households try to increase their holdings of money. Consequently, income and output will be pulled back down by the limited money stock.

Stated somewhat differently, any increase in Government expenditures (not accompanied by an appropriate increase in the money stock) will be matched by an equal decline in private expenditures; any decrease in Government expenditures (not accompanied by an appropriate decline in the money stock) will be matched by an equal increase in private expenditures.

The key that allowed monetary policy to work in the simple world just described is the constancy of desired *relative* money balances. In order to achieve an equilibrium, annual national income will always adjust so that it is ten times the stock of money. If we can control the money supply, we can control national income. The key that locked fiscal policy out is that Government taxing and spending policies have no effect on desired relative money balances. No matter what fiscal policies are followed, annual national income will always tend to be ten times higher than the stock of money. In these two keys are the germs of the Monetarist position: (1) Although demand for relative money balances is not fixed, it is the most stable and predictable variable on which we can count for economic policy. (2) Although fiscal policies may have some influence on desired relative money balances, they do not have a strong, predictable influence; therefore, fiscal policies are of relatively little or no use.

A LOOK AT THE NEW ECONOMICS FROM THE MONEY SIDE

Advocates of the New Economics do not agree that income is the only variable that exerts a strong, predictable influence on the demand for money. They argue that a typical family might find it very convenient at some given level of income to go about its daily business with an average checking account balance of $100. But convenience must be balanced against cost. One hundred dollars in the checking account is not earning interest. When the interest rate on savings accounts is very low, the household may indeed hold a $100 checking account balance. But let the interest rate rise substantially and the household may decide that it can get by with only $75 or $50 worth of money. The lower money balance might mean more bother—more accurate balancing of the checkbook, more trips to the bank—but the bother is compensated by the greater interest income. In short, the New Economists argue that both the level of income and the interest rate determine the desired stock of money. By adding this additional ingredient—interest rates—the New Economist can salvage the argument for the expenditure-income chain.

Keynesians expect roughly the same kind of initial response to fiscal policy as do the Monetarists. An increase in Government expenditures drives income up, and the existing stock of money becomes inadequate to handle the additional income. In an effort to acquire more money, people try to sell nonmonetary financial assets such as bonds. As the supply of these assets rises relative to demand, interest rates begin to rise to make them more attractive to buyers. This hike in interest rates is the key that is supposed to let fiscal policy back in. Higher interest rates mean that the economy will be able to support a higher level of income with the given stock of money. With higher interest rates, households and businesses find it advantageous to economize on the use of money—to make the existing stock "go farther." The economy will, after the initial shock of added Government expenditures, come to rest at a higher level of national income—and higher interest rates. The higher interest rates are necessary; otherwise, the public could not be induced to hold the same quantity of money at the higher level of activity. Put in slightly different terms, the ratio of desired money balances to income will decline because interest rates have risen.

An extreme version of the Keynesian view gives rise to the so-called liquidity trap. Imagine what would happen if the public were willing to hold whatever money balances were offered at the prevailing interest rate. The public would make no attempt to convert new money balances into other assets, regardless of how much money the authorities pumped into the economy. Any new money that was placed in the economy would be willingly held at the existing interest rate and income. Monetary policy is completely frustrated if and when we get into the trap because then the public's actions are unaffected by changes in the money supply.

In contrast, recall that in the simple Monetarist case the demand for *relative* money balances doesn't change. Individual members of the public never will be willing to hold unlimited quantities of money. If new money is added to the economy, the public will have "too much" money and will try to get rid of the excess. This process will drive income up to a new equilibrium.

DOES IT MATTER IF THE INTEREST RATE MATTERS?

The single most revealing element in the encounter between Monetarists and New Economists is that they cannot agree on the relevance of the relevance of the interest rate. The Monetarist Milton Friedman wrote:

> . . . in my opinion no "fundamental issues" in either monetary theory or monetary policy hinge on whether [the demand for money depends on interest rates].

The Keynesian Paul Samuelson wrote:

> . . . the minute you believe that [the demand for money depends on interest rates], you have moved to . . . the post-Keynesian position.

Keynesians insist that the interest rate is the added gear in the mechanism that allows fiscal policy to work. For them, fiscal policy (viewed from the money side of the economy) gives authorities control over the interest rate and, through the interest rate, control over desired *relative* money balances. The Monetarists insist that this control must be inconsequential because they see no evidence that it has worked in the past (New Economists, of course, dispute the charge of lack of evidence). For the Monetarists there are two possibilities: (1) fiscal policy has had an erratic, unsystematic effect on the interest rate and, hence, an unobservable effect on national income, or (2) fiscal policies have been so mild as to have only a small effect on interest rates.

The issue (regarding the demand for money) that is of primary importance to the Monetarist is the stability and predictability of desired relative money balances. Evidence of a highly unstable and unpredictable ratio of money balances to national income would directly contradict the efficacy of monetary policy. In terms of the Keynesian theory, the instability would arise if we fell into a liquidity trap. The Monetarists are therefore considerably more interested in whether a trap exists than in whether the demand for money is sensitive to the interest rate.

HISTORICAL EVIDENCE: THE DEMAND FOR MONEY

It is time to fish or cut bait. A number of issues have been raised and questions asked about the demand for money. What kinds of answers does history provide? To make things manageable, we can concentrate on three key questions: (1) Does the demand for money depend on income? (2) Is the demand for money sensitive to interest rates? (3) Have we ever been caught in a liquidity trap?

Question One: What Role for Income?

Virtually every empirical study undertaken has shown that the demand for money depends on the level of income. Sometimes the relationship is based on a linkage between current income and money demand through the level of transactions of the sort we discussed earlier. Sometimes the relationship is based on more subtle arguments.

These more subtle discussions generally presume that economic well-being is a more important determinant of the demand for money than is the volume of transactions. The discussions take as their point of departure the notion that improved economic status for a nation (or an individual) means a greater demand for most assets, including money. In fact, at least one economist believes that money is a luxury in the sense that the demand for it rises very rapidly as a nation (or individual) moves up the economic ladder.

The two measures of economic well-being that have been used to explain the demand for money are wealth and permanent income. Everyone is familiar with the notion of wealth, and there should be no dispute that it is one measure of economic well-being. The meaning of permanent income, however, is not widely known.

Permanent income is most simply described as expected average lifetime income. It is a good measure of economic well-being because it is adjusted for temporary ups and downs. A day laborer who happens to be working his way through medical school has a higher *permanent* income than his co-worker whose actual or *measured* income is the same but whose ambitions and income expectations are more modest.

Economists who take the permanent income approach do not deny the importance of measured income. They argue that current and past levels of measured income are the most important influences on permanent income. They claim that expectations are largely formulated on the basis of past experience.

Question Two: How Important Is the Interest Rate?

Historically, the interest rate has influenced the demand for money. This much we know with virtual certainty—that is, if unanimity of opinion implies certainty of knowledge. There is some disagreement, however, on just how important the interest rate has been. Some economists, like Milton Friedman and Maurice Allais, take the view that the interest rate is so unimportant in determining the demand for money that little is lost if it is ignored. Other investigators, however, have presented evidence that the demand for money is highly sensitive to changes in the rate of interest. Perhaps the most sensitive relationship was found by Allan Meltzer who estimated on one occasion that any given percentage change in long-term interest rates would be matched by an equal percentage change (in the opposite direction) in the demand for money.

The disagreement over the importance of the interest does not follow "party lines." As it turns out, all three of the economists mentioned in the last paragraph are Monetarists. Estimates of the interest sensitivity by Keynesians are greater than zero but less than Meltzer's.

A major reason for all this disagreement about the importance of the interest rate is that it is often difficult to untangle the influence of interest rates from other influences on the demand for money. Interest rates vary in a more or less systematic way over the business cycle—they generally go up during expansions and down during economic contractions.

Other variables that are likely to influence the demand for money also behave more or less predictably over the cycle. This raises the possibility that an investigator will wrongly attribute the influence of some other variable to interest rates, or the influence of interest rates to other variables.

Milton Friedman and Anna J. Schwartz, in particular, argue that an uncritical reading of history has led to an over-emphasis on the role of the interest rate in determining the demand for money.

It is well known that relative money balances (the ratio of money balances to income) fall during expansions and rise during contractions. Generally speaking, therefore, relative money balances are high when interest rates are low (during slumps), and are low when interest rates are high (during booms). The interest rate seems to do a good job in explaining movements in the demand for relative money balances.

Friedman and Schwartz argue that there is another factor to explain movements in relative money balances over the cycle. It is based on the idea of permanent income (expected average lifetime income) mentioned earlier. During economic downturns, people anticipate that things will get better; so permanent income is higher than measured income. During periods of prosperity, people guess that incomes are unusually high; so permanent income is lower than measured income. Over the cycle, permanent income fluctuates much less than measured income because people recognize that a good deal of income fluctuations are transitory. If the demand for money depends on permanent income, it will fluctuate relatively little over the business cycle because permanent income is relatively stable over the cycle. Therefore, during periods of recovery, the demand for money will rise more slowly than measured income, so relative money balances (the ratio of money balances to measured national income) will fall. During periods of contraction, the demand for money will fall more slowly than measured income, and relative money balances will rise.

Friedman and Schwartz offer some evidence in support of their views in their famous study *A Monetary History of the United States.* For example, they point to the period, 1932–1937, during which both interest rates and relative money balances fell. This pattern is clearly inconsistent with the interest-rate explanation of movements in the demand for money. The 1932–1937 experience is very easily explained by the permanent income concept. In the mid-1930's, the economy started to climb out of the depths of the Great Depression. Income was rising. Nevertheless, vivid memories of 1929, 1930, and 1931 lingered. People were not so sure that the recovery was going to be sustained. Permanent income rose, but not so fast as measured income. Desired money balances, which respond to permanent income, grew more slowly than measured income. So, the ratio of money balances to measured income fell.

Not all economists agree that the Friedman and Schwartz evidence is convincing. A number of studies have shown that the interest rate has had a strong influence even if one accepts the permanent income hypothesis. In fact, Friedman and Schwartz seem to have retreated slightly on this point. In 1966, Friedman wrote "most estimates [of the interest rate sensitivity], including some we have obtained in our own subsequent work are higher . . . than the estimate Anna J. Schwartz and I used in *A Monetary History.*"

Question Three: Have We Ever Been Trapped?

The answer to this question can be stated very succinctly: The great weight of historical evidence indicates that we have never been in a liquidity trap. A number of studies have attempted to find periods in American history when the public was willing to hold whatever quantity of money balances made available. Over the periods investigated, the public has always made attempts to unload excess money balances in exchange for other assets.

A Summary

Studies of the demand for money can be thought of as the first round in the debate over the efficacy of monetary and fiscal policy. The nice thing about the first round is that each side can go back to its corner confident that it took the round on points. Monetarists smell victory because of the absence of any evidence of the existence of a trap. To them this is the crucial issue. Keynesians are delighted with the outcome because of the overwhelming evidence of the interest sensitivity of the demand for money.

There has been a marked shift in the great economic debate since the initial victories of the New Economics. In the late 1940's and early 1950's, it was generally believed by Keynesians that money didn't matter at all. By the early and mid 1960's, the Monetarists had made sufficient headway to shift the question from "does money matter?" to "does fiscal policy matter?" The New Economists have largely recognized the importance of money, but not its dominance. The Monetarists, however, continue to question the empirical relevance of fiscal policy.

READING 18
Monetarism Objectively Evaluated
Paul A. Samuelson

Paul A. Samuelson, Institute Professor at M.I.T., is a world renowned American economist who critically reviews the claims of Monetarism in this reading. Professor Samuelson, who studied under Alvin Hansen at Harvard University and received his Ph.D. in 1941, was awarded the Nobel Memorial Prize in 1970 by the Royal Swedish Academy of Sciences. His scientific contributions to economic theory and his incisive contributions to analysis of economic problems and issues are well-known in the field of economics, and these same qualities are visible in this appraisal of Monetarism. Not a narrow-minded fiscalist alone, the author does, nonetheless, debunk what he regards as the excesses of the Chicago School view so succinctly expressed by Professor Milton Friedman.

Professor Samuelson explains the two extreme positions—the older Keynesian view that "money does not matter" and the Monetarist view that "money alone matters," both of which he regards as being wide of the mark. This position is one which does not deny the inherent difficulties in gauging and forecasting the state of the economy, nor does it imply that "fine tuning" is a science of perfection. What the author does reveal is the usefulness of both fiscal and monetary policy along with the continual need to search for better and more effective ways to achieve price stability and full employment.

Guideposts for Thought While Reading

Contrast the statements "Money does not matter," "Money matters," and "Money alone matters." How do Friedman Monetarism and Keynesian economics fit within this three-fold statement about the importance of money? Analyze the historical period 1966–1969 with respect to fiscal and monetary policy. Summarize the positions you would expect to hear repeated in a debate between Professor Samuelson and Professor Friedman. Assuming that you have to take a position on the issue of Monetarism, how would you defend your views?

There are fashions within science. Nowhere is the oscillating pendulum of opinion more marked in the field of economics than in the area of money. By the end of the 1930s, after the so-called Keynesian revolution, courses and textbooks continued to be devoted to money. But in fact money had almost completely dropped out of them and the emphasis had shifted to analysis of income determination in terms of such Keynesian concepts as the multiplier and the propensity to consume.

If the market quotation for monetary theory sagged in the decade after 1936, by the early 1950s there were unmistakable signs of a comeback. It was Professor Howard S. Ellis of the University of California who coined in those years the expression, "the rediscovery of money." And the famous Accord of 1951, which gave back to the Federal Reserve its freedom to pursue an autonomous monetary policy independently of the needs and desires of President Truman's Treasury, was the objective counterpart of the reappearance of money in the theoretical models of academic scholars.

FRIEDMAN AND THE CHICAGO SCHOOL

Undoubtedly the popularity of monetarism can be traced in large part to one man, namely Professor Milton Friedman of the University of Chicago. His monumental *Monetary History of the United States, 1867–1960,* written with Mrs. Anna Schwartz, is the bible of the movement; and let me say as an infidel that it is a classic source of data and analysis to which all scholars will turn for years to come. In addition to this scholarly work, Professor Friedman has published numerous statistical studies in learned economic journals. He has testified before Congress and lectured before lay groups. His influential columns in *Newsweek* and writings for the financial press have hammered away at one simple message:

> It is the rate of growth of the money supply that is the prime determinant of the state of aggregate dollar demand. If the Federal Reserve will keep the money supply growing at a steady rate—say 4 to 5 percent by one or another definition of the money supply, but the fact of steadiness being more important than the rate agreed upon—then it will be doing all a central bank can usefully do to cope with the problems of inflation, unemployment, and business instability.
>
> *Fiscal policy as such has no independent, systematic effect upon aggregate dollar demand. Increasing tax rates,* but with the understanding that money growth remains unchanged, *will have no effect* in lessening the degree of inflation; it will have no *independent* effect in increasing the level of unemployment in a period of deflation; changes in public expenditure out of the budget (it being understood that the rate of growth of the money supply is held unchanged) will also have *no lasting effects on inflationary or deflationary gaps.*
>
> In the past, budgetary deficits and budgetary surpluses have often been accompanied by central bank creation of new money or deceleration of growth of new money. Therefore, many people have wrongly inferred that fiscal deficits and surpluses have *predictable* expansionary and contracting effects upon the total of aggregate spending. But this is a complete confusion. *It is the changes in the rate of growth of the money supply which alone have substantive effects.* After we have controlled or allowed for monetary changes, fiscal policy has negligible independent potency.[1]

[1] Professor Friedman is careful to specify that fiscal policy does have important effects upon the *composition* of any given total of gross national product. Thus increases in government expenditures will pull resources out of the private sector into the public. John Kenneth Galbraith might like this but Milton Friedman does not. Also, increasing taxation relative to

This is my summary of the Friedman-type monetarism. No doubt he would word things somewhat differently. And I should like to emphasize that there are many qualifications in his scientific writing which do not logically entail the *simpliste* version of monetarism outlined above. Indeed it is one of the purposes of this article to demonstrate and emphasize the point that the weight of the evidence on money, theoretical and empirical, does not imply the correctness of crude monetarism.

Among the central bankers of the world, financial journalists, statesmen and politicians, business and academic economists, and men of affairs generally, monetarism seems almost paradoxically simple and perverse. Can President Nixon really suppose that it makes no difference for the control of the 1969–70 American inflation, whether or not he proposes to extend into 1970 the tax surcharge? Professor Friedman is but one of his advisers, and it is evident that Paul McCracken, Chairman of the Council of Economic Advisers, and Arthur F. Burns, the new chairman of the Federal Reserve Board named by Nixon, do *not* see eye to eye with Friedman in this matter.

Yet Professor Friedman does not stand alone. His mountains of data, cogency of reasoning, and formidable powers of patient persuasion have raised unto him a host of followers. Graduates of the Chicago workshops in monetary theory carry to new universities the message. A number of other scholars, such as Professors Allan Meltzer at Carnegie-Mellon University in Pittsburgh and Karl Brunner of Ohio State University, have also produced research in support of monetarism. Professor Harry Johnson leads the campaign to export monetarism to the British Isles. One of our twelve regional Federal Reserve Banks, that of St. Louis, has carried the torch for monetarism, providing up-to-date numerical information on the vagaries of the money supply, and promoting quantitative research on the lagged potency of money. Distinguished graduates of the University of Chicago, such as Dr. Beryl Sprinkel of the Harris Trust Company Bank in

---

public expenditure, although having no independent effect on aggregate demand, will tend to lower consumption and reduce interest rates. This contrived increase in thriftiness will move the mix of full-employment output in the direction of more rapid capital formation; it will speed up the rate of growth of productivity and real output, and will increase the rate of growth of real wages. If the trend of the money supply remains unchanged, this will tend toward a lower price level in the future or a less rapidly rising one. (See the introduction to the Reading 82 for Friedman's exact wording.)

Chicago, and Dr. James Meigs, of the First National City Bank of New York, profess to be monetarists who improve the accuracy of their business forecasts by concentrating primarily on money. At one time or another the editorial pages of the influential *Washington Post* and *New York Times* have become permeated by monetarism. Finally, the Joint Economic Committee of Congress, when it was under the chairmanship of Senator William Proxmire, reacted strongly against the use of fiscal policy as a stabilization device, and recommended to the Federal Reserve Board that it never permit the money supply to grow at rates widely different from some agreed-upon constant.

KEYNESIAN ECONOMICS

Thus monetarism is a movement to reckon with. I believe monetarism could be deemed fruitful, to the degree that is has pushed economists away from a *simpliste* Keynesian model, popular in the United States during the Great Depression and still lingering on in Britain, and made economists more willing to recognize that monetary policy is an important stabilization weapon, fully coordinate with fiscal policy as a macro-economic control instrument. However, my reading of the development of modern economic doctrine does not suggest to me that the post-Keynesian position that I myself hold, and of which Professor James Tobin of Yale and Franco Modigliani of M.I.T. are leading exponents, has been materially influenced by monetarism. Indeed, speaking for myself, the excessive claims for money as an exclusive determinant of aggregate demand would, if anything, have slowed down and delayed my appreciation of money's true quantitative and qualitative role.[2]

Although the neglect of money is often said to be a characteristic of Keynesian economists and a heritage of the analysis in Keynes' 1936 classic *General Theory of Employment, Interest and Money*, it is doubtful that Keynes himself can be properly described as ever having believed that "money does not mat-

[2] To clarify my point, let me state my belief that Professor Friedman has been a force of the first magnitude in getting economists generally to realize the desirability of flexible exchange rates. He, and Professors Frank Knight and Henry Simons at Chicago before him, deserve an honored place in the history of economic thought in influencing economists to appreciate the merits of market pricing as against direct government interventions. But I do not believe that the positions today of the Tobins and Modiglianis of the modern scene would be very different if a Chicago School had never existed.

ter."[3] If one writes down in the form of equations or graphs the boney structure of the *General Theory,* he sees that money enters into the liquidity-preference function in such a way that an increase in the money supply lowers interest rates, thereby inducing an increase in investment, and through multiplier mechanism causes a rise in employment and production, or, if employment is already full and output at capacity levels, causes upward pressure on the price level.

How is it that some Keynesians should ever have become identified with the doctrine that money does not matter? Most converts to Keynesianism became converts during the slump years of the late 1930s. Then the deep-depression polar case did seem to be the realistic case. It is a sad fact about many scholars that they learn and unlearn nothing after the age of 29, so that there exist in chairs of economics around the world many economists who still live mentally in the year 1938. For 1938, when the interest rate on Treasury Bills was often a fraction of a fraction of a percent, even a monetarist might despair of the potency of central bank monetary policy.

HOW IT WORKS

By the 1950s and 1960s a body of analysis and data had been accumulated which led to a positive, strong belief that open-market and discount operations by the central bank could have *pronounced macroeconomic effects upon investment and consumption spending in the succeeding several months and quarters.* One of the principal preoccupations of the post-Keynesian economists, which is to say of the ruling orthodoxy of American establishment economics, has been to trace out the *causal* mechanisms whereby monetary and fiscal variables produce their effects upon the total of spending and its composition.

[3] When an author writes as much as did Keynes, it is inevitable that certain of his passages might seem to contradict others. There are *some* of his paragraphs written in the 1930s that do seem to play down the quantitative potency of monetary policy in times of deep depression. And those many writers, such as Sir John Hicks, Sir Roy Harrod, Professor James Meade, and the late Oskar Lange, who have codified the *General Theory* in the form of simple equations and graphs, are able to formulate a "deep-depression" polar case in which money does not matter (either because the liquidity-preference schedule displays infinite elasticity at a "liquidity trap," or the marginal efficiency schedule of investment displays complete inelasticity to interest rate changes). But note that this is not the general case of the *General Theory,* but only a special polar case, just as the classical quantity theory of money is the special case at the opposite pole.

Thus, an open-market purchase of Treasury bills by the Fed first bids up bond prices and lowers their yield; this spreads to *a reduction* in *yields* on competing securities, such as longer-term government bonds or corporate bonds or home mortgages. The lowering of interest costs will typically be accompanied by *a relaxation in the degree of credit rationing,* and this can be expected *to stimulate investment spending* that would otherwise not have taken place. The lowering of interest rates generally also brings about an *upward capitalization of the value of existing assets,* and this increase in the money value of wealth can be expected to have a certain *expansionary influence on consumer spending,* and in a degree on business spending for investment. As a limit upon the stimulus stemming from money creation by orthodox open-market operations, must be reckoned the fact that as the central bank pumps new money into the system, it is in return taking from the system *an almost equal quantum of money substitutes* in the form of government securities. In a sense the Federal Reserve or the Bank of England is merely a dealer in second-hand assets, contriving transfer exchanges of one type of asset for another, and in the process affecting the interest rate structure that constitutes the terms of trade among them.

What needs to be stressed is the fact that one cannot expect money created by this process of central-bank open-market operations *alone,* with say the fiscal budget held always in balance, to have at all the same functional relationship to the level of the GNP and of the price index that could be the case for money created by gold mining or money created by the printing press of national governments or the Fed and used to finance public expenditures in excess of tax receipts. Not only would the creation of these last kinds of money involve a flow of production and spendable income in their very *act of being born,* but in addition the community would be *left permanently richer* in its ownership of monetary wealth. In money terms the community *feels* richer, in money terms the community *is* richer. And this can be expected to reflect itself in a higher price level or a lower rate of unemployment or both.

By contrast, money created through conventional central-bank operations quite divorced from the financing of fiscal deficits or the production of mining output does not entail an equivalent permanent increase in net wealth as viewed by people in the community. Post-Keynesians emphasize that extinguishing the outstanding interest-bearing public debt, whether by a capital levy or by open-market purchase of it, does rationally make the community *feel poorer* than would be the case if the same amount of money existed and the public debt had been unreduced. All men are mortal. Most men do not concern themselves with the wellbeing of their remote posterity. Hence, government bonds as an asset are not completely offset in their minds by the recognition of the liability of paying in perpetuity taxes to carry the interest on those bonds. Only if people live forever, foreseeing correctly the tax payments they (or the posterity as dear to them in the most remote future as is their own lifetime wellbeing) must make on account of the perpetual future interest payments on government bonds—only then would it be true to say that retirement of public debt would have no substantive effects upon the reckoning of wealth, the levels of spending, and the level of prices generally. Rejecting such a perpetual-life model as extreme and unrealistic, we must debit against an increase in money through open-market operations a partial offset in the form of retirement of some of the outstanding public debt.

Finally, to clarify the significant difference between the post-Keynesian analysis which most modern economists believe to be plausible as against the tenets of monetarism, I must point out that even when the money supply is held constant:

1. Any significant changes in thriftiness and the propensity to consume can be expected to have systematic independent effects on the money value of current output, affecting average prices or aggregate production or both.
2. Likewise an exogenous burst of investment opportunities or animal spirits on the part of business can be expected to have systematic effects on total GNP.
3. Increases in public expenditure, or reductions in tax rates—and even increases in public expenditure balanced by increases in taxation—can be expected to have systematic effects upon aggregate GNP.

All these tenets of the modern eclectic position are quite incompatible with monetarism. (Indeed that is the differentiating definition by which we distinguish the Chicago School monetarism from the post-Keynesian positions with which it has so much overlap.) The eclectic position is incompatible with monetarism, but it is not incompatible with a *sophisticated* version of the Quantity Theory of Money. For as soon as one follows the logic of neoclassical analysis (expecting that less of any kind of inventory will be held if, other things equal, the cost of holding it has gone up) and postulates that the *velocity of circulation of money is a rising function of the interest rate,* the post-Keynesian (and even the simple Keynesian) model becomes compatible with the Quantity Theory. One way of looking at Keynesian liquidity preference is as *a theory of the velocity of circulation*.

FAULTY LOGIC

When post-Keynesians study recent economic history, they find that interest rates and money do enter into their estimating equations and with the theoretically expected algebraic signs. Case studies bear out the importance for investment decisions of the cost and availability of credit. Properly phrased questionnaires to business elicit answers that point in the same direction. And plausible theories to explain how businessmen make their investment decisions and how they ought to also bear out the fact that monetary policy does matter. So there is simply no excuse for living in a 1938 dream world in which money does not matter.

The bearing of all this on monetarism is well illustrated by an incident a few years ago at an American Bankers Association symposium where leading academic economists were commenting upon Professor Friedman's writings. Professor James Tobin went to the blackboard and wrote down three sentences:

1. MONEY DOES NOT MATTER.
2. MONEY MATTERS.
3. MONEY ALONE MATTERS.

He went on to say: Professor Friedman produces evidence to prove that the first proposition, Money doesn't matter, is false: he purports to have demonstrated from this that the third proposition, Money alone matters, is true; whereas the correct logical conclusion is that the second proposition, Money does matter, is all that follows. And on that there is no quarrel among leading modern macroeconomic economists.

I think there is much wisdom in this. When Professor Friedman defends monetarism, as for example in a late-1968 debate at New York University with new economist Walter Heller [see Reading 82], he refers to a mountain of evidence that supports monetarism. But how many members of the thousands in the overflow crowd attending that debate were able to appraise that evidence to see whether it supports the proposition 2, that money matters, rather than the central tenet of monetarism, that (when it comes to predictable systematic effects on aggregate demand and on inflationary or deflationary gaps) money alone matters? Sir Ronald Fisher, the greatest statistician of our age, pointed out that replication a thousandfold of an inconclusive experiment does nothing to add to its value. In terms of the language of statistics, most of the evidence compiled about money has little or no power to differentiate between propositions 2 and 3.

What does a monetarist do when confronted with the fact that his causal factor, money, does not empirically lead his response factor, general business? One desperate artifice is to change his focus from the *stock* of money to its *time derivative,* its *rate of growth.* It is a mathematical fact that any periodic fluctuation that behaves a bit like a sine curve will have its derivative turndown a quarter cycle before itself; so if money itself does not lag business by as much as one quarter, one cannot help but get some lead at turning points by using the rate of change of money. But by that kind of frivolous action, one could use the derivative of production, its rate of change, to predict the turning points of the stock of money: or, with recognition of noise in the data, use production's own rate of change to predict its turning points.

Dimensional traps. Obviously, we have to find the reason for using dM/dt, the rate of change of money, rather than M, the stock of money, as our causal variable. One ridiculous argument for using the former is dimensional: both the level of GNP and the rate of growth of the money supply are measured in terms of dollars *per year.* Therefore, relate GNP and dM/dt, not GNP and M. This argument is ridiculous because the whole basis of the quantity theory of money is that V, the velocity of circulation of money or its reciprocal, is the dimensional constant that exists to relate the stock of money and the flow of national product. Professor Friedman, more than any other modern economist, has sloshed through the mountains of Yugoslavia to demonstrate that every peasant holds seventeen-weeks purchasing power in his pockets. The whole demand-for-money concept is for the purpose of making hypotheses about how that number 17 will change when interest rates, branch banking, or price expectations change. Moreover, there is involved a profound misunderstanding of how dimensional analysis is to be used in any science. The behavioral equation of a simple pendulum has for its very purpose the relating of two dimensionally different magnitudes—the position of the pendulum as measured in centimeters or dimensionless angular degrees and its acceleration as measured in centimeters per time squared. Nor is this a special example: Newton's universal law of gravitation, the greatest system of the world produced by man's thoughts, relates dimensionally different magnitudes in precisely the way that Dr. Friedman criticizes.

CRUCIAL TESTS IN 1966–1967 AND 1968–1969

Personally, as a scientist, I would cheerfully accept *any hypothesis that would deliver the goods and explain the facts.* As a fallible human being, I do not relish having to change my mind but if economists had to hang from the ceiling in order to do their job, then there would be nothing for it than to do so. But monetarism does not deliver the goods. I could make a fortune giving good predictions to large corporations and banks based on monetarism if it would work. But I have tried every version of it. And none do.

To this there are two standard answers. The first is that nothing works well. Fine tuning is an illusion. There is much "noise" in the data. No one can claim that monetarism would enable the Federal Reserve to iron out all the variation in the economy. All we can say for it is that stabilizing the growth rate of money is the best policy that the ingenuity of man can ever arrive at. All this involves what I call the chipmunk syndrome. The nimble monetarist sticks his neck out in an occasional prediction: that prediction is not always free of ambiguity, but it does seem to point qualitatively in one direction, often a direction counter to the conventional wisdom of the moment: then if subsequent events do seem to go in the indicated direction, the prediction is trumpeted to be a feather in the cap of monetarism. If, as is happening all the time, events do not particularly go in that direction—or if as happens often, events go somewhat in a direction that neither competing theory has been subjected to a test of any resolving power—the chipmunk pulls in his head, saying that there is no way of fine tuning the economy or making completely accurate predictions.

The other argument against the view that monetarism simply does not work is the assertion, "Monetarism does work. So and so at the Blank bank uses it and he beats the crowd in batting average." I believe this to be a serious and important subject for investigation. Let me therefore, because of space limitations, confine myself to a few observations based upon preliminary investigations of the matter.

1. Those analysts who use their monetarism *neat* really do *not* perform well.

2. A number of bank economists, who give great weight to the

money factor but who *also* pay attention to what is happening to defense spending and inventories and a host of other factors, seem to me to have compiled an excellent record at forecasting. Not a perfect record. Who has a perfect record? And not, as far as quantitative studies known to me suggest, a better record than the best macroeconomic forecasters who do not consciously put special stress on the money factor (but who do not neglect it either!). In short, it is impossible to separate "flair" in forecasting from success attributable primarily to use of money-supply variables.

3. The years 1966–67 are often referred to as years of a crucial test in which monetarism defeated Keynesianism. I have gone over all the main forecasts used by both schools during that period and I must report that this is a misapprehension. There was *wide range* of forecasts by practitioners of both schools: there was a *wide overlap* between these two ranges. On the whole, the monetarists averaged better and *earlier* in their perception of the slowdown beginning to be seen in late 1966 in consequence of the money crunch of 1966. And one would expect this to be the case from an eclectic viewpoint since the independent variable of money received the biggest alteration in *that* period. But many of the monetarists went overboard in predicting a recession in 1967 of the National Bureau type: indeed some of the more astute monetarists warned their brethren against following the logic of the method, lest it discredit the method! And some of the largest squared errors of estimate for 1967 that I have in my files came from dogmatic monetarists who did not heed the warning from inside their own camp.

4. Again, the year 1969 is thought by some to provide a test of some power between the two theories. Yet I, who am an eclectic, have my own GNP forecast for the year nicely bracketed by the two banks that have been most successful in the past in using monetarism in their projections. And though I must admit that the last part of 1968 was stronger than those who believe in the potency of fiscal policy and the mid-1969 tax surcharge to be, I do not interpret that extra strength as being a negation of any such potency or as due solely or primarily to the behavior of money during the last 12 months. Without the tax surcharge, I believe the GNP would have surprised us by soaring even faster above predictions. Since history cannot be rerun to perform controlled experiments, I cannot prove this. But the weight of all the evidence known to me does point in this direction. In a soft science like economics, that is all even the best practitioner can say.

CONCLUSION

The bulk of my remarks have been critical of an overly simple doctrine of monetarism. But they must not be interpreted as supporting the view that money does not matter. There are parts of the world, particularly in Britain and the Commonwealth, where it might be better to believe in overly simple monetarism than in overly simple denial of the role of money.

In the *Sunday Telegraph* (London, December 15, 1968) I was able to invert the Tobin syllogisms to isolate the fatal flaw in the reasoning of the Radcliffe Report. The Radcliffe Committee heard much convincing testimony to show that there existed no invariable velocity of circulation of money to enable one to predict GNP accurately from the money supply alone. In effect then, Radcliffe established the falsity of Tobin's third proposition, Money alone matters. And, in a *nonsequitur*, they concluded the truth of his first proposition, that Money does not matter. For all their talking around the subject of liquidity as a substitute concept for money alone, they and the fossil-Keynesians who hailed their report should have recognized the fact that both theory and experience give to money (along with fiscal and other variables) an important role in the macroeconomic scenario of modern times.

READING 19
Regulation Q: An Instrument of Monetary Policy
Jimmie R. Monhollon

Regulation Q has become an instrument of considerable importance in the implementation of monetary policy. Dr. Monhollon, vice-president of the Federal Reserve Bank of Richmond, points out the uses of Regulation Q as a general, as well as a selective, policy instrument. The arguments for and against the use of Regulation Q as a method

Reprinted by permission of the Federal Reserve Bank of Richmond, from Jimmie R. Monhollon, "Regulation Q: An Instrument of Monetary Policy," *Monthly Review*, July 1970, pp. 2–8.

of policy implementation are summarized. The author concludes that continued use of Regulation Q for general policy implementation is being questioned seriously within the Federal Reserve System.

Guideposts for Thought While Reading
How is Regulation Q used as a general and a selective policy instrument? Why is there dissatisfaction within the Federal Reserve System over the use of Regulation Q as a general policy instrument?

In recent months Regulation Q, the regulation which specifies maximum interest rates banks are permitted to pay on time and savings deposits, has become increasingly the subject of controversy. Debate has centered around two major questions: (1) Is Regulation Q effective as an instrument of general monetary control? (2) Are the selective impacts of Regulation Q desirable or undesirable? This article will describe experience with Regulation Q through the years and then catalog the major points in the current debate about whether Regulation Q is an effective policy tool.

EXPERIENCE WITH REGULATION Q

Regulation Q was not initially intended as an instrument of credit policy. The Banking Act of 1933 amended the Federal Reserve Act to permit the Federal Reserve Board to regulate the rate of interest which member banks pay on time deposits and to prescribe different rates on deposits having different maturities, different conditions of withdrawal or repayment, or different locations. The rationale for the legislation and subsequent regulation grew out of the widespread bank failures of the 1920's and 1930's. It was believed that interest rate competition encouraged banks to move into high-risk assets in order to be able to cover ever-rising deposit costs and therefore weakened the internal soundness of the banking system. Thus, the amendment granting authority to regulate interest rates on deposits was just one of many pieces of legislation passed during the 1930's to protect the banking system by limiting competition and maintaining the solvency of individual institutions.

Banks were flooded with reserves in the late 1930's as a result of huge inflows of gold and, in the 1940's, as a result of the Federal Reserve's policy of pegging the prices of U.S. Government bonds. During this period market interest rates remained substantially below the established Regulation Q ceilings, and for all practical purposes the ceilings were inoperative, either as a regulatory device or as an instrument of monetary policy.

Period of Accommodation

The situation changed in the mid-1950's. The ceilings, which had remained unchanged for almost 20 years, finally became binding in late 1955. The combination of strong loan demand and restrictive monetary policy drove market rates of interest up to and then beyond the Q ceilings. The growth of time and savings deposits at commercial banks promptly slowed. Depository institutions which were not subject to Regulation Q continued to experience rapid inflows of savings. In order "to permit individual member banks greater flexibility to encourage the accumulation of savings" and to compete "actively for time and savings balances by offering rates more nearly in line with other market rates," the Board of Governors raised the Regulation Q ceilings effective January 1, 1957.

With this change, a period began which might be described as one of accommodation of Q ceilings to market interest rates. During the period from 1957 to 1966, the Board generally raised the maximum permissible rate when rising market rates of interest made time and savings deposits unattractive. The only notable exception was the period of high interest rates in 1959 and early 1960. From mid-1960 to mid-1966, the Board tended to keep the Q ceilings comfortably above market rates. The volume of time deposits grew at the rapid rate of about 14 per cent per year.

The underlying rationale of the rate increases in this period was to permit banks to compete for time and savings deposits as yields on closely substitutable investments were irregularly rising. The ability to compete was viewed as having various desirable consequences. The early 1960's was a period of dual concern —about sluggish economic expansion on the one hand and about the balance of payments deficit on the other. In explaining all of the increases in the early 1960's, the Board cited the higher permissible rates as a marginal factor which would benefit the external accounts as banks were allowed to compete more vigorously for foreign deposits. The higher ceilings were also regarded as desirable "to provide an added incentive for accumulation of the savings necessary to finance . . . future economic growth. . . ."

Regulation Q took on new significance when negotiable certificates of deposit came into widespread use in 1961. At that time the large commerical banks in New York began to offer large-denomination certificates of deposit in order to retain the deposits of large corporate customers who were making strenuous efforts to economize on demand balances. A secondary market for CD's developed, and as the practice of issuing negotiable CD's spread throughout the country, the volume outstanding grew rapidly. The sensitivity of CD customers to interest rate differentials enhanced the potential of Regulation Q as a policy instrument.

So far as commerical banks were concerned the growing popularity of the CD and other time deposit instruments prompted the emergence of a new concept of liquidity. Banks began to rely to a greater degree on their ability to attract money market funds. This led to liquidity management from the liability rather than the asset side of the balance sheet.

Active Use of Q as a Policy Instrument

The policy of accommodation to market changes ended in 1966. In December 1965, the Q ceilings on time and savings deposits were raised substantially to a uniform 5½ per cent on all maturities. The aim of this larger-than-usual increase was to make the Q ceilings inoperative by raising them to a level well above market rates. But the new ceilings quickly became binding. Interest rates rose sharply as Government and agency borrowings became very heavy and as the economy expanded rapidly, leading to a substantial increase in borrowing of the private sector. This time, the Board of Governors did not raise the Q ceilings when they became restrictive. Banks generally had heavy loan commitments outstanding, and keeping the ceilings unchanged caused a severe squeeze, especially at those banks which had made commitments in anticipation of being able to acquire funds by issuing CD's at attractive rates.

In failing to raise the rates, the Board aimed at two objectives. First, it hoped that a runoff of CD's would result in a slowdown in the rate of growth of bank credit and in particular that it would force banks to cut back their lending to business borrowers, thereby removing some of the financing that was spurring the investment boom. Second, it hoped to reduce bank competition with the financial intermediaries which specialized in mortgage lending. Savings and loan associations and mutual savings banks found themselves experiencing the severest liquidity squeeze of the postwar period and the housing market was severely depressed.

The Board of Governors was very concerned about the

mortgage market. It wanted to lower maximum rates payable on those classes of commercial bank time and savings deposits which competed most vigorously with the liabilities emitted by the other thrift institutions. But it had only limited authority to set differential rates on different classes of time and savings deposits. Using the authority it had, the Board, on July 20, 1966, scaled bank rates on multiple maturity time deposits—all the way to 4 per cent in the case of those deposits having a maturity of less than 90 days. On September 21, the President signed into law a bill which gave the Board wide latitude to set differential rates according to numerous criteria, including size of deposit. Five days later the Board scaled back the maximum rate payable on single maturity time deposits of less than $100,000 to 5 per cent. These small rollbacks in the ceilings probably had only a marginal impact on the thrift institutions and the housing market, but they served to demonstrate the Board's concern that the incidence of monetary restraint was falling disproportionately onto the housing industry.

Banks confronted with heavy CD attrition, particularly the large money market banks, attempted to meet firm loan commitments and gain time in which to make orderly asset adjustments by tapping nondeposit sources of funds. U.S. banks borrowed large amounts in the Eurodollar market and sold increasing amounts of short-term notes. For the banking system as a whole, this amounted to a conversion of deposit liabilities into nondeposit liabilities having no reserve requirements. Thus, the Eurodollar market and the market for short-term notes provided not only a safety valve for individual banks, but also a means whereby banks collectively could reduce average required reserves at their own initiative. This only partly compensated, however, for the extraordinarily high rates which banks had to pay in the Eurodollar market. Thus, they had strong incentive to ration credit aggressively, and the Board added to this incentive by plugging the loophole of short-term promissory notes effective September 1, 1966. These were defined as deposits subject to Regulations D and Q. The purpose was "to prevent the future use of those instruments as a means of circumventing the regulations governing reserve requirements and payments of interest on deposits."

Since 1965, time deposit growth has fluctuated widely as interest rates have fluctuated above and below the Q ceilings. The sharp decline in time deposits in late 1966 was followed by an even sharper rise in the first three quarters of 1967 as market rates fell well below the ceiling rates. Growth moderated in late

1967 and early 1968 as rising market rates reduced the relative attractiveness of CD's. Growth spurted following the increase in the Q ceilings in April 1968 and remained rapid through the rest of the year. The spurt was not intended. The Board raised maximum permissible rates only on large-denomination CD's having maturities of 60 days or more. The intent of the new graduated scale of ceiling rates was to set them at levels which would "enable banks to resist further large reductions in such deposits, but not so high as to permit significant expansion in the outstanding volume of CD's and thus in bank credit." Early in 1969 rising market rates made CD's unattractive, the Board did not raise the Q ceilings, and CD attrition became massive. Outstandings declined about $13 billion, or 44 per cent during the course of the year.

As in 1966, banks sought to compensate for the CD losses by turning in large volume to nondeposit sources of funds—Eurodollars, sale of assets under repurchase agreement, and sale of commercial paper by bank holding companies and affiliates. The Board looked upon this development with disfavor for several reasons. First, the regulatory power of the Board was being eroded as the liability structure of the banking system shifted from deposits subject to regulation to nondeposit liabilities not subject to regulation. Second, equity considerations were involved. While some banks, mainly by virtue of size and structure, had ready access to nondeposit sources of funds, other banks had little access to such sources. Third, monetary restriction was being eroded as average reserve requirements were in effect being reduced by the shift of liabilities from deposit to nondeposit status. Of course, this evasion of monetary restraint could have been offset, or more than offset, by further tightening through open market operations, but the Board chose instead to reclassify all these nondeposit sources of funds as deposits subject to reserve requirements, or Q ceilings, or both.

In January 1970, despite concern that raising the Q ceilings might be interpreted as a relaxation of monetary policy, the Board of Governors raised the Q ceilings on most classes of time and savings deposits. It held the increases to "moderate size so as not to foster sudden and large movements of funds into the banking system that could . . . lead to an upsurge in bank lending." Sharp declines in market rates of interest in February made longer-term time deposits competitive with market instruments. The volume of time and savings deposits outstanding has increased at about 15 per cent annual rate since early February.

Effects of Regulation Q on Bank Credit

What have been the effects of Regulation Q and the ebb and flow of time deposits on the growth and composition of bank credit? This is a difficult question to answer because so many other variables are involved, such as the strength and composition of private loan demand, Treasury financing needs, the effects of other policy instruments, etc. But in general, periods of rapid growth in time deposits have been associated with rapid growth of bank credit, and vice versa. Moreover, Regulation Q has affected the composition of bank credit as well as the total. As a rule, banks have tended to invest the proceeds of time deposits in high yield assets, particularly tax-exempt securities. The relationship between the rate of change of time deposits and the rate of change of other securities (mainly tax-exempts) has been very close. During periods of rapid time deposit growth banks have been the mainstay of the tax-exempt market, buying at such times as much as three-fourths or more of all new issues. On the other hand, during periods of declining time deposits, banks have sometimes become net sellers. This shifting pattern of bank behavior has resulted in very large swings in interest rates on tax-exempt securities. To the extent that state and local expenditures are affected by the shifting fortunes of the tax-exempt market, Regulation Q can be said to have had a selective economic impact.

Summary of Experience

This historical review reveals that, rightly or wrongly, Regulation Q has become an instrument of policy. Obviously, the use of Q has had two dimensions. It has been both a general control and a selective control. As a general control, the Board has looked upon Q as a means of influencing the total quantity of bank credit. For example, restraint has been attempted by encouraging or allowing market rates to rise above the Q ceilings. The resulting conversion of time to demand deposits has been tantamount to an increase in average reserve requirements. Moreover, Q has perhaps been regarded as a means of speeding the effect of restraint by quickly exerting pressure on the reserve positions of those big banks which rely heavily on CD's. Raising Q ceilings when they are restrictive has been thought of as a move toward less restraint. This argument was frequently cited as a reason for not raising Q ceilings in 1969.

The year 1966 serves as the best example of using Q as a selective control. Failure to raise rates on large-denomination

CD's was looked upon as a way of forcing quick rationing of credit to business customers. Reducing rates payable on consumer-type deposits was viewed as a means of reducing the impact of tight money on savings and loan associations, the mortgage market, and housing. In short, Regulation Q was used in such a way as to try to shift the composition of total credit flows. Regulation Q was used in essentially the same way in 1969. Ceilings on savings deposits and consumer-type time deposits were kept at the 1966 levels, and while ceilings on large-denomination CD's were higher, they became binding as market rates rose to new highs. The debate about the efficacy and the desirability of using Regulation Q as a policy instrument has become more vigorous in recent months. Space is not available for a detailed examination of all the arguments pro and con. What follows is a mere listing and a brief discussion of the major arguments.

ARGUMENTS SUPPORTING REGULATION Q

Regulation Q Is a Good Tool of General Monetary Control

The basic argument for Q as a general control probably rests on the degree to which Q influences the extent of financial intermediation in the economy. Other things equal, it is generally assumed that increased intermediation is stimulative and vice versa. Since banks are the largest intermediaries, any policy instrument which affects the extent of their intermediation has considerable leverage. Keeping ceiling rates high relative to market rates encourages the channeling of funds from savers to ultimate investors through an efficient intermediary with the result that funds are more readily available and at lower cost than would otherwise be the case. Conversely, relatively low ceilings tend to force funds to flow from savers to ultimate investors via various routes which are less efficient and more costly.

Given that banks want to compete for time and savings deposits, it is probably true that Regulation Q can be used both to stimulate and to restrain the economy. Whether it is the best available instrument is, of course, another matter. To answer this question one must compare Regulation Q with other instruments, including in the analysis the possible selective impacts of the various alternatives. The incidence effects cannot be ignored.

Regulation Q Produces Desirable Allocative Effects

While Regulation Q may be useful as a general control, most arguments in favor of Regulation Q seem ultimately to boil down to the idea that Q produces desirable allocative effects, especially during periods of tight money when Q ceilings may reduce the pressure which would otherwise be exerted on the mortgage market and the housing industry. The linkages in this case are seen as both direct and indirect. The straightforward argument is simply that during inflationary periods Q ceilings reduce bank competition with those intermediaries which specialize in mortgage lending. The indirect argument is that use of Regulation Q results in a smaller run-up of interest rates and therefore a lesser effect on the mortgage market than would be the case if the same degree of restraint were achieved by use of other tools. This argument is implicit in Duesenberry's article, "Policy Effects on Thrift Institutions," which appeared in the 1969 *Conference on Savings and Residential Financing.*

ARGUMENTS AGAINST REGULATION Q

The arguments against Regulation Q have multiplied in recent months. In general they fall into two categories: (1) The effects of Regulation Q are either perverse or neutral. (2) The effects are discriminatory and produce distortions in credit flows. Each category will be considered in turn.

Regulation Q Produces Perverse or Neutral Effects

Different people arrive by different routes at the conclusion that the effects of Q may be the opposite of those intended. The conclusion is easily reached by those who attach preeminent importance to the narrowly defined money supply as an indicator of the ease or tightness of policy. If the Federal Reserve injects reserves at a given rate and if holders of time deposits choose to switch into some other asset (Treasury bills or whatever), demand deposits and the money supply will grow at a faster pace. The monetarist who excludes time deposits from his definition of money would conclude that monetary policy has eased, not tightened. This view, of course, regards as unimportant the behavior of total deposits and bank credit which would grow at a slower rate.

But some who focus on total credit (bank plus nonbank) also say that the effect of a CD runoff is at best neutral and perhaps expansionary. Their argument is two-pronged. First, they say that bank lending power is not greatly reduced because of banker ingenuity in designing and issuing liabilities not subject to regulation. Second, such reduction of bank lending power as occurs does not curb spending because the financing of economic activity is merely diverted from the banks to the nonbank public. The August 1969 issue of the Morgan Guaranty Survey puts the matter as follows:

> . . . Business borrowers . . . obviously can be accommodated by lenders other than banks, and there is ample reason to think that many of the funds disgorged from bank certificate-of-deposit accounts flowed directly into the commercial paper market and thus were put at the disposal of exactly those people whose credit usage the authorities were seeking to curb.

These and similar arguments have been put forward recently as a possible explanation for the failure of the economy to slow down as quickly in 1969 as was generally expected.

Regulation Q Is Discriminatory and Leads to Distortion of Credit Flows

Perhaps most of the criticism of Regulation Q has centered on its being discriminatory and leading to distortions of credit flows. The idea is that rates payable on time and savings deposits are prices which should be allowed to fluctuate in accordance with changes in supply and demand conditions in the market. When the Federal Reserve sets a ceiling which becomes binding, it departs to some appreciable extent from its normal practice of using "general controls" which create a climate within which the interaction of private decisions produces particular prices with their implications for reserve allocation. Presumably, this allocation achieved by the free market is in accordance with the tastes and preferences of the public and therefore superior to the allocation achieved when particular prices are set outside the market.

Numerous alleged distortions resulting from Q have been reported in the financial press. It is frequently heard, for example, that Regulation Q discriminates against those large banks which rely heavily on CD's as a source of funds. This discrimination presumably forces credit to flow through other, less-well-developed channels, with loss of economic efficiency. Of course, these large banks are the first to turn to nondeposit sources of funds, but as these sources are made subject to regulation, the argument comes to the fore again. In any case, opponents of Regulation Q argue that it is time consuming, costly, and therefore inefficient for banks to be forced to invent new access routes to the money market. Banker ingenuity in turn forces the monetary authorities to invest scarce legal and regulatory talent plugging loopholes. The end result is the use of scarce resources in unproductive lines of activity.

Second, the rechanneling of credit flows is said to work hardships on particular sectors. For example, as has already been explained, the tax-exempt market has been a frequent casualty in recent years. Also, the effects of Q have spread beyond our own shores. In terms of volume, Eurodollars have been the largest nondeposit source of funds. Heavy bidding by the few U.S. banks with access to the Eurodollar market helped push Eurodollar rates to unusually high levels. These high rates led to reserve losses by several countries which requested changes in our regulations to limit the access of U.S. banks to the Eurodollar market. This sentiment was certainly one factor in the imposition of the marginal reserve requirement against Eurodollar borrowings.

These are just a few of many examples of altered credit flows brought about by Regulation Q. Of course, one cannot object to altered credit flows per se. It is in the very nature of monetary policy, however conducted, to lead to alterations in credit flows, specifically, to dry up or expand that portion flowing through the commercial banking system. One objection to Q is that it tends arbitrarily to redirect flows without sufficient regard for private preferences.

CONCLUSION

This article has reviewed the experience with Regulation Q and has simply cataloged some of the arguments which have swirled around it recently. No analysis has been attempted here.

At the present time there appears to be a growing dissatisfaction within the Federal Reserve System with the use of Q for purposes of general monetary control. In a recent speech, Chairman Burns expressed the following sentiments:

> . . . I regard interest rate ceilings on deposits as one device that is overdue for serious re-examination. As a matter of personal economic philosophy, I would like to see an evolution away from reliance upon interest rate ceilings as an ancillary device of monetary policy, at least as far as instruments of the money-market type are concerned.

When and as circumstances permit, I believe an element of greater economic rationality would be introduced into the financial system if interest rates on such instruments were permitted to find their own level as a result of market forces.[1]

[1] Arthur F. Burns, Chairman, Board of Governors of the Federal Reserve System, "The Federal Reserve and the Banking System," Speech before the 59th Annual Meeting of the Association of Reserve City Bankers, Boca Raton, Florida, April 6, 1970, p. 10–11.

READING 20
An Overview of the Development of the U.S. Economy
Douglass C. North

This overview is by the well known economic historian, Douglass C. North of the University of Washington.

Study of historical development of the economy of the United States can provide useful insights into its future development, as well as to provide knowledge to aid in the development of less advanced nations. Of course, circumstances and conditions change—modern technology and consumer tastes and preferences, for example, differ greatly from those of colonial times. The trick then, is to infer basic principles which apply for economic development regardless of the setting. Professor North notes in the preface of the book from which this reading is taken that "If history is to be something more than a subjective recording of the facts of the past as man's perspective changes with each generation, we must apply the disciplines of the social sciences to historical research, and apply the methods of scientific inquiry to testing the resultant hypotheses. Economic history is better equipped to pioneer in this approach than are other social sciences, because of its well articulated body of theory. . . . Current historical inquiry for earlier periods uses implicit (and usually bad) theory and implicit quantitative measurements arrived at by the weight given to facts presented as evidence. Surely, it is better that the theory be explicit and consistent with the state of theorizing in the discipline and that the implicit quantitative weights be made explicit."

Guideposts for Thought While Reading

What factors accounted for the extensive and the intensive growth of the United States? As the American economy developed, what new institutions were required? What accounted for the expansion of governmental influence in the market economy?

Since the earliest national income estimate of 1840, the economy has grown at a rate of about 1.6 per cent per year in real terms. This means that in terms of constant prices, the average per capita income has risen by that figure, and this is roughly analogous to what has actually happened to the average standard of life or the average well-being of people, although it is well to remember that there are real limitations to using per capita income figures and drawing too neat a pattern from them. At first glance, the figure of 1.6 per cent may not sound like a very impressive annual growth rate; but it turns out to have quite spectacular compound results. It means that every 43 years, income per capita, in constant prices, has doubled in America. In today's prices, average income per head is around $2,400, whereas back in 1840, when measurements began, it was $400 in today's prices. This raises the question, what happened before 1840? We lack information on income before that date. Less is known about the economy, and the statistics are still far from adequate. It is probable, however, that per capita real income grew at a slower pace.

The growth rate of 1.6 per cent per year probably did not exist much earlier than 1840. Projected back before that date, the same growth rate very rapidly reaches unreasonably low levels of per capita income. In today's dollars, per capita annual income would have been $145 in 1776; $80 in 1740, and $30 in 1680. Since the early Americans did not starve, these are ridiculous figures, having no real significance. It therefore appears likely that the rate of growth of the economy must have been slower in the period before 1840 (although when the change takes place, we don't know).

THE COLONIAL ECONOMY, AGRICULTURE, AND FOREIGN TRADE

What were some of the salient features of the Colonial economy? First of all, most people worked on the land, and this was the main source of economic activity; a preponderant 90 per cent of the population engaged in farming or in pursuits directly related to farming. There was little increase in the efficiency of farming in the Colonial period, and therefore little growth in per capita income resulting from productivity gains in agriculture. It is to be expected that some improvements in efficiency did occur with increases in the size of the market and with better marketing methods; but there was comparatively little shift to better land during this period, and it is doubtful that living standards rose rapidly.

Meanwhile, really substantial gains in efficiency were taking place in another part of our economy that was another main source of income—international shipping. In Colonial times, America was already a major shipping power, engaging in fishing, whaling, and particularly in carrying the goods of the world—not only from our own shores to other nations, but between foreign countries. Colonial efficiency in shipping improved substantially during that period and became an important feature of the total economy. A good share of credit for the increased efficiency goes to an event seldom thought of today—the decline in piracy. As freebooters were driven from the seas, fewer men and guns were needed for protection on ships, and this turned out to be an important source of lowering the real cost of ocean transportation.

In Colonial times there was little manufacturing. Shipbuilding was an important activity, and there were some small-scale manufacturing activities like making iron. By and large, however, it was a farming, shipping, and commercial society, not heavily involved in manufacturing. Since America of that day was a small market with relatively expensive labor, it is not surprising that the English provided most of our manufacturing.

One would expect to find that the Colonial economy improved only gradually and probably not at the 1.6 per cent per year figure cited for more recent times. There was little technological change in agriculture, the major source of income. And improvements that were occurring in economic organization were still very gradual, in the forms of increasing efficiency in shipping, of larger markets, of the beginnings of towns, and of better communication and transportation. It is doubtful, therefore, that the Colonial economy could have been expected to grow as strikingly, over-all, as it did after 1840.

What about the *extensive* growth of the Colonial period? Rapid population growth certainly characterized the period. Population increased from negligible numbers up to 331,000 by 1710, then soared to more than 2,000,000 at the time of the Revolutionary War. Immigrants made up much of this increase. Many came voluntarily, free and clear; others put themselves into indenture, agreeing to work for someone for a prescribed period in return for payment of their passage and for specified benefits at the end of the indenture. Still others, in substantial numbers, were brought in as slaves who provided a great share of the labor force in the southern colonies. Extensive growth in the Colonial period, therefore, consisted of a notable increase of population; settlements along the coasts, a gradual movement into the interior, and the beginning of an economy based upon agriculture and shipping.

Colonial days were turbulent. The settlers frequently had grievances against the British, against the French and Spanish on their borders, against the Indians along the frontier, and at times against each other. These disputes reflected the Colonists' views that their welfare was being adversely affected, and at times they led to open warfare. The actual income effects of these controversies have not been measured. The most significant for American history were the issues between the Crown and the Colonists from 1763 to 1775.

THE NINETEENTH CENTURY, EXPANSION IN NONAGRICULTURAL ACTIVITY

Turning now to the nineteenth century we may take a sweeping look at the pattern of that century's economy. In 1839, agriculture accounted for 70 per cent of the value of commodity output of the economy and certain agricultural commodities were particularly important. Of these, cotton played a dominant early role and was a large part of total exports. Cotton comprised more than half of American exports in the years before the Civil War. After the war, it continued as an important part of the agricultural economy, although the value of wheat exports became a significant and growing challenger.

Agriculture expanded with the opening up and settlement of the West. It is not surprising, therefore, that as new, rich lands were developed, the agricultural output continually expanded and the kinds of agriculture became diversified. Although agriculture grew all through the century in absolute terms of value of output, *relatively*, it declined. Whereas it was 70 per cent of commodity output in 1839, it was only 33 per cent of output by the end of that century. How were people employed? The earliest available figures, in 1820, show 2 million out of 2.8 million people working on the land; other aspects of the economy were relatively negligible. But as the century moved forward, the change in the employment pattern is striking. It is true that the number of agricultural workers increased; but growing much more rapidly were the tallies of those working in manufacturing, construction, transportation, and trade. Later in the century, proportionately more and more were working in activities other than agriculture; as a matter of fact, 1910 was a peak year in absolute terms for agricultural workers, whose total has been declining ever since that date. The distribution of the labor force mirrors strikingly that while we were a rapidly growing agricultural economy, other sectors, particularly manufacturing, were growing even more rapidly. By 1880, only one half of our people were working in agriculture.

Now if people shift from agriculture to other activities, comparable shifts are expected in how they live. Logically, they will move off the farms to the cities, and that is exactly what occurred. Classing "urban" population as those living in communities of 2,500 or more, and "rural" as communities of less than that number, the distribution is continually moving in the direction of an increasingly urban society. By the twentieth century, America was becoming predominantly urban, but not until 1920 did urban territory include more people than rural territory. The whole process of westward movement and shift from farm to city is tied to where people worked and the kinds of jobs they had. A sidelight to this pattern of rural-urban relationship is the domestic birth rate in America. The decline from 55 per thousand in 1820 to 18.4 per thousand in 1936 appears to be related to the shift of people from the farm to the city. Demographers have speculated that children are not only a greater asset on the farm but are less costly for the farmer than for the city dweller to bring up; so that as people became more urbanized, their families grew smaller. In modern times, this pattern tends to be reversed in urban areas, and there has been an increase in birth rates, but this phenomenon is observable only in very recent times.

An integral part of nineteenth century expansion was the growth of our banking system, of wholesale and retail marketing organization, and a more efficient transportation network. All contributed significantly to productivity increase by lowering the real costs of credit and of handling and moving goods.

The high cost of carrying bulk goods in Colonial times limited commerical production to areas adjacent to navigable waterways. Improved roads and then turnpikes after the Revolutionary War widened local markets, but the major improvements in internal transportation came with the growth of water transport on the Mississippi River system (particularly with the innovation of the steamboat for upriver carriage of goods in 1816) and the growth of a canal system connecting the Great Lakes with both the Mississippi system and with the eastern seaboard. The development of the railroad after 1830, in turn, displaced the canal and dominated internal transport history during the rest of the nineteenth century.

The orientation of the Colonies toward external markets (and the purchase of goods from abroad) led to rather well-developed merchant houses dealing in exports and imports; however, as internal trade and commerce grew, institutions to move goods from producers to consumers also grew and necessarily became more complex. The evolution from the itinerant peddler, jobber, roving merchant, and general store (often associated with a local factory) to specialized wholesale houses and equally specialized retail outlets was a nineteenth century development, and it is mirrored in the growing percentage of the labor force engaged in trade, increasing from about 6 per cent in 1850 to more than 10 per cent by the turn of the century.

Banking was in its infancy the decade after Independence was achieved. The first chartered bank was established in 1784, but banking growth was slow in early years. The establishment of the First United States Bank in 1791 provided an important impetus for tying together government fiscal activities with the early banking community. Although the bank was an important step in the growth of the capital market, it engendered considerable opposition, and its charter was not renewed after its initial twenty-year term. Five years later, however, in 1816, the Second United States Bank was chartered. After a rocky start under undistinguished leadership it became, under Nicholas Biddle, a major influence in regulating the commercial banks, in acting as a reserve bank when banks needed additional specie, and in integrating the banking system. In short, it anticipated in many respects the role expected of a modern central bank in influencing the money supply and tying together federal government fiscal activities with the banking system. It became an even more controversial institution than its predecessor and a central issue in the election of 1832. When Andrew Jackson triumphed the bank's fate was settled; and with the expiration of its charter, central banking was not again to be revived until the next century.

The demise of the second bank resulted in a mounting number of banks, each issuing its own notes. By 1860 there were 1500 banks individually issuing, on the average, six different types of notes. Moreover, the worth of the notes varied strikingly—some were "as good as gold," others were the worthless paper of broken banks. The Civil War and growing pressure for a national banking system led to the passage in 1864 of the National Banking Act, which permitted federal charter of banks and required that such banks keep reserves in cash or as deposits with a national bank in one of seventeen large cities. Similarly, banks in these large cities had the same option to keep part of their reserves in New York City banks. The result was the beginning of a nationwide banking system. A central banking system to unite federal government fiscal policy with the banking system did not occur, however, until the creation of the Federal Reserve System in 1914.

One more aspect, important to the economy in the nineteenth century (and particularly in its first half) was our relationship with the rest of the world. We were yet a small part of the great world, and the fact that foreigners wanted our goods and services contributed significantly to our extensive expansion. Cotton and shipping have already been discussed. But foreigners also wanted other kinds of goods—agricultural products in the early part of the nineteenth century and then, as the century wore on and we became an industrial nation, our manufactured goods as well.

Perhaps more important than the role of trade in the country's growth was immigration. Beginning in the 1840's with the Irish famine and its consequences, vast numbers of people turned to America in a tide that flowed through the decades until World War I. This was a swelling movement of unprecedented numbers willing to take their chances in a New World. Undoubtedly, it was one of the important formative aspects of our expansion.

Foreigners also invested heavily in the new nation. This was particularly true of the British who, having confidence in America's future, invested in canals, railroads, and cotton plantations. Although foreign investment was significant, it probably has been overstressed in the history of national development. Foreign capital was important in the 1830's, but thereafter its proportion of total capital formation dwindled, even though the absolute amount grew substantially.

Over-all, the international economy contributed through investment; it contributed through people; and it contributed through trading goods that could be produced more efficiently elsewhere in exchange for those that we could produce relatively efficiently. It also contributed in one essential way that cannot be shown in graphic form—ideas. The technology America borrowed in the nineteenth century, basically from Europe and particularly from Great Britain, was a major source of improvement in productivity.

By 1860 the United States had become a major industrial nation, second only to Britain. From 23 per cent in 1870, the nation's share rose to more than 40 per cent of the world's manufacturing output by 1926–1929. Between the Civil War and World War I, an already thriving manufacturing enormously expanded.

At the same time, population was redistributing itself around the United States. In the early days, of course, all settlement was along the coastal line; by 1860, the population was moving out across the Appalachian Mountains into the Great Lakes area, the middle Atlantic area, and into the cotton-producing South. The Gold Rush of 1848 pushed the frontiers of population westward to California and Oregon. After the Civil War, the movement was primarily across the Mississippi into the rich area of the plains, that whole vast area from the Mississippi to the Rocky Mountains, which became peopled and settled during that period. Population expanded from New England, the oldest area, into the Midwest and then into the Far West. Not only were people relocating, but they were continually moving into new and rich agricultural lands. At the same time that America rose to first place among manufacturing nations of the world, it also became the world's leading agricultural nation. In short, America became a supplier to the world both of industrial products and of greatly increased output of agricultural products.

The nineteenth century, therefore, was marked not only by an unprecedented increase in people, capital, and land—spurring its extensive growth—but also by increasing efficiency of these production factors, resulting in intensive growth. The most noteworthy aspects were (1) adoption of the most efficient techniques in the world in manufacturing and in agriculture; (2) significant increase in education in America, making possible the use of the latest technology and a new efficiency stemming from substantial research both in industry and in agriculture; and (3) availability of a vast new United States market of unprecedented size, which made feasible all the efficiency of large-scale production.

If over-all growth characterized this period, so did frequently recurring economic distress and hardship for diverse groups. The most important sources of such distress were the recurrent depressions and recessions of the nineteenth century; 1819, 1837, 1839, 1857, 1873, and 1893 were all years that marked the onset of falling income and increasing unemployment of varying degrees of severity. There are no accurate statistics to measure the fall in income or the amount of unemployment during these periods. As an increasing percentage of the population shifted from self-sufficient agriculture to production for the market, the impact of these depressions became greater, since they affected more and more people. There is no evidence that the depressions themselves became more severe, however (in fact, probably the depression of 1839 was the most severe of the century).

The immigrant or the farm boy who left the farm was likely to seek employment in the new factory towns as manufacturing grew. His hours were long and the conditions onerous by present standards. Factory towns were frequently unsanitary, overlaid with coal dust, and housing conditions were grim. Although it is doubtful that the new factory worker's real income fell, he bore the serious costs of monotonous discipline during long hours at a machine and the insecurity of employment as workers were let out during depressions.

The farmer's well-being, too, was becoming more dependent upon the market. On top of drought, locusts, and other natural disasters, wide fluctuations in prices received for crops made his income subject to broad swings. His lot improved in the nineteenth century, but this undeniable statement hides the diversity of economic experience that held disaster in the short run for many.

It is not surprising, therefore, that the nineteenth century was characterized by a variety of protest movements against working conditions, job insecurity, low prices, and monopoly.

Utopian schemes and programs of reform were continually advanced as solutions to these problems. Trade-union membership was never a significant percentage of the labor force until well into the twentieth century. Attempts to form a nationwide labor organization such as the National Labor Union in 1866 and the Knights of Labor (which had its major expansion in the

1870's and early Eighties) turned out to be temporary, and it was not until the founding of the American Federation of Labor in 1881 that trade unions achieved permanent organization on a national basis. Farm protest movements had a larger impact upon public policy. Between the Civil War and 1900, the Greenback, Granger, and Populist movements attempted to increase prices and to undertake basic economic reforms in the expectation that they would raise farm real income.

THE TWENTIETH CENTURY, THE PROBLEMS OF AN AFFLUENT FREE MARKET ECONOMY

A growing source of concern to worker and farmer alike was the development of the trust and of other forms of organization having significant monopoly power. The publication of Henry Demarest Lloyd's *Wealth Against Commonwealth* and Ida Tarbell's *History of the Standard Oil Company* provided early examples of the growing literature of reformers and "muckrakers" protesting against the growth of monopoly. The reformers not only pointed up the dangers of the trust but exposed political graft and corruption and made Americans aware of the importance of conserving and setting aside the rich natural-resource heritage of forests and scenic attractions in the face of the onrushing extensive expansion of the economy.

World War I marks the end of an era, a boundary beyond which nations became more self-contained. America dammed the stream of immigration, and other countries erected tariff barriers, as we had done earlier. An international economy in which people, capital, and ideas had enjoyed free interchanges for a century became hampered by restrictions on the movement of people and by restrictions on trade. World War I also marked the end of a relatively peaceful century and the beginning of a century marked by global war and a global depression. The decade of the Twenties was prosperous, but the 1929 crash and subsequent decade of depression resulted in a greater fall in income and a more cataclysmic economic period than any ever experienced before. It had long-run implications for our future views about how to cope with comparable situations and about the policies to be pursued. The depression of the Thirties continued in some measure until our 1941 entry into World War II and the resultant explosive expansion to meet war needs.

In taking this overview of what happened in the twentieth century—a notable growth of the economy interrupted by the Great Depression but continued thereafter—a few salient changes should be recognized. One was the development of new products. The twentieth century introduced the automobile, the electric refrigerator, and all the other comforts known as durable consumer goods; and it inspired a vast concern with services as compared with goods. The result was a significant change in the employment pattern and in the structure of the economy to meet these new demands of a prospering people. A second change was a turnabout in America's international role: instead of being a debtor nation, as at the turn of the century, it became a creditor; and since World War II, it has expended vast sums attempting to promote and assist the development of the rest of the world. No longer is America "just another nation," but a dominant nation viewing itself as having a responsibility to other countries in the world. And a third transformation was one that took place in the role of government in the American economy. When the federal government first emerged in 1790, it spent but a tiny fraction of national income and was involved in relatively few concerns. Contrast the role of government in the American economy today! The federal government alone (forgetting for the moment state and local governments) has an annual budget in the neighborhood of $100 billion. Government at all levels expends somewhere around a quarter of total national income. Obviously, government now has a role different from any it has ever had before—one of vastly more scope in regulating and ordering the working of our economy.

READING 21
Sources of Economic Growth
Robert M. Solow

Robert M. Solow, a professor of economics at M.I.T. has authored numerous theoretical papers on production, capital, and economic growth. In this paper, he discusses the conventional determinants of economic growth in developed countries, as well as considering both sides of some of the more controversial growth topics.

Reprinted by permission of the publisher from Robert M. Solow, "Sources of Economic Growth," a paper presented at the Conference on Savings and Residential Financing, U.S. Savings and Loan League, 1966.

Guideposts for Thought While Reading
What are the main sources of increases in potential output? Which of these sources does Solow feel are of importance to current growth efforts? What arguments does he use to support a full-employment policy as not detrimental and perhaps even helpful in the quest for greater economic growth?

GROWTHMANSHIP AND THE ECONOMISTS

I should perhaps say a word about the fact that so many of the world's leading growthmen are either academic economists or so close to being academic economists as to make the distinction hardly worth having. There are at least three reasons why the economics of long-run growth is such a popular subject in universities and learned journals these days.

One reason is the way in which the problem of the economic development of preindustrial areas has captured the attention and the imagination of the postwar world and become a matter of some international political importance.

A second reason is purely intellectual. The dominant Keynesian approach to macroeconomics left a yawning gap through its concentration on short-run flow equilibrium with the stock of capital held constant. Harrod and Domar leaped in and we are still going.

My final reason would seem less strange anywhere but in Chicago. I think that most economists feel that short-run macroeconomic theory is pretty well in hand. The basic outlines of the dominant theory have not changed in years. All that is left is the trivial job of filling in the empty boxes, and that will not take more than 50 years of concentrated effort at a maximum. This has the implication that most economists think that knowledge is adequate for at least a crudely rational full employment policy—only the rest of the population does not realize it yet. So, given that feeling, it is natural to look for new and slightly different problems.

Remember that by economic growth I mean fundamentally the growth of capacity to produce rather than the growth of demand, although that is an important but separate problem. So the foundation of any broad view of economic growth has to be an evaluation of the major determinants of potential output and productivity in an economy, the chances of influencing them and the effectiveness of changes in the determinants on capacity output itself.

DETERMINANTS OF POTENTIAL OUTPUT

Everyone is in broad agreement about the nature of the major determinants of potential output, but there is some disagreement about their relative influence, and recent research has led to some revision of earlier opinions. The main sources of potential output we can name pretty clearly:

1. The first determinant is the number of people available for employment; the number of hours they wish to work; and the level and distribution of skills, education, health and attitudes toward work. I suppose one ought to include managerial and entrepreneurial knowledge and ability as a special kind of labor, or perhaps it deserves a heading to itself.

2. The second broad and important determinant is the size of the existing stock of capital goods and its distribution by age, by industry and by location.

3. The third important determinant is the level of technology. Here one must distinguish between the extent of technological knowledge and the degree to which it can be made effective, because that may depend in large part on the age distribution of the existing capital stock. There is a sense in which the whole civilized world shares the discoveries of modern science and engineering on an equal basis, but an economy saddled with an antiquated stock of capital may be unable to use what in principle it knows.

4. The fourth determinant, I would say, is the terms on which the economy has access to natural resources, whether through domestic production or through imports.

5. The fifth determinant is the efficiency with which resources are allocated to different economic ends; the extent of monopolistic or other barriers to the movement of capital and labor from low productivity to high productivity uses; and the degree of resistance to the introduction of new technology.

If these are the basic determinants of potential output, then the growth of productive capacity is largely limited by the rate at which the basic determinants can be expanded and improved. That, in turn, depends upon the ease with which these determinants themselves can be influenced by conscious policy or fortuitous events, and upon the sensitivity of potential output to changes in the determinants themselves.

Opinions about this have changed drastically over the last century, and even over the last dozen years. The classical economists believed that the ultimate limit to economic growth was given by the finite availability of natural resources. It has always been a source of wonder to me how such intelligent and perceptive men, writing at a time when the industrial revolution had clearly taken secure hold on England, could so underestimate the power of technological progress in offsetting the effects of diminishing returns. Maybe this is a high standard to apply. We still occasionally read dire predictions that we are about to run out of natural resources.

TECHNOLOGY AND RESOURCE SCARCITY

The truth is, of course, that as certain raw materials become physically scarce, it becomes more expensive to extract them from nature; but this tendency is offset partly by technical progress, partly by investment in improved methods and management, partly by increased reliance on imports and partly by the substitution of cheap raw materials for expensive ones. Even these "partly's" may not add up to the whole. If the offsets are not fully effective, resources can be obtained at somewhat higher cost by digging deeper, using leaner ores, conserving wastes and using heavier equipment. The necessity of devoting more labor and capital to extractive industry is indeed equivalent to a net decline in the productivity of the economy as a whole; but it certainly does not set, as far as we can see, an absolute limit to the growth of the economy.

One way of measuring the effects of resource scarcity is by looking at the long-term trend of raw materials prices relative to finished product prices in general. When one does so, one finds that all raw materials are now about 25% more expensive relative to finished products than they were at the turn of the century, but only 5% more expensive than they were in 1925-1929. More interesting than this very gentle tendency toward increased real cost of raw materials is the wide variety of behavior exhibited by different classes of raw materials. Lumber products have indeed increased rapidly in relative price, almost doubling since 1925-1929, and almost tripling since the turn of the century. This is the way Ricardo presumably expected all raw materials to behave. But there actually may have been some tendency for this trend to moderate in recent years. Mineral construction materials, on the other hand, are cheaper relative to finished goods in general than they were at the turn of the century, though not quite as cheap as they were just before 1914. In any case, the only sound conclusion is that there is much less to natural resource scarcity than meets the eye.

We are a long way from having reliable quantitative answers

to the kind of question I am now discussing, but about some gross facts I think we can be fairly confident. I believe, for instance, that it would now be generally accepted that earlier thinking on this subject substantially underestimated the influence of improving the quality of human resources on the economy's capacity to produce.

EDUCATIONAL LEVEL AND INCOME

This is a particularly tricky area in which to make quantitative inferences, mainly because of the difficulty of imputing observed differences in income at different educational levels in part to differences in native ability and in part to education itself. But if one takes Edward Denison's recent estimates as a fair example, he attributes some 40% of the average annual growth between 1929 and 1957 in national income per person employed to the effects of education in improving the quality of the average man-hour of work. Between 1909 and 1929, he estimates the contribution of education to have been only about a quarter of the annual growth rate in productivity. Notice that this estimate excludes the contribution of education to the advance of knowledge itself.

In other words, had the educational level of the labor force remained stationary where it was in 1929, national income per person employed would have risen not at an average annual rate of 1.6%, as it did between 1929 and 1957, but at something less than 1.0% per year. That is a big difference. I do not know the exact present state of knowledge in this area; it is changing rapidly as new research is completed, much of it here in Chicago.

The other big revaluation that has taken place in recent years has to do with the relative importance of capital investment and technical change. The older economists seemed to think of increases in output per man-hour (of constant quality, though they did not often mention that) as being primarily or exclusively a matter of the deepening of capital, of increased capital per worker. Within the last 10 years, research done by Schmookler, Abramovitz, Kendrick and others, including myself, seemed to show that this was not the case. An explanation of the macroeconomic facts appeared to require the conclusion that observed increases in output per man-hour over a 50-year period had only little to do with the increase in capital per worker. The bulk of the explanation, between 85% and 90%, had to come from other sources such as labor quality, technological progress and the like.

CAPITAL INVESTMENT AND ECONOMIC GROWTH

This downgrading of fixed investment as a source of growth had genuine policy implications. Calculations based on these ideas suggested that substantial rates of growth were obtainable with little or no net investment, and that any visible acceleration of growth through the stimulation of capital formation would require fantastic amounts of investment—although people sometimes forget that with net investment only about half of gross, a 10% increase in the rate of gross investment means in the short run a 20% increase in the rate of net investment.

I finally came to think that this undervaluation, or downgrading, of the importance of capital investment was really a little implausible and that all reasoning like that, including my own, overlooked the fact that at least some technological progress requires being embodied in newly designed types of fixed capital before it becomes effective in production. Investment thus serves the purpose not only of adding to the stock of capital per worker, but also of improving its quality, of carrying new technology into operation.

You could easily devise numerical examples that would convince you that this could make a real difference in the story. When account is taken of "embodied" inventions, the kind of inventions that need new kinds of capital to become effective, then a surge in the rate of capital formation will have bigger effects on potential output than the simple notion of "residual" productivity increase would lead one to expect.

Some rough econometric estimates I once made seem to me to give a plausible figure for the size of the investment effort needed to support a somewhat higher growth rate over the next 10 years. For example, a growth rate of 4% annually in potential GNP between 1960 and 1970, which means a growth rate of some 4½% in realized GNP if 1970, unlike 1960, is a year of full utilization, would require investment in plant and equipment of roughly 11% of GNP as compared with about 9% in the last few years and slightly higher than we had in 1955-1957. This is on the assumption that all technical changes need to be embodied in new fixed capital.

One of the troubles with this whole line of thought is that it is just about impossible to make aggregate data tell anything about the extent to which innovations are of the embodied kind and the extent to which they are disembodied. Denison simply assumes it is half and half, and comes to the conclusion that between 1929 and 1957 less than 10% of the annual growth rate of national income per person employed can be imputed to the increase in reproducible capital per employee, while over a third of the annual growth rate of productivity in the same period can be attributed to the advance of knowledge. My casual guess would be that more than half of technical progress is the embodied kind, but I do not know how to find out.

CAPITAL STOCK: SIZE, AGE DISTRIBUTION

The extra "oomph" one gets from investment in this new view comes from the fact that a burst of investment changes not only the size of the capital stock, but also its age distribution. Lowering the average age of the capital stock gives a productivity bonus. But it is not easy to change the average age of a long-lived stock. An increase in plant and equipment investment relative to GNP will eventually move the age distribution of capital as far as it is ever going to move it, and then it will not move it any further. Then the average age remains stationary and the higher growth rate lapses back to what it was when the investment quota was lower, relative to GNP. Output will be forever at a higher level, but the very long-run growth rate will not change. But over a 10- or 20-year period, the change in the investment quota might make a substantial difference.

I might conclude this section by remarking that we probably know least about the contribution to economic growth that could be made by more efficient allocation of resources, the costs of monopoly, restriction and immobility. In some areas—agriculture, perhaps—the costs may be great, and therefore the growth advantage, temporary of course, from removing the restriction may be correspondingly great. But not much is known about the economic costs of monopoly and similar sources or malallocation.

FULL EMPLOYMENT AND ECONOMIC GROWTH

There are a number of subquestions here which need to be disentangled. The view has recently been expressed in the United Kingdom by Paish, and recently again by Phillips, that some decrease in the average pressure of demand on resources, accompanied by a small increase in the unemployment rate, would be desirable for several reasons and could be engineered without any deterioration in the growth rate and perhaps with some improvement.

I am not sufficiently well acquainted with conditions in the United Kingdom to hold a strong opinion on this subject, but I do not find this view wholly implausible. For one thing, continuous full employment may tend to generate inflationary pressure on prices (whether originating in labor markets or product markets) and recurrent balance-of-payments crises, which require that the upward march of demand be halted frequently.

In turn, the necessary restriction of demand, either through credit tightness or tax policy, may for one reason or another fall heavily on fixed investment. I can easily imagine that this chain of events could make it true that a little extra slack could be engineered without ultimately reducing the growth rate, and perhaps even help it over a decent interval of time.

Secondly, it is often said that a perpetually tight economy builds up immobilities, barriers to the adoption of new technology and resistance to competition. This may be so. It has been so long since the American economy operated with that degree of tightness that I have no fresh observations to report. What I have observed in the United States is the reverse phenomenon. Too much slack in an economy can build up the same kinds of pressures against innovation, against technological advance, against the mobility of labor and capital from declining to advancing sectors of the economy. In the United States, at least, one even observes an ebb and flow of sentiment for a shortening of the workweek with the business cycle, which relates not to any real preferences for leisure as against income but to a feeling that there is simply not enough employment to go around without a decrease in weekly hours.

Other examples are not hard to find. The movement of labor out of agriculture, for instance, is clearly intimately related to labor market conditions in industry. When urban unemployment is low, the rate of migration out of agriculture is high, and vice versa. Of course the rate of migration is also sensitive to the market for agricultural products. When farmers are doing well, as during the Korean war, even a tight demand for labor in industry will not pull up the migration rate. But that does not contradict my observations.

To take another example, the recent report of a presidentially appointed commission to study work rules on the railroads showed a majority, including all the public members, agreeing that there is altogether too much featherbedding, too much stultification of technical progress by clinging to antiquated work rules. Such commissions usually try hard, too hard, to be neutral, so the finding is almost certainly true. Now, even in a full-employment economy, an elite occupational group would probably cling to its quasi-rents, but I do not believe the resistance to change would be so great if the demand for labor in the economy at large were considerably higher.

GROWTH AND ECONOMIC EFFICIENCY

Even if I am right and the American economy loses some efficiency because the level of demand is too low, it might still be true that other economies lose some efficiency because the pressure of demand is too high. There might indeed, from this point of view, be an optimal degree of tightness. I am only concerned to say that the United States is clearly on the slack side of that. There exists no conflict on these grounds between the goals of full, or at least fuller, employment and rapid growth.

This position that—to quote the recent Report of the Council of Economic Advisers—"a full employment economy can achieve more rapid growth than an economy alternating between boom and recession; for that reason effective stabilization policy is the first step toward a policy of economic growth" has been attacked as theoretically weak and even anti-Schumpeterian. I suppose it is the latter, but not the former.

Schumpeter, who was a teacher of mine, argued that the business cycle is the way in which a capitalistic economy makes progress. Eliminate or damp the business cycle, and you slow down the rate of progress. More specifically, of course, Schumpeter had a theory of the bunching of technical innovations. The depression is a way of shaking the unsuccessful or obsolete ones out of the system. Anyone who believes this doctrine believes in strong medicine. The business cycle Schumpeter was thinking of, which is supposed to be necessary for capitalist progress, was not the minor postwar business cycle, but the deeper 10-year major cycle of the 19th century and the prewar years. If that is necessary for economic growth, then the almost world-wide acceleration of growth during the last 15 years becomes very difficult to explain.

SHORT BUSINESS CYCLE AND ECONOMIC GROWTH

Indeed, even the belief that the short business cycle is an indispensable midwife for economic growth is hard to maintain in the face of the postwar history of western European countries. Most of them have experienced faster productivity growth than we have; most of them have shown a sharper acceleration of their prewar trends; and all of them have maintained a consistently tighter pressure of demand and a consistently lower unemployment rate than we have, even allowing for differences in definition and statistical practice.

I have been arguing that steady full employment need not prejudice the growth of potential output. It is a more difficult question whether steady full employment might itself increase the rate of growth. This is once again largely a question of the rate of investment. Despite the fact that plant and equipment spending falls off in recession and rises in recovery, it is logically possible that wiping out the business cycle might not increase the average rate of investment relative to aggregate output. It might be that over a complete business cycle we get all the investment we would get even if the business cycle were not there, only we get it concentrated in periods of high employment, filling in the holes left by periods of low employment.

If, for example, investment were governed simply by the acceleration principle, this would be the case. Nobody can say for sure what the true state of affairs is. I am inclined to believe that the main effect of high-level stability on the volume of investment would be a reduction in the riskiness of investment. It seems plausible that one of the reasons businesses seem to demand a high expected rate of return on new projects is to compensate for the risk of inadequate markets.

The confident expectation of full employment by reducing that risk would probably make for a somewhat lower acceptable average rate of return. In my neoclassical view, that is an important part of the battle to generate higher capacity through the deepening of capital, for, apart from the effects of technical progress, each successive increment to productivity bought in this way involves diminished profitability. If I am right on this, an aggressive full-employment policy would elicit more investment averaged over a cycle than we now have, and this would contribute to economic growth. This argument also suggests that an important part of a fiscal policy designed to add to growth through investment might be an extension of income averaging for tax purposes, more complete loss offsets for corporations and, in this way, some socialization of risk.

PART 3
Microeconomics: Prices and the Allocation of Resources

READING 22
The Economic Organisation of a P.O.W. Camp
R. A. Radford

The neoclassical theory of price encompasses buyers and sellers exchanging goods, services, and a medium of exchange (such as dollars) when such trade is to their mutual advantage. An elegant theoretical model has been developed by economists to explain the interaction of buyers and sellers. Economists classify these buyers and sellers into groups on the basis of economic criteria. Consumers, entrepreneurs, wage earners, and investors are examples of the type of groups economists analyze. Intensive development of the implications of supply and demand has lead to many testable propositions resulting from optimizing behavior on the part of the individuals which make up the economic groups.

One essential question remains: Is the formation of these economic groups and the optimizing behavior assumed by economic theorists common, or is it a result of a particular institutional framework? The following paper by R. A. Radford provides an example that exchange and all of its resultant implications will occur even in the artificial and restricted environment of a German prisoner of war camp. It is interesting to note that well-defined markets and other economic institutions arose just as economic theory would predict.

Guideposts for Thought While Reading
How did Radford find prison life different from the outside world with regard to economic activities? What institutions developed in the prison which we can observe in any market system? What public-sector activities were initiated by the prisoners?

After allowance has been made for abnormal circumstances, the social institutions, ideas and habits of groups in the outside world are to be found reflected in a Prisoner of War Camp. It is an unusual but a vital society. Camp organisation and politics

Reprinted by permission of the publisher from R. A. Radford, "The Economic Organisation of a P.O.W. Camp," *Economica*, November 1945, pp. 189–201.

are matters of real concern to the inmates, as affecting their present and perhaps their future existences. Nor does this indicate any loss of proportion. No one pretends that camp matters are of any but local importance or of more than transient interest, but their importance there is great. They bulk large in a world of narrow horizons and it is suggested that any distortion of values lies rather in the minimisation than in the exaggeration of their importance. Human affairs are essentially practical matters and the measure of immediate effect on the lives of those directly concerned in them is to a large extent the criterion of their importance at that time and place. A prisoner can hold strong views on such subjects as whether or not all tinned meats shall be issued to individuals cold or be centrally cooked, without losing sight of the significance of the Atlantic Charter.

One aspect of social organisation is to be found in economic activity, and this, along with other manifestations of a group existence, is to be found in any P.O.W. camp. True, a prisoner is not dependent on his exertions for the provision of the necessaries, or even the luxuries of life, but through his economic activity, the exchange of goods and services, his standard of material comfort is considerably enhanced. And this is a serious matter to the prisoner: he is not "playing at shops" even though the small scale of the transactions and the simple expression of comfort and wants in terms of cigarettes and jam, razor blades and writing paper, make the urgency of those needs difficult to appreciate, even by an ex-prisoner of some three months' standing.

Nevertheless, it cannot be too strongly emphasised that economic activities do not bulk so large in prison society as they do in the larger world. There can be little production; as has been said the prisoner is independent of his exertions for the provision of the necessities and luxuries of life; the emphasis lies in exchange and the media of exchange. A prison camp is not to be compared with the seething crowd of higglers in a street market, any more than it is to be compared with the economic inertia of a family dinner table.

Naturally then, entertainment, academic and literary interests, games and discussions of the "other world" bulk larger in everyday life than they do in the life of more normal societies. But it would be wrong to underestimate the importance of economic activity. Everyone receives a roughly equal share of essentials; it is by trade that individual preferences are given expression and comfort increased. All at some time, and most people regularly, make exchanges of one sort or another.

Although a P.O.W. camp provides a living example of a simple economy which might be used as an alternative to the Robinson Crusoe economy beloved by the text-books, and its simplicity renders the demonstration of certain economic hypotheses both amusing and instructive, it is suggested that the principal significance is sociological. True, there is interest in observing the growth of economic institutions and customs in a brand new society, small and simple enough to prevent detail from obscuring the basic pattern and disequilibrium from obscuring the working of the system. But the essential interest lies in the universality and the spontaneity of this economic life; it came into existence not by conscious imitation but as a response to the immediate needs and circumstances. Any similarity between prison organisation and outside organisation arises from similar stimuli evoking similar responses.

The following is as brief an account of the essential data as may render the narrative intelligible. The camps of which the writer had experience were Oflags and consequently the economy was not complicated by payments for work by the detaining power. They consisted normally of between 1,200 and 2,500 people, housed in a number of separate but intercommunicating bungalows, one company of 200 or so to a building. Each company formed a group within the main organisation and inside the company the room and the messing syndicate, a voluntary and spontaneous group who fed together, formed the constituent units.

Between individuals there was active trading in all consumer goods and in some services. Most trading was for food against cigarettes or other foodstuffs, but cigarettes rose from the status of a normal commodity to that of currency. RMk.s existed but had no circulation save for gambling debts, as few articles could be purchased with them from the canteen.

Our supplies consisted of rations provided by the detaining power and (principally) the contents of Red Cross food parcels —tinned milk, jam, butter, biscuits, bully, chocolate, sugar, etc., and cigarettes. So far the supplies to each person were equal and regular. Private parcels of clothing, toilet requisites and cigarettes were also received, and here equality ceased owing to the different numbers despatched and the vagaries of the post. All these articles were the subject of trade and exchange.

THE DEVELOPMENT AND ORGANISATION OF THE MARKET

Very soon after capture people realised that it was both undesirable and unnecessary, in view of the limited size and the equality of supplies, to give away or to accept gifts of cigarettes or food. "Goodwill" developed into trading as a more equitable means of maximising individual satisfaction.

We reached a transit camp in Italy about a fortnight after capture and received ¼ of a Red Cross food parcel each a week later. At once exchanges, already established, multiplied in volume. Starting with simple direct barter, such as a non-smoker giving a smoker friend his cigarette issue in exchange for a chocolate ration, more complex exchanges soon became an accepted custom. Stories circulated of a padre who started off round the camp with a tin of cheese and five cigarettes and returned to his bed with a complete parcel in addition to his original cheese and cigarettes; the market was not yet perfect. Within a week or two, as the volume of trade grew, rough scales of exchange values came into existence. Sikhs, who had at first exchanged tinned beef for practically any other foodstuff, began to insist on jam and margarine. It was realised that a tin of jam was worth ½ lb. of margarine plus something else; that a cigarette issue was worth several chocolate issues, and a tin of diced carrots was worth practically nothing.

In this camp we did not visit other bungalows very much and prices varied from place to place; hence the germ of truth in the story of the itinerant priest. By the end of a month, when we reached our permanent camp, there was a lively trade in all commodities and their relative values were well known, and expressed not in terms of one another—one didn't quote bully in terms of sugar—but in terms of cigarettes. The cigarette became the standard of value. In the permanent camp people started by wandering through the bungalows calling their offers—"cheese for seven" (cigarettes)—and the hours after parcel issue were Bedlam. The inconveniences of this system soon led to its replacement by an Exchange and Mart notice board in every bungalow, where under the headings "name", "room number", "wanted" and "offered" sales and wants were advertised. When a deal went through, it was crossed off the board. The public and semipermanent records of transactions led to cigarette prices being well known and thus tending to equality throughout the camp, although there were always opportunities for an astute trader to make a profit from arbitrage. With this development everyone, including non-smokers, was willing to sell for cigarettes, using them to buy at another time and place. Cigarettes became the normal currency, though, of course, barter was never extinguished.

The unity of the market and the prevalence of a single price varied directly with the general level of organisation and comfort in the camp. A transit camp was always chaotic and uncomfortable: people were overcrowded, no one knew where anyone else was living, and few took the trouble to find out. Organisation was too slender to include an Exchange and Mart board, and private advertisements were the most that appeared. Consequently a transit camp was not one market but many. The price of a tin of salmon is known to have varied by two cigarettes in 20 between one end of a hut and the other. Despite a high level of organisation in Italy, the market was morcellated in this manner at the first transit camp we reached after our removal to Germany in the autumn of 1943. In this camp—Stalag VIIA at Moosburg in Bavaria—there were up to 50,000 prisoners of all nationalities. French, Russians, Italians and Jugo-Slavs were free to move about within the camp: British and Americans were confined to their compounds, although a few cigarettes given to a sentry would always procure permission for one or two men to visit other compounds. The people who first visited the highly organised French trading centre, with its stalls and known prices, found coffee extract—relatively cheap among the tea-drinking English—commanding a fancy price in biscuits or cigarettes, and some enterprising people made small fortunes that way. (Incidentally we found out later that much of the coffee went "over the wire" and sold for phenomenal prices at black market cafés in Munich: some of the French prisoners were said to have made substantial sums in RMk.s. This was one of the few occasions on which our normally closed economy came into contact with other economic worlds.)

Eventually public opinion grew hostile to these monopoly profits—not everyone could make contact with the French—and trading with them was put on a regulated basis. Each group of beds was given a quota of articles to offer and the transaction was carried out by accredited representatives from the British compound, with monopoly rights. The same method was used for trading with sentries elsewhere, as in this trade secrecy and reasonable prices had a peculiar importance, but as is ever the case with regulated companies, the interloper proved too strong.

The permanent camps in Germany saw the highest level of commercial organisation. In addition to the Exchange and Mart notice boards, a shop was organised as a public utility, controlled by representatives of the Senior British Officer, on a no profit basis. People left their surplus clothing, toilet requisites and food there until they were sold at a fixed price in cigarettes. Only sales in cigarettes were accepted—there was no barter—and there was no higgling. For food at least there were standard prices: clothing is less homogeneous and the price was decided around a norm by the seller and the shop manager in agreement; shirts would average say 80, ranging from 60 to 120 according to quality and age. Of food, the shop carried small stocks for convenience; the capital was provided by a loan from the bulk store of Red Cross cigarettes and repaid by a small commission taken on the first transactions. Thus the cigarette attained its fullest currency status, and the market was almost completely unified.

It is thus to be seen that a market came into existence without labour or production. The B.R.C.S. may be considered as "Nature" of the text-book, and the articles of trade—food, clothing and cigarettes—as free gifts—land or manna. Despite this, and despite a roughly equal distribution of resources, a market came into spontaneous operation, and prices were fixed by the operation of supply and demand. It is difficult to reconcile this fact with the labour theory of value.

Actually there was an embryo labour market. Even when cigarettes were not scarce, there was usually some unlucky person willing to perform services for them. Laundrymen advertised at two cigarettes a garment. Battle-dress was scrubbed and pressed and a pair of trousers lent for the interim period for twelve. A good pastel portrait cost thirty or a tin of "Kam". Odd tailoring and other jobs similarly had their prices.

There were also entrepreneurial services. There was a coffee stall owner who sold tea, coffee or cocoa at two cigarettes a cup, buying his raw materials at market prices and hiring labour to gather fuel and to stoke; he actually enjoyed the services of a chartered accountant at one stage. After a period of great prosperity he overreached himself and failed disastrously for several hundred cigarettes. Such large-scale private enterprise was rare but several middlemen or professional traders existed. The padre in Italy, or the men at Moosburg who opened trading relations with the French, are examples: the more subdivided the market, the less perfect the advertisement of prices, and the less stable the prices, the greater was the scope for these operators. One man capitalised his knowledge of Urdu by buying meat from the Sikhs and selling butter and jam in return: as his operations became better known more and more people entered this trade, prices in the Indian Wing approximated more nearly to those elsewhere, though to the end a "contact" among the Indians was valuable, as linguistic difficulties prevented the trade from being quite free. Some were specialists in the Indian trade, the food, clothing or even the watch trade. Middlemen traded on their own account or on commission. Price rings and agreements were suspected and the traders certainly co-operated. Nor did they welcome newcomers. Unfortunately the writer knows little of the workings of these people: public opinion was hostile and the professionals were usually of a retiring disposition.

One trader in food and cigarettes, operating in a period of dearth, enjoyed a high reputation. His capital, carefully saved, was originally about 50 cigarettes, with which he bought rations on issue days and held them until the price rose just before the next issue. He also picked up a little by arbitrage; several times a day he visited every Exchange or Mart notice board and took advantage of every discrepancy between prices of goods offered and wanted. His knowledge of prices, markets and names of those who had received cigarette parcels was phenomenal. By these means he kept himself smoking steadily—his profits—while his capital remained intact.

Sugar was issued on Saturday. About Tuesday two of us used to visit Sam and make a deal; as old customers he would advance as much of the price as he could spare then, and entered the transaction in a book. On Saturday morning he left cocoa tins on our beds for the ration, and picked them up on Saturday afternoon. We were hoping for a calendar at Christmas, but Sam failed too. He was left holding a big black treacle issue when the price fell, and in this weakened state was unable to withstand an unexpected arrival of parcels and the consequent price fluctuations. He paid in full, but from his capital. The next Tuesday, when I paid my usual visit he was out of business.

Credit entered into many, perhaps into most, transactions, in one form or another. Sam paid in advance as a rule for his purchases of future deliveries of sugar, but many buyers asked for credit, whether the commodity was sold spot or future. Naturally prices varied according to the terms of sale. A treacle ration might be advertised for four cigarettes now or five next week. And in the future market "bread now" was a vastly different thing from "bread Thursday". Bread was issued on Thursday and Monday, four and three days' rations respectively, and by

Wednesday and Sunday night it had risen at least one cigarette per ration, from seven to eight, by supper time. One man always saved a ration to sell then at the peak price: his offer of "bread now" stood out on the board among a number of "bread Monday's" fetching one or two less, or not selling at all—and he always smoked on Sunday night.

THE CIGARETTE CURRENCY

Although cigarettes as currency exhibited certain peculiarities, they performed all the functions of a metallic currency as a unit of account, as a measure of value and as a store of value, and shared most of its characteristics. They were homogeneous, reasonably durable, and of convenient size for the smallest or, in packets, for the largest transactions. Incidentally, they could be clipped or sweated by rolling them between the fingers so that tobacco fell out.

Cigarettes were also subject to the working of Gresham's Law. Certain brands were more popular than others as smokes, but for currency purposes a cigarette was a cigarette. Consequently buyers used the poorer qualities and the Shop rarely saw the more popular brands: cigarettes such as Churchman's No. 1 were rarely used for trading. At one time cigarettes hand-rolled from pipe tobacco began to circulate. Pipe tobacco was issued in lieu of cigarettes by the Red Cross at a rate of 25 cigarettes to the ounce and this rate was standard in exchanges, but an ounce would produce 30 home-made cigarettes. Naturally, people with machine-made cigarettes broke them down and re-rolled the tobacco, and the real cigarette virtually disappeared from the market. Hand-rolled cigarettes were not homogeneous and prices could no longer be quoted in them with safety: each cigarette was examined before it was accepted and thin ones were rejected, or extra demanded as a make-weight. For a time we suffered all the inconveniences of a debased currency.

Machine-made cigarettes were always universally acceptable, both for what they would buy and for themselves. It was this intrinsic value which gave rise to their principal disadvantage as currency, a disadvantage which exists, but to a far smaller extent, in the case of metallic currency;—that is, a strong demand for non-monetary purposes. Consequently our economy was repeatedly subject to deflation and to periods of monetary stringency. While the Red Cross issue of 50 or 25 cigarettes per man per week came in regularly, and while there were fair stocks held, the cigarette currency suited its purpose admirably. But when the issue was interrupted, stocks soon ran out, prices fell, trading declined in volume and became increasingly a matter of barter. This deflationary tendency was periodically offset by the sudden injection of new currency. Private cigarette parcels arrived in a trickle throughout the year, but the big numbers came in quarterly when the Red Cross received its allocation of transport. Several hundred thousand cigarettes might arrive in the space of a fortnight. Prices soared, and then began to fall, slowly at first but with increasing rapidity as stocks ran out, until the next big delivery. Most of our economic troubles could be attributed to this fundamental instability.

PRICE MOVEMENTS

Many factors affected prices, the strongest and most noticeable being the periodical currency inflation and deflation described in the last paragraphs. The periodicity of this price cycle depended on cigarette and, to a far lesser extent, on food deliveries. At one time in the early days, before any private parcels had arrived and when there were no individual stocks, the weekly issue of cigarettes and food parcels occurred on a Monday. The non-monetary demand for cigarettes was great, and less elastic than the demand for food: consequently prices fluctuated weekly, falling towards Sunday night and rising sharply on Monday morning. Later, when many people held reserves, the weekly issue had no such effect, being too small a proportion of the total available. Credit allowed people with no reserves to meet their non-monetary demand over the week-end.

The general price level was affected by other factors. An influx of new prisoners, proverbially hungry, raised it. Heavy air raids in the vicinity of the camp probably increased the non-monetary demand for cigarettes and accentuated deflation. Good and bad war news certainly had its effect, and the general waves of optimism and pessimism which swept the camp were reflected in prices. Before breakfast one morning in March of this year, a rumour of the arrival of parcels and cigarettes was circulated. Within ten minutes I sold a treacle ration, for four cigarettes (hitherto offered in vain for three), and many similar deals went through. By 10 o'clock the rumour was denied, and treacle that day found no more buyers even at two cigarettes.

More interesting than changes in the general price level were changes in the price structure. Changes in the supply of a commodity, in the German ration scale or in the make-up of Red Cross parcels, would raise the price of one commodity relative to others. Tins of oatmeal, once a rare and much sought after luxury in the parcels, became a commonplace in 1943, and the price fell. In hot weather the demand for cocoa fell, and that for soap rose. A new recipe would be reflected in the price level: the discovery that raisins and sugar could be turned into an alcoholic liquor of remarkable potency reacted permanently on the dried fruit market. The invention of electric immersion heaters run off the power points made tea, a drug on the market in Italy, a certain seller in Germany.

In August, 1944, the supplies of parcels and cigarettes were both halved. Since both sides of the equation were changed in the same degree, changes in prices were not anticipated. But this was not the case: the non-monetary demand for cigarettes was less elastic than the demand for food, and food prices fell a little. More important however were the changes in the price structure. German margarine and jam, hitherto valueless owing to adequate supplies of Canadian butter and marmalade, acquired a new value. Chocolate, popular and a certain seller, and sugar, fell. Bread rose; several standing contracts of bread for cigarettes were broken, especially when the bread ration was reduced a few weeks later.

PAPER CURRENCY—BULLY MARKS

Around D-Day, food and cigarettes were plentiful, business was brisk and the camp in an optimistic mood. Consequently the Entertainments Committee felt the moment opportune to launch a restaurant, where food and hot drinks were sold while a band and variety turns performed. Earlier experiments, both public and private, had pointed the way, and the scheme was a great success. Food was bought at market prices to provide the meals and the small profits were devoted to a reserve fund and used to bribe Germans to provide grease-paints and other necessities for the camp theatre. Originally meals were sold for cigarettes but this meant that the whole scheme was vulnerable to the periodic deflationary waves, and furthermore heavy smokers were unlikely to attend much. The whole success of the scheme depended on an adequate amount of food being offered for sale in the normal manner.

To increase and facilitate trade, and to stimulate supplies and customers therefore, and secondarily to avoid the worst effects of deflation when it should come, a paper currency was organised by the Restaurant and the Shop. The Shop bought food on behalf of the Restaurant with paper notes and the paper was accepted equally with the cigarettes in the Restaurant or Shop, and passed back to the Shop to purchase more food. The Shop acted as a bank of issue. The paper money was backed 100 per cent. by food; hence its name, the Bully Mark. The BMk. was backed 100 per cent. by food: there could be no over-issues, as is permissible with a normal bank of issue, since the eventual dispersal of the camp and consequent redemption of all BMk.s was anticipated in the near future.

Originally one BMk. was worth one cigarette and for a short time both circulated freely inside and outside the Restaurant. Prices were quoted in BMk.s and cigarettes with equal freedom —and for a short time the BMk. showed signs of replacing the cigarette as currency. The BMk. was tied to food, but not to cigarettes: as it was issued against food, say 45 for a tin of milk and so on, any reduction in the BMk. prices of food would have meant that there were unbacked BMk.s in circulation. But the price of both food and BMk.s could and did fluctuate with the supply of cigarettes.

While the Restaurant flourished, the scheme was a success: the Restaurant bought heavily, all foods were saleable and prices were stable.

PUBLIC OPINION

Public opinion on the subject of trading was vocal if confused and changeable, and generalisations as to its direction are difficult and dangerous. A tiny minority held that all trading was undesirable as it engendered an unsavoury atmosphere; occasional frauds and sharp practices were cited as proof. Certain forms of trading were more generally condemned; trade with the Germans was criticised by many. Red Cross toilet articles, which were in short supply and only issued in cases of actual need, were excluded from trade by law and opinion working in unshakable harmony. At one time, when there had been several cases of malnutrition reported among the more devoted smokers, no trade in German rations was permitted, as the victims became an additional burden on the depleted food reserves of the Hospital. But while certain activities were condemned as antisocial, trade itself was practised, and its utility appreciated, by almost everyone in the camp.

More interesting was opinion on middlemen and prices. Taken as a whole, opinion was hostile to the middleman. His function, and his hard work in bringing buyer and seller together, were ignored; profits were not regarded as a reward for labour, but as the result of sharp practices. Despite the fact that his very existence was proof to the contrary, the middleman was held to be redundant in view of the existence of an official Shop and the Exchange and Mart. Appreciation only came his way when he was willing to advance the price of a sugar ration, or to buy goods spot and carry them against a future sale. In these cases the element of risk was obvious to all, and the convenience of the service was felt to merit some reward. Particularly unpopular was the middleman with an element of monopoly, the man who contacted the ration wagon driver, or the man who utilised his knowledge of Urdu. And middlemen as a group were blamed for reducing prices. Opinion notwithstanding, most people dealt with a middleman, whether consciously or unconsciously, at some time or another.

There was a strong feeling that everything had its "just price" in cigarettes. While the assessment of the just price, which incidentally varied between camps, was impossible of explanation, this price was nevertheless pretty closely known. It can best be defined as the price usually fetched by an article in good times when cigarettes were plentiful. The "just price" changed slowly; it was unaffected by short-term variations in supply, and while opinion might be resigned to departures from the "just price", a strong feeling of resentment persisted. A more satisfactory definition of the "just price" is impossible. Everyone knew what it was, though no one could explain why it should be so.

As soon as prices began to fall with a cigarette shortage, a clamour arose, particularly against those who held reserves and who bought at reduced prices. Sellers at cut prices were criticised and their activities referred to as the black market. In every period of dearth the explosive question of "should non-smokers receive a cigarette ration?" was discussed to profitless length. Unfortunately, it was the non-smoker, or the light smoker with his reserves, along with the hated middleman, who weathered the storm most easily.

Curious arguments were advanced to justify price fixing. The recommended prices were in some way related to the calorific values of the foods offered: hence some were overvalued and never sold at these prices. One argument ran as follows:—not everyone has private cigarette parcels: thus, when prices were high and trade good in the summer of 1944, only the lucky rich could buy. This was unfair to the man with few cigarettes. When prices fell in the following winter, prices should be pegged high so that the rich, who had enjoyed life in the summer, should put many cigarettes into circulation. The fact that those who sold to the rich in the summer had also enjoyed life then, and the fact that in the winter there was always someone willing to sell at low prices were ignored. Such arguments were hotly debated each night after the approach of Allied aircraft extinguished all lights at 8 p.m. But prices moved with the supply of cigarettes, and refused to stay fixed in accordance with a theory of ethics.

By April, 1945, chaos had replaced order in the economic sphere: sales were difficult, prices lacked stability. Economics has been defined as the science of distributing limited means among unlimited and competing ends. On 12th April, with the arrival of elements of the 30th U.S. Infantry Division, the ushering in of an age of plenty demonstrated the hypothesis that with infinite means economic organisation and activity would be redundant, as every want could be satisfied without effort.

READING 23
How To Free TV
Milton Friedman

In this reading, Dr. Friedman disclaims any knowledge of the consequences of a free market for television programs but does insist that the outcome cannot help but be an improvement over existing legally enforced giveaway programming. Contrasting television and the publishing industry, Friedman points to the superior product offering and many consumer alternatives made available by the publishing industry.

Reprinted by permission of the publisher from "How To Free TV," *Newsweek*, December 1, 1969, p. 82. Copyright Newsweek Inc., Dec. 1, 1969.

Guideposts for Thought While Reading

How do the FCC and other government agencies work against the public interest which they are hired to protect? What method does Friedman suggest for implementing a free-market system in the television medium?

In his powerful attack on TV news coverage, Vice President Agnew accurately described the present lack of diversity, but touched only lightly on causes and cures.

The causes are not to be found in the character of the men who present the news or who run the networks. Both groups try to present the news fairly. Yet, with the best of intentions, three collections of men breathing the same intellectual atmosphere and with a strong incentive to appeal to the same audience in the same way will inevitably present a one-sided point of view.

CAUSES

This narrow range of views has its origins in two related features of TV: first, the requirement of a government license in order to operate a TV station; second, the effective stifling of pay-TV for well over a decade by the Federal Communications Commission under the pressure and influence of the networks.

To see the importance of the second feature, suppose that it were made illegal for any reading matter to be sold directly to the public. Reading matter could be distributed only if it were given away to all comers, financed, as TV programs now are, by advertising, philanthropy or government subsidy.

What would happen to our present variety of reading matter —to which Mr. Agnew referred so aptly? Would advertisers finance newspapers and magazines of the kind we now have? Perhaps a few, but surely not many, and hardly any that would take a strong, independent and unpopular position, or that, like the New Republic, National Review, Harper's, Atlantic Monthly, would appeal to very limited audiences.

What kind of books would be published? Some time ago, I bought a magnificent collection of reproductions of Andrew Wyeth's paintings, which sells for $75. Can you conceive of an advertiser finding it in his interest to use so expensive a book with such limited appeal as a vehicle for selling his product? No, the books published would be mostly the kind that are now printed by the millions in paperback—the kind we "effete snobs" call "trash."

The books published would appeal to the masses—in this sense the advertisers could say that they were giving the public what it wants, just as the TV networks now claim. Yet the public would not get what it wants in the meaningful sense of getting everything that it was willing to pay for. It would get only those items that could be produced cheaply enough to serve as fillers between the advertisements.

This is precisely the situation in TV today. The insistence that programs must be "given away"—that is, paid for by the public through its purchase of advertised products—has led to precisely the results that it would lead to with reading matter: deadening uniformity; limited choice; low-cost, low-quality programs. It has also fostered the dominance of networks and their geographical concentration, because their special advantage is in merchandising nationwide advertising. That is why they have bitterly opposed pay-TV.

The networks have been able to maintain their monopoly position because of the requirement of a government license to operate a TV station. Without this requirement, it would have been impossible for them to have prevented the development of pay-TV on a large scale—and, for all I know, of still other alternatives to present-day commercial TV.

The FCC supposedly regulates the radio and TV industry in the public interest. But like just about every other regulatory agency—ICC, CAB, FPC, and so on through the dreary alphabet—it has in fact become an instrument of the industry it supposedly regulates. It has been used by that industry to preserve monopoly and to prevent competition. Its abolition is essential if we are to have truly free TV.

CURE

But, you will say, the number of TV channels is limited—not to three but to a fairly small number. Surely, government must decide who is to use them. That is a non sequitur. Gold mines are limited. Must the government therefore decide who is to operate them? Land is limited. That may call for zoning requirements, but does it require the licensing of the use of particular parcels to particular people? Precisely the same solution is available for the allocation of TV channels as for the allocation of land. Just as the U.S. sold much of its public land a century ago, let the FCC sell now to the highest bidder the rights now covered by a license (to broadcast at a specified frequency and power in a specified way during specified hours of the day, from a particular location). And then let it go out of business.

The owners of these rights would have private property in them, which they would protect from trespass as you and I protect our land from trespass, through the courts. They could buy and sell the rights, subdivide them, recombine them, as you and I do with our land.[1] They would have the full protection of the Bill of Rights just as the press now does.

Monopolies, if any developed, would be subject to the antitrust laws, not, as now, protected by a government agency. And they would be far less likely to develop because advertisers and networks would be denied the special privileges that they are now granted.

CONSEQUENCES

What kind of TV system would emerge from the free and unfettered operation of market forces? No one can say in detail. The market is most ingenious and always produces surprises. But certain things are clear. First, there would still be programs supported entirely by advertising—as giveaway newspapers are now. Second, there would be many programs supported partly by advertising, partly by fees—as many newspapers and magazines are now. Third, there would be many programs supported entirely by fees—as so many books and other publications are now. Fourth, the TV bill of fare would be far richer than it now is. It would cater to all viewers, not just those influenced by advertising. It would provide expensive programs for limited audiences as well as low-cost programs for mass audiences.

Here, Mr. Agnew, is a far better road to a cure than asking listeners to write and telephone TV stations. Give the viewer the power that makes the consumer the boss in other areas, the power to buy from whom he wants what he wants to buy. That is the way to a truly free TV.

[1] The technical feasibility of this proposal is examined and demonstrated in R. H. Coase, "The Federal Communications Commission," Journal of Law and Economics, October 1959, and in Arthur S. DeVany, Ross D. Eckert, Charles J. Meyers, Donald J. O'Hara, Richard C. Scott, "A Property System for Market Allocation of the Electro-magnetic Spectrum: A Legal-economic-engineering Study," Stanford Law Review, June 1969.

READING 24
Opportunity Versus Outlay Costs
Joel Dean

The following is a brief excerpt from Joel Dean's *Managerial Economics*, in which Dean points out the distinction between opportunity costs and standard accounting costs. Joel Dean has served as a professor of Business Administration and is a well known economic consultant.

Guideposts for Thought While Reading
When does consideration of alternative or opportunity cost become of paramount importance for decision-making by the firm? Can this criteria be carried over to public-spending decisions?

A distinction can be drawn between outlay costs and opportunity costs on the basis of the nature of the sacrifice. Outlay costs are those that involve financial expenditure at some time and hence are recorded in the books of account. Opportunity costs take the form of profits from alternative ventures that are foregone by using limited facilities for a particular purpose. Since they represent only sacrificed alternatives, they are never recorded as such in the financial accounts.

Whenever the problem allows an opportunity to buy all input factors for cash, outlay cost is the correct concept to use. In this situation, cash is the scarce factor and the standard of value of input factors relative to all other conceivable uses of cash.

Such complete market access is almost never within the bounds of practicability, and thus some concept of opportunity cost is usually relevant. Indeed, for many problems, opportunity cost is the more important cost. In a cloth mill that spins its own yarn, for example, the cost of yarn is really the price at which the yarn could be sold if it were not woven into cloth. For the problem of measuring the profitability of the weaving operations in order to decide whether to expand them or abandon them, it is this opportunity cost—the foregone revenue from not selling the yarn—that is relevant. In periods of boom demand, the use of a versatile bottleneck factor, such as scarce steel or scarce loom capacity, for making one product, involves the opportunity cost of not using it to make some other product that can also produce profits. The opportunity cost of producing heating oil in a modern, flexible refinery, for example, is the value of the gasoline that might otherwise have been made. For this reason, "gasoline equivalent" costing has considerable acceptance in this industry.

For short-run decisions like those illustrated above, the alternatives are clear, and the opportunity cost of foregoing them is calculable. But opportunity cost has a broader meaning and a wider usefulness than is implied in these straightforward applications. It is useful for long-run decisions involving problems of major strategy. For example, the cost of getting a college education is not confined to the outlays on tuition and books, but also includes the earnings that are foregone by not working full time.

In military affairs, to cite another example, the cost of sending bombers on a particular mission is not the price of the gasoline and ammunition but, rather, the damage that they would have done the enemy had they been sent on a substitute mission. Opportunity costs also play a role in sales strategy. For example, in determining whether a gasoline station should do major automotive repair work, the owner should consider the cost of such work in terms of the amount of gasoline and oil that will not be sold because the attendant is flat on his back under a truck. Managerial skill is scarce in most companies. Ventures that demand executive time must have high productivity to cover the opportunity cost of foregone management activities.

Opportunity cost plays an important role in capital expenditure budgeting. Under conditions of capital rationing, the cost of acquiring a $100,000 gasoline station in New York City is not usually the interest that would have to be paid on the borrowed money but, rather, the profits or cost savings that could have been achieved if the $100,000 had been invested in four suburban gasoline stations, or in pipelines or refinery facilities. Investing equity money in the venture involves opportunity costs measurable in terms of sacrificed income from alternative investments. Estimates of cost of capital are essentially founded on an opportunity concept of investment return.

Opportunity cost is the cost concept to use when the supply

of input factors is strictly limited. Such rigid supply may occur for technical reasons, e.g., the limited number of television channels available in a single locality; for social reasons, e.g., wartime rationing; for private reasons, such as lack of ready cash, or because the problem is too short-run to adapt facilities to their most profitable long-run relation to the job. In business problems the message of opportunity costs is that it is dangerous to confine cost knowledge to what the firm is doing. What the firm is not doing but could do is frequently the critical cost consideration which it is perilous but easy to ignore.

READING 25
Can Anyone Explain Capitalism?
R. Joseph Monsen

The ideologies of modern American capitalism range from the rugged individualism of Adam Smith's laissez-faire economy to the social-goods orientation of John Kenneth Galbraith and his disciples. Professor R. Joseph Monsen, as a specialist in the study of business behavior and motivation at the College of Business of the University of Washington, has written the following provocative article which shows the several viewpoints of capitalism and relates capitalistic ideology to the goals of the groups which manifest it.

Guideposts for Thought While Reading

According to Monsen, what are the predominant capitalistic ideologies in America? How do these ideologies buttress the economic welfare or rationalize the activities of the groups which espouse them?

If people on the streets of Moscow and New York were stopped and asked to define capitalism (assuming that anyone on a New

Reprinted by permission of the publisher from R. Joseph Monsen, "Can Anyone Explain Capitalism," *Saturday Review*, December 14, 1963.

York street could be stopped), the Russians, I suspect, would have little trouble in answering such a question, the Americans a great deal. While the description of capitalism given by the Muscovites might sound like something out of Dickens, they would probably be quite unanimous and positive about it. The New Yorkers, however, would be uneasy about even the word "capitalism," and their definitions would be both varied and vague. Without drawing a moral from such an imaginary poll, it is quite clear that in the United States today there are a number of ideas about what this thing called capitalism really is.

Schools in this country are making increasing efforts to explain American capitalism and our economic system within the classrooms. In most plans to develop a program that will explain our economic system to students, however, two crucial factors are overlooked: the bias of those developing such material and the attitude of the teacher toward capitalism. These factors will necessarily color any explanation the student receives. It may be argued that this is true of all education. I would agree. But in the case of capitalism the problem is considerably more involved and controversial than in most. For even if capitalism is defined quite neutrally as a system in which private ownership operates in a market environment for profit-making, the critical role of government remains to be interpreted. Yet in the United States today no issue is more hotly debated than the extent to which government should participate in economic affairs. There is little doubt that the role of government as perceived by J. K. Galbraith or by Arthur Schlesinger, Jr., is considerably larger than that accepted by Barry Goldwater, William Buckley, or the National Association of Manufacturers.

This difference of opinion concerning the role of government brings us to the central point of this article: that in the United States today at least five major versions of capitalism can be found. The role of government in these versions is a major [distinguishing] characteristic.

These separate versions of capitalism may, in fact, be considered as separate ideologies—ideologies because they present explanations or rationalizations that are used by groups to justify their own positions. Economic ideologies, like religious dogmas, have their "true believers" as well as those adherents who espouse them for more practical ends.

To understand our economy today one must have some idea of what our major ideologies about capitalism are and who espouses them. Congressional debates and public argument in the press on major issues become much easier to follow once the positions for various groups are linked to their ideologies. We frequently hear that we have no economic ideology in this country, or that we have finally reached, as Daniel Bell entitled his book, *The End of Ideology*. Nothing could be further from the truth. Even though Marxian and collectivist ideologies are not significant in the mainstream of American thought today, to argue that we have no other economic ideologies is extremely naive.

THE CLASSICAL IDEOLOGY

Of the ideologies of American capitalism prominently in print today, the oldest is what has been called the classical ideology of capitalism. It is disseminated in the United States largely by the National Association of Manufacturers, the Foundation for Economic Education, the Committee for Constitutional Government, the United States Chamber of Commerce, and the American Enterprise Association, to name only some of the better-known organizations. While at times these groups may vary, through their many publications they present the major interpretation of this most traditional version of the American capitalist ideology. The importance of this ideology in business circles is indicated by a report estimating that out of more than $32,000,000 spent by corporations to influence legislation, some $27,000,000 was in the form of donations for use by the organizations disseminating the classical ideology.

The essence of the classical ideology is its concept of individually owned private property in a decentralized market operated by the forces of supply and demand in the quest for profit. The official stand of the NAM concerning the role of government in the economy is that the solutions to the basic economic problems of what, how, for whom, and at what price goods should be produced must be left to the voluntary adjustments of a free market rather than to the central authority of government. While this view does not demand that there be no government regulation, it does argue that because of the effectiveness of competition as a regulatory device, government intervention and regulation of the market are seldom needed. The classical ideology maintains, then, that there is no need for government countercyclical spending. Deficit spending is not only unnecessary but, according to the classical ideology, "irresponsible" on the grounds that it produces inflation, raises the specter of national bankruptcy, and may create recessions by interfering with the natural, competitive market.

This ideology, opposed to deficit spending, is reinforced in the public mind by the analogy between private and public finance; just as individuals risk bankruptcy by deficit spending, so it is argued, does government. Such ideological statements carry highly emotional and moral overtones. America's traditional Puritan ethic stresses economic independence, thrift, and freedom from debt, all of which buttress the charge that the government is acting "irresponsibly," "profligately," "immorally," if it utilizes deficit spending—no matter what the conditions of the economy. When the classical capitalist ideology applies the Puritan ethic of personal finance to government financial policy in this way, it is apparent that the central idea of deficit spending and Keynesian economics is in direct conflict with it.

The anachronism involved in the classical ideology (as espoused by both Barry Goldwater and Harry S. Byrd) is that for more than a decade both Republican and Democratic Administrations have followed the Keynesian idea of using deficit spending to bolster the economy in times of recessions and unemployment. The further notion that deficit spending should also take place in periods of prosperity is a recent elaboration of Keynes's original theory. Deficit spending in non-recessionary periods is justified today largely as a means of stimulating greater economic growth.

THE MANAGERIAL IDEOLOGY

If the classical ideology had been more flexible in accepting a somewhat greater economic role for government, as well as in allowing the use of deficit spending under certain circumstances, its main rival as a business creed, known increasingly as the managerial ideology, would probably never have developed. The managerial ideology had its birth with the formation of the Committee for Economic Development in 1942. Since that time, this ideology has been vigorously disseminated by the CED and such business magazines as *Fortune*.

Politically the managerial ideology received its greatest patronage during the Eisenhower Administration. For there was, as *Business Week* observed, "a marked similarity between the CED and the new Administration (Eisenhower's) that involved more than the names of men. Both represent the views of a forward-looking businessman, a sort of progressive conservative."

The managerial ideology of capitalism takes its name from the increasing control by professional management of the large corporation. While the managerial ideology is a reaction to the traditional classical creed, there are great similarities between them. The issues in which similarities occur, however, are usually those about which the managerial ideology is silent. The managerial ideology points largely to the basic changes that have occurred within the economy in the past few decades. It attempts to portray the manager of the large corporation as a trustee for the worker, consumer, and owner.

The dispute over the proper function of government not only partially caused the development of the managerial ideology but indeed remains one of the principle differences between it and the classical ideology. The managerialists accept a considerably greater role for government than the traditionalists will approve. The CED has taken the position that government action is essential in attempting to control business fluctuations—even if such a policy includes deficit spending (though here the managerialists talk in terms of balancing the budget over the whole business cycle and not necessarily in every year, as the NAM requires). The editors of *Fortune* expressed the managerial position by saying: "It is now almost universally accepted that . . . in the event of a serious depression government . . . undertakes very large countercyclical spending programs."

The managerial ideology's acceptance of a larger role for government is considerably more realistic today than the classical ideology's on this issue. In this regard, the classical ideology is less descriptive and more normative than the managerial creed, for it must argue that it represents the way things "ought" to be, not necessarily the way they are. The managerial ideology deemphasizes the traditional forces of supply and demand as the determinants of prices and accepts a governmental role deeply involved in business affairs, attempting to face what it feels are the realities of modern capitalism. To a large degree, the managerial ideology of capitalism is successful in that it provides arguments in currently accepted terms.

THE IDEOLOGY OF COUNTERVAILING POWER

After its election in 1960 the Kennedy Administration had on a number of occasions used a sort of semi-official ideology attributed to the well-known Harvard economist and former Ambassador to India, John Kenneth Galbraith. With the publication in 1952 of his book, *American Capitalism: The Concept of Countervailing Power*, Professor Galbraith set forth the main themes of this ideology. Since then, we have seen the term "countervailing power" spread until today it is hard to find any discussion about American capitalism that does not make some reference to it. In fact, Galbraith is now probably the most widely known economist in this country. While countervailing power cannot be considered as full-blown an ideology as the classical ideology, it has nonetheless become one of the most popular explanations of modern American capitalism.

What is the concept of countervailing power upon which the ideology is based? Most succinctly, it is "the neutralization of one position of power by another." For Galbraith argues that "private economic power begets the countervailing power of those who are subject to it." The development of strong unions, then, in this argument, was inevitable in America to neutralize or balance the power of large companies. While this may not be historically correct, the thesis is that as one group develops in power, others arise to offset its power and prevent their own exploitation. By this reasoning, the strongest unions should develop in those industries where the strongest corporations exist.

The role of government in this interpretation is to assist the development of checks and balances of power. Thus, under this view, the concept of competition as the autonomous regulator of economic activity has been superseded. The potential role of government is, therefore, perhaps greater under the ideology of countervailing power than in any of the other major ideologies of modern American capitalism. In this sense, it may be expected to gain more supporters from among politically liberal citizens than from among conservatives, who are more apt to endorse the classical ideology.

While the countervailing power thesis as an economic theory has been subject to much criticism, as an ideological explanation of modern American capitalism it has become internationally known and suggests the basic flavor of modern American capitalism abroad perhaps more than any other capitalist ideology. Whether countervailing power as an ideology will develop independently or will merely be appended to one of the others, only time will tell. The concept of countervailing power appears, in the last analysis, to be far more adaptable as an ideology for the defense of American capitalism than as an economic theory to explain it; this feature, I might add, it shares with the other major ideologies of capitalism.

THE IDEOLOGY OF PEOPLE'S CAPITALISM

The label "people's capitalism" has become increasingly fashionable as a title for the contemporary American economic system. The United States Information Agency, which at one time made use of the slogan, admitted quite frankly that "this type of terminology is designed as an eye-catcher, as a thought-provoker. The aim is to suggest at the outset that the American system is a far cry from nineteenth-century stereotypes of capitalism."

The central focus of the ideology of people's capitalism is the widening of both equity ownership and decision-making power among the populace. To its supporters, people's capitalism in America today is distinguished more by its emphasis on this system of property diffusion than by its present structure.

The origin of the term "people's capitalism" is alleged to have been developed in 1956 by the American Advertising Council for the USIA, which used the concept abroad. General Electric and Standard Oil of New Jersey have used the phrase in their ads in this country. Business economists such as Marcus Nadler and corporation executives such as Roger Blough of U.S. Steel have publicly used the term often. As Victor Perlo noted in the scholarly *American Economic Review*, "Future editions of economics texts can hardly fail to discuss the theory—or slogan—of people's capitalism."

The most important challenge to the ideology comes from those, such as Perlo, who question whether there has been any significant increase, in recent decades, in the relative diffusion of ownership and decision-making in the U.S.

Incomplete as the concept may be for a full explanation of modern American capitalism, there is little doubt that the ideology of people's capitalism is widely used as a defense, justification, and explanation of our contemporary economic system both at home and abroad. As such, it is one of the primary American capitalist ideologies.

THE EXPORT IDEOLOGY

A synthesis of the major American capitalist ideologies, as described by USIA, has been called enterprise democracy. This ideology, perhaps best thought of as our "export" ideology, has been developed over several Administrations. In his book *What We Are For,* Arthur Larson, former head of the USIA under President Eisenhower, has given one of the few explanations specifically intended for home use of what our "export" ideology is.

The argument of enterprise democracy is that class conflict cannot explain American history. Rather, the practice of cooperation between business, labor, and government—out of the necessity of mutual self-interest—explains the American system. Hence, while the traditional competitive spirit in America is cited as important for the development of an industrial economy, alongside competitiveness, modifying it, is the "strong strain of cooperation." The feature that distinguishes modern enterprise democracy from laissez-faire capitalism is the recognition of necessary cooperation and mutual interest among society's basic groups; this includes recognition of government's positive duty to act when necessary for the varying needs of society's members. Government is different, however, from the other countervailing groups in the economy: "Its power over our freedoms, our fortunes, and our lives can be ultimate and absolute. Every other power in our society is secondary. The power of government is final. That is why we instinctively resist its increase."

The key to enterprise democracy is the role assigned to government. Sometimes called by the USIA "the Lincoln Formula," this ideology proclaims that the function of government is to do only that which needs to be done and cannot be done so well privately.

From this thesis, three corollaries are developed: 1) that more than one group should exist to act for the needs of the community; 2) that the major groups in modern industrial society do not basically conflict but rather mutually support one another (i.e., business, labor, and government); and 3) that private methods are always inherently preferable to government action. This, then, means a preference for as little governmental action "as possible." The phrase "as possible" is, of course, elastic and vague.

Other concepts that the ideology of enterprise democracy emphasizes are freedom, property, justice, individuality, group allegiance, and religion. The traditional criticisms of capitalism —competitiveness, class conflict, and inequality of income distribution—are, needless to say, not emphasized.

Essentially, enterprise democracy represents a composite or

compromise ideology that, the USIA hopes, will receive a minimum of domestic criticism to let it function abroad as representative of American capitalism. But no term has been made official. Rather, local USIA officers are allowed to describe the American economic system in any terms they feel are appropriate. The basic ideology called enterprise democracy by Larson has not, however, been repudiated by the USIA or the Administration.

The main purpose of the ideology is to produce something that both the two main political parties and the other major groups in this country can agree upon for use in portraying the United States to the world. Its basic outline, therefore, cannot be thought of as inherently Democratic or Republican. If such an identification should occur, enterprise democracy as an export ideology would lose its usefulness as a propaganda instrument.

Like the classical and managerial ideologies, enterprise democracy is backed by an organized group. The main difference is that its support comes from an agency of the government—the USIA which functions abroad as our propaganda instrument. The operation of the USIA is of tremendous scope but, even so, it is not always a match in size or strength for its Communist counterparts. Through the Voice of America, newspapers, magazines, cultural, educational, and scientific exhibits, motion pictures, and libraries, the USIA attempts to project America's image abroad. This may also explain why the enterprise democracy ideology is better known abroad than at home.

The ideology's adherence to reality is a matter of opinion. Since it offers no body of economic theory, as does the classical ideology of capitalism, the way in which the various groups work out their mutual interests is left quite vague. One must assume the presence of countervailing power, a vague answer in itself. What will prevent the government from going beyond the constraints set up by the concept of limited government is indefinite. One assumes that political pressures and traditions are the constraints.

In newer, developing countries the following of such a nebulous prototype as this would present serious problems. The essentially synthetic character of the enterprise democracy ideology—since it is an attempt to mesh a number of ideological strands from the classical, managerial, countervailing power, and people's capitalism creeds—creates a number of paradoxical, contradictory elements within the ideology. This, of course, is not uncommon in ideologies. There are, however, limits of tolerance as to how many opposing strains can be fitted within the frame of a single ideology and still leave it viable and appealing.

Many observers have commented on our demand that a greater amount of laissez-faire exist in nations receiving foreign aid than exists within our own country, and this attitude is occasionally apparent in our "export" ideologies. But as one studies the pressures under which the USIA must operate and the need to propagandize an ideology inoffensive to any Congressman or group apt to oppose its annual budget, it becomes clear that under our present system the United States cannot expect any other type of "export" ideology, no matter how unrealistic, that is not a compromise. This fact, of course, presents certain problems for effective propaganda. Since it must inevitably attempt to incur a minimum amount of criticism in Congress rather than focusing solely on presenting American capitalism effectively to other nations, our "export" ideology may seem somewhat unrealistic to the folks at home. Perhaps even more important, however, is the question whether it seems as strange to the folks abroad.

This short perusal of the various ideologies found within contemporary America suggests reasons why we commonly have difficulty defining our economic system and specifying what the role of government should be. Without some knowledge, however, of the prevalent ideologies of capitalism in our country, it is doubtful that the basic issues and arguments within our economy can be brought clearly into the open, as they must be.

Meanwhile, it may be worthwhile to remember that American capitalism is, in one way at least, a little like electricity: Nobody knows exactly what it is, but it works—and works well.

READING 26
The Unemployment-Inflation Problem

This study paper was prepared by the staff of a Cabinet Committee on Price Stability constituted by President Nixon to investigate the sources of inflation that cannot be attacked effectively through monetary or fiscal policy alone. The study paper focuses on factors which might shift the alleged inverse relationship between rates of inflation and the percentage of the labor force unemployed, commonly known as Phillips curves. It should be noted that the *U-I* limit curve shown in Figure 3 is essentially a Phillips relationship, while the curve M_I–M_U shows the acceptable tradeoff between inflation and unemployment. This latter curve is concave because as unemployment reaches low levels, more inflation is acceptable only if a relatively large decrease in unemployment can be traded for it, and as the rate of inflation reaches low levels higher unemployment is acceptable only if increasingly larger cuts in the rate of inflation can be traded for it.

Guideposts for Thought While Reading

What is the difference between micro and macro policies geared to attack the U-I dilemma? Why are micro policies necessary to solve what appears to be a macro question? How do expectations enter into the price-formation mechanism? What policies are recommended to reduce the conflict between the unemployment and inflation goals?

THE NATURE OF THE PROBLEM

Figure 1 registers the relationship between the percentage change in the Consumer Price Index (CPI) and the rate of unemployment for each year since 1960; it also shows the relationship between the percentage change in the industrial component of the Wholesale Price Index (WPI) and the rate of unemployment over the same period. Using the CPI and WPI as alternate

Reprinted from "The Unemployment-Inflation Problem?" Study Paper Number 4, Studies by the Staff of the Cabinet Committee on Price Stability, January 1969, pp. 125–151.

FIGURE 1 Price Level Changes and Unemployment Rates: 1960–1968

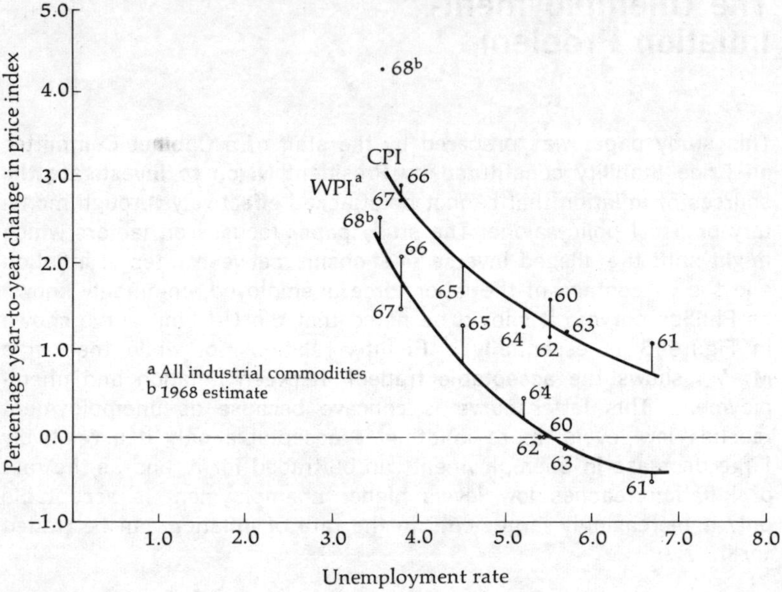

SOURCE: Department of Labor (Bureau of Labor Statistics)

measures of inflation, two curves are depicted; one relates percentage changes in CPI to the unemployment rate and the other similarly relates the WPI to unemployment.

Many observers have seen in this relationship the existence of an unemployment-inflation trade-off problem: Can we simultaneously achieve high employment and price stability or must we trade off higher rates of inflation for lower levels of unemployment? The fact, however, that price stability has not been achieved in the past with low unemployment rates does not imply the existence of an immutable relationship.

Unemployment and the price level are each influenced by a great many factors. The relationship between unemployment and the price level is neither simple nor direct. Because a low level of unemployment has been an important public objective, analytical attention has often focused on the overall unemployment rate as the proxy for a wide range of economic forces, e.g., general prosperity, the rate of utilization of economic resources, trends in wage rates and profits. The separate impact on the price level of these other economic characteristics has only recently begun to receive detailed study. The following analysis suggests a variety of public policies and private actions that can be expected not only to reduce the inflation problem without incurring higher unemployment rates, but also to lessen the uneven burden of unemployment among subgroups of the labor force without undue inflationary pressures.

This apparent inverse relationship between unemployment and inflation, associated with growth and high employment, has been variously called the unemployment-inflation dilemma and the Phillips curve. Technically, the Phillips curve refers to the relationship between the unemployment rate and the change in wages, a relationship in which unemployment is considered to be a major determinant of wage changes. Popular usage has also tagged the unemployment-inflation relationship as the Phillips curve, but we shall refer to it as the unemployment-inflation or U-I relationship.

Two important measures of a problem are a widespread recognition of its existence and the persistence and variety of attempts to solve it. By these measures, the unemployment-inflation relationship is a problem of the first magnitude. Every major free industrial nation has recognized the problem and has experimented with policies and institutions in attempts to cope with the problem.

Free societies, of course, pursue other economic goals besides high employment and price stability. These include an acceptable rate of economic growth, a balance of payments equilibrium, an equitable distribution of income, and free institutions.

Macro Economic Factors

Macro economic factors include such *broad* or *aggregative* phenomena as aggregate demand, employment, growth, and the general level of prices. Monetary and fiscal policies—our principal demand-related policies—are frequently called macro policies because they are attempts to influence these aggregate factors. For example, monetary policy, by easing credit and increasing the supply of money, and fiscal policy, by lowering taxes and increasing government expenditures, increase aggregate demand and decrease unemployment. These macro policies can differ in a wide array; for example, they can differ as to pace, purpose, timing, and chosen instrument.

Type and Mix of Policies

In addition to the usual distinction between monetary and fiscal policies, it is convenient to differentiate countercyclical, expansion, and growth policies. Countercyclical policies are essentially defensive or reactive; they are less concerned with sustaining growth or closing the GNP gap than that growth not get out of hand. Their drama is provided mainly by reactive and restrictive measures.

Expansion policies, on the other hand, attempt to expand actual GNP up to potential GNP, i.e., to close the GNP gap. In the same context, growth policies aim to stimulate the growth of potential GNP; consequently, expansion policies tend to be more demand oriented and growth policies more capacity oriented. Both, however, represent an affirmation to impart a direction to our economic development, reaching for higher utilization of men and equipment and for greater output. Their drama is provided mainly by stimulative measures.

There is no unique countercyclical, expansion, or growth policy. Each of these policies can be implemented by highly diversified mixes of policy instruments and timing. It is significant to the development of our U-I performance, for example, whether fiscal policy stresses taxes or expenditures, investment or consumption. And shifts in policy or changes in policy mix can cause a change in the composition of demand; this change, as we note later, can contribute to "sectoral" or "demand-shift" inflation. Macro policies can also be used to increase unemployment and decrease the rate of inflation. In fact, when designed to achieve price stability, such policies rely heavily on increasing unemployment and have an adverse effect on the short-run rate of growth.

Micro Economic Factors

Macro policies are essentially demand-related influences. They are, however, only a part of the U-I story; they are one blade of the scissors. Individual prices change because of demand-related and supply-related influences in their respective markets. The aggregate price level rises because price increases on individual items are not offset by decreases on other items. Macro policy affects demand in individual markets because of its impact generally on the evolution of aggregate demand and directly, through specific programs or expenditures, on the development of demand in particular markets. *Micro* economic factors include both supply-related and demand-related characteristics of *in-*

dividual product and labor markets. In the present context we emphasize those micro factors that operate essentially from the supply side; they influence reaction, in terms of price and output response, to changes in demand. These supply-related influences provide the second blade of the scissors.

If individual markets were perfect, they would adjust smoothly to changes in demand. Labor, material, and capital equipment would move readily to small changes in prices: labor would quickly acquire new skills; information generated by product and labor markets would be accurate and timely; buyers and sellers would be well informed; and markets would be competitive. If these conditions were characteristic of individual markets, macro policy could expand output and lower unemployment, maintaining stable prices, until the economy reached some hypothetical level of full employment. Expansion would encounter no resistance or assertive action from the supply side. At full employment, attempts to utilize additional, non-existent labor and equipment would dissipate in inflation (Figure 2A depicts a relevant U-I curve). Under these circumstances, the only impediment to the simultaneous achievement of full employment and price stability would be faulty macro policies. There would be no U-I problem.

Market conditions, however, are not perfect; they do not always effect smooth adjustments. Generally speaking, market imperfections are of three types: those associated with immobilities, inadequate information available to buyers and sellers, and discretionary power in product and labor markets. Before proceeding to a discussion of these imperfections, however, we shall try to conceptualize their significance.

Given a policy goal, we assume an optimum macro policy for any given set of micro conditions. These micro conditions will be limited to (1) the structures of particular markets and (2) the observed pattern of conduct by private decision-makers. Market structure consists of the mobility, information, and competitive characteristics of individual markets. Both structure and observed conduct reflect a given set of micro policies, as enforced. The given set of supply-related influences will change, therefore, if any of these four factors change: market structure, observed conduct, micro policies, or their enforcement.

These given micro factors provide resistance to or assert themselves against macro policy as it directs or conditions the private decision-making sector. As the optimum macro policy reduces unemployment, these supply-related and demand-related forces interact. As a result, a U-I curve unfolds that represents the best U-I performance that macro policy, given the micro conditions, can achieve. We shall call this curve the U-I limit or the macro boundary; macro policy, given the structure and conduct characteristics of individual markets, cannot penetrate the line and achieve U-I combinations which lie below it (See Figure 2B).

The inflation represented by the macro boundary is what has usually been called supply inflation. It can be the result of involuntary and defensive response or of aggressive and assertive behavior in the private sector. This type of inflation or variants of it have been called: nondemand, seller's, cost-push, cost, premature, administered, etc.

Any U-I combination above the limit is possible. Given the micro set, such combinations would result from inappropriate or faulty macro policy. For example, macro policy that pushed too rapidly against supply resistance would record U-I combinations above the boundary. Such inflation would be both supply and demand inflation; demand inflation would be measured up from the U-I limit. This has also been called demand-pull inflation.

The macro boundary can be shifted up or down by private or public decisions. Increased militance by labor or management in their reach for income gains greater than productivity increases will shift the boundary up. On the other hand, behavior that conformed to the wage-price guideposts would shift the limit down. Changes or innovations in government micro policies that affected structure or conduct would also change the U-I limit.

FIGURE 2-A U-I Curve: Perfect Market Conditions

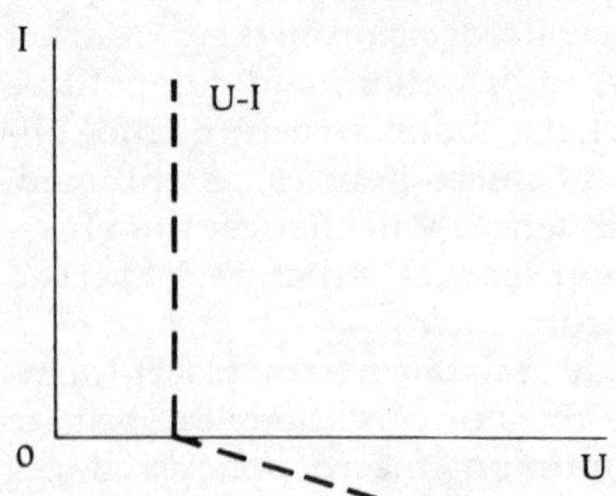

FIGURE 2-B U-I Curve: Imperfect Market Conditions

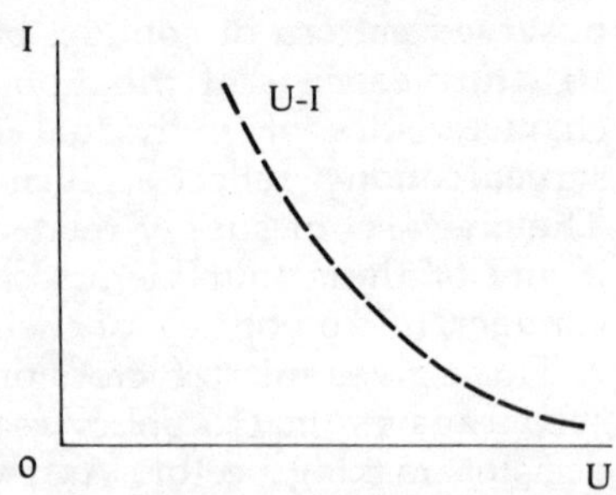

In short, our quest for a suitable U-I performance must involve not only an appropriate macro policy but also micro policies that can effectively alter market structure and conduct. These micro policies are attempts to make market conditions more nearly perfect: to enable labor and capital to be more mobile, to improve information, and to reduce or influence discretionary power in product and labor markets.

Immobilities

The distribution of labor and output shifts among industries in response to changes in relative wages and prices. If supplies of labor, material, and capital equipment do not react to small changes in price, then larger price increases are necessary to overcome immobilities or to increase supplies. Alternatively, materials and equipment whose supplies are sluggishly adapted to change or labor that is slow to acquire new skills can cause significant levels of excess capacity or unemployment to persist at relatively high rates of inflation. Furthermore, the impact of these market imperfections on prices is aggravated when demand surges against such immobilities and rigidities; a more deliberate expansion of demand would generate less upward pressure on prices.

Price rigidity: The ability to maintain price against excess capacity has particular relevance to the question of inflation. This type of discretionary power differs among industries just as does the power to exploit a discretionary markup; and the latter need not always be associated to the same degree with the former. Uncertainty which results from an oligopolist's recognition of mutual interdependence with other large firms in the industry, causes him to be hesitant toward changing prices in the face of changed demand and supply conditions. Prices become particularly sticky on the downward side. The discretionary ability to maintain prices contributes to inflation by enabling firms to prevent prices from falling despite the existence of excess capacity necessary to effect deflation. Such power gives rise to what has been called "demand-shift" or "sectoral" inflation and is an important element in the ratchet mechanism by which our economy resists downward pressure on prices and wages.

Assume a two sector economy. If inflation is to be avoided and if prices in sector A rise because of a shift in demand to sector A, prices must fall in sector B. If the monetary authorities refuse to expand the money supply and thereby refuse both to validate the price increase in A and to stabilize prices in B, the shift of demand away from B will cause prices to fall in the latter. However, if firms in sector B possess the power to stabilize prices against excess capacity, they can decide to maintain their prices and accept the resulting unemployment and excess capacity. The refusal of the monetary authorities to validate will have resulted in inflation, unemployment, and excess capacity rather than the desired price stability. And if the authorities validate by expanding the money supply, unemployment and excess capacity will probably decline less but prices will rise more.

The resistance of prices and wages to downward pressures constitutes one of the toughest problems confronting achievement of an effective stabilization policy. One of the difficulties is the simple matter of identification. Rising prices can be seen; prices that should have fallen are not as obvious. If the competitive forces of individual markets cannot effect warranted price reductions, other sanctions must be used if inflation is to be avoided.

It has also been argued that this power to maintain prices can temporarily retard the manifestations of inflationary pressures. During a recovery period, an industry whose firms possess such discretion will record relatively stable prices as long as it is experiencing excess capacity and no significant increases in industry-wide costs. Rising prices, however, can be expected when such a cost increase occurs or when excess capacity gives way to excess demand, and in the absence of special considerations such as the fear of market losses to a cheaper substitute.

Discretionary Power in Labor Market

Although corporations hire individual workers, labor is not sold by unions. Unions negotiate jointly with management to establish the rules within which individuals are hired, rewarded, and disciplined. This joint negotiation is collective bargaining. Collective bargaining is not a simple, impersonal exchange relationship; it is essentially a political relationship designed to achieve certain economic consequences.

Collective bargaining is a rule-making process from which derives a system of industrial jurisprudence that regulates the ongoing relationship between labor and management. The continuity of this relationship and the conflicts that arise out of it have values that weigh heavily at the bargaining table. Although the interests that initiate the relationship may be economic in nature, this is no assurance that the considerations that determine the rules negotiated at the table are predominately economic. Collective bargaining reflects a clash of values as well as a clash of economic interests. Collective bargaining involves the distribution of power within the production process as well as the distribution of income generated by that process. In short, the relationship of a union to an employer is not simply that of another supplier of productive factors.

The above is by way of explaining that the nature of and limitations upon the market power of organized labor are complex and not well understood. For present purposes, it is probably sufficient to postulate that, in a particular bargaining situation, product and labor market forces combine to determine a range within which labor and management can contend until, through negotiation that involves both economic and non-economic considerations, an agreement is reached. In this private decision-making process that resolves economic and political issues, both labor and management usually possess discretionary power; therefore, attitudes and goals of the parties, as well as relative power, are instrumental in determining the terms of the agreement.

Considerations germane to collective bargaining on economic issues would undoubtedly include: acceptable standard of living, living cost changes, wage comparability, ability to pay, productivity, and effect of settlement on inflation and employment. There seems to be some agreement that the three considerations of greatest significance in the outcome of a negotiation are: living cost changes, wage comparability, and ability to pay. It is noteworthy that two of these three significant considerations—changes in living costs and wage comparability—are reactions to events outside the scope of the industry directly involved. In this sense, they represent a defensive reaction to events beyond the control of the unions or of the particular bargaining relationships. They also provide a mechanism by which inflationary pressures can be diffused and thereby become cumulative.

The ability to pay can be measured by the ability and willingness of management to resist demands based on living cost changes and comparability. This resistance tends to be low where management possesses appreciable discretionary power; the unusually large profits allowed such firms by the market attract and enlarge labor's demands, and the power to pass through cost increases reduces resistance. Productivity is given short shrift. In brief, discretionary power to *demand* and to *grant* wage increases in excess of average productivity gains can give an upward thrust to the price level. The ability to pay can also be easily pushed over into an attempt to effect an income shift. Unfortunately, attempts to shift income by demanding wage increases in excess of productivity increases, without effective constraints on product price increases, are also inflationary.

Discretionary power possessed by union leaders at the bargaining table is influenced not only by forces derived from the relevant product and labor markets but also by pressures generated by political relationships internal to the union. Pressures from the rank-and-file, implemented by internal union democracy, are in many instances a powerful constraint upon leadership; they are, however, unfortunately a constraint that rarely induces leadership to make a more "responsible" settlement. Given the relevant laws and the nature of the organizations, union leaders must be more responsive to their membership than corporate management must be to stockholders. And union members, witnesses to obvious asset inflation, fearful of an adverse income shift, and suspicious of their tax burden, seek theirs at the bargaining table.

Expectations and Discretionary Power

The role of expectations gives an additional dynamic quality to the interaction of discretionary power as exercised by labor and management representatives. The result is what might be called a consensual explanation of the wage-price spiral, although it also depends upon the possession of discretionary power by both labor and management.

According to this view, collective bargaining contains a conventional element: a consensus of expectations that parties bring to the table. This consensus is shaped by such events as a conspicuous settlement, recent price movements (including increases in the competitive sector), implicit or explicit action by the government, statements by influential private parties, etc. These events, of course, are not a grin without a cat; they reflect the accelerating realities of the imperfect market conditions that underlie the U-I curve. As E. H. Phelps Brown observed:

> Once formed, it (consensus on a wage and price rise) tends to realize itself. Any one party to a negotiation feels himself no longer a free agent but impelled by all around him. No one is conscious of pushing out in front; the union is only struggling to overtake arrears, the employer cannot afford to be left behind. To resist a claim for the expected amount will be costly and ultimately futile, to grant it will

prove harmless because the others will be granting it too. The same spontaneous collusion permits the subsequent price rises that enable higher costs to be borne without squeezing profit margins. A tacit combination thus develops the capacity for self-propulsion.

Such "tacit" combinations of labor and management, reflecting a change in the shared consensus of expectations, change the micro conditions that determine the macro boundary. The boundary shifts up and, unless macro policies are changed, a less desirable U-I performance results.

GOALS IN CONFLICT

Implicit in the unemployment-inflation dilemma is the proposition that full employment and price stability, as goals, are in conflict. They are, however, not in effective conflict unless there is no desirable combination of the two that can be achieved under existing circumstances. In Figure 3, it is assumed that M_I is the maximum rate of inflation that will be tolerated by whatever constitutes the effective decision-making group. This rate is associated with zero unemployment because, presumably, higher rates of unemployment have to be compensated for by lower rates of inflation. Similarly, M_U represents the maximum tolerable rate of unemployment and is associated with complete price stability. M_U and M_I can be connected by a curved line that

FIGURE 3 U-I Limit and Acceptable U-I Combinations

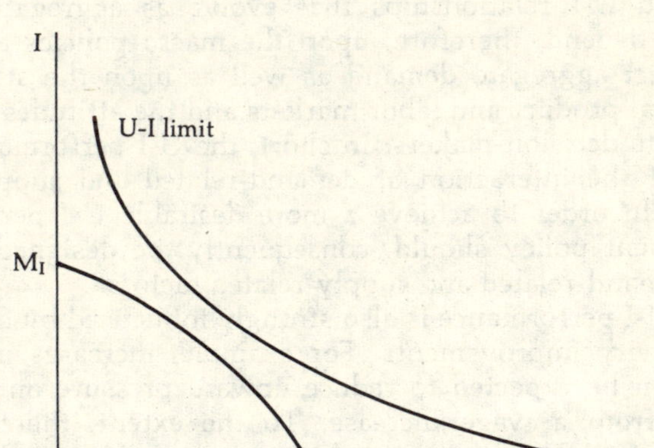

reflects the maximum tolerable rate of inflation for every rate of unemployment up to M_U and vice versa. In short, all U-I points located on or within the M_IM_U curve are acceptable; each point represents a combination of an acceptable rate of inflation and an acceptable rate of unemployment. Not all points inside the curve, however, are equally desirable.

If the U-I limit curve neither touches nor intersects M_IM_U, the goals of full employment and price stability are in effective conflict. A tolerable rate of unemployment must be paid for by an unacceptable rate of inflation. And the opposite holds. If, on the other hand, the macro boundary intersects the M_IM_U curve, an acceptable rate of unemployment can be combined with an acceptable rate of inflation. Although a trade-off must still be made between a lower rate of inflation or a lower rate of unemployment, there is no effective conflict in the sense that one of the choices in the trade-off must be unacceptable. Experience, both ours and that of other free industrial nations, suggests that high employment and price stability are in effective conflict. Nevertheless, this analysis argues that an appropriate mix of micro stabilization policies can shift the macro boundary down so that the two goals are no longer in such conflict.

POLICY CONSIDERATIONS

Relevant policies derive from the identification of the problem. In our view, U-I performance is strongly influenced by aggregate demand as it is distributed over particular supply conditions. Observed U-I relationships that evolve as aggregate demand changes depend, therefore, upon the macro policies and forces that affect aggregate demand as well as upon the structure of individual product and labor markets and the attitudes and goals of private decision-makers. In short, the U-I performance is the result of the interaction of demand-related and supply-related factors. In order to achieve a more desirable U-I performance, government policy should, consequently, be designed to affect both demand-related and supply-related factors.

The U-I performance is also strongly influenced by the pace of productivity improvements. For example, increases in productivity can be expected to reduce upward pressure on prices resulting from a wage increase. To the extent, therefore, that wages rise with decreases in the unemployment rate, we should expect productivity increases to reduce the rate of inflation at given rates of unemployment.

Productivity is an extraordinarily complex measure of performance. Simplistically, we can distinguish between changes in productivity that result from changes in the rate at which capital equipment is utilized and from longer run improvements in the capital plant itself. As the economy expands—actual GNP approaching potential GNP—productivity increases up to some point principally because fixed costs are being spread over a larger output. Such productivity increases can reduce the inflationary impact of wage increases during the period of expansion. However, as the gap closes, increases in productivity from this source may tend to level off or decrease significantly; consequently, at this time wage increases begin to press more directly upon profits and prices. Accordingly, productivity changes that are a function of the rate at which existing capital equipment is utilized cannot be relied upon to reduce inflationary pressures as the rate of unemployment declines and industry capacity becomes fully utilized.

Productivity can also increase because of the introduction of improved capital equipment. This is a long-run source of productivity improvement and can be expected to moderate inflationary pressures at low rates of unemployment. Other sources of long-run productivity improvement include improvements in the quality of the labor force, shifts of labor and capital from less productive use to more productive use in response to enduring shifts of demand, and increases in the stock of capital. As the GNP gap closes and we shift from expansion to growth, we must rely on these long-run types of productivity improvements if stability is to accompany growth.

Macro Policies

The first step in pursuit of a better U-I performance is the adoption of appropriate monetary and fiscal policies. Even an optimum mix of such policies, however, cannot assure an acceptable U-I relationship because of the resistance and assertive action of those product and labor markets that are relatively inefficient and imperfect. The second step, therefore, is the development and application of micro stabilization policies that are designed to make markets function more efficiently and less imperfectly.

Micro Stabilization Policies

Micro stabilization policies are complementary to macro policies. In general, they are attempts to increase mobility, to improve information, and to reduce or influence the exercise of discretionary power and, thereby, to improve the U-I performance. The general outline of such policies can be observed in existing legislation and governmental action. They can affect both demand and supply conditions of individual markets. Manpower programs, for example, function as both demand-related and supply-related policies. Manpower employment programs—in contrast to supply-related training programs—are demand-related; work experience and public service employment programs reduce unemployment among selected subgroups of the labor force experiencing comparatively high unemployment rates. The Nation has not yet developed an efficient and effective set of micro stabilization policies. Much innovation, experimentation, and coordination remain to be done.

At present, four basic micro stabilization policies are operative in the United States. Manpower policies, competition and international trade policies, a guidepost or incomes policy, and the consumer information program. Although in their present form these policies and programs do not constitute an adequate and coordinated micro policy set, they provide a foundation upon which effective micro stabilization policies can be built.

Competition and wage-price guidepost policies are complementary in product markets characterized by discretionary power. Competition policy, through antitrust action on the structure and conduct of industry, attempts to narrow the range of prices within which private parties exercise their discretion. Guidepost policy, in seeking to influence the exercise of discretion, introduces the national interest as an important criterion in labor and management decisions. These policies are complementary in product markets because each seeks to influence the exercise of discretionary power; competition policy by reducing it and voluntary restraint policies by influencing its exercise.

A different relationship of complementarity exists in labor markets between manpower and guidepost policies than exists between competition and guidepost policies in product markets. In the latter instance, the exercise of discretionary power is the objective of both policies. Guidepost policies function similarly as attempts to influence the discretionary power of labor and management at the collective bargaining table. Manpower programs, on the other hand, attempt to facilitate the supply adjustment process of labor markets whether or not they are characterized by discretionary power. More often, however, they function to improve the supply adjustment process; market inefficiencies and frictions, not discretionary power, are involved.

The manifold activities of the Federal Government have

significant impact on many individual prices. Some prices are directly regulated by the Government; others are indirectly regulated. For many goods and services the Government is the only or, at least, the dominant buyer. In other cases it provides the funds to finance purchases by others. To the extent possible, efforts by the Government to minimize the inflationary impact of these many direct and indirect purchases as well as the inflationary impact of price changes for which the Government has singular responsibility (e.g., regulated industries and relevant agricultural programs) would aid in our pursuit of a better U-I performance.

READING 27
Ownership and Management: The Effect of Separation on Performance

R. Joseph Monsen

The corporate form of organization is predominant in the American business scene. Although outnumbered by the multitude of small proprietorships, the giant corporation is responsible for the bulk of the nation's business. The loss of direct control of business organizations by their owners may have ramifications for the allocation of resources and the distribution of wealth in the United States. In order to probe this question more deeply, Professor R. Joseph Monsen of the College of Business at the University of Washington has carried out an empirical investigation of the performance of corporations which are under the control of their owners and those that are effectively controlled by hired managers. The results of this study given in this reading show that important changes occur when ownership is separated from control of the business firm.

Guideposts for Thought While Reading

In terms of the welfare of society, why, according to Monsen, is the owner-controlled firm preferable to the manager-controlled firm? Given current trends toward manager control, what government policies might be suggested by the results of this study?

The separation of ownership from control in the large corporation has been recognized for many years. What has not been understood, however, is the effect of such separation on the performance of the firm. Evidence now indicates that large owner-controlled companies outperform manager-controlled ones in terms of return on investment by a significant degree.

A few economists in the past, including the author, have suggested that the separation of ownership from control of the corporation creates a quite different motivation between owners and managers. Such difference in motivation may be ascribed to goal conflict of owners and managers that exists in our modern economic system because of the asymmetry between risks and rewards. This asymmetry appears to take the form of greater incentives and rewards for owners than managers in terms of risk-taking. Since recent research has suggested that motivation has far greater consequences upon economic efficiency than economists or others have commonly supposed, differences in goals and motivations between owner-managers and nonowner managers may indeed explain the differential performance between the owner- and manager-controlled companies.

If owners and managers are motivated differently, do these differences affect corporate policy? In other words, we may ask whether owner- and manager-controlled companies are basically different in terms of goals, outlook, and policies, or are differentiated only because owner-controlled firms try harder to produce a higher rate of return on their investment? The research cited offers inconclusive proof on this point. However, some recent evidence suggests that there are very basic policy differences between owner-controlled and manager-controlled companies—beyond mere return. The author has assembled data which show that dividend policies are very different between the two types of companies. It now appears that manager-controlled firms tend to have higher earnings/pay-out ratios than firms controlled by their owners. While the industry in which the firm is located has a significant effect upon its dividend pay-out, the type of control appears to be even more significant in explaining the difference in dividend policy.

Such differences appear quite understandable if we look at the goals and incentives of both owners and managers. Due to the tax differential between capital gains and dividend income, a preference for a smaller dividend pay-out and greater earnings retention is a reasonable policy for a company controlled by a wealthy owner-manager. Further, there are noneconomic reasons (desire to rule a financial empire or continuance of family name or tradition) that can supply other explanations as to why an owner-managed firm would prefer to finance itself through high retained earnings rather than risk loss of control by participating extensively in outside capital markets.

Thus it appears that overt policy decisions, such as dividend pay-out, are influenced significantly by what type of manager controls the company. Differences between these two types of firms in both performance and policy suggest that fundamentally there are quite separate goals and motivations at work for owners and managers. Such differences in outlook result in distinctly different behavior patterns between the two types of firms.

If we admit such differences do in fact exist, what are the implications? A number of questions come to mind.

Is motivation really the crux of the issue? Is motivation sufficiently crucial for efficiency that it affects the firm as strongly as our data suggest?

Are professional managers themselves merely less proficient than the owner-managers in large firms? Are business schools training professional but inefficient managers? Could this account for the difference in performance and behavior we observed?

Would different compensation schemes for management alter their behavior and goals? If so, what kind of a system could be devised that might be successful?

Most critically for the economy, are current tax policies eliminating the most efficient firms, forcing them to merge with and become manager controlled? Is profit becoming less important to the largest corporations?

If owner-controlled firms are more efficient in terms of return on investment, are manager-controlled firms more responsive to the demands of workers, consumers, and government? Which is better?

These questions will be explored briefly after we have examined in more detail several of the studies mentioned above.

SUMMARY OF RESULTS

In an attempt to shed some light on the behavior of owner-controlled and manager-controlled large firms, 72 corporations were studied from *Fortune*'s list of the 500 largest industrial firms by sales in this country for a twelve-year period (1952–63). Six firms (three owner-controlled and three manager-controlled) from twelve different industries were compared. A firm was considered owner-controlled if 10 percent or more of the corporation stock was owned by one party. An analysis of the data revealed that the owner-controlled group of firms outperformed the manager-controlled firms by a considerable margin. The net income to net worth ratio was 75 percent higher for owner-controlled corporations over the twelve-year period. This indicates that these firms provide a much better return on the original investment, and suggests a better-managed capital structure and more efficient allocation of resources.

The effect of the type of industry on the net income to net worth ratio was statistically significant but only one-third the strength of the control-type effect; the size of the firm was not a significant factor. No other effect, including the control plus industry interaction, was statistically significant, indicating that *the owner- or manager-control factor affects all industries tested.*

In an attempt to look at policy differences, particularly dividend policy, 69 owner- and manager-controlled firms were studied from among the 200 largest nonfinancial corporations in this country. Again, owner control was defined as a minimum of 10 percent stock ownership in the corporation by one party, and firms of roughly the same size and same industry were compared. Utilizing an analysis of variance statistical technique, as in the first study, the results were once again quite clear. The type of industrial classification to which a firm belonged did influence the firm's dividend pay-out ratio. However, the ownership type of the company had an even stronger effect, statistically, upon the dividend policy than the type of industry to which the firm belonged. Further, no evidence was found that industry interaction with ownership type produces special effects upon dividend pay-out ratios. Thus, the evidence supports the existence of distinct dividend pay-out policies between owner-controlled and manager-controlled firms of approximately similar size in the same industry.

These two studies support the idea that the type of control strongly affects both the performance and the policy decisions of a company. In this sense, the traditional economic approach addressing firms from this aspect as simply one aggregate of behavior is seriously oversimplified.

Why, in the first study, should the owner-controlled firms outperform the manager-controlled firms? And why, in the second study, should the two types have very different and distinct dividend policies? The answer that seems most convincing is that two quite different motivational incentive systems are at work, emanating from the pursuit of different goals. It would seem that our business system is not generally structured to provide the same set of motivations or goals for both owners and managers. As a result, the behavior of our largest firms differs widely depending upon what group controls them.

SOME PRACTICAL IMPLICATIONS

Motivation

In the past, economists have tended to ignore the effect of motivation upon economic activity. Only recently have some studies been made which yield evidence that motivation is considerably more important in influencing efficiency in the economy as a whole than economists traditionally have believed. Thus, the effect of the modern separation of ownership from management may have a motivational impact upon the performance of the firm—perhaps of greater consequence than allocative efficiency, which has been the main concern of past economic efficiency studies.

If motivation does have a significant effect upon the performance of the firm, what factors influence motivation? Does the separation of ownership and control in most large corporations have an effect upon motivation of management? Does such motivational difference, if it exists, between owners and managers affect the behavior of the firm? The data of the studies we have cited here certainly do suggest that owner- and manager-controlled firms behave differently. The differences in goals and motivations that we have posited seem the most plausible explanation. However, while the differences in behavior of the two types of firms can be observed empirically, our motivational explanation, sound as it may seem, is not definitely established. We can in final analysis only suggest explanations that seem consistent with the data.

While traditional economic theory recognizes only one motive for firm management—to maximize profit—economic theorists have recently suggested that the large firm attempts to maximize sales, growth, or the management's own lifetime income. In fact, different types of firms may pursue one or a combination of these and other goals, and in the real world the owner-controlled firm appears more likely to fit the picture of the world painted by traditional economic theory. Distinguishing between types of firms is important because the behavior of each firm with respect to profits depends upon certain elements of its internal structure.

The professional manager, unlike the owner-manager, is probably more responsive to pressures from the various constituent groups of the firm such as workers, consumers, suppliers, or stockholders, and the government. The professional manager is apt to respond to conflicting demands from these groups by balancing one off against the other or by utilizing compromise as an issue-settling device. The owner-manager, who views each dollar given to workers, suppliers, consumers, or the government as coming from his own pocket, is less likely to compromise. Further, the position of the owner-manager is a good deal more secure regarding his tenure in office than that of the professional manager. For, although professional management is generally autonomous in the large corporation, an executive may be sidetracked or replaced if he makes a bad blunder. The owner-manager, because of his stock ownership, seldom faces this problem. The risk and reward system for owners and managers is therefore quite different.

Because of these basic differences in the security and financial reward of their respective positions, the strategy to maximize the income of an owner-manager may be considerably different from that of a nonowner manager. Given the same goal, to maximize their wealth, the strategy, policies, and performance of the firm would probably be quite different depending on whether the company was owner- or manager-controlled.

Further study may reveal that there are also differences in behavior between various subtypes of owner- and manager-controlled firms. Mutually owned corporations are a specific category needing further research, for they appear to form a quite distinct category of their own. All told, if motivation is a major factor influencing firm behavior, we could hypothesize that wherever the motivations of corporate leadership patterns have a distinct character, firm behavior should reflect that fact. Finally, if motivations and behavior are different between groups of firms, should this cause any change in current tax or antitrust policies to either encourage or discourage certain forms of economic behavior?

The studies discussed here offer empirical evidence that the separation of ownership from control has indeed produced different and distinct types of economic behavior. Both performance and policy differences are observable. Large owner-controlled firms in the same industry have much higher rates of return on investment and lower dividend pay-outs than manager-controlled firms. The first finding may or may not be the result of conscious policy; nonetheless, the performance differential is certainly there. The finding on dividend pay-out is the conscious result of policy decisions.

Our observation that the owner-controlled firm is more efficient but is gradually being eliminated was suggested by both Berle and Means in their original study nearly forty years ago and confirmed by Larner's recent one. Since this is a problem of both private and public concern, it should be investigated to see if the public policy which encourages it should be changed.

At the very least, managers, directors, investors, and government officials should give immediate attention to the reasons why owner-controlled firms have higher rates of return than comparable manager-controlled firms. There may be considerable opportunities for increasing the rate of return in manager-controlled companies. Managers and directors can hardly ignore this challenge to their internal operations, and government officials should not let this opportunity pass to investigate a neglected area of significance for public policy. Could a case be made that manager-controlled firms should be constrained from acquiring owner-controlled ones? What would be the total effect upon our economy and society? The relative social responsiveness of the two types of firms could settle argument as to whether large owner-controlled firms should be gradually eliminated from our economy as present public policy encourages.

The main justification for the present public policy is either (1) that redistribution of economic power is encouraged by permitting managers to replace owners in controlling our largest firms, or (2) that manager-controlled firms have a higher social worth to society in some way, perhaps in greater social responsiveness to environmental problems. As we have said, the latter has yet to be established. Thus, this whole area of public policy needs investigation. It may well be that drastic changes in our taxation and antitrust laws need to be made. It is time, as well, that directors and management looked into their own motivation to determine what goals they are attempting to achieve and in what order of preference. The data here certainly cast suspicion on the assumption that manager-controlled firms are placing return on investment as their prime goal. If they are, they are inexplicably less efficient in pursuing this goal than the owner-controlled firms. It would seem more likely at this stage of investigation to posit motivational and goal differences between owner- and manager-controlled firms as the critical factors in influencing their performance and policies.

We can only hope that the studies cited here will create greater concern and further research. Both public and corporate policy may be badly in need of overhauling—how and where is the next question.

PART 4
Domestic Economic Issues

READING 28
Galbraith, Solow, and the Truth About Corporations

Robin Marris

Dr. Marris teaches economics at King's College, Cambridge, England, and is the author of *The Economic Theory of "Managerial" Capitalism* which was referred to by Professors Solow and Galbraith in papers to which this comment pertains. Marris envisages the giant corporation as effectively directed by management toward its goal of growth rather than maximum profits. Growth is constrained by the ability of the firm to create demand and simultaneously finance growth of capacity, and profits are just sufficient to allow growth of sales—but high enough to finance the major share of expenses incurred to increase capacity.

Guideposts for Thought While Reading

What arguments does Marris present against advertising? Why does he argue that consumers' sovereignty is a myth? Why should giant corporations seek goals other than maximum profits? How does Marris differ from Galbraith in his conclusions and policy recommendations? Marris argues that subsidies to promote low-income housing could be smaller for "managerial capitalism" than for a profit-oriented firm. Why?

I have volunteered to intervene in the Solow-Galbraith controversy, which began in the Fall issue of this journal, because I have some doubts whether, at the end of the day, the lay reader was left clear about the basic issues. As will become apparent, however, I am politically biased in favor of Galbraith and will probably be unfair to Solow.

It is true that Galbraith relies largely on assertion (or, shall we say, on persuasive writing) in contrast to large-scale evidence to make his case—especially his case about advertising. It is also true that, by a great deal of hard work and by painstaking de-

Reprinted by permission of the publisher from Robin Marris, "Galbraith, Solow, and the Truth About Corporations," *The Public Interest*, Spring 1968, pp. 37–46. Copyright by National Affairs, Inc., 1968.

velopment of mathematical and statistical methods, economists over the last twenty years have learned to work more scientifically. But, for reasons which seem to be as much cultural as technical, the leading exponents of the new methods have chosen largely to confine themselves within the framework of the traditional assumptions. The form of their experiments has tended to preclude answering many of the questions here in debate. The influence of advertising, for example, has not been tested, but when the question arises it is customary to say that the traditional framework, now endowed with statistical flesh, provides a reasonable explanation of observed behavior, so that it is probably unnecessary to worry about Madison Avenue. If asked for a further opinion, exponents of this school usually themselves resort to assertions: specifically, they assert that the effects of large-scale advertising largely cancel themselves out, leaving the broad pattern of consumer expenditure undisturbed. Solow's review of Galbraith followed this line of argument almost precisely.

THE QUESTION OF ADVERTISING

The statistical studies which are said to support the argument are not referred to in detail. But I think I know the literature Solow has in mind (even if Galbraith does not!), and I would suggest that, when it is carefully examined, the implications change considerably. When econometric studies look at the problem from the producers' side (i.e., when they test the hypothesis that variations in selling prices and profits can be explained, in Solow's words, by "supply and demand"), the results in fact leave a great deal of variation unexplained. When they start from the consumer end, they succeed in explaining a good deal of the observed variations in demand for individual commodities only by introducing factors other than conventional economic variables. These other factors, however, are not directly observable; they have to be inferred from the statistical results[1] and described as the trend of tastes, rate of habit formation, reaction to existing stocks of consumer durables, and so on. It is by no means unlikely that advertising has significant net effects on the strength of these relationships. But at present we cannot say whether this is so or not, because, after a quarter-

[1] I should make it clear that like most of my colleagues I regard these methods as not only valid, but often brilliantly conceived.

century during which advertising has become one of the outstanding features of our economic life, and scientific economics has been intensively developed, the relevant experiments have never been tried.

There is substantial technical justification for the situation, since the experiments required would stretch our capacity for rigorous testing to the limit. On the other hand, if the great majority of applied economists in this country are really so sure that they already know the answer, i.e., they are sure that most advertising results in a stand-off, the profession has clearly been guilty of a grave dereliction of duty to the public. They should have been shouting loudly and with one voice, "Here is an activity that has no significant net economic effect, good or bad; it is a total waste; it should be prohibited like arson." The discussion would then be thrown back into the sociological arena. I personally regard the cultural effects of advertising as debasing to language, to truth, and to logic, and as especially despicable because advertising is known to be most effective where the consumer has the least capacity to obtain the information necessary to evaluate products. There are sociologists who argue that the modern style of advertising (especially television) has a function in integrating the working class into the mass society and that the less well-educated obtain satisfaction from being wooed by advertisers. It is true that it is mostly the educated who scoff at advertising. We know from British experience that the working class positively prefers commercial programs and that BBC's audience is largely confined to the better educated. On the other hand, one has to count the cost of the recent effects in the United States of parading television commercials before people living in squalid conditions who can see no hope of buying many of the goods displayed. These are sorts of questions which economists have not equipped themselves to judge, and here I would align myself with Galbraith (in his rejoinder) in a plea for the broadening of both economics and sociology.

THE MYTH OF "CONSUMERS' SOVEREIGNTY"

This said, I must confess that the picture which, in my book, I drew in support of my own theory was more complex than Galbraith's and put considerably less emphasis on the effects of advertising as such. The picture was not strictly confirmed by "hard" evidence, although it is considerably supported by evidence drawn from the work of sociologists and market researchers. I saw the process by which consumer tastes develop as a complicated interaction of personal influence (meaning the influence of consumers on other consumers), greatly helped at critical points by advertising and marketing efforts generally. Sociologists have shown, in rather carefully designed experiments, that consumption decisions are effectly influenced, on the one hand, by a variety of advertising media and, on the other, by the recommendations of other persons known to the individual consumer. Each factor—advertising and personal recommendation—is responsible, very broadly, for about an equal share of the total result. The experiments cannot contribute directly to the present controversy, because they relate to decisions between alternative brands of the same product at given prices; but they remain suggestive.

The implications for the "affluent society" thesis, and for economic theory, are also clear. A complex, dynamic, socioeconomic system of this kind must be considered to be something like a biological phenomenon. Chance constellations of small individual factors at a particular time can have a considerable influence on the future direction of a plant's development. The needs, interests, and performance of producers are a particularly potent example of such influence, and one way of reading Galbraith is to take "advertising" as a portmanteau word for all these kinds of effects. In any event, once we accept this kind of picture, the notion of "consumers' sovereignty" becomes vague, to say the least, and we are provided with a virtually complete justification for a wide range of political action to impose social value judgments in the direction of consumption patterns. Here, quite likely, Solow would want to raise his hand and say, "I do not disagree." But the fact remains that the notion of consumers' sovereignty, essentially an *economic* theory, retains very considerable political force in defense of the status quo. Anyone who doubts the close political relationship should take a look at an advertisement in the January 1968 issue of *Fortune* magazine,[2] paid for by the Magazine Publishers' Association. This advertisement pointed to the alleged relative economic failure of East Germany, as compared with West Germany, in a defense of the activity of United States mass media in fostering demand for a wide range of, and variety among, individual consumers' goods (using the example of

[2] Page 228. Ironically the issue was devoted to the United States Urban Crisis.

stuffed olives). A dramatic juxtaposition of a representation of the Berlin Wall was clearly intended to create a mental association between political repression and government intervention in the pattern of consumption.

THE LARGE CORPORATION

The other basic issue between Galbraith and Solow concerned the role of the large corporations. Of course it is true that important sectors of the American economy are still traditionally organized. Supermarkets were an important social innovation, and still more important was the discovery that they can be operated successfully by quite small businesses. But does Solow or anyone else *really* believe that these small-business sectors have a significant influence on the speed and pattern of economic development? The drive of our system comes manifestly from the large-scale sector, now increasingly including the government as well as the large "profit-making" corporations.

And there is a major exception that marvelously tests the rule. The temporary visitor to this country cannot help being impressed by the apparently general dissatisfaction with the economic and social performance in the field of urban development, dissatisfaction which ranges from the fact of the existence of slums (and the associated difficulty in providing low-cost housing) to the more general question of the adequacy of city planning, the development of the suburbs, and so on. From overseas, the United States appears so prosperous that the "urban" problem is widely assumed to be no more than a euphemism for the race problem. But is it a coincidence that the production sector most closely concerned (namely the construction industries and the real estate business) happens to represent the most prominent exception to the rule of "managerial" capitalism? In this sector, medium-scale organization is typical, and large-scale organizations are usually owned by traditional capitalists. In particular, the free market in urban land (which is at the bed of this whole sea of troubles) displays one of the purest forms of traditional capitalism still surviving. And the cream of the joke is that most qualified observers of the scene other than economists are asking that the great managerial corporations come to the rescue.

Galbraith, on the other hand, thinks that the "Technostructure" cannot or will not undertake the task, because its performance would lack technical virtuosity. I am not convinced.

Although put across with characteristic force, the argument is not in fact very strong. There is not firm evidence that, if money were provided for massive urban projects on a scale comparable with current military and space programs, opportunities for exercising technical virtuosity would not be found or would be rejected, especially if the new programs made liberal use of such labels as "Componentization Research" and "Systems Analysis." Galbraith's later argument (in his chapter on the Cold War), that one reason why this kind of money is not in practice available is the indirect political (and indirectly bellicose) influence of the existing Technostructure, is much more convincing, but was not referred to by Solow.

THE REAL WORLD OF THE FIRM

When we reach the core of the debate—i.e., the economic theory of corporate behavior—the truth is that Solow was disingenuous, but that Galbraith had left out vital elements and laid himself open to legitimate attack. What Solow omitted to tell was that my theory implies that *in spite* of the existence of "an important discipline in the capital market," the real-world system almost certainly behaves very differently from the way implied in the conventional theory: the conventional theory would imply that corporations would choose to grow considerably more slowly and reward stockholders significantly better. Galbraith, however, in failing to meet the argument that profits are needed for growth, failed to explain how this divergence can occur. In offering to put the record straight, I am motivated not only by vanity, but also by the conviction that an accurate theory about corporate growth is essential for a correct understanding of a wide range of contemporary problems of economic and social policy. The theory cannot be made simple, but can be summarized as follows.

A growing corporation faces two problems: the problem of creating a growing demand for its products, and the problem of financing the necessary growth of capacity. The corporation may strive to be as efficient as possible, in the sense of squeezing the maximum profit from its existing markets; but the search for (or creation of) *new* markets inevitably costs money (in research, marketing, and losses from failures), and so, as the growth process is accelerated, the average return realized on the *total* assets of the corporation must be adversely affected (even if the development expenditure is deployed as efficiently as possible). In theoretical language, we say there is consequently a "functional relationship" between the rate of return and the rate of growth of saleable output, which varies from corporation to corporation (in the sense that some can get a better return with a given growth rate than others) and from time to time, but that at a given phase in a particular corporation's history, when all the facts are known, the relationship is unique. At the same time, any given growth rate of sales must be supported by a corresponding growth rate of production capacity and hence requires an adequate supply of financial capital. If the main source of finance is internal, the existing level of profits is obviously a major factor governing the sums available, so we get a "feedback" loop in which the rate of growth both influences and is influenced by the rate of profit. In fact, it is not difficult to see that if retained earnings were the only source of finance, and if the *proportion* retained were arbitrarily fixed by law or convention, we would already have what is called a "closed model": given the relationships described, for each individual corporation there would be only one rate of growth which could satisfy both conditions simultaneously (the unique value would, however, vary *between* corporations). This would be an "equilibrium" relationship between growth rate and profit rate, in the sense that the profit rate was at the same time just *low* enough to be consistent with the growth rate of sales and just *high* enough to provide adequate finance. This is about the simplest and neatest "theory of the growth of the corporation" one can conceive. To the best of my knowledge it was invented by Carl Kaysen, now Director of the Institute for Advanced Studies at Princeton, New Jersey, in an unpublished seminar paper given in England about ten years ago. It is not difficult to make the theory more realistic by allowing for flexibility in the retention/pay-out decisions and by bringing in outside finance. In my earlier work I put considerable emphasis on the role of internal finance, and more particularly on the balance between internal and external finance in "closing" a more realistic model. More recently, I have become increasingly impressed by the theoretical work of other economists which suggests that the basic implications are much the same whether one assumes finance to be all internal, all external, or a mixture of the two. In other words, I now think it may not matter too much whether Galbraith or Solow was most right in their confrontation on this point. But to explain the next step in the argument most easily (and for that reason only), it is convenient to write as if all finance were internal.

If we accept that, within very wide limits, the retention ratio is effectively decided by the management, the basic structure of the theory remains unchanged—but it is turned around. If the management chooses to go for a certain growth rate, this will determine the profits rate, so there is now only one value of the retention ratio which will provide the continuous finance required. Once the management has decided its target growth rate, it *must* adopt a corresponding retention ratio; if not, the corporation will either (1) run out of money or (2) fail to achieve its target. Of course, Boards of Directors do not see their problems in these precise terms; but there is considerable evidence that they feel and understand the essential structure of the problem in this way.

PROFITS AND/OR GROWTH

If the process of growth were steady and continuous, and if the numerical values of the relations involved remained unchanged (neither conditions, of course, being satisfied in real life), a decision by the management to grow at a certain rate, and to choose the consistent retention ratio, must also evidently imply a unique level and expected rate of growth of the dividend; and so, in a rational stock market, the decision must imply a unique current price and prospective capital gain in the corporation's stock. Up to a point, actual or potential stockholders may be content to see increased growth creating prospects of future gain at the expense of current dividends; beyond this point, any further increase in the growth rate chosen by the management must have a depressing effect on the stock price. There is no reason to suppose that a growth-oriented management will always refrain from accelerating beyond this point; and if they go too far they will undoubtedly lay themselves open to a variety of dangers (e.g., a take-over raid). I suggested in my theory that we might describe a typical "managerial" objective as maximum growth subject to a *minimum* on the stock price.

Solow said that my theory, in recognizing the minimum stock-price constraint, "came closer to the conventional view." On the contrary, in the conventional view management exists only to serve stockholders, and the essential technical problem is to find decision rules that would establish the policy which will, in fact, *maximize* the price of the stock. The two theories become "similar" only in the special conditions where the minimum and maximum position lie close together. These conditions are most improbable; in other words, the traditional theory is literally a "special case."

Because large-scale, professional management, not personally owning large supplies of finance, has such predominant technical advantages in the modern economy; because, although it may *use* stockmarket investors and bankers, it no longer *depends* on them; because the (not insubstantial) true capitalists who remain in our system avoid speculating in large manufacturing businesses unless these are going very cheap (they prefer real estate); because the other potential take-over raiders are typically themselves management-controlled—because of all this and much more, it is inevitable that the safe minimum level of the price of a corporation's stock will be significantly lower, and the safe maximum growth rate correspondingly higher, than the values which would be chosen by a management that really did care only for the welfare of the stockholders. Numerical calculations based on statistical observation suggest that a rather growth-conscious management could typically grow almost twice as fast, setting the stock market value at all times about one-third lower, as compared to the values which would be obtained in an otherwise comparable corporation dominated by stockholders who knew all the facts. Furthermore, the growth-oriented management could safely continue the policy indefinitely, even if there were quite a number of others who chose to behave otherwise. Since the growth-oriented managements will by definition be located in the faster growing corporations, this type of behavior must in time drive out other types—a process which, I suggest, has been going on for some time. The further the process goes, the weaker is the power of the stock market to resist. Since the growth-oriented firms are technically efficient, they display not unattractive levels and growth rates of dividends, the incentive to resistance is dampened, and the latent preference for slower growth and higher current dividends remains unrecognized.

Furthermore, because managements, in fostering growth, also create technical progress, new wants, new goods, and a generally different dynamic environment, the implications of the two types of theory cannot easily be compared. We cannot possibly assert that it would necessarily be in the public interest to compel managements to conform to the traditional norm; we might very likely make many people worse off and few better off. Galbraith, however, imposed the value judgment (the "affluent-society" thesis) that the higher rate of consumer innovation resulting from "managerial" behavior by the corporations is undesirable, because it is biased against the expression of leisure preferences and against the development of "public" goods. He does not, however (as maybe does Solow in saying "it might perhaps be better if companies were forced more often into the capital market") suggest that the remedies lie in the direction of the traditional model.

The conclusion I draw (and it is an implication which I suspect to be one of the causes of the considerable ideological drive of "neoclassical" economics in the United States) would probably be disliked by both parties: namely, that once the classical idealization of capitalism is thus destroyed, there is no *economic* case for its superiority over socialism. Consequently, the attempt to impose capitalism all around the world, in some cases virtually by force, can only be justified on political grounds. The latter, however, seem to get thinner every day. In the miserable developing countries of the "free" world, where we cheerfully give aid to almost any form of dictatorship provided no industries are nationalized (the case of Tito being a historical freak, much disliked by the Congress, I understand), there is no dearth of greedy *profit* maximizers, many living in considerable luxury. What the nonaffluent majority of the world's population so badly needs is a much greater number of *growth* maximizers.

THE NEED FOR "RESTRUCTURING"

More domestic and less inflammatory implications of the truth about the corporations are varied and pervasive. I will conclude with an example which may be of some topical interest. Suppose it is desired to get the corporations interested in replacing slums with wholesome low-rental dwellings, and suppose that the political conditions for the necessary diversion of national resources have already been created. Suppose federal contracts provide a massive injection of technical stimulus into the construction sector. We would still face the difficulty that low-income housing is an unprofitable line of business. This keeps out the traditionally motivated corporation and also discourages the growth-motivated corporation, because it means growing in directions that offer a particularly unfavorable relationship between growth and profitability, and consequently, means low "equilibrium" rates of growth in accordance with the theory. Under present conditions, therefore, a growth-oriented management undertaking these desirable activities *will be penalized in terms of its own motives*—a point which, once seen, appears rather obvious, but is not in fact generally well understood, and seems to have been missed by Galbraith.

Solow and many of his colleagues would then say, of course, that here is a perfect example of the traditional assumptions being good enough for policy purposes. On the contrary, it provides an excellent example of the serious practical errors which can result from that attitude. Suppose a certain senator, who may be nameless, proposes a scheme of tax credits to firms which will undertake socially oriented urban renewal projects. On the traditional assumptions, the function of the subsidy is simply to compensate stockholders for a reduced pre-tax rate of return. In my kind of model, the function is to compensate the management for lost growth-opportunity by offsetting the reduction in cash flow. If we follow this through, we will find that the size of the tax credit needed to obtain a given amount of housing would be substantially smaller, and the general political appeal of the project consequently more attractive.

Finally, I would suggest, if we were to "restructure" our economic system so that the units of production were endowed with the social norm of growth maximization (subject to financial constraints), and were freed from the embarrassments of stockholders and other trappings of private property, manipulation of the financial rules to offset various kinds of built in bias, and generally to foster a good society, would be much easier. We would be freed from the inhibitions and costs resulting from our archaic but powerful custom of assigning a private owner or part owner to most of our means of production. We should be able to concentrate on the task of finding the most efficient ways of organizing all the things we want to do, and to stop wasting our time discussing whether the old corporations did, or were supposed to, "maximize profits." But that is a longer story.

READING 29
External Diseconomies in the Modern Economy
Tibor Scitovsky

Professor Scitovsky of Harvard University presents a summary of the technical situations under which a market economy fails to allocate resources efficiently. He further shows that society is often reluctant to act to eliminate external costs due to fear of personal loss. The most striking argument made by Scitovsky entails the interaction of private wants and underpriced social spending. The production of public goods in order to complement private wants can lead to disasterous long-term effects on social welfare. Often the use of public spending to overcome one externality only leads to different problems later on. If a solution to this dilemma exists it may be through more careful consideration of the interaction effects and long-run consequences of regulation or spending by the public sector to "correct" some alleged externality.

Guideposts for Thought While Reading

How does the use of money as measures of welfare tend to bias economic development? What are the shortcomings of the public-expenditure approach to overcoming external diseconomies?

Perhaps the main reason for the fast growth of the capitalist economy during past centuries was its capacity to inculcate the habit of thinking in terms of money. That Americans have carried this habit the farthest is proverbial; and their also being farthest along the road of economic development may well have something to do with it. Money is a common denominator in terms of which to express and so render comparable the values of otherwise incomparable things and quantities; and there are many reasons why the habit of translating and comparing values in money terms promotes progress. First and most important, the acquisition of this habit is essential for the rational

Reprinted by permission of the publisher from Tibor Scitovsky, "External Diseconomies in the Modern Economy," *Western Economic Journal*, Vol. IV, No. 3, Summer 1966, pp. 197–202.

behavior of sellers when they decide what to specialize on, and of buyers when they try to combine in the best proportions the things they buy. Exactness, precision, and rational calculation hinge on the use of money. In the words of Georg Simmel, "Money economy and the dominance of the intellect are intrinsically connected. They share a matter-of-fact attitude in dealing with men and with things." Second, when sellers consider themselves makers of money rather than of shoes or ladies' garments, their occupational and geographical mobility becomes greater, thus enabling the economy to adjust faster to changing requirements. Third, the profit-maximizing manufacturer probably conforms more closely to consumers' preferences than one for whom pride of craftsmanship or professional reputation are more important. For the latter will produce the best by his own standards, while the former gains by producing the best by the customer's standards; and the two need not coincide. In the case of an artifact, the maker's (artist's or artisan's) standards are usually better than the customer's; but for most consumers' goods, this is not necessarily so. The manufacturer will usually stress workmanship and engineering design where the customer is interested in variety, novelty, and esthetic appeal. Also, the manufacturer's standards tend to be more conservative than the customer's and often slow progress. He is likely to manufacture to finer specifications and for greater durability than are needed in practical use; and this tends to raise costs, restrict availability, and hamper the development of new manufacturing methods.

A fourth reason why thinking in money terms furthers growth is that consciousness of market prices is consciousness of society's valuations; and when a person's actions are influenced by market prices, they conform that much more closely to society's needs and limitations. Fifth, man's system of values is inevitably influenced by other people's values; and his recognition of market prices as reflections of society's collective values is likely to make him adopt, to some extent, these values as his own. In other words, general knowledge of a common set of market prices is likely to foster similarity in preference scales. In short, the use of money has made man into a more rational being, especially in his economic actions; it has integrated his actions more closely with those of other members of the economy; it has rendered our economy more mobile, able to respond faster to changing requirements as reflected in changing market conditions; and it tends to inspire similar ambitions in the hearts of men and so harness more resources to a single cause.

THE LAYMAN'S COMPLAINTS AGAINST MONEY

While the use of money has great advantages, it also has its drawbacks—and these will be the main subject of this paper. It may be best to approach these drawbacks by first examining the layman's complaints against money. These are of two kinds. One is that man applies the measure of money also to those things in life that should not be so measured. The other is that man neglects those values in life that cannot be expressed in money terms in favor of those that can.

The two complaints, only seemingly contradictory, both stem from the fear that man in the modern, rationally calculating world will neglect the higher things in life. The first is a protest against expressing in money the *cost* of things that are of the spirit, on the ground that man should decide on the relative importance in his life of material and spiritual values, irrespective of their relative costs. The second voices the fear that spiritual, ethical and esthetic values will be neglected because their *benefits* cannot be or are not expressed in money, and man is increasingly getting used to taking seriously only those benefits that are so expressed.

These are fascinating and important issues; but they are not in my field, and I shall leave them therefore to others to resolve.

INTERDEPENDENCE AND THE TENDENCY TO BIASED DECISIONS

However, the tendency to undervalue costs and benefits not expressed in terms of money and the related tendency also to undervalue costs and benefits that, though expressed in money, are not actually collected or disbursed are affecting and biasing many decisions beyond those involving the choice between things of the flesh and those of the spirit; and such a bias is quite likely to interfere with further economic development and divert it into undesirable directions.

Much of this problem stems from increasing interaction among different people and their activities. In a simpler age, there was relatively little interdependence between different people's actions and welfare; and most of it was easily taken care of either in the market where one man paid another for goods bought and services rendered, or in the courts where damages were awarded for suffering harm through another's action. Much harmful interaction was easily prevented by traffic laws, zoning regulations, and so forth.

Today, an increasing density of population and a rising standard of living have greatly increased the degree of interdependence in our economy; but we have not yet developed machinery adequate to deal with the new problems created by the new interdependence. Indeed, in many cases we have not even recognized the existence of this interdependence.

Perhaps the most striking example is the creation of waste as we process resources into goods and consume these goods. This has now reached dimensions where one man's waste can seriously affect other people's welfare, endangering health, comfort, and esthetic sensibilities. Hence, to dispose of waste and to restrain its creation have become an economic problem; but we are as yet unprepared and unequipped for dealing with it. The notion dies hard that man has an inalienable right free of charge to emit fumes into the atmosphere and dump solid and liquid waste into the lap of nature. The American public produces solid waste at a daily rate of almost ½ million tons and pays the cost (about $3 billion annually) merely for its removal from the front door to the local dump. But in San Francisco, for example, the local dump is San Francisco Bay, which is gradually disappearing, because it happens to be the most convenient and cheapest hole into which to sink garbage of which San Francisco and San Mateo counties alone produce enough to fill a square mile ten feet deep each year. The "Save The Bay Association" has been fighting this for a long time; but the champions of esthetic values always have a difficult time fighting against the champions of hard cash.

Another place into which a lot of garbage gets dumped is the air we breathe. Burning reduces garbage to one-quarter of its original bulk; the other three-quarters are added to the smog problem. In fact, San Francisco Bay is to some extent the victim of Air Pollution Control; we dump so much garbage into the Bay because the Bay Area is among the few places where burning is forbidden.

Another problem, whose full magnitude is only now beginning to be realized, is that created by our production of sewage and other liquid waste, which spread infection, reduce the availability of drinking water, kill the trout, perch and whitefish in our rivers, and make an ever-increasing number of our lakes and rivers unsafe for swimming and fishing. Raw sewage is infesting not only Lake Erie but even California's Lake Tahoe with the algae that change a clear blue color into a dirty green and create foul odors and an unpleasant taste. And lest I create the impression that this problem exists only in the United States, let me mention that few fish are left in European rivers, and Lake Geneva in Switzerland, the original "picture-postcard," is becoming unsafe for swimming. According to a recent issue of *The Wall Street Journal*, the Maroning River, which meanders through Ohio and Pennsylvania, has reached a state where "oil and grease coat its surface and discolor its banks, suspended solids destroy its clarity, sludge covers its bed, and oil clings to tree limbs and bushes." Some 90 rivers in this country and over 7000 miles of waterways are contaminated in some such way.

A third problem, about which little is known and less is done but which may be the worst of all, is air pollution. We know that nearly 6000 communities in the United States are affected, including all 310 cities with populations above 50,000. Many of the large cities of Japan and England have serious smog problems, and also many cities and parts of the Continent. Smog causes material damage to crops, livestock, rubber, and textile fibers; it corrodes metal and attacks and soils many other substances. The total material damage caused by smog in the United States is estimated at $11 billion annually. Damage to health caused by smog has not been estimated yet in monetary terms, nor has it been fully assessed in medical terms. To give an impressionistic idea, let me recall that a 5-day London smog killed 4000 people in 1952; in the little town of Donora, Pennsylvania, a single freak of the weather made over 40 percent of the 13,000 population acutely sick and killed off 20 people; and a recent New York City report about smog estimated its effect on New Yorkers as being equivalent to the smoking of two packs of cigarettes per day. In Los Angeles, 10,000 people annually are advised by their doctors to leave and seek jobs elsewhere; and according to a questionnaire survey, one-third of all Los Angeles physicians have seriously considered leaving that paradise of the profession to look for less lucrative but healthier jobs elsewhere. Lung cancer, emphysema, bronchial asthma, and chronic bronchitis are among the diseases caused by smog—and there may be more. After all, there are many air pollutants and many types of smog. The death rate from pulmonary emphysema has increased sevenfold in a decade. If we judge by Social Security payments for total disability, this disease in now the second most important illness (after heart disease) in the United States. Whether smog is the main cause is not yet established, but there are few other suspects.

Another and different type of interaction is the traffic problem. All of us contribute to traffic and traffic jams; and the noise, the smell, the waiting, and the frustration shorten tempers and lives, and spoil a lot of fun for a lot of people. Traffic in and around New York and other large cities is a nightmare; and the nightmare is expected to get worse and spread to still other cities within the next ten years. As urbanization proceeds, and we are approaching our latest ideal of the three-car family, we are also approaching a volume of wheeled city traffic so enormous that either we shall have to abandon the traditional concept of the large city as we have learned to know and like it, or we shall have to adopt a drastically different approach to city transportation. For example, according to a projection of the growth of traffic in Washington, D.C., 16th Street, which today is an ordinary wide street facing the White House, would by 1975 need 12 lanes to accommodate normal traffic if its growth continues unchecked.

All these are examples of external diseconomies, where one man's enjoyment of life, or the manufacture of products for his enjoyment, creates for others discomforts, ugliness, and hazards to life, limb, and health. These are true economic costs that ought to be minimized and compensated for; but they are not expressed in terms of money, they do not look like costs incurred in the market, and their diffuseness makes it hard to identify the people who suffer the diseconomies and sometimes those who create them. For all these reasons the public is reluctant to accept and treat them as costs, and what little is done to prevent or eliminate external diseconomies is done by regulation or public expenditure, both of which have their uses but also their limitations.

THE RELUCTANCE OF THE PUBLIC TO DEAL WITH EXTERNALITIES

A good example of the public's reluctance to face these problems and of the limited usefulness of regulation in dealing with them is provided by air pollution. Its existence and harmful nature have been known for at least 700 years. A London ordinance of 1273 was the first of a long series of regulations to prohibit the use of coal as prejudicial to health, at least one person is known to have been tried, condemned, and executed (in 1306) for this offense; yet the prohibition remained completely ineffective throughout. According to a 1661 entry in John Evelyn's diary, "Her [London's] inhabitants breathe nothing but an impure and thick Mist, accompanied by a fuliginous and filthy vapour, which renders them obnoxious to a thousand inconveniences, corrupting the lungs, and disordering the entire habit of their Bodies, so that Catarrhs, Phthisicks, Coughs and Consumptions, rage more in this one City, than in the whole Earth besides." Yet, London had to wait another 300 years, until the 1952 disaster (in which a week's smog caused 4000 excess deaths) brought in its wake regulation truly effective—at least to the extent that by 1963 a smog of similar duration killed off merely 750 people.

REGULATION EFFORTS

The public has willingly accepted dirt, smell, discomfort, a darkened sky, and an increased incidence of respiratory diseases as the inevitable costs of progress, probably because these costs were not expressed in money and because of the lack of machinery through which to collect and induce a minimization of these costs. Regulation seemed the only feasible, and remains to this day the only existing, means of dealing with the problem; and even this is accepted very slowly. Public opinion is hostile to all new regulation and accepts it grudgingly, only under the impact of conclusive and incontrovertible evidence that it will prevent or mitigate serious loss. And the trouble with regulation is the difficulty of enforcement. Regulations that prohibit are much easier to enforce than those that would merely limit activity; usually they are the only ones practicable. At the same time, prohibition is more drastic than limitation; and this militates against its acceptance by public opinion. For example, the outright prohibition to burn smog-creating fuels proved too drastic an action and therefore unenforceable. We had to wait for centuries—and in some areas we are still waiting—for the development of technical means to purify the smoke and fumes emitted, so that prohibition of burning fuels without the use of such purifiers should become less drastic, more palatable to public opinion, and thus more enforceable. At no time have we succeeded in persuading the public to "economize" in the creation of air pollutants or industry to speed up the development of technology to filter them.

SPENDING BY THE PUBLIC SECTOR

Public expenditure, the other customary means of dealing with external diseconomies, also has its shortcomings. These are best illustrated in connection with the traffic problem, although they are endemic to all public expenditure and not confined to public expenditure when used to deal with the problem of external diseconomies. Public opinion is beginning to recognize that some consumers' services are better or cheaper to provide collectively by government than privately through the market; but unfortunately we have no way at present to allocate resources efficiently between the public and private sectors.

THE TENDENCY FOR EXCESS GOVERNMENT SPENDING

Collectively provided, services are usually made available to the consumer at no marginal cost, thus causing the demand for them to be filled to saturation and their production to be greater than it ought to be on economic principles. Hence the general feeling that government squanders resources and does not know how to economize. Yet whenever the public wants to have a good provided by the government, it insists on it being provided in the excessive quantities needed to saturate demand. An example is the almost universal feeling that governments should build highways and city streets in the profusion needed to fill to saturation every driver's demand for roadway. It is true that highway building is financed from gasoline taxes, but these fall far short of paying the full cost of providing, maintaining, and policing both highways and city streets.

As a result, highway building has encouraged the excessive use of the private car or truck; and if the widening of city streets has not kept in step in all cities, it is not for want of trying. It is becoming apparent that to fill to saturation the demand for city streets is physically impossible and would destroy the very concept and nature of the large city. That the free provision of roadway encourages the use of private car and truck far beyond what is economical becomes especially apparent when one takes into account the full social cost of their use. We worry about smog, about the wear and tear traffic puts on the city-dwellers' nerves, and about the decline and declining profitability of the railroads and metropolitan transportation, but at the same time we build bigger and better highways and never stop to think about their interconnection and conflict. If car and truck users had to pay the full social cost of their use, including the social cost of their contribution to smog and traffic, the resulting limitation of such use would go a long way toward solving all these problems. Smog and traffic problems would be eased and public transportation would become more viable.

On the other hand, we have developed no machinery as yet to make drivers pay for their contribution to congestion in traffic and hydrocarbons in the atmosphere; and public opinion may not yet be ready for it. People find it hard to accept the idea of having to pay for something that was free in the past. Yet, until the time when machinery is available to collect, and the public ready to pay, fees for the creation of external diseconomies, we shall have to suffer the losses, the discomforts, and the misdirection of resources that they entail.

READING 30
Government Investment: How Scientific Can It Be?
Neil W. Chamberlain

In this reading Dr. Chamberlain, a professor of economics at Columbia Graduate School of Business, describes the current popularity of the cost-benefit criteria for appraising investment projects by the public sector. Chamberlain presents arguments for and against the cost-benefit measuring rod. He shows that while cost-benefit provides a framework which may increase efficiency in decision-making, it is no substitute for human judgment on the many intangibles involved with public projects.

Guideposts for Thought While Reading

How does benefit-cost differ from investment criteria used by private business? Why does this difference lead to some unsolved problems in public decision-making? Where is benefit-cost used by the public sector? What are the main criticisms of benefit-cost analysis?

Before making a new investment, the key question a businessman must ask himself is, "How much will it cost, and how much will I get back?" He then allocates his capital to those investment possibilities that appear to give him the highest return.

Reprinted by permission of International Arts and Sciences Press, Inc., White Plains, N.Y., from Neil W. Chamberlain, "Government Investment: How Scientific Can It Be?," *Challenge*, July–August 1966, pp. 32–35, 44.

So that he could administer the Pentagon's huge expenditures with some degree of rationality, Robert McNamara—abetted by his former Assistant Secretary, economist Charles J. Hitch—reshaped defense decision making along similar lines. As a consequence, the businessman's venerable question of "What will I get for what I spend?" has now entered the public sector as cost-benefit analysis. In fact, the new concept—at least for government—has spread so rapidly that today no respectable administrator can propose, and no up-to-date legislator can approve, any project over which the cost-benefit liturgy has not been said.

WHAT IS COST-BENEFIT ANALYSIS?

How can we best describe this new analytic aid to government economic decision making? Prof. Robert Dorfman of Harvard, has given it a succinct formulation. "Benefit-cost analysis is closely analogous to the methods of investment project appraisal used by businessmen. The only difference is that estimates of social values are used in place of estimates of sales value when appropriate."

Others have said that the intent is to maximize the net value of all benefits streaming from the public investment process. Maximizing must, of course, be subject to certain constraints or conditions, such as a budgetary limit, or an equitable geographical spread of benefits, or a balance of payments restriction. But within such confines, government officials should allocate capital funds to those projects promising the greatest measurable value for the amount of money spent.

Actually, it is misleading to call this formal analytical technique new. Two English economists recently surveyed the literature in this field and traced it back as far as 1844, when a pioneering work was published by a Frenchman, Dupuit, on "The Measurement of Utility of Public Works." But there was little follow-up until the present century, and then the stimulus came not from theoretical European economists but from practical American legislators, who wrote a provision for it into the River and Harbor Act of 1902. That Act required a board of engineers to report on the desirability of proposed projects, taking into account the amount of commerce benefited and the cost of the undertaking. Faced with this directive, the Army Corps of Engineers developed a set of valuation principles and techniques.

For some time the new procedures were confined to water-use

projects. The Flood Control Act of 1936, for example, authorized federal involvement in that area of activity "if the benefits to whomsoever they may accrue are in excess of the estimated costs." (While this formulation would be viewed as crude by today's refined standards, it had the important effect of broadening the concept of social benefit.)

Two years later Oregon experimented with cost-benefit application to highway construction. Since then applications have been made to urban renewal, recreation, land reclamation, health, education, research and development, and, of course, defense. The 1963 Brookings conference called for trial runs in such more difficult areas as the prevention of high school dropouts and venereal disease control programs.

Aside from McNamara's interest in getting a grip on the Pentagon behemoth, why the recent spread of interest in governmental investment efficiency? The two English economists, Prest and Turvey, who made the previously mentioned survey, suggest three reasons: the public sector is expanding, so that its investment decisions have greater economic consequence; the number of really large-scale investments has grown in recent years, as illustrated by the costs of developing a supersonic plane, making a manned moon shot or engineering a high-speed Boston-to-Washington rail system; and, finally, mathematical techniques such as operations research and systems analysis, which have proved invaluable in making the current more sophisticated quantitative studies, are primarily of post-World War II vintage.

APPLICATIONS OF COST-BENEFIT ANALYSIS

There are several ways in which cost-benefit analysis can be used. The earliest on the scene, and perhaps still the most common, is its application to a particular project—say, the building of a large dam—to ascertain whether the stream of benefits which it is expected to provide, both direct and indirect, exceed its cost of construction and maintenance. This is the coarsest sieve through which any investment proposal must pass, since it says nothing about whether the particular capital expenditure yields a better return than other possible uses of the government's limited investment funds.

Cost-benefit analysis may also be used to choose among alternative ways of accomplishing the same objective. The single large dam may be only one possible way of achieving the flood control and irrigation which are really wanted. A series of smaller dams may be another possibility, or a dam located at a different site. By quantifying the particular benefits expected to flow from each of the competing methods, and laying these alongside their respective costs, choice can be based on something more than artful judgment or political pressure.

These are the two most common usages of the cost-benefit technique—to determine whether a project is worth its expense, or which of several competing projects will accomplish a set objective the most economically.

A third application is also claimed by partisans of this new analytical tool. It can, they say, be used to choose among projects which have differing objectives. The dam for flood control and irrigation can be ranked relative to a subway system for Washington, D.C., or federal aid to higher education, or a low-income housing program. Public funds are simply not available to finance all such worthy ventures, so that the selection of some necessarily means the exclusion of others. Which to choose? Again the answer lies in calculating as well as one can the value of the benefits to be derived from each, taking into account the time when these benefits will be realized.

The outlays required can similarly be estimated. The ratio of costs and benefits establishes the yield of each project. Those which promise the highest yields receive priority in the government's investment program. The process is similar to a business firm's forced choice of, say, increasing its R&D budget or installing more highly automated equipment or modernizing a plant when budgetary limitations prevent its doing all of these.

The objectivity of the cost-benefit approach in solving such problems of public investment, coupled with its logical precision, carries an enormous appeal. Analysis replaces the pork barrel. The measuring rod curbs excess ardor for "public welfare" projects. A scientifically based decision process substitutes for the politician's hunch. Business techniques help to avoid traditional governmental inefficiency and wastefulness.

DEFECTS IN THE COST-BENEFIT APPROACH

But before joining in too vigorous applause for this manifestation of our increasing economic sophistication, let us pause and appraise. Even among economists there are skeptics and critics, although the sharpest sniping has come from government administrators. Could it be that there are bugs in benefit analysis?

The clash between the advocates and opponents of the new technique was perhaps most sharply displayed in the Brookings conference already mentioned. In the words of the conference chairman, Prof. Dorfman, "The battle lines were clearly drawn . . . Most of the academicians among the conference participants were hopeful that the benefits of government investment projects could be appraised objectively and even quantitatively . . . The practitioners were very skeptical and inclined to doubt whether the most important social effects of government investments could ever be appraised quantitatively by cost-benefit analysis or any other formalized method."

Before considering the most forceful objections of the skeptics, we may as well dismiss two often-cited but actually irrelevant contentions. One concerns the political unit within which benefits are measured. Expenditures by one community to improve a highway may have the effect of rechanneling traffic so that more cars empty into a bottle-neck area or a residential section of an adjacent community. The latter adverse effect is not likely to enter into the cost-benefit calculations of the highway-improving community.

This can hardly be viewed as a flaw in the analytical technique, however. It is simply a consequence of the way political boundaries have been drawn. The solution is a political one, such as redrafting jurisdictions or—more feasibly—devising instruments for intergovernmental collaboration.

A second alleged defect is the difficulty of including, in any benefit measure, all the effects which will flow from an investment, since some of these cannot be foreseen. How can one foretell all the technological applications of an investment in military research, for example, even though such applications may profoundly affect the scale of benefits? How can one predict that a purchase of public land may have its value either reduced or enhanced by shifts in population, or by scientific discoveries or technical developments affecting the value of the land's resources?

But lack of foresight—or of omniscience—can scarcely be viewed as a flaw in any analytical system. The absence of "perfect knowledge"—that assumption through which the classical economists designed and defended a beautiful but unreal competitive system—haunts every process of judgment known to man. Cost-benefit analysis may still be useful, if it succeeds only in identifying and evaluating as many effects of a project as can "reasonably" be foreseen.

Even after dispelling these inconsequential detractions there remains a number of far more damaging criticisms. Most of these are based on the subjective nature of the quantitative measures which are presumed to make the analysis scientific. Estimating future benefits from an investment project is at best a matter of expertise, professional wisdom and informed guesswork, with the inevitable consequence that the apparent precision which a number suggests is purely illusory.

One consequence of this inevitable play of judgment in the "scientific" analysis is that supporters of particular projects can be counted on to give as favorable estimates of benefits and costs as they can get away with. (The same phenomenon has been observed in the business world when subjective judgments are made about such matters as how consumers will respond to a new product, how effective a new production process will be when transferred from the drawing boards to the plant floor, or whether rival firms will come out with a similar or better product.)

An illustration of how this works out in the public domain is provided by two cost-benefit estimates made by different agencies for the same project, a cross-Florida barge canal. The Army Corps of Engineers, by a conservative judgment on costs of construction and maintenance, and generous estimates of the resulting savings in transportation costs and other incidental favorable effects (fishing, recreation, flood control), concluded that total benefits would run 20 per cent more than total costs. A consulting firm—retained by a group of railroads which could be presumed to be less than happy about the prospective water route—countered with figures showing that costs would be a third again as much as the Engineers had estimated, that the savings in transportation would be at most only one-sixth of the Engineers' optimistic computation, and that no measurable incidental benefits could be counted on. As they figured it, the proposed canal would return no more than 13 per cent of its cost.

The play of judgment is most in evidence in putting values on the intangible or noneconomic effects of a prospective investment. What "benefit"—in money terms—can be imputed to the esthetic appeal of one public building, for example, in contrast to the cold functional efficiency of a competing architectural design? What price can be placed on the qualitative difference which urban redevelopment and slum clearance make in the lives of those affected? What estimates of value can we "scientifically" derive for the prolongation of life of the aged, the ill, or the mentally retarded?

Perhaps the most searching question we can ask is: What is the objective measure of the worth of a human life that should be cranked into the cost-benefit analysis of projects like traffic control, health maintenance, and police and fire protection?

There are other valid and significant criticisms which may be directed against cost-benefit analysis. One is the difficulty of establishing an unambiguous cause-effect relation between a project and its presumed benefits. With multiple influences simultaneously affecting people's health, productivity, and civic responsibility, for example, how can we identify that degree of influence which can be attributed to some particular social program?

Even dismissing most of the difficulties concerned with the problem of measurement, and even assuming that reliable and objective estimates of costs and returns could be obtained, there remains a dilemma of choice which the analysis does not resolve. The differential scales of competing investment alternatives present a separate and significant issue demanding the exercise of judgment.

Willis Shapley of the U.S. Bureau of the Budget has pointed out that even if the yield from some grandiose project, such as a lunar landing or a Martian mission, came out unmistakably higher than the yield from all alternative investments, we might choose not to put all our investment eggs in one basket. We might prefer smaller yields from a variety of projects than a somewhat greater yield from a single program. Conceptually, this problem could be handled by incorporating in the comparisons a statistical measure of our preference for spreading risk and benefit over many activities rather than one, but this "resolution" simply brings us back to the thorny problem of measuring intangibles.

READING 31
The Public Be Damned
Milton Friedman

In this article, Professor Milton Friedman argues against the socialization of postal services as it is currently enforced through laws prohibiting private enterprise from competing with the United States Post Office. Friedman discusses the advantages of private enterprise for postal delivery, but concludes that the widespread, but relatively minor, individual benefits from competition in postal services cannot sway politicians to legislate in favor of free enterprise when faced with existing pressure groups.

Guideposts for Thought While Reading
Why are congressmen unwilling to support a bill allowing private enterprise in postal services? How can a democracy function without losing control to coalitions of special interest groups?

A Presidential commission has just made official what you and I have long known from experience. The Post Office "each year . . . slips further behind the rest of the economy in service, in efficiency and in meeting its responsibilities as an employer."

The commission recommended that the Post Office be converted from a government department to a nonprofit government corporation. That might improve matters some, but since the Post Office would still be a monopoly and a government organization, it would remain high-priced and inefficient. A far better solution is one I suggested many months ago (*Newsweek*, Oct. 9, 1967)—simply repeal the present provision making it illegal for private enterprise to provide mail service. Competition would quickly set modern technology to work in the transmission of mail, and simultaneously lower the cost to the consumer. The government system would have to shape up or ship out.

PRESSURE GROUPS UP . . . .

But neither the one proposal nor the other will be adopted. The facts of political life that make this prediction a near-certainty were brought home to me when I was writing my earlier column on the Post Office. Why not, I thought, use it to persuade a congressman to introduce a bill to repeal the present prohibition on private delivery of mail? That would have started desirable legislation on its way, made the column more topical, and given the Congressional sponsor some publicity. So I spoke to a number of friends in Congress.

All were favorable to the substance of the bill, yet none was willing to introduce it. As one congressman said to me, "Can you suggest any unions we might conceivably persuade to testify in favor of it?" I could not do so.

Strong pressure groups will oppose changing present arrangements: the postal unions that have become experts in lobbying before Congress; the users of third- and fourth-class mail, who fear that the subsidy they now enjoy would be threatened if Congress no longer finances postal deficits.

No strong pressure groups will favor the proposed changes—which serve only the widespread general interest of the public. If the proposed changes were made—if, for example, private competition were permitted—pressure groups would emerge. Enterprises that succeeded in the new business and their employees and customers would become such groups. But these are only potential, not actual.

A congressman has limited time and influence. It is wise for him to husband that time and influence to promote measures that have some chance of being adopted, or, at least, of bringing him some political support. What can he gain by the purely quixotic gesture of sponsoring a bill to introduce competition into the postal service? Only the active hostility of present special interests. True, many more persons would be benefited than would be harmed and the aggregate benefit would greatly exceed any transitional harm. *But,* and it is a big but, the few persons who believe that they would be harmed will be aware of that fact, and each will expect significant harm, so it will pay them to fight the bill. Most persons who would benefit will not be aware of that fact. Even if they were, the benefit to most would be small. Hence, they are unlikely to devote much effort to promoting the bill—or even to have their vote influenced by its introduction. Their vote is likely to be determined by the matters with respect to which they are members of special interest groups.

. . . DIFFUSED GENERAL INTEREST

Many citizens regard it as a paradox that a democratic government, supposed to promote the general welfare, should enact so many measures that promote special interests. It is not a paradox. It is the result to be expected when government engages in activities that have concentrated effects on small groups and widely diffused effects on the rest of the citizens. A majority rules in a political democracy, but the majority that rules is typically a coalition of special interests—not a majority promoting the general interest.

In the heyday of nineteenth-century capitalism, William H. Vanderbilt, a railroad tycoon, is said to have remarked, "The public be damned" to an inquiring reporter. That may have been his attitude but it was never an accurate description of how private enterprise behaved. Competition saw to that. Enterprises that damned the public did not survive for long. But however accurate it may have been then, today the phrase fits Washington to a T.

READING 32
A Rationale for Public Expenditures

Richard A. Musgrave

In this article, Professor Musgrave who is well known for his writing in the field of public finance, provides us a concise statement showing a basis upon which to allocate resources between the private and public sectors.

Reprinted from Federal Expenditure Policy for Economic Growth and Stability, Hearings before Subcommittee on Fiscal Policy, Joint Economic Committee, 85th Congress, 1st Session, pp. 42–44.

Guideposts for Thought While Reading

Why are public expenditures needed? Why is it a fallacy to think of public-sector spending simply as diverting part of the output that has been produced? According to Musgrave, what is an optimal budget? What is wrong with the concept of taxable capacity?

Public expenditures are needed because the market mechanism, while ideally equipped to provide for the satisfaction of most of our wants, cannot provide for all of them. There are certain wants which must be provided for through the budget. This does not mean that the goods and services in question must be produced by government, although some of them are; my main point is that they must be paid for in taxes rather than through consumer purchases in the market. This is so because these goods are consumed in equal amount by all, so that all individual consumers are benefited whether they contribute to the cost or not. Voluntary bidding, which is the essence of the market mechanism, will not be forthcoming. A political process is needed to determine these wants, involving decisions by majority vote and compulsory contributions in accordance with a common tax formula.

1. Social wants involve certain characteristics which require that they be provided for through the budget. As such they differ from private wants which may be satisfied and paid for through the market. The fact that this difference exists does not establish a presumption that social wants are either more or less important than private wants.

In other words, we are easily given to considering the national income that is produced by the private sector as being the primary factor in the economy, and to thinking of the budgetary activity as diverting part of the output that has been produced. I think this is a fallacy. We have to look at both as inherently interrelated parts which contribute equally in their way to the total want satisfaction.

2. The proper allocation of resources between the satisfaction of social wants and the satisfaction of private wants is that which selects the most important wants of both types, and leaves unsatisfied the less important wants of both types. A budget which does this may be called an optimal budget.

3. This concept of optimal budget is concerned just as much with avoiding too low a lower limit as with avoiding too high an

upper limit to public expenditures. The concept of taxable capacity by the very semantics of the term is concerned with the upper limit only. It is a biased concept designed from the outset to give a biased answer.

4. At the same time, note that the division of resources between the satisfaction of private and of social wants is not only a question of which final wants are to be recognized. The satisfaction of social wants, in scope and content, may affect the functioning of the market system. Public services may improve the efficiency of private enterprise in many ways. Indeed, the private-enterprise sector of the economy could not function without a minimum level of public services. Taxes, if excessively high, and especially if ill designed, may interfere with the functioning of private enterprise. Thus, the proper scope of public services or satisfaction of social wants must be determined with due allowance for its repercussions, favorable and unfavorable, on the private-enterprise section of the economy.

READING 33
The Case Against Big Business
George J. Stigler

In this article Dr. Stigler, who is a professor of economics and business at the University of Chicago, defines big business and criticizes its monopoly power and the tendency for bigness in business to beget bigness in labor and government. Stigler concludes with some recommendations concerning antitrust policy.

Guideposts for Thought While Reading

What is Stigler's definition of a big business? In what way is this definition important to his arguments? Why is Stigler unsatisfied with present antitrust activity? What alternative solutions does Stigler present and why does he choose dissolution as the best remedy?

Reprinted by permission of the publisher from George J. Stigler, "The Case Against Big Business," *Fortune*, May 1952, pp. 123, 158, 162, 164.

WHAT IS BIGNESS?

Bigness in business has two primary meanings. First, bigness may be defined in terms of the company's share of the industry in which it operates: a big company is one that has a big share of the market or industry. By this test Texas Gulf Sulphur is big because it produces more than half the sulfur in America, and Macy's (whose annual sales are much larger) is small because it sells only a very small fraction of the goods sold by New York City retail stores. By this definition, many companies that are small in absolute size are nevertheless big—the only brick company in a region, for example—and many companies that are big in absolute size (Inland Steel, for example) are small. Second, bigness may mean absolute size—the measure of size being assets, sales, or employment as a rule. Then General Motors and U.S. Steel are the prototypes of bigness.

These two meanings overlap because most companies that are big in absolute size are also big in relation to their industries. There are two types of cases, however, in which the two meanings conflict. On the one hand, many companies of small absolute size are dominant in small markets or industries. I shall not discuss them here (although they require attention in a well-rounded antitrust program) for two reasons: they seldom have anywhere near so much power as the companies that are big relative to large markets and industries; and they raise few political problems of the type I shall discuss below. On the other hand, there are a few companies that are big in absolute size but small relative to their markets—I have already given Macy's as an example. These companies are not very important in the total picture, and I shall also put them aside in the following discussion.

For my purposes, then, big businesses will mean businesses that are absolutely large in size and large also relative to the industries in which they operate. They are an impressive list: U.S. Steel, Bethlehem, and Republic in steel, General Electric and Westinghouse in electrical equipment, General Motors, Ford, and Chrysler in automobiles, du Pont, Union Carbide, and Allied Chemical among others in chemicals, Reynolds, Liggett & Myers, and American Tobacco in cigarettes.

What bigness does not mean is perhaps equally important. Bigness has no reference to the size of industries. I for one am tired of the charge that the critics of the steel industry vacillate between finding the output too large and too small: at various times the industry's output has been too small; for fifty years the largest firm has been too large. Concerted action by many small companies often leads to over-capacity in an industry: it is the basic criticism of resale price maintenance, for example, that it encourages the proliferation of small units by fixing excessive retail margins. Industries dominated by one or a few firms—that is, big businesses—seldom err in this direction. Nor does bigness have any direct reference to the methods of production, and opposition to big business is usually compatible with a decent respect for the "economies of large-scale production," on which more later.

The fundamental objection to bigness stems from the fact that big companies have monopolistic power, and this fundamental objection is clearly applicable outside the realm of corporate business. In particular, big unions are open to all the criticisms (and possibly more) that can be levied against big business. I shall not discuss labor unions, but my silence should not be construed as a belief that we should have a less stringent code for unions than for business.

THE INDICTMENT OF BIGNESS

There are two fundamental criticisms to be made of big businesses: they act monopolistically, and they encourage and justify bigness in labor and government.

First, as to monopoly. When a small number of firms control most or all of the output of an industry, they can individually and collectively profit more by cooperation than by competition. This is fairly evident, since cooperatively they can do everything they can do individually, and other things (such as the charging of non-competitive prices) besides. These few companies, therefore, will usually cooperate.

From this conclusion many reasonable men, including several Supreme Court Justices, will dissent. Does not each brand of cigarettes spend huge sums in advertising to lure us away from some other brand? Do not the big companies—oligopolists, the economists call them—employ salesmen? Do not the big companies introduce constant innovations in their products?

Competition of a Kind

The answer is that they do compete—but not enough, and not in all the socially desirable ways. Those tobacco companies did not act competitively, but with a view to extermination, against the 10-cent brands in the 1930's, nor have they engaged in price competition in decades. The steel companies, with all their salesmen, abandoned cartel pricing via basing-point prices only when this price system was judged a conspiracy in restraint of trade in cement. The plain fact is that big businesses do not engage in continuous price competition.

Nor is price the only area of agreement. Patent licensing has frequently been used to deprive the licensees of any incentive to engage in research; General Electric used such agreements also to limit other companies' output and fix the prices of incandescent lamps. The hearings of the Bone Committee are adorned with numerous examples of the deliberate deterioration of goods in order to maintain sales. For example, Standard Oil Development (a subsidiary of the Jersey company) persuaded Socony-Vacuum to give up the sale of a higher-potency commodity (pour-point depressant) whose sale at the same price had been characterized as "merely price cutting."

Very well, big businesses often engage in monopolistic practices. It may still be objected that it has not been shown that all big businesses engage in monopolistic practices, or that they engage in such practices all, or even most of, the time. These things cannot be shown or even fully illustrated in a brief survey, and it is also not possible to summarize the many court decisions and the many academic studies of big business. But it is fair to say that these decisions and studies show that big businesses usually possess monopolistic power, and use it. And that is enough.

For economic policy must be contrived with a view to the typical rather than the exceptional, just as all other policies are contrived. That some drivers can safely proceed at eighty miles an hour is no objection to a maximum-speed law. So it is no objection to an antitrust policy that some unexercised monopoly power is thereby abolished. (Should there be some big businesses that forgo the use of their dominant position, it is difficult to see what advantage accrues from private ownership, for the profit motive is already absent.)

Second, as to bigness in labor and government. Big companies have a large—I would say an utterly disproportionate—effect on public thinking. The great expansion of our labor unions has been due largely to favoring legislation and administration by the federal government. This policy of favoring unions rests fundamentally upon the popular belief that workers individually competing for jobs will be exploited by big-business employers —that U.S. Steel can in separate negotiation (a pretty picture!)

overwhelm each of its hundreds of thousands of employees. In good part this is an absurd fear: U.S. Steel must compete with many other industries, and not merely other steel companies, for good workers.

Yet the fear may not be wholly absurd: there may be times and places where big businesses have "beaten down" wages, although I believe such cases are relatively infrequent. (In any event, the reaction to the fear has been unwise: for every case where big business has held down workers there are surely many cases where big unions have held up employers). But it cannot be denied that this public attitude underlies our national labor policy, the policy of local governments of condoning violence in labor disputes, etc.

Big business has also made substantial contributions to the growth of big government. The whole agricultural program has been justified as necessary to equalize agriculture's bargaining power with "industry," meaning big business. The federally sponsored milkshed cartels are defended as necessary to deal with the giant dairy companies.

Business Across the Board

Big business is thus a fundamental excuse for big unions and big government. It is true that the scope and evils of big business are usually enormously exaggerated, especially with reference to labor and agriculture, and that more often than not these evils are merely a soapbox excuse for shoddy policies elsewhere. To this large extent, there is need for extensive education of the public on how small a part of the economy is controlled by big business. But in light of the widespread monopolistic practices—our first criticism of bigness—it is impossible to tell the public that its fears of big business are groundless. We have no right to ask public opinion to veer away from big unions and big government—and toward big business.

EFFICIENCY AND BIG BUSINESS

Are we dependent upon big businesses for efficient methods of production and rapid advances in production methods? If we are, the policy of breaking up big businesses would lower our future standard of living and many people would cast about for other ways than dissolution to meet the problems of bigness.

A company may be efficient because it produces and sells a given amount of product with relatively small amounts of material, capital, and labor, or it may be efficient because it acquires the power to buy its supplies at unusually low prices and sell its products at unusually high prices. Economists refer to these as the social and the private costs of production respectively. Big businesses may be efficient in the social sense, and usually they also possess, because of their monopoly position, private advantages. But the ability of a company to employ its dominant position to coerce unusually low prices from suppliers is not of any social advantage.

It follows that even if big companies had larger profit rates or smaller costs per unit of output than other companies, this would not prove that they were more efficient in socially desirable ways. Actually, big businesses are generally no more and no less efficient than medium-sized businesses even when the gains wrung by monopoly power are included in efficiency. This is the one general finding in comparative cost studies and comparative profitability studies.

Indeed, if one reflects upon the persistence of small and medium-sized companies in the industries dominated by big businesses, it is apparent that there can be no great advantages to size. If size were a great advantage, the smaller companies would soon lose the unequal race and disappear.

When we recall that most big businesses have numerous complete plants at various points throughout the country, this finding is not surprising. Why should U.S. Steel be more efficient than Inland Steel, when U.S. Steel is simply a dozen or more Inland Steels strewn about the country? Why should G.M. be appreciably more efficient than say a once-again independent Buick Motors? A few years ago Peter Drucker reported:

> The divisional manager . . . is in complete charge of production and sales. He hires, fires and promotes; and it is up to him to decide how many men he needs, with what qualifications and in what salary range —except for top executives whose employment is subject to a central-management veto. The divisional manager decides the factory layout, the technical methods and equipment used. . . . He buys his supplies independently from suppliers of his own choice. He determines the distribution of production within the several plants under his jurisdiction, decides which lines to push and decides on the methods of sale and distribution. . . . In everything pertaining to operations he is as much the real head as if his division were indeed an independent business.

If big businesses are not more efficient as a rule, how did they get big? The answer is that most giant firms arose out of mergers of many competing firms, and were created to eliminate competition. Standard Oil, General Electric, Westinghouse, U.S. Steel, Bethlehem, the meat packers, Borden, National Dairy, American Can, etc.—the full list of merger-created big businesses is most of the list of big businesses. A few big businesses owe their position to an industrial genius like Ford, and of course future geniuses would be hampered by an effective antitrust law—but less so than by entrenched monopolies or by public regulatory commissions.

We do not know what share of improvements in technology has been contributed by big businesses. Big businesses have made some signal contributions, and so also have small businesses, universities, and private individuals. It can be said that manufacturing industries dominated by big businesses have had no larger increases in output per worker on average than other manufacturing industries. This fact is sufficient to undermine the easy identification of economic progress with the laboratories of big businesses, but it does not inform us of the net effect of monopolies on economic progress.

At present, then, no definite effect of big business on economic progress can be established. I personally believe that future study will confirm the traditional belief that big businesses, for all their resources, cannot rival the infinite resource and cold scrutiny of many independent and competing companies. If the real alternative to bigness is government regulation or ownership, as I am about to argue, then the long-run consequences of big business are going to be highly adverse to economic progress.

REMEDIES FOR BIG BUSINESS

Let me restate the main points of the foregoing discussion in a less emphatic—and I think also a less accurate—manner:

1. Big businesses often possess and use monopoly power.
2. Big businesses weaken the political support for a private-enterprise system.
3. Big businesses are not appreciably more efficient or enterprising than medium-size businesses.

Few disinterested people will deny these facts—where do they lead?

A considerable section of the big-business community seems to have taken the following position. The proper way to deal with monopolistic practices is to replace the general prohibitions of the Sherman Act by a specific list of prohibited practices, so businessmen may know in advance and avoid committing monopolistic practices. The proper way to deal with the declining political support for private enterprise is to advertise the merits of private enterprise, at the same time claiming many of its achievements for big business. Much of this advertising has taken literally that form, apparently in the belief that one can sell a social system in exactly the same way and with exactly the same copywriters and media that one sells a brand of cigarettes.

Guard the Sherman Act

The request for a list of specifically prohibited monopolistic practices will be looked upon by many persons as a surreptitious attack upon the Sherman Act. I am among these cynics: the powerful drive in 1949 to pass a law legalizing basing-point price systems is sufficient evidence that large sectors of big business are wholly unreconciled to the law against conspiracies in restraint of trade. Even when the request for a specific list of prohibitions is made in all sincerity, however, it cannot be granted: No one can write down a full list of all the forms that objectionable monopoly power has taken and may someday take. Moreover, almost all uncertainties over the legality of conduct arise out of the Robinson-Patman Act, not the Sherman Act, and I would welcome the complete repeal of the former act.

We must look elsewhere for the solution of the problems raised by big business, and a satisfactory solution must deal with the facts I listed at the head of this section. Our present policy is not a satisfactory solution. The Sherman Act is admirable in dealing with formal conspiracies of many firms, but—at least with the Supreme Court's present conception of competition and of the proper remedies for demonstrated restraint of trade in oligopolistic industries—it cannot cope effectively with the problem posed by big business. In industries dominated by a few firms there is no need for formal conspiracies, with their trappings of quotas, a price-fixing committee, and the like. The big companies know they must "live with" one another, and the phrase means much the same thing as in the relationships between man and woman. Any competitive action one big company takes will lead to retaliation by the others. An informal code of behavior gradually develops in the industry: Firm X announces the new price, and except in very unusual circumstances Y and Z can be relied upon to follow. So long as there are a few big businesses in an industry, we simply cannot expect more than the tokens of competitive behavior. Antitrust decrees that the big businesses should ignore each other's existence serve no important purpose.

This conclusion, I must emphasize, is not merely that of "economic theorists," although most (academic) economists will subscribe to it. It is also the conclusion our generation is reaching, for our generation is not satisfied with the behavior of big business. More and more, big businesses are being asked to act in "the social interest," and more and more, government is interfering in their routine operation. The steel industry, for example, what with congressional review of prices and presidential coercion of wages, is drifting rapidly into a public-utility status. And the drift will not be stopped by slick advertising.

Dissolution the Remedy

No such drastic and ominous remedy as the central direction of economic life is necessary to deal with the problems raised by big business. The obvious and economical solution, as I have already amply implied, is to break up the giant companies.

READING 34
Planning, Regulation, and Competition

John Kenneth Galbraith
Willard F. Mueller

Among economists today there is a fundamental difference of opinion which is over neither politics nor economic and social goals. Both groups espouse the advantages of a free-market system under competition. The debate concerns the possibility of obtaining workable competition. Professor John Kenneth Galbraith of Harvard University and his followers believe that far-reaching market power over consumers in combination with a strong security motivation leads giant corporations to manage consumer behavior. This bureaucratic manipulation prevents consumers from spending in a way which maximizes their own and thus the welfare of society. Neoclassical economists see no evidence to support such alarmist conclusions. The following congressional testimony by Galbraith and Dr. Willard Mueller, representing the Federal Trade Commission, pinpoints some of the essential arguments on both sides of the issue.

Guideposts for Thought While Reading
Why does Galbraith argue that antitrust enforcement by the federal government is a charade? What solution, if any, does Galbraith suggest to maintain competitive markets? What are the points used by Mueller to defend current antitrust laws and enforcement efforts?

STATEMENT OF DR. JOHN KENNETH GALBRAITH, PAUL M. WARBURG PROFESSOR OF ECONOMICS, HARVARD UNIVERSITY, CAMBRIDGE, MASS.

In the lectures that precipitated this discussion and the book I have just published,[1] I took it for granted that American business has become very big.

The element of surprise in this conclusion is very small; I

Reprinted from *Planning, Regulation, and Competition*, Hearing before Subcommittees of the Select Committee on Small Business, United States Senate, Ninetieth Congress, First Session, A Seminar Discussion of the Question: "Are Planning and Regulation Replacing Competition in the New Industrial State?" U.S. Government Printing Office, Washington, 1967, pp. 4–27.

[1] *The New Industrial State* (Boston: Houghton Mifflin Co., 1967).

doubt that this conclusion will be much disputed. There are still a large number of small firms and small farms in the United States. They are, however, no longer characteristic of the American economy. In 1962, the five largest industrial corporations in the United States, with combined assets in excess of $36 billion, possessed over 12 percent of all assets used in manufacturing. The 50 largest corporations had over a third of all manufacturing assets. The 500 largest corporations had well over two-thirds. Corporations with assets in excess of $10 million, some 2,000 in all, accounted for about 80 percent of all the resources used in manufacturing in the United States.

In the mid-1950's, 28 corporations provided approximately 10 percent of all employment in manufacturing, mining, and retail and wholesale trade. Twenty-three corporations provided 15 percent of all the employment in manufacturing. In the first half of that decade—June 1950–June 1956—a hundred firms received two-thirds by value of all defense contracts; 10 firms received one-third. In 1960 four corporations accounted for an estimated 22 percent of all industrial research and development expenditure. Three hundred and eighty four corporations employing 5,000 or more workers accounted for 85 percent of these research and development expenditures; 260,000 firms employing fewer than 1,000 accounted for only 7 percent.

If I might continue this somewhat exaggerated dose of statistics for just a minute, in 1965, three industrial corporations, General Motors, Standard Oil of New Jersey, and Ford Motor Co., had more gross income than all of the farms in the country. This is relevant to my statement that these are the typical, characteristic parts of the economy. The income of General Motors, of $20.7 billion, about equalled that of the 3 million smallest farms in the country—around .90 percent of all farms. The gross revenues of each of the three corporations just mentioned far exceed those of any single State. The revenues of General Motors in 1963 were 50 times those of Nevada, eight times those of New York, and slightly less than one-fifth those of the Federal Government.

These figures, like all statistics, are subject to minor query on matters of detail. As orders of magnitude they are not, I believe, subject to any serious question. Nor are the consequences.

PLANNING REPLACES THE MARKET

The large firms that dominate the nonservice and nonagricultural sector of the economy have extensive power over their prices. They have large influence over the prices that they pay—at least those costs that are important to their operations. And also the wages they pay. They supply themselves with capital; some three-quarters of all savings now come from the retained earnings of corporations, which is to say that the latter have largely exempted themselves from dependence on the capital market. And, with varying degrees of success, firms with the resources to do so go beyond the prices that they set to persuade their customers as to what they should buy. This is a persuasion that, in various and subtle ways, extends to the State. There is great room for difference of opinion, and accordingly for debate, on how decisive are these several manifestations of power. But nearly all will agree that "There is a large correlation between the concentration of output in the hands of a small number of large producers and the existence of firms with significant degrees of market power." The observation just cited is that of Mr. Carl Kaysen and Mr. Donald F. Turner in their authoritative volume, *A Policy for Antitrust Law.*

They add, as would I, that a policy that deals with "the existence and significance of market power is not aimed at *merely marginal or special phenomena, but at phenomena spread widely through the economy.*" Still quoting Professor Kaysen and Mr. Turner.

In my own volume I have gone on, at no slight length, to argue that this trend to the large corporation and this resulting exercise of substantial power over the prices, costs, wages, capital sources, and consumers is part of the broad sweep of economic development. Technology; the extensive use of capital; affluent and hence malleable customers; the imperatives of organization; the role of the union; the requirements imposed by public tasks, including arms development and space exploration, have all weakened the authority of the market. At the same time, these developments have both enabled and required firms to substitute planning with its management of markets for a simple response to the market. Bigness and market power, in other words, are but one part of a much larger current of change. To see them in isolation from other change is artificial. In part it is what results when a social discipline passes however partially from the custody of scholars to that of specialists and mechanics.

I have also been concerned in this book with the problem of how we are to survive, and in civilized fashion, in a world of great organizations which, not surprisingly, impose both their values and their needs on the society they are assumed to serve.

But these further matters are not directly at issue this morning. In any case they do not directly involve the question of the antitrust laws.

ANTITRUST IS A CHARADE

The issue of the antitrust laws arises in response to a prior question. That question is whether we can escape the concentration and the attendant market control and planning which I have outlined and whether the antitrust laws, as now used, are an effective instrument for this escape. The present hearings materialized when I urged the contrary—when I said that the trend to great size and associated control was immutable, given our desire for economic development, and that the present antitrust efforts to deal with size and market power were a charade. I noted that the antitrust laws legitimatize the real exercise of market power on the part of the large firms by a rather diligent harassment of those who have less of it. Thus, they serve to reassure us on the condition they are assumed to correct.

The facts which lead to the foregoing conclusions are not at all obscure. Nor are they matters of great subtlety. They are accepted by most competent economists and lawyers including the very distinguished men here this morning. Only the rather obvious conclusions to be drawn from these facts encounter a measure of resistance. This, no doubt, is purely temporary, but while it persists it does cause a measure of confusion.

The most effective manifestation of economic power, all must agree, is simply the big firm. To be big in general and big in an industry is by far the best way of influencing prices and costs, commanding capital, having access to advertising, and selling resources, and possessing the other requisites of market power. And, as we have seen, by common agreement the heartland of the industrial economy is now dominated by large firms. The great bulk of American business is transacted by very large corporations.

And here enters the element of charade in the antitrust laws. If a firm is already large it is substantially immune under the antitrust laws. If you already have the basic requisite of market power, you are safe. The Assistant Attorney General in Charge of the Antitrust Laws in the distinguished book to which I have already adverted argues that the market power of the large firm should now be made subject to the antitrust laws. This indeed is the main thrust of Mr. Turner's and Mr. Kaysen's book. If something needs to be done, he would not, of course, argue that it has been done. And in responding to the questions of this committee on May 2 of this year he affirmed the point, if in slightly more cautious language:

> It is more difficult under present law to bring a case attacking ex*isting* concentration in an industry than to prevent further concentrations which firms attempt to realize through merger.

But this we see is no minor qualification. If firms are already large—if concentration is already great—if the resulting power to use Mr. Turner's own words, is not "merely marginal" but is "spread widely through the economy" as he says, then it means that all so favored have won immunity or virtual immunity from the antitrust laws. And this, of course, is the case.

Meanwhile, the antitrust laws are effective in two instances where the firms do not have market power but are seeking to achieve it. Where firms are few and large they can, without overt collusion, establish and maintain a price that is generally satisfactory to all participants. Nor is this an especially difficult calculation, this exercise of power. This is what we economists with our genius for the neat phrase have come to call oligopolistic rationality. And this market power is legally immune or very nearly so. It is everyday practice in autos, steel, rubber, and virtually every other industry shared or dominated by, relatively, a few large firms. But if there are 20 or 30 or more significant firms in the industry, this kind of tacit pricemaking—this calculation as to what is mutually advantageous but without overt communication—becomes more difficult, maybe very difficult. The same result can only be achieved by having a meeting or by exchanging information on prices and costs and price intentions. But this is illegal. It is also legally vulnerable. And it is, in fact, an everyday object of prosecution as the Department of Justice will confirm. What the big firm in the concentrated industry can accomplish legally and effortlessly because of its size, the small firm in the unconcentrated industry does at the pain of civil and even criminal prosecution. Moreover, with this my colleagues will, I believe, agree.

The second manifestation of the charade has to do with mergers. If a firm is already large, it has as a practical matter nothing to fear under antimerger provisions of the Clayton Act. It will not be demerged. It can continue to grow from its own earnings; if discreet, it can even, from time to time, pick up a small and impecunious competitor, for it can reasonably claim that this does little to alter the pattern of competition in the industry. But if two medium-sized firms unite in order to deal more effectively with this giant, the law will be on them like a tiger. Again if large, you are exempt. If you seek to become as large, or even if you seek to become somewhat larger, although still much smaller, you are in trouble. And again I doubt that the committee will encounter a great deal of dissent.

Here we have the nature of modern antitrust activity. It conducts a fairly effective war on small firms which seek the same market power that the big firms already, by their nature, possess. Behind this impressive facade the big participants who have the most power bask in nearly total immunity. And since the competitive market, like God and a sound family life, is something that no sound businessman can actively oppose, even the smaller entrepreneurs who are the natural victims of this arrangement do not actively protest. It is possible that they do not know how they are being used.

As I say all of this is agreed—or at least is supported by the past writings and speeches of participants in this discussion. All I have done—I wish I could lay claim to greater novelty—is to state the rather disagreeable conclusion flowing from this agreement. The antitrust laws give the impression of protecting the market and competition by attacking those who exercise it most effectively. I wonder if the committee thinks that charade is an unjust word?

Now let me clear up two or three secondary matters which may seem to affect this discussion but really do not. The first requires me, I think for the first time—in substance as distinct from terminology—to quit company with Attorney General Turner. Mr. Turner, while conceding that the law is largely helpless in attacking achieved as distinct from aspired-to power, holds that it is important to act preventatively to keep smaller firms from getting larger. This he has emphasized in his responses to this committee. It will surely have occurred to the committee, as it must have occurred to Mr. Turner, that this does not meet the issue of gross discrimination as between those who already have and those who aspire to market power. Nor, one imagines, can a major law officer of the Government be entirely happy about such discrimination. It condones professional and accomplished wrongdoing, as it were, but stresses the importance of cracking down on amateur wickedness. Surely this is bad law. Also, given the size and market power that has already been achieved, and given its immunity, it will be evident that this justification amounts to locking the stable door not alone after the horse has been stolen but after the entire stud has been galloped away.

Next, I must correct a misapprehension of Attorney General Turner. His responses to the committee and his extremely interesting lecture attacking my general position in London convey the impression that I am concerned with making the economic case for the large corporation. I am, he suggests, especially concerned to defend its efficiency and technical virtuosity. To this he responds by arguing that, while the big corporation is more efficient than the small firm, there is no great difference between the big corporation and the giant corporation. He doesn't make altogether clear, incidentally, how big a big as distinct from a giant corporation is. All would, I imagine, be among the five hundred or thousand firms that dominate industrial activity. But I have a more fundamental objection. He attacks me on a point that concerns me little and which is of no importance for my case.

I am not concerned with making the case for big business. Nor am I especially concerned about its efficiency or inefficiency. Doubtless efficiency is worth having. But, like truth, regular bathing and better traffic regulation, it has an adequate number of exponents. I have always thought it unwise to compete with the commonplace. Mr. Turner may be correct in his conclusions about the giants. I am content to argue that we have big business, and that the antitrust laws notwithstanding we will continue to have it, and that they give an impression of alternative possibilities that do not exist.

I conclude also that while big business and giant business may not be more efficient, their market power as manifested only on what they sell and what they buy and over buyers does give them advantages in planning their own future and insuring their own survival. Since big business is inevitable and will not be affected by the antitrust laws, I naturally go on to consider how we may come to terms with it. Much of my book is concerned with that. If my colleagues this morning disagree, as is their right, they must tell you how the antitrust laws are to be brought effectively to bear on the large corporation. Otherwise —and here let me interpolate an important point—there is no escape from the conclusion that the antitrust laws, so far from being a threat to big business are a facade behind which it operates with yet greater impunity. They create the impression, the antitrust laws, that the market is a viable control. Then, if a drug firm has exorbitant profits, it can say this is what the market allows. Or if an automobile firm does not want to install safety appliances, it can say that the market does not demand it. Or if there is resistance to Government price guideposts to prevent inflation, it can be said that these interfere with the market.

In each case, the antitrust laws effectively protect the large business from social pressure or regulation by maintaining the myth that the market does the regulating instead.

Finally, I agree that the antitrust laws have purposes other than those related to the structure of industry and the resulting power and planning. I agree in particular they are a code of what is deemed fair and decent as between seller and buyers. They exclude the resort to activities—naked aggression, as in the case of the old Standard Oil Co. in the last century—based on superior economic resources, favoritism, surreptitious and unfair discounts, numerous other practices which the civilized commercial community holds in disesteem. I have no complaint about these aspects of the antitrust laws. On the contrary, I consider them serviceable. But only in the most marginal fashion do they thus affect the structure of industry. They are, in large part, a separate matter and do not affect the discussion here.

THE DISSOLUTION DILEMMA

To what then does this all lead? It is possible that my distinguished colleagues here this morning will call for an all-out attack on achieved market power along the lines which Attorney General Turner has adumbrated in his book, which Prof. Walter Adams has long favored, and which I have just said would be necessary if they disagree with my conclusions on the inevitability of market power. This means action, including enabling legislation leading to all-out dissolution proceedings against General Motors, Ford, the oil majors, United States Steel, General Electric, IBM, Western Electric, Du Pont, Swift, Bethlehem, International Harvester, North American Aviation, Goodyear, Boeing, National Dairy Products, Procter & Gamble, Eastman Kodak, and all of comparable size and scope. For there can be no doubt: All are giants. All have market power. All enjoy an immunity not accorded to those who merely aspire to their power. Such an onslaught, tantamount, given the role of the big firms in the economy as I described it, to declaring the heartland of the modern economy illegal, would go far to make legitimate the objections to my position. It would mean that achieved market power was subject to the same legal attack as that which is only a matter of aspiration.

But I will be a trifle surprised if my distinguished colleagues from the Government are willing to proclaim such a crusade. I am frank to say I would not favor it myself; as I indicated at the outset, I do not think that the growth of the modern corporation can be isolated from other and intricately related changes in modern economic development. I doubt that one can operate on one part of this fabric. The political problems in proclaiming much of the modern economy illegal will also strike many as impressive.

If this crusade is not to be launched, then my good friends have no alternative but to agree with me. They are good men; they cannot acquiesce in a policy which by their own admission attacks the small man for seeking what the big firm enjoys with impunity. I readily concede that it would be quixotic to ask the repeal of the antitrust laws although other industrial countries function quite competently without them. But the antitrust laws are part of the American folklore. They receive strong support from the legal profession and vice versa. They have a reserve value for dealing with extreme and sanguinary abuse of power as occasionally occurs. I would be content were we simply to withdraw our faith from the antitrust laws—were we to cease to imagine that there is any chance that they will affect the structure of American industry or its market power and, having in mind the present discrimination in their application, were we then to allow them quietly to atrophy. Then we would face the real problem, which is how to live with the vast organizations—and the values they impose—that we have and will continue to have. This being so, nostalgia will no longer be a disguise for that necessity.

STATEMENT OF DR. WILLARD F. MUELLER, CHIEF ECONOMIST AND DIRECTOR, BUREAU OF ECONOMICS, FEDERAL TRADE COMMISSION, WASHINGTON, D.C.[2]

At the outset, let there be no mistake about it: Although Galbraith has articulated a provocative thesis concerning the causes and implications of "the new industrial state," he has not borne the burden of mustering the evidence to validate this thesis.

Time permits joining issues on only his key points. I shall challenge three of his major contentions:

[2] The views expressed herein are those of the author and not necessarily those of the Federal Trade Commission.

1. Technological imperatives dictate vast industrial concerns and high levels of market concentration and, hence, the death of the market.

2. Public policy aimed at maintaining a market economy has failed in the past and is doomed to fail in the future.

3. The necessity for State planning in certain areas further diminishes the need for reliance on the market as a regulating and planning agent.

THE TECHNOLOGICAL IMPERATIVES

Most fundamental to Galbraith's thesis are the so-called technological imperatives which he views as the root causes of modern industrial organization. He asserts that we must have very large industrial complexes and high market concentration because of the requirements of large-scale production, invention, and innovation. As he puts it, "The enemy of the market is not ideology but technology." But what are the facts on this point?

Recent studies of this subject are almost unanimous in concluding that productive efficiency dictates high concentration in only a small and declining share of all manufacturing industries. On this point, there seems to be little disagreement.

There is a growing body of research into the extent to which economies of large scale dictate large business enterprise and high market concentration. The evidence is sharpest in the area of productive efficiency. This is an especially crucial area because of the public policy dilemma posed by industries with increasing returns to large scale. In clear-cut cases where large-scale production dictates monopoly, as with telephone and electric power, the American answer has been either regulation or Government ownership. But, if such industries prove the rule rather than the exception, this raises a basic question as to the compatibility of productive efficiency and a competitively structured economy. It is, therefore, extremely significant that recent studies are unanimous in concluding that productive efficiency dictates high concentration in only a small—and declining—share of all manufacturing industries.

But Galbraith does not rest his case on the requirement of large-scale production. He further argues that economies of scale in research and innovation make high concentration and near monopoly an inevitable outcome of modern capitalism. Since Joseph Schumpeter first set forth this doctrine in 1942 and Galbraith expanded upon it in 1952, it has been subjected to extensive empirical testing. There has been a virtual flood of studies in recent years. All students of the subject are not in complete agreement. But as a minimum, a careful reading of the evidence shows that the theory has no general validity in explaining inventive and innovative activity in American experience. Indeed, recent studies indicate that the thesis is on the verge of collapse. One of Schumpeter's disciples recently discovered no systematic relationship between the degree of market power and inventive success. He concluded:

> These findings among other things raise doubts whether the big, monopolistic conglomerate corporation is as efficient an engine of technological change as disciples of Schumpeter (including myself) have supposed it to be. Perhaps a bevy of fact-mechanics can still rescue the Schumpeter engine from disgrace, but at present the outlook seems pessimistic.

Students of the problem owe a debt of gratitude to the Senate Subcommittee on Antitrust and Monopoly, chaired by Senator Philip A. Hart, for the exhaustive hearings it has held on the subject of the role of technology and industrial organization. Over the past 3 years these hearings have reviewed systematically nearly all of the recent authoritative work on this subject. I shall not review this evidence here, but it is must reading for anyone genuinely interested in getting at the facts in this area. Regrettably, Professor Galbraith apparently has failed to explore this and other authoritative work on the subject. Until he, or others, can come up with contrary evidence, the chief pillar of his thesis lacks an empirical foundation.

Perhaps no industry fits as snugly the Galbraith model for ideal planning as the American steel industry. Since the creation of United States Steel in 1901, the American steel industry has been highly concentrated and dominated by big enterprises. Presumably this market structure provided what Galbraith views as the "prime requirement" of planning: "control over decision."

There can be no doubt but that the market structure of the industry gave big steel considerable discretion in planning. But the relevant question is whether this discretion was used as Galbraith's theory predicts. Fortunately in this case we need not rely on speculation. The leading steel companies clearly had a lackluster record as inventive and innovative forces in this most basic industry. The accomplishments of United States Steel have been especially disappointing. After an exhaustive study of the corporation, an engineering consulting firm reported to United States Steel in 1939 that it was lagging badly in many respects. Nor have United States Steel or other large steel companies performed much better since 1939. A study of the 13 major innovations in the American steel industry between 1940 and 1955 reveals none was the outgrowth of American steel companies. Four were based on inventions of European steel companies (generally small by American standards) and seven came from independent inventors.

Especially instructive is the postwar record concerning the introduction of the oxygen steelmaking process by dominant American steel firms. The basic oxygen process has been called the only major technological breakthrough at the ingot level of steelmaking since before 1900.

Not only did the largest steel companies play no role in the discovery and initial development of this important innovation, but they lagged badly in introducing it. A small Austrian steel company (which was one-third the size of a single plant of United States Steel) perfected and introduced the oxygen process. The first American company to adopt the new process was McLouth Steel, which had less than 1 percent of industry capacity. Although other smaller companies followed McLouth's lead, not until 1964 did United States Steel and Bethlehem introduce the process. This was fully 10 years after McLouth and 14 years after the small pioneering Austrian firm had introduced this revolutionary process.

Does Galbraith really want more industries structured like the American steel industry? Would he have permitted this industry to become even more concentrated through mergers among small enterprises (e.g., Bethlehem and Youngstown, which you will recall was one of the first merger cases) so that they could better emulate the performance of U.S. Steel?

IS THE MARKET DEAD?

As a corollary of his assumptions concerning technology, Galbraith argues that we can no longer rely on market forces to allocate resources. Because of this, he continues, the struggle to maintain competition alive "has obviously been a losing one. Indeed, it has been lost." These assertions go to the heart of Galbraith's thesis, for it is because the market has perished that we must be saved by extensive extra market planning. Should this premise prove faulty, Galbraith's thesis comes tumbling down.

We have already seen that the evidence does not support his thesis that as a general rule technological imperatives require high levels of industrial concentration. It should therefore come as no surprise that in many industries competitive forces are considerably stronger than Galbraith suggests and that in many industries where concentration is highest, the market position of industry leaders is being eroded. I recently presented to this committee a rather comprehensive summary of postwar concentration trends. Very briefly, during the postwar years—between 1947 and 1963—market concentration tended to decline across a broad front in the producer goods sector of manufacturing. While this is in direct conflict with the predictions of Galbraith's thesis, it is entirely consistent with the empirical evidence referred to earlier and which Professor Adams has mentioned. While in some industries technology may make it impossible for very small companies to operate efficiently, it does not dictate mammoth size and high levels of market concentration. Most American markets have become so large that they can sustain a rather considerable number of efficient-size enterprises.

Surprisingly, it is in consumer goods manufacturing industries where concentration has been on the rise in the postwar years. Surprisingly, I say, because the technological requirements in these industries demand relatively smaller enterprises than in producer goods manufacturing. Of course, the reasons for increasing concentration in consumer goods manufacturing are to be found in the requirements of product differentiation (especially the costs of large-scale promotion) and distribution, not in the technological imperatives that Galbraith assumes to be the kingpins of market power.

When postwar concentration trends are viewed together with the recent findings concerning the relationship between technology and industrial organization, we have a valuable insight into the future viability of the market as a regulator and planner of economic activity. Modern technology has not made obsolete our competitive, market-oriented economy. For it is precisely in the producer goods manufacturing industries where economies of large-scale invention, innovation, and production are most pronounced. Yet these industries have experienced a significant drop in market concentration. This has occurred because many industrial markets have grown more rapidly than have the requirements of large-scale business organization.

These trends in market concentration may yet be irrelevant if Galbraith's concept of market power is correct. Throughout his discussion he implies that, "characteristically," American industries are concentrated "oligopolies," and that the firms operating in them have great discretionary pricing power independent of the market. But like Gertrude Stein, Galbraith has difficulties with shades of difference. Fortunately, however, all oligopolies are not alike and there are important differences in the degree of market power conferred by varying market structures. The accumulating evidence of the relationship between an industry's structure and its performance leaves little room for agnosticism concerning the powerful role played by the market in limiting discretionary pricing power. And, importantly, there is now persuasive evidence demonstrating that in the larger part of American manufacturing industry market forces limit quite severely the discretionary pricing power of firms. But, again, Galbraith has ignored the mounting evidence which runs counter to one of his central premises.

This isn't to imply that there are no strong positions of entrenched power in our economy—there are. Again, however, Galbraith greatly overstates his case. But, importantly, whereas he pays tribute to the firms with substantial market power—indeed, he believes such power is essential—the evidence indicates that firms with great power perform less admirably than he assumes. Hence, the facts support a precisely opposite public policy than that advocated by Galbraith—we need more competition, not less. (We shall consider shortly whether or not this is feasible.)

The rising concentration in consumer-goods industries at first blush seems to bear out Galbraith's thesis of managing consumer wants to suit the needs of the business enterprise. But the causes of developments here are not rooted in Galbraith's technological imperatives. As noted earlier, the requirements of large-scale production, invention, and innovation are less demanding in the manufacture of consumer goods than in other areas of manufacturing. It is true that many sellers try to manage consumer wants. But this is because of the form which competition takes where opportunities for product differentiation exist. True, the market operates less perfectly as a result—though I suspect it operates better than Galbraith assumes. If

Americans really are strongly dissatisfied, however, they can do something about this problem; though they probably won't. Nor will Galbraith's "new industrial state" change things on this score.

Despite its shortcomings, particularly in the area of some consumer goods, the market clearly has not disappeared as the key coordinating and integrating force in allocating resources in most of the economy. The picture that emerges when one studies the entire industrial landscape is not that painted by Galbraith. Whereas he concedes his thesis does not encompass the entire economy, close inspection shows it captures only a small part of the real world.

IS ANTITRUST A CHARADE?

But the mere absence of factors requiring high market concentration does not guarantee that excessive concentration will not arise or that it will decline in industries where it already is too high. Simply put, effective competition is not a flower that thrives unattended. Powerful firms may engage in competitive strategies which counteract the forces working toward deconcentration. Specifically, until the passage of the Celler-Kefauver Act in 1950, horizontal and vertical mergers often had the effect of offsetting these forces, with the result that in many industries concentration remained unchanged or even increased.

Again, I feel that Professor Galbraith has neglected his homework. He has not kept abreast of contemporary antitrust policy or its effects. He asserts that it is a "charade" acted out, "not to prevent exploitation of the public," but, "to persuade people in general and British Socialists and American liberals in particular, that the market is still extant." He sums up his views of current antitrust policy as follows (he has already mentioned them this morning):

> A great corporation wielding vast power over its markets is substantially immune * * *. But if two small firms seek to unite, this corporate matrimony will be meticulously scrutinized. And, very possibly, it will be forbidden.

These assertions simply do not square with the facts. Antimerger effort has been directed almost exclusively against the largest industrial concerns. It has not, as he suggested, been an attack on industrial midgets. Over 60 percent of the largest, those with over a billion dollars, and merely a third of the top 200 have been subjects of antimerger complaints. Practically all of these complaints have not involved the challenging of miniscule mergers, but rather have involved an attack upon mergers by large concerns. I have discussed this at greater length elsewhere. My major conclusion, however, is that there has been an enormous effort. Perhaps Professor Galbraith would say that my intellectual outlook has been affected somewhat by the technostructure within which I now operate. But even if I were back at the University of Wisconsin—or even at Harvard—I would still come to the same conclusion, as I am sure he will when he reads my other statement. In my opinion, this enforcement effort represents a great victory for competition, as well as a clear demonstration that antitrust policy can be an effective instrument of public policy in the last half of the 20th century.

It is true that antitrust policy cannot easily—and certainly not quickly—solve problems of deeply entrenched power. Fifty years of ineffective public policy toward mergers resulted in unnecessarily high concentration in many industries. But recent developments show that much can be accomplished. I say categorically: Whether or not the market survives in the greater part of our economy, or is destroyed by vast aggregations of market power, will not be determined by technological imperatives but by public policy toward the achievement and retention of power. The market may well be destroyed in the next generation as Galbraith predicts, but not for his reasons. It will be a matter of public will or neglect, not technology.

PLANNING AND THE STATE

In the "new industrial state" the Government plays a central role in economic planning with a concomitant diminution in reliance upon the market. Specifically, it stabilizes aggregate demand, underwrites expensive technology, restrains wages and prices in limiting inflation, provides technical and educational manpower, and buys upwards of a fifth of our economic output.

It is true that the Government does these things, and more. But Galbraith exaggerates the role of the state (as opposed to the market) in the planning process. He points out correctly that one of the main responsibilities of the modern state is to sustain aggregate demand and stimulate economic growth. He fails to perceive, however, that the state's planning in this respect is neither in competition with, nor a substitute for, planning by business enterprise, and it certainly does not require abandonment of the market. On the contrary, the basic philosophy of the Employment Act of 1946 is that the state create a general economic environment within which private enterprise can generate economic growth. Within this environment the basic "planning" decisions of what and how much of each product to produce are left to private enterprise responding to aggregate demand.

Experience increasingly demonstrates the heavy role played by the market in implementing or frustrating monetary and fiscal policy aimed at full employment. Only if competition is effective are extensive price controls not a necessary adjunct to planning for rapid economic growth without inflation.

The wage and price guideposts of the Council of Economic Advisers are a symptom of the absence of effective competition in some segments of the economy. But, happily, these segments are in the minority. Were it otherwise, it probably would be impossible to push toward full employment without implementing extensive wage and price controls.

None appreciate these facts of life so keenly as those economists responsible for public policy in this area. Dr. Walter Heller, the former Chairman of the Council of Economic Advisers and prime mover in gaining public acceptance for the "new economics," has emphasized the importance of keeping competition alive. He does not believe that planning for rapid economic growth requires abandonment of the market. Rather, he argues forcibly in his recent book that we must make competition more, not less, effective. As he puts it:

> There are substantial differences among economists on how far the government should go in protecting consumers or setting guideposts for wages and prices. But there is little difference—at least among the vast majority of economists—in supporting strong measures to protect the free play of market forces against monopoly and price-fixing, and in strongly opposing direct wage and price controls as inefficient and inequitable substitutes for market forces, to be considered only as a last resort in a war economy.

In a similar vein, the Joint Economic Committee of the Congress has repeatedly emphasized the importance of maintaining effectively competitive markets, and I do not think they are merely playing charades. Its most recent report on the Economic Report of the President concluded, "Antitrust must be assigned a central role in national economic policy of no less significance than monetary and fiscal policy."

Do not misunderstand me. Certainly, many of the most pressing problems of the day—water and air pollution, job retraining, urban and rural poverty, preservation of our natural resources, promotion of basic research, to name a few—require action and planning by the state. But it is wrong to infer that the failure of the market to solve these kinds of problems represents a fatal flaw in the system. Unfortunately, many persons are inclined to damn the market—which to them means the businesses operating within it—for failing to do jobs better left to the state. And, unfortunately, the defensively hostile responses of some business leaders to every social welfare proposal lend credence to the argument that the real issue at stake is the market system. Actually, however, the real issue usually is whether or not a particular job should be done at all, and who is going to pay for it. Once it is agreed that there is nothing inherently un-American or antimarket in admitting that some things are best left to the state, the state and the market can live in happy coexistence. In truth, they are indispensable complements of one another, rather than rivals or substitutes. But this has little to do with economic imperatives and the abandonment of the market.

READING 35
The Military-Industrial Complex
Dwight D. Eisenhower

In his farewell address to the nation on January 17, 1961, President Dwight Eisenhower warned against the dangers of excessive economic-political influence lodged in the "military-industrial complex." The rapid rise in government spending is, in large part, military spending. Thus, a significant portion of the market economy has as

Taken from the text of a radio-TV address to the nation by President Dwight D. Eisenhower, January 17, 1961.

its consumer the federal government. Many of the industries producing for the military market are highly concentrated. Bargaining is between giant government and giant firms, a big step from the Invisible Hand. An unusual and significant aspect of Eisenhower's final speech as president of the United States provided a warning that the similar interests of governmental bureaucrats and the manufacturers of military hardware may make them closer to co-conspirators than to the buyers and sellers in a free market.

Guideposts for Thought While Reading

Do you agree that there are dangers to the American way of life implicit in the "military-industrial complex"?

A vital element in keeping the peace is our military establishment. Our arms must be mighty, ready for instant action, so that no potential aggressor may be tempted to risk his own destruction.

Our military organization today bears little relation to that known by any of my predecessors in peacetime, or indeed by the fighting men of World War II or Korea.

Until the latest of our world conflicts, the United States had no armaments industry. American makers of plowshares could, with time and as required, make swords as well. But now we can no longer risk emergency improvisation of national defense; we have been compelled to create a permanent armaments industry of vast proportions. Added to this, 3.5 million men and women are directly engaged in the defense establishment. We annually spend on military security alone more than the net income of all United States corporations.

This conjunction of an immense military establishment and a large arms industry is new in the American experience. The total influence—economic, political, even spiritual—is felt in every city, every statehouse, every office of the Federal Government. We recognize the imperative need for this development. Yet we must not fail to comprehend its grave implications. Our toil, resources and livelihood are all involved; so is the very structure of our society.

In the councils of Government, we must guard against the acquisition of unwarranted influence, whether sought or unsought, by the military-industrial complex. The potential for the disastrous rise of misplaced power exists and will persist.

We must never let the weight of this combination endanger our liberties or democratic processes. We should take nothing for granted. Only an alert and knowledgeable citizenry can compel the proper meshing of the huge industrial and military machinery of defense with our peaceful methods and goals, so that security and liberty may prosper together.

Akin to, and largely responsible for the sweeping changes in our industrial-military posture, has been the technological revolution during recent decades.

In this revolution, research has become central; it also becomes more formalized, complex and costly. A steadily increasing share is conducted for, by, or at the direction of the Federal Government.

Today, the solitary inventor, tinkering in his shop, has been overshadowed by task forces of scientists in laboratories and testing fields. In the same fashion, the free university, historically the fountainhead of free ideas and scientific discovery, has experienced a revolution in the conduct of research. Partly because of the huge costs involved, a Government contract becomes virtually a substitute for intellectual curiosity. For every blackboard there are now hundreds of new electronic computers.

The prospect of domination of the nation's scholars by federal employment, project allocations, and the power of money is ever present—and is gravely to be regarded.

Yet, in holding scientific research and discovery in respect, as we should, we must also be alert to the equal and opposite danger that public policy could itself become the captive of a scientific-technological elite.

It is the task of statesmanship to mold, to balance and to integrate these and other forces, new and old, within the principles of our democratic system—ever aiming toward the supreme goals of our free society.

READINGS 36 AND 37
Ralph Nader and the New Citizenship

As a self-appointed, and unpaid, public defender, Ralph Nader has recently laid bare monopolistic, illegal, and inequitable business operations in his writing and his Congressional testimony which is recorded in the public archives. Reading 55 serves to introduce the reader to the many varied business practices which Mr. Nader has attacked in his defense of the public interest. Reading 56 gives excerpts from Nader's testimony before a Congressional committee with respect to the monopolistic practices of the automobile industry. It will be readily apparent that Nader does not pull his punches!

Guideposts for Thought While Reading

How does Ralph Nader succeed in attacking the many monopolistic business practices without resorting to legal battles? How many different charges by Nader against illicit activity by big industry and big government can you find in these two readings? Why is it that none of Nader's targets have yet sued him for libel?

Midway through lunch at a fashionable Washington restaurant not long ago, a young man named Ralph Nader stopped suddenly and gazed down in disgust at his chef's salad. There, nestled among the lettuce leaves, lay a dead fly. Nader spun in his chair and jabbed both arms into the air to summon a waiter. Pointing accusingly at the intruder on his plate, he ordered: "Take it away!" The waiter apologized and rushed to produce a fresh salad, but Nader's anger only rose. While his luncheon companions watched the turmoil that had erupted around him, Nader launched into a detailed indictment of sanitation in restaurants. He pointed out that flies killed by insect spray often fall into food, thereby providing customers not only with an unappetizing bonus but also with a dose of DDT—or something even stronger.

Restaurant owners had better take heed. Nader is by now an

almost legendary crusader who would—and could—use a fly to instigate a congressional investigation. As the self-appointed and unpaid guardian of the interests of 204 million U.S. consumers, he has championed dozens of causes, prompted much of U.S. industry to reappraise its responsibilities and, against considerable odds, created a new climate of concern for the consumer among both politicians and businessmen. Nader's influence is greater now than ever before. That is partly because the consumer, who has suffered the steady ravishes of inflation upon his income, is less willing to tolerate substandard, unsafe or misadvertised goods. It is also because Nader's ideas have won acceptance in some surprising places. Last week, for example, Henry Ford II went farther than any other automobile executive ever has in acknowledging the industry's responsibility for polluting the air and asked—indeed, prodded—the Government to help correct the situation. The auto companies must develop, said Ford, "a virtually emission-free" car, and soon. Ford did not mention Ralph Nader, but it was not really necessary. Nader is widely known as a strong critic of the auto industry for, among other things, its pollution of the atmosphere.

Nader was able to force off the market General Motors' Corvair, which was withdrawn from production this year. Corvair's sales had plunged by 93% after Nader condemned the car as a safety hazard in his bestseller, *Unsafe at Any Speed*. That influential book, and Nader's later speeches, articles and congressional appearances, also forced the Department of Transportation to impose stricter safety standards on automobile and tire manufacturers.

Advocate, muckraker and crusader, Nader has also been almost solely responsible for the passage of five major federal laws. They are the National Traffic and Motor Vehicle Safety Act of 1966, the Wholesome Meat Act of 1967, the Natural Gas Pipeline Safety Act, the Radiation Control for Health and Safety Act and the Wholesale Poultry Products Act, all of 1968. This week Congress will almost certainly pass the Federal Coal Mine Health and Safety Act, which Nader and a group of insurgent mine workers supported against the wishes of complacent union leadership. The act contains stiff preventive measures against working conditions that can cause black lung.

Nader was the first to accuse baby-food manufacturers of imperiling the health of infants by using monosodium glutamate, a taste enhancer that medical research shows can cause brain damage in some animals. The three largest producers of baby food have since stopped using it. In addition, Nader's repeated warnings about the dangers of cyclamates and DDT helped to nudge the Department of Health, Education and Welfare to press research that led to recent federal restrictions on their use. From witness chairs and podiums, he has also taken aim at excessively fatty hot dogs, unclean fish, tractors that tip over and kill farmers, and the dangerous misuse of medical X rays. He has revealed that some color-television sets were recalled for leaking excessive amounts of radiation. (The Federal Trade Commission has publicly warned viewers to sit at least six feet away from color tubes.)

THE EROSION OF LIFE

To many Americans, Nader, at 35, has become something of a folk hero, a symbol of constructive protest against the status quo. When this peaceful revolutionary does battle against modern bureaucracies, he uses only the weapons available to any citizen—the law and public opinion. He has never picketed, let alone occupied, a corporate office or public agency. Yet Nader has managed to cut through all the protective layers and achieve results. He has shown that in an increasingly computerized, complex and impersonal society, one persistent man can actually do something about the forces that often seem to badger him—that he can indeed even shake and change big business, big labor and even bigger Government.

"My job is to bring issues out in the open where they cannot be ignored," says Nader, chopping his hands, as he often does when he speaks. "There is a revolt against the aristocratic uses of technology and a demand for democratic uses. We have got to know what we are doing to ourselves. Life can be—and is being—eroded." To prevent that erosion, he unmercifully nags consumer-minded U.S. Senators, pushing them to pass new bills. When their committees stall, he phones them by day, by night, and often on Sundays. "This is Ralph," he announces, and nobody has to ask, "Ralph *who*?"

Nader today is widening his sights. A lawyer by training, he is investigating the affairs of Covington & Burling, the Washington law firm headed by former Secretary of State Dean Acheson. At one time or another, Covington & Burling has numbered among its clients 200 of the nation's 500 biggest corporations, and Nader wants to determine just how much influence the firm has inside the Government. Most of all, he is probing into the affairs of ossified federal bureaucracies. "We hear a lot about law and order on the streets," he says, with a mischievous twinkle in his eyes. "I thought we ought to find out how law and order operates in the regulatory agencies." How does it? "It doesn't."

DEFERRED BRIBES TO REGULATORS

He issued a report (now in hardcover) that scaldingly criticized the FTC and called for its reorganization: recently several FTC officials have agreed with him. He is examining laxity within agencies as diverse as the National Air Pollution Control Administration and the Federal Railroad Administration, which he says shares the blame for the fact that U.S. railways have 100 accidents a day, accounting for 2,400 deaths a year. "Regulatory agencies have failed by the most modest of standards," Nader contends in great part because their top men are too cozy with the industries that they oversee and often use their Government jobs as stepping-stones to lucrative private careers in the same field. By his count, 75% of former commissioners of the Federal Communications Commission are employed or retained by the communications industry. This, he charges, amounts to a "deferred bribe." Agency officials who resign their jobs, Nader contends, should be barred from accepting immediate employment in the industry that they were supposedly policing.

NADER'S RAIDERS

To multiply the manpower for his campaigns, Nader has enlisted the help of vacationing students for the past two summers. Their Zola-like zeal for investigating bureaucracies has earned them the name "Nader's Raiders." Last year there were only seven Raiders, but this year the number grew to 102 law, engineering and medical students. The Raiders, who were paid a meager living allowance ($500 to $1,000 for ten weeks), delved energetically into the Department of Agriculture, the Food and Drug Administration, the National Water Pollution Control Administration, occupational health agencies, the Interstate Commerce Commission and several other fiefdoms.

In anticipation of their findings, which are due to be released beginning early next year, at least one ICC official has already resigned. Meanwhile, Nader and his Raiders have accused Government authorities in general of "systematically and routinely" violating the 2½-year-old Freedom of Information Act, which is supposed to entitle public access to much federal information. "If Government officials displayed as much imagination and initiative in administering their programs as they do in denying information about them," he says, "many national problems now in the grip of bureaucratic blight might become vulnerable to resolution." In line with that philosophy, one group of Raiders last month filed a suit in federal court to force the Civil Aeronautics Board to release findings on passenger complaints. Nader expects similar suits to be filed soon against the Departments of Labor and Agriculture.

Over the long run, the inspiration that Ralph Nader is providing for young Americans may prove as important to the country as his own lone battle. The Harvard Law School newspaper has somewhat generously called him "the most outstanding man ever to receive a degree from this institution," which has counted among its graduates Oliver Wendell Holmes and Felix Frankfurter. Nader is a major hero in most law schools. Two of last summer's Raiders canvassed Texas colleges and returned with 700 applications for next summer.

UNSAFE AT ANY SPEED

What makes Nader so effective today? Much of the answer lies in his lawyer's dedication to hard facts. He makes accusations almost daily that would be libelous if untrue; yet no one has ever sued him on his charges against companies or products. He collects facts everywhere—from his audiences on campus speaking tours, from obscure trade journals and Government publications, from interviews with high officials, from secret informers in public office and private industry, from thousands of letters addressed simply to "Ralph Nader, Washington, D.C." Nader receives more mail than the majority of U.S. Senators and Congressmen, reads all the letters—but can answer few.

His first inkling that all was not well with the Corvair's suspension system came from a disgruntled General Motors auto worker who wrote him a letter. In *Unsafe at Any Speed,* Nader went on to single out the sporty car's rear-suspension system as an example of hazardous compromise between engineering and styling. At certain speeds and tire pressures, or in certain types of turns, he charged, the rear wheels could "tuck under," causing a driver to lose control. G.M., which eventually redesigned the system, at first did not even recall the model for checking.

But executives were disturbed enough by Nader's charges to hire a Washington law firm to look into the matter. The lawyer, in turn, engaged the Vincent Gillen private detective agency to trail Nader. Purely on a fishing expedition that was to find nothing, the agency's head urged his men to uncover what they could about Nader's "women, boys, etc." Tipped by friends that investigators were looking into his private life. Nader charged publicly that he was being harassed. G.M.'s use of grade-B spy-movie tactics was fully exposed when its president, James Roche (now chairman), was summoned before a Senate subcommittee and twice apologized to Nader for the company's investigation.

In his battle for pipeline-safety legislation, Nader secured important technical data from an engineer who was fighting the installation of a gas main near his home. He first learned of the damage that pipeline explosions could cause from a professor whom he met at an M.I.T. conference. "Sometimes the things these professors casually drop at conferences send me up the wall," says Nader.

INFLUENCE ON THE LAW

Typical of Nader's battle style was his campaign for more stringent federal meat inspection at packing plants. While speed-reading the small print of a House report on Agriculture Department appropriations, Nader noticed that it urged "further studies" of the U.S. meat-inspection program. Did that mean that there had been earlier studies showing that the U.S. had a meat problem? Indeed it did, as Nader found out when he requested a copy of the little-known study at the Agriculture Department. "Nobody ever asked for this before," said the employee who handed it to him. The study gave graphic descriptions of conditions in some meat plants.

Now Nader had his ammunition. He sent a summary of the study to the House Agriculture Committee, which was about to hold "clean meat" hearings for the first time in eight years. He quickly wrote an article for *The New Republic* titled "We're Back in the Jungle"—a title that echoed Upton Sinclair's classic indictment of the meat industry 60 years ago, *The Jungle*. He sent press releases to newspapers located near the worst plants. As a result, Nader was deluged by letters from meat handlers, meat buyers and anonymous Agriculture Department officials. He gave tips and new evidence to the Senate sponsor of the meat bill, Minnesota's Walter Mondale. What Nader's activity produced was the Wholesome Meat Act, which brings small, intrastate meat-packing plants under federal interstate jurisdiction.

One campaign leads to another. Many doctors who wrote Nader about meat urged him to investigate the steadily rising fat content of the venerable hot dog, which they said was contributing to heart disease. Nader found that average frank fat has increased in 15 years from 17% to 33% of the total content. The "fatfurter" campaign was on, and he now emphasizes it frequently in his speeches. Nader cultivates mutually helpful friendships among Congressmen, offering to let them take credit for his digging and even drafting legislative proposals for them. His chief contacts in the Senate are Magnuson, Moss, Teddy Kennedy, Wisconsin's Gaylord Nelson and William Proxmire, Texas' Ralph Yarborough, Connecticut's Abraham Ribicoff and Indiana's Vance Hartke.

As a result of Nader's indictments, the Government is making many changes. "When Nader issued his report on the Federal Trade Commission, my first feeling was irritation," says an FTC commissioner, Mary Gardiner Jones. "But I feel now that the commission has pulled itself together more, and faster, than if it had not come out." Though the FTC still has a long way to go, it has lately begun to take more vigorous actions. Sample: after nearly a decade of indecision, the commission in August ordered gasoline stations and food stores that use giveaway games for promotion to inform customers as to just how infinitesimal are their chances of winning.

Though Nader has rarely done his fighting in the courtroom, he has exerted a profound influence on the law. Before his auto-safety crusade, accident injuries were blamed on faulty drivers —not faulty cars. In order to collect damages, an accident victim was usually required to prove negligence on the part of a manufacturer. But Nader contended that automakers should build "crashworthy" cars that would not cause bodily injury in a "second collision" after the accident itself. The second-collision concept is now recognized by many courts. A 22-year-old Pennsylvania college student, who suffered permanent injury when the roof of a car buckled in an accident, recently won the right to use the "second-collision" principle in a damage suit against General Motors. U.S. District Judge John A. Fullam ruled that the roof should have been built to withstand the car's roll-over and that automakers are required "to provide more than merely a movable platform capable of transporting passengers from one point to another." Since the second-collision principle could be applicable to other products as well, manufacturers may become more safety-conscious and design their products to avoid injury in case of mishap.

THE NEW CITIZENSHIP

The entire legal profession must be reformed, Nader maintains, if society is to alleviate its ailments. "The best lawyers should be spending their time on the great problems—on water and air pollution, on racial justice, on poverty and juvenile delinquency, on the joke that ordinary rights have become," he says. "But they are not. They are spending their time defending Geritol, Rice Krispies and the oil-import quota."

That is changing, in no small part because of Nader. Of the 39 *Harvard Law Review* editors who will be graduated next June, not one intends to join a high-paying Wall Street law firm. Instead, most plan to enter neighborhood agencies or government service—and represent the individual against the institutions. Nader believes that the rise of the youthful protester, which began in the '60s, will accelerate into the '70s. "You watch," he predicts. "General Motors will be picketed by young activists against air pollution."

Student demonstrators, he believes, will increasingly choose to become student investigators. Many of them will move to Washington and, like Nader, spend their early careers prowling among the Government filing cabinets, searching for examples of abuse and seeking means of reform in the existing system. "This is a new form of citizenship," Nader says. At heart, he is teaching the oldest form of citizenship: that one man, simply by determined complaining, can still accomplish a great deal in a free society.

READING 37 Nader and the Automobile Industry

STATEMENT OF DAVID HOUSMAN, PRESIDENT, AUTOMATIC RADIO MANUFACTURING CO., MELROSE, MASS.; ACCOMPANIED BY WORTH ROWLEY, WALKER B. COMEGYS, JR., AND ROGER P. STOKEY, COUNSEL

Automatic Radio depends for its sales in very large measure upon the market represented by the automobile dealer. About 80 percent of our radios are custom radios sold for installation in new cars and for installation by the dealer at the time he sells the car.

We sell our custom car radios to these dealers through 50 major distributors located throughout the United States and in foreign countries. These distributors are small, independent businessmen who buy radios from us, stock them, and resell them to new car dealers. We have no franchise arrangements or contracts of any sort with our distributors. These distributors also handle related product lines of other independent manufacturers which they sell to new car dealers. For example, they sell seat covers, hub caps, mirrors, and antifreeze, spark plugs, floormats, et cetera. However, in most instances, our radios account for much more than half of our distributors' entire business. A distributer's total annual sales for all products range from $100,000 for a small distributor to $1 to $2 million for a large one.

We also sell car radios to mail-order houses and other retailers of electronic equipment. These sales account for about 20 percent of our car radio sales. The vast majority of radios sold to this market are universal radios. We cannot survive on this business in and by itself.

THE IMPACT OF THE AUTOMOBILE FRANCHISE SYSTEM UPON THE AUTOMOBILE RADIO BUSINESS

Just as soon as our company came to be a factor in the market for sales of custom radios to new car dealers, we immediately

Reprinted from "Planning, Regulation, and Competition: Automobile Industry—1968" Hearing before subcommittees of the Select Committee on Small Business, United States Senate, 90th Congress, 2nd Session, 1968.

found ourselves to be a victim of the automobile franchise system. Franchising in the automobile business takes a very special form. I do not feel qualified to discuss the pros and cons of franchising in general, because my experience has been limited to the automobile field, and even there it has been experience from the outside, looking in. However, I am firmly convinced, on the basis of my company's experiences, that the automobile franchise system is a means whereby the colossal automobile manufacturing companies control the marketing, not only of new cars, but of all products sold in conjunction with new cars.

The automobile manufacturing business is concentrated in three of the largest and most powerful companies in the world—General Motors, Ford, and Chrysler. These industrial giants use the franchise system of distribution to add to their power to control the marketing of new automobiles and associated products, such as radios.

Now, the automobile maker has a big advantage in sales of accessory products, such as car radios, to its franchised dealers. It would have an advantage even if it took no action to push the sales of its own accessories. The new car dealer should be an independent businessman, but in the franchise system he operates under the domination of the automaker. He is primarily in the business of selling cars. His franchise is his license to do so. If he loses his franchise to sell cars for one manufacturer, he is not likely to get a franchise from another car manufacturer. As an independent businessman, with many thousands of dollars invested in his dealership, it is not surprising that he feels obliged to favor accessory products marketed by his franchiser as a middleman over the same products offered to him directly by the accessory manufacturer from whom the franchiser obtains them. Therefore it is not surprising that the franchising system presents a severe marketing problem to Automatic Radio.

If a car radio manufacturer, like Automatic, wants to sell custom radios for new cars, there are two choices open to it. First, Automatic could attempt to sell to the automobile companies. It is a fact of business life that if a car radio manufacturer sells to a company such as Ford, he cannot compete with Ford by attempting to sell custom car radios to Ford dealers. Bendix and Motorola, who sell custom radios to Ford and Chrysler, do not sell these custom radios to Chrysler dealers or Ford dealers. However, both Bendix and Motorola produce a full line of custom radios for General Motors automobiles which they sell to General Motors franchised dealers. They are free to do this because neither company sells car radios to General Motors.

Because Automatic Radio has been unable to negotiate satisfactory sales arrangements with the automakers, it has to take the second route; that is, sales to the franchised new car dealers. In order to overcome the advantage the franchise system of retailing gives to Ford, General Motors, and Chrysler, Automatic has had to furnish a better product, at a lower price, on more favorable terms, and with a superior warranty; and Automatic has survived only because it has done so.

You can classify car radio manufacturers according to the way they sell to the new car market:

First, there are independent radio manufacturers, such as Bendix and Motorola, which sell to the carmakers and thereby get the carmakers' advantage in selling to the franchised automobile dealer.

Second, there are the carmaker's own subsidiaries which make car radios. These include Delco, with a stranglehold on the radio market represented by General Motors cars, and Philco, which Ford acquired and which is now taking over the manufacturing of Ford's car radio requirements.

Finally, there are the independent radio manufacturers which sell to franchised dealers through distributors, and which must compete directly with the carmakers in the market they control. These include Automatic, Tenna (Cleveland), Soundex (Brockton, Mass.), and formerly Peptone, which is now out of business.

SOME ABUSES OF THE AUTOMOBILE FRANCHISE SYSTEM

Unfortunately for Automatic, the carmakers have not been content with the franchising advantage they have over us in the sales of car radios to the automobile dealers. To increase their advantage, they have abused their power under the franchise system.

This committee has already heard testimony from representatives of the Pennzoil Co. and of the Kendall Refining Co. about their experiences with the Ford franchise system in the marketing of motor oil. I would like to list for you, by way of further example, some of the experiences in connection with the marketing of automobile radios that my company has had with all three big automobile manufacturers—Chrysler and General Motors, as well as Ford.

The Chastity Belt

In about 1960, Chrysler Corp. designed a half-size radio to mount behind the instrument panel for the Plymouth model, with an iron bar—chastity belt—snugly fitted around the radio, welded to the instrument panel, to prevent any other manufacturer's radio from being installed.

General Motors has consistently delivered unordered radios to their Chevrolet dealerships, and when the dealers protested, they were told, "If you do not want the radios, forget about the cars."

In recent years, Ford Motor Co. has set and enforced quotas for sales of its radios. These quotas have been presented to Ford dealers as an ultimatum. It is not surprising that in the end the quotas were achieved. Remember, Ford's franchised dealers are utterly dependent upon Ford for the cars that they sell. Ford dealers are told to "get your cars where you buy your radios," and frankly, Mr. Chairman, I do not think our company should have to bring out a line of cars in order to compete with Ford Motor Co. in sales of car radios.

Other threats of franchise cancellation are less veiled.

Where the dealer has ordered the car from the manufacturer without a car radio, so that he could install our Automatic car radio, the cars have been delivered with a radio already installed by the automobile manufacturer.

Tied Sales

Several years ago Ford made the radio "standard equipment" in the Thunderbird. This of course, means that the radio is installed at the factory and that neither the dealer nor the consumer can buy a Thunderbird without a Ford radio preinstalled. As a result of this sudden action, our distributors were left with large inventories of Automatic Thunderbird radios, which we, as the factory, felt morally obliged to take back from them, not to mention the 10,000 radios that the factory had on hand, which they could not dispose of.

In 1961 Ford acquired Philco. Philco had formerly supplied Ford with car radios, though it was not doing so at the time of the acquisition. Today, Philco is supplying the bulk of Ford's needs. The acquisition of Philco is more proof of the drive on the part of Ford Motor Co. to complete its monopoly of radio sales by Ford car dealers. This acquisition hurts not only the independent, such as Automatic (because Ford has increased its pressure to manufacture Philco radios), but it also cuts Bendix and Motorola off as Ford's suppliers. Moreover, it gives Ford added leverage with radio parts manufacturers which Ford can use to our competitive disadvantages.

Henry Ford II has admitted in testifying about the Philco acquisition and its role as a radio supplier that his company has—and I quote: "... a general company policy that we try to integrate as much as possible, and when we feel we can integrate up to 100 percent, we move toward that 100 percent. When we review the Philco budget in December of this year (1965), we will have a discussion, I assume, probably about radios in part, and at that time we will probably discuss what the future holds."

Why does Mr. Ford concern himself about automobile radios? Because they are big business, that is why. With the committee's permission, I would like to submit as an exhibit for the record of this hearing a copy of a September 27, 1962 intracompany memorandum prepared by Mr. Iococca, who, as you know, is a principal Ford executive. Mr. Iococca's memorandum shows that Ford is intentionally forcing independents, such as Automatic, out of the Ford franchised dealerships. This memorandum also shows that Ford, whose profits on automobile radios are greater than our total auto radio sales, is not content with the lion's share of the car radio business—it wants it all.

Senator Hart. I think I should indicate that the memorandum will be received.

Mr. Housman. The competition of Automatic Radio in the car radio market is important to the consumer—that is, to everyone who keeps a car. Not only have we developed and brought out such innovations as the first all-transistor automobile radio, we have brought down prices of car radios to less than one-half of their former level. While a new-car radio used to cost over $100, today it is $50 or less—except, of course, where the automobile manufacturer makes you buy its radio by calling it "standard equipment" and refuses to sell the car without it. Here I cite specifically the General Motors Cadillac, the Chrysler Imperial, the Ford Continental and the Ford Thunderbird. For the radio on each of these cars except the Thunderbird, the buyer is forced to pay more than $150, and in the case of the Thunderbird, he is forced to pay about $100. In all cases the radio is virtually identical to radios which, as optional equipment, they price at approximately $50.

We at Automatic would like to have our rightful share of the car radio business—that is, a share wholly determined by free competition. We are not a monopoly. We have no illegal power to coerce, to engage in tied selling, to sell at a loss so as to exterminate competition, or to gouge the consumer in the absence of competition. We think we can earn a major share of the market if we get a fair chance to compete, on the basis of our better product and lower price.

The great problem, gentlemen, is that General Motors, Ford, and Chrysler are using their power as automobile manufacturers to monopolize a market in radios. They are denying the automobile dealers and the public the freedom of choice—the freedom of choosing between the products they offer and the products of others, including ours, in open and fair competition. The automobile dealer should be left free to decide which radio to buy, on the basis of its relative merit. The public should not be denied access to a competitive radio market.

My lawyers tell me that the existing law, if honestly adhered to and firmly enforced, is quite adequate to remedy the situation. This may be so, but a private suit is expensive, long drawn out, and disruptive of our day-to-day business in producing and selling automobile radios. Although we have filed suit against Ford and intend to press it vigorously, nevertheless it is my hope that we will not have to go the road alone. We do not have the resources of the U.S. Government. Ford is a formidable opponent. The Government forces are necessary in order to penetrate the Ford complex. They should be used, not merely for us, but for our competitors as well, and for the benefit of the public generally.

Moreover, the problem is not confined to Ford, but extends to General Motors and to Chrysler as well. Neither the Antitrust Division nor the Federal Trade Commission is dealing effectively or aggressively with any of them. These public enforcement authorities will, I hope, in the light of the information this hearing is bringing out, promptly begin to discharge the responsibilities Congress has entrusted to them, and thus secure for the benefit of the public fair competition in the automobile radio market.

Thank you.

THE MASSIVE STATISTICS OF GENERAL MOTORS

The description of General Motors as a nation unto itself is usually offered, and accepted, as hyperbole. In some respects, though, General Motors *is* as big as a country. In fact, its net operating revenues last year exceeded the 1964 gross national product of all but nine nations in the free world. G.M.'s "value added" (sales less the cost of materials and services purchased) in 1965 was $11,217,000,000—more than the G.N.P., in a recent year, of Argentina, Denmark, Greece, or Norway.

The figures compiled by G.M. make an astonishing contour that stands out even against the ten-year backdrop of the 500 companies in FORTUNE's directory and the U.S. industrial economy as a whole. G.M.'s 1965 sales of $20,734,000,000 were not only greater than those of any other corporate entity, they were also greater than the combined general revenues of the state and local governments of New York, New Jersey, Pennsylvania, Ohio, Delaware, and the six New England states.

General Motors is the only company in the world to have had net earnings of more than $2 billion in a single year. Its 1965 profits of $2,125,606,000 came to 10.6 percent of the total net earnings of all the 500 industrials. Even more startling, G.M.'s profits amounted to 7.6 percent of the earnings of the 500 *and* all the other industrial companies in the U.S. G.M.'s 1,310,000 stockholders collected $1,500,000,000 in dividends last year. Just mailing out one quarter's dividend checks cost General Motors more than $65,000 in postage.

More than 735,000 people work for General Motors worldwide—a total greater than the population of Boston. These employees work in 127 plants in the U.S. and forty-five in other countries. They were paid $5,448,343,000 last year—more than twice the personal income of all the citizens of Ireland—and had an additional $603 million set aside for them by the company for benefits such as medical insurance and retirement pensions. The figures, of course, would be even more impressive if they included the employees, payrolls, and benefit payments of G.M.'s, 35,000 suppliers and more than 16,000 franchised dealers.

As a heavy taxpayer, G.M. is the best single source of income for a good many governments. In the U.S. alone, the company paid $2,307,000,000 in local, state, and federal taxes in 1965; that figure does not include an additional $1,451,000,000 in sales and excise taxes paid by purchasers of the 5,348,568 G.M. cars, buses, and trucks sold in the U.S. during the year. G.M.'s federal income tax of $1,742,000,000 represented 1.87 percent of the federal government's receipts in 1965 and 6.83 percent of all corporation income taxes paid during the year.

Among all G.M.'s firsts, there is one that is often overlooked. G.M. not only makes more cars than any other company in the world, but also more automotive cigarette lighters. There's one in almost every car, and G.M. makes its own—some five million last year.

ASTONISHING PROFITS

Mr. Nader. Perhaps the most intriguing expression of inordinate market power is GM's long-established practice of a target rate of profit. The method used is basically similar to that of a public utility, except that GM sets its own upper limit several orders of magnitude above the average utility and there is no public supervision of its cost formulations and pricing practices. To set its target rate of return, ranging from 15 to 20 percent on net worth but always managing to exceed that level substantially, GM has to possess the market power requisite for fixing its prices in advance of the new model year without having to concern itself with the possible effects of competitive pricing on its planned percentage profits and on its share of the market.

Analysis of the yearly outcome of GM's pricing formula suggests that a sufficient margin is taken into account to cover estimated income taxes. Income tax rates have not affected GM's rate of return. Taxes for GM have been treated as another cost which it can pass on to its customers. In a way it is like a disguised sales tax. After taxes, for example, the 1929 rate of return was 36.2 percent, while the 1950 rate of return was 37.5 percent. The 1929 rate was attained with a pretax earnings rate of 38.5 percent on average stockholders' investment while in 1950 GM made a pretax profit of 77.4 percent to earn 37.5 percent after taxes.

In an article that appeared in "The Corporate Director" (July 1956), the American Institute of Management marveled at GM's phenomenal rate of return, and this is really an exceptional description of the company's profit level. I quote:

> The astonishing fact emerges . . . that, from 1949 through 1955, the average rate of operating profit (net sales less cost of sales, selling and administrative expenses and depreciation), in proportion to total assets employed, including debt, has exceeded 40 per cent per annum. The operating profit on net stock and surplus, defined to include minority interest and special reserves, has exceeded 55 per cent per annum in the average of these years. It has averaged 140 per cent of the average net plant account in these same years.

At the 1955 rate of profit, the American Institute of Management noted that GM's net earnings (after interest and income taxes), were sufficient to recoup the company's entire net plant investment in 2 years. AIM took note that this kind of return is "in fact, a continuing characteristic of the enterprise, being equaled or bettered in 12 of the preceding 20 years."

The price leadership of GM vis-à-vis Ford and Chrysler, for example, is indicative of its power. On occasion Ford and Chrysler have announced their annual model prices before GM but they continually have to adapt closely to GM's prices if they guessed wrong. In 1957, Ford guessed wrong and *raised* its prices to meet GM's.

THE CUSTOMER CEASES TO BE KING

Mr. Nader. There is even less incentive to compete on price, under a target pricing policy by the dominant firm in the industry, when that firm has pursued a product policy that emphasizes nonprice competition. With little price competition at the producer level and with the camouflaging complexities of financing, and trade-in gimmicks at the retail level, the emphasis long ago shifted to the area of style, intimations of aggression, power, vacation-land image and the "personality" of the particular make or model. You can see the growing stress on the personality of the vehicle, not only in terms of product differentiation but also in terms of advertisement. For example, in January 1967, when Pontiac introduced its Firebird with four or five variations of Tweedledee and Tweedledum, the radio advertisement beamed to women was:

> Girls, fall in love with a Firebird. When you get into a Firebird you will feel better, look better and be the envy of all those girls when you are with all those boys in that Firebird.

This is hardly a trivial example. I consider automobile advertising as among the most impressive examples of applied social science that this country has ever known.

The bulk of the communication process between auto company and customer stresses these themes and garnishes them with animistic appellations taken from the mountains, such as Cougar, jungles and ocean depths, such as Barracuda. In the attenuated competition of a tight oligopoly, the range of competition is continually narrowed as each company competes more and more about less and less. In this game, GM has excelled. It has led the way with wraparound windshields, hardtop models, protruding dash panels, low profile vehicles, dagger fins and ornaments and other creative lethalities which the other domestic companies felt compelled to emulate.

As George Romney said 10 years ago, GM's share of the market was so great that its styles determined the modernity of American cars. He gave an example of the wraparound windshield which enormously increased the cost of replacement and distorted vision at the sides, which horrified optometrists. When GM introduced that wraparound windshield because of its large share of the market, over 50 percent, that became the index of what a new car looked like in that year and the stage, as an illustration, the stage was repeatedly set for what economists call protective imitation.

On the other side of the vehicle design, although disc brakes and radial ply tires were available on some mass production cars in Europe as early as 1953 and 1949 respectively, only when GM, commencing in 1965, tiptoed into these radical offerings, as extra cost options, did the other companies follow suit. Clearly, a competitive industry would have seen one or more companies forge ahead here with such tested innovations. But again and again, one hears and has heard the plaint of Ford and Chrysler personnel bemoaning the risks attendant upon not following the product leadership of GM. GM's planning and regulation in these price and product areas is possible, of course, by the effective insulation from a critical consuming body having available real choices whose differences are revealed at the point of sale. I might take note here in the perfect model of competition, buyers are assumed to have perfect knowledge. That is the chief discipline on sellers. And in this economy of growing concentration in the auto industry and other industries, the trend, of course, has been toward packaging; the trend along with more complex products has been to reduce the amount of knowledge held by the consumer at the point of sale, or even if he wished to inquire into the matter as an avocation.

Again, Mr. Romney put it candidly—

When you get an inadequate number of companies in an industry, the customer ceases to be king. He begins to be dictated to by the concepts that a few have as to what he ought to have, and that is what I am here talking about as far as this whole product situation is concerned, because there is inadequate and deficient product competition in the automobile business.

That was before the Senate Antitrust Committee.

One worsening area is that the price of entry into automobile production with national distribution most certainly has gone up from an estimated 1 billion made by Mr. Romney in 1958 when he headed American Motors. Very high barriers to entry help preserve the status quo. They are another dominant criteria for what constitutes unreasonable or monopolistic market power.

The many ramifications of target pricing was discussed in a 1963 article by Gardiner Means. I think that is an extremely concise statement of the public interest consequence of target prices. And I quote:

> . . . it is important to see just how pricing for an excessive rate of return does damage to the public interest. It does this in four important ways. It operates to slow up economic growth. It distorts the use of resources. It intensifies the conflict between labor and management and it distorts the distribution of income.

Another way of saying part of this is that it amounts to a reduction in real income to the consumer.

Mr. Means discusses each of these points in some detail. His first point bears on product innovation and quality, which bears on some very, very fundamental consumer hazards. He says:

> The tendency to delay the introduction of improved techniques and improved products. If a new technique must promise a 16 or 20 percent return on capital before it is substituted for the old, it will not be introduced if it only promises an eight or 10-percent return. The same applies to new products.

LACK OF ANTITRUST ENFORCEMENT

The history and attainments of GM's market power make it a classic candidate for antitrust enforcement under Sherman 1 and 2 and Clayton 7. In law and in economics there are solid grounds for proceeding toward dissolution or divestiture of General Motors under the two antitrust laws.

I might state that both the present antitrust chief, Mr. Zimmerman, and the prior antitrust chief, Mr. Turner, would concur with this statement.

The only obstacle is political, to move in against General Motors under these antitrust laws.

How ironic indeed, for the political power of highly concentrated economic firms was a fundamental concern of the Republican Congress that passed the Sherman Antitrust Act in 1890. History has come full circle, when General Motors can succeed in transforming a fait accompli into de facto immunity from this basic antitrust action.

Mr. Nader. This is not the place for a detailed legal analysis of such an antitrust action. Suffice it to say that General Motors passes the test of unreasonable market power in terms of its size and the source of that power growth through mergers and acquisitions of over 100 companies including the Olds Motors Works, Cadillac Motor Co., Fisher Body, et cetera. The *Standard Oil* case, *Alcoa,* and *Du Pont* cases, among others, are relevant authoritative interpretations of the antitrust laws for application to the GM situation. The Justice Department, more than anyone, knows the case against General Motors. Beginning near the end of the Eisenhower administration and continuing into the Kennedy and Johnson administrations, Antitrust Division lawyers conducted a detailed examination into the company's anticompetitive and monopolistic behavior, both vertically and horizontally. A grand jury was convened in New York for 18 months. In May 1966 a 120-page memorandum, together with a 104-page draft complaint, was completed by staff. Succeeding inquiries to the Department of Justice have received the same reply: "The matter is still under study." Antitrust chiefs come and go and the reply remains the same. And it will remain the same until there rises a private constituency for antitrust that Mr. Turner has on occasion felt would be necessary for going forward with the big cases.

In issuing its merger guidelines last month, the Justice Department declared that it would generally challenge mergers between two firms which each account for 4 percent of a highly concentrated market. Pitifully small in comparison with GM's 50–55 percent market share was the share of the local market held by Von's and Shopping Bag Grocery chains which desired a merger that would have given them 7.5 percent of the Los Angeles grocery market. The Justice Department sued and prevented the merger under Clayton 7 in 1966 (*U.S. v. Von's Grocery Company,* 384 U.S. 270).

THE LABOR INPUT IN AUTOMOBILE PRODUCTION

Senator Nelson. Mr. Nader, where do you get your figure that the direct and indirect labor costs of medium-priced cars do not exceed $300?

Mr. Nader. From several sources, Senator.

The Wall Street Journal made a study 10 years ago by Mr. Cordtz, which approximated that figure. Now, the answer to that is, well, wages have gone up since then. Of course, the counter-answer to that is productivity has gone up even faster and the critical point is not what the wage is per hour but what is the number of hours required to produce an automobile. And that total number has been decreasing in dollar results faster than the increase in labor costs.

Also there was an estimate made by the Senate Antitrust and Monopoly Subcommittee in its hearings and also I have here cost data relating to Ford Motor Co. which indicates in specific ways just what a trivial component labor cost is in the overall cost of producing an automobile.

Senator Nelson. Do the auto manufacturers contest that figure?

Mr. Nader. When it was stated in the Wall Street Journal and noted by the Antitrust Committee, I did not see a challenge to that figure. I am not certain that there was no challenge, because I do not have access to the correspondence files obviously, of the Senate Antitrust Committee, but we can certainly provide them with another opportunity to challenge that figure if they so wish and to back it up with recent data.

Senator Nelson. I think it is a dramatically significant figure, even if it were twice that much, and I would hope the chairman here will agree with me that the auto industry ought to respond to that figure because so frequently they tell the public that the excuse for the increase of prices is an increase in the wages secured by labor.

SAFETY DOESN'T SELL

Mr. Nader. My third point, because it conflicted with GM's sales formula of visible obsolescence and invisible permanence, safety became encapsuled in a slogan that was merchandised. "Safety doesn't sell." Taking safety out of the competitive race occurred years ago and the consumer was never asked. His choice was made for him by corporate planning. This is a very important dimension of corporate planning, narrowing the range of competition in a way, of course, that affects very intimately the lives and limbs of American motorists.

To illustrate this, consider the argument hypothetically that safety can be incorporated as part of competitive behavior. It certainly is not difficult to conceive. Safety is mostly engineered into the vehicle and is not visible for a consumer's supposed esthetic rejection. I do not think the consumer would rush down to the dealer and tear out his disc brakes and ask for their replacement by inferior drum brakes. Better brakes, tires, handling, safer instrument panels, steering columns and door locks are all "passive" safety features hardly in the category of enraging a car buyer. Viewed as an innovative segment of product quality, it becomes part of vehicular progress, not a nasty nuisance.

A few safety features, of course, were add-on components and required passenger cooperation. The companies deliberately ignored these features (seat belts, for example, were prominent in aviation in the twenties) and when they could no longer ignore them, offered some as optional extra-cost equipment with very little communication to motorists of their protective qualities.

Senator Nelson. May I interrupt just a moment?

Senator Morse. Go right ahead.

Senator Nelson. Are you aware, Mr. Nader, as a matter of fact, the auto companies lobbied around the country against compulsory legislation for safety seatbelts?

Mr. Nader. Definitely.

Senator Nelson. It was introduced while I was in the legislature in Wisconsin. They lobbied against seatbelts and finally in 1959 when I was Governor, one of the major companies came to my office, privately, and said they wanted me to know—privately—they were not against seatbelts but did not want to say anything publicly or make any disclosures because it would infuriate the other auto companies. And that was as recently as 1959.

Mr. Nader. That is symptomatic of the attitudes of the smaller companies. I might add that one of the reasons why the industry fought seatbelts long after their great lifesaving utility was available to them was that it was like a spotlight on interior safety in the automobile. The very existence of a seatbelt says that people are injured when they crash against the insides of the car, and obviously, when you begin the process of focusing on that problem, then people begin to say, well, how about instrument panels, how about rearward displacing steering columns, et cetera. In other words, you would unleash a public concern and dialog about the crash worthiness of a car.

Later they put seatbelts as standard equipment. I might note here that the first company that put seatbelts in as standard equipment was the tiniest company of all, Studebaker, in January 1964. Note where the leadership came from. But the seatbelts are still awkwardly designed and the installation reflects low seat and door pillar strength, which impedes customer usage.

THE "FRIENDLY" ANTITRUST DIVISION

My fourth point, one of these neglected needs is that of breathing pure air. Roughly half of the Nation's air pollution proceeds from the internal combustion engine and its emissions of hydrocarbons, carbon monoxide, nitrogen oxides, and lead. Here, once again, it was not the industry that defined the problem but a professor (Haagen-Smit), at California Institute of Technology, who observed the connection between photochemical smog and auto emissions in 1951. A lesson, I think, we should all remember, that many of these problems which come from industry are never defined by industry. They show no interest in defining or learning the extent of these hazards. They have to be defined by forces external to the industry which is why I believe that the Government has such a critical role to play here in terms of research, development, and prototype work.

The agonizing experience of Los Angeles County and the State of California in trying to move the auto industry toward less polluting engines has been told elsewhere. Here one may note that the Antitrust Division of the Justice Department thought there was serious evidence of concerted and collusive behavior by the domestic auto companies in restraining the development and marketing of auto exhaust control systems to keep a grand jury busy for 18 months in Los Angeles. But, just as a groundbreaking suit for "product fixing" was about to be filed, the anticipated criminal action was dropped over the dissent of Government counsel who handled the proceedings before the grand jury. This was in January 1968. The civil action that could end up with the judicial relief of "go and sin no more," was to be instituted instead. Yet, as of this day there has been no action whatsoever. This is another indication of the charmed life that General Motors leads whenever it comes into the nitty-gritty potential antitrust action with the Justice Department.

I might indicate I think it is time now to become a little candid about General Motors' relationship with the Antitrust Division. As far as I am concerned, there is entirely too much interchange both on an informal and private level between General Motors and the Antitrust Division. This interchange has been institutionalized in ways which may not seem objectionable but if you look at the heads of various antitrust sections in General Motors Corp., you will see time after time that they are recruited from the Antitrust Division. The process goes fullfold. Oftentimes firms representing General Motors in antitrust work devotedly release one of their young associates for public service as assistants to antitrust chiefs and deputy chiefs, and after 2 or 3 years of on-the-job training, these people go right back into the law firms or go to work for General Motors or other companies' legal counsel.

Again, I have heard, and unfortunately cannot document, but I have heard from reliable oral sources that the leaks from the Antitrust Division in the direction of the auto industry have been proverbial, that the auto industry learns about what is going on ahead of time, that the Division is a sieve as far as the auto industry is concerned, but it is an iron door as far as any other access is concerned. I have heard that, for example, attorneys who used to work for the Antitrust Division marvel at the communication and intelligence process that auto company representatives have developed in this regard. I cannot but conclude this comment by saying the following, that I agree wholeheartedly with Prof. Kenneth Culp Davis that the Antitrust Division should develop an information policy whereby it tells the public why it does not take action, not only explains when it takes action, that not taking action is a very, very important form of policymaking and the grounds for not taking action should be explicit and made public.

Continuing with the area of pollution, a particularly clear illustration of continuing industry intransigence on pollution-free engines was afforded this May before the Senate Commerce Committee. Hearings were held on nonpolluting steam cars. Both General Motors and Ford came in with testimony so patently erroneous or misleading that independent authorities in the room blinked or grimaced with incredulity. One could be charitable with some of these statements and call them the products of ignorance; one could be more accurate and chalk them up to corporate prevarication—a common affliction of executives before public committees or agencies.

I might add as a footnote here an enlightening attempt to explain this phenomenon is contained in the January–February 1968 issue of the Harvard Business Review. ("Is Business Bluffing Ethical?") by Albert Z. Carr. Mr. Carr quotes the advice of Paul Babcock, an associate of John D. Rockefeller, to Standard Oil Co. executives who were about to testify before a Government investigating committee in 1888: "Parry every question with answers which, while perfectly truthful, are evasive of *bottom* facts" (his emphasis).

THE COST OF STYLE CHANGE

Fifth, even in the area of supposed consumer acceptance, that of product differentiation over style, comfort, and gadgetry, the industry maintains an adhesion to adjectives and an aversion to factual disclosure.

Let's take their pride and joy, the area of style which they consider so important and which they say—they say this is what the consumer wants. "We are only giving him what he wants." Let's take this area.

Would the consumer crave for styling changes if he knew that they are costing him at least $700 of the price of his new car? This was discussed in an article by a number of Harvard and MIT economists in some detail, the cost of the annual model change. Especially if he had a choice of not having them and saving the difference? The difference in money?

Do consumers really want those chrome eyebrows, called bumpers, whose chief function appears to be self-protection or the fostering of a multimillion-dollar industry selling bumper guards to make up for stylistic idiocy? Ask them after they see that $200 repair bill following a 3-mile-per-hour crash into another car while parking. Was there a clamor by consumers to put eyelids on Cougars, particularly the kinds of eyelids that sometimes refuse to flutter open at night (such a defect led to the recall of 85,000 Cougars last spring)? These eyelids were standard equipment. What popular demonstration demanded hidden windshield wipers and the consequent freezing problem in northern climates?

Mr. Nader. It is important that the committee inquire into the problems represented by these suggestions for actions.

I don't want to give the impression that antitrust is, of course, even the chief tool here. It is an extremely important tool and it has an important spinoff, but to engage corporations in a continual context of responsiveness takes a good deal of complex restructuring of their economic and political environment.

Let me give you two very brief examples here. In 1958 the domestic auto industry had 38,000 franchised auto dealers. There was not a single Negro franchised auto dealer in that number, 38,000. Three years ago I believe there still was no Negro franchised dealer. But under the pressure of the times in the area of civil rights, the auto industry is beginning to respond and as of the end of last year, Ford now has one Negro dealer, Chrysler, I believe, has one, and General Motors has two, out of about 30,000 franchised dealers.

Senator Nelson. That is 30,000 General Motors franchised dealers?

Mr. Nader. 30,000 General Motors, Chrysler, Ford, and American Motors. That is roughly 30,000 domestic franchised dealers.

MEAGER RESOURCES FOR ANTITRUST

Mr. Nader. One of the functions of corporate planning is to make sure that the Antitrust Division and the Federal Trade Commission never receive adequate funds for their work. For a $900 billion economy, both the combined budgets of the Federal Trade Commission and the Antitrust Division of the Justice Department directed toward the problem of competition and fair trade practices in the economy does not exceed $14 million a year. Compare this with a gross hourly return by General Motors, 24 hours a day, of $2.3 million.

This indicates that you simply cannot regulate or determine or plan for competition, certainly not to make the requisite studies and develop the requisite data, with that level of manpower.

The distance of corporate behavior and influence from these norms declared by Mr. Orrick and Mr. Simons is the measure of the intensity of the radicalism of corporate collectivism today. For if radicalism be defined as the operational aberration from the traditional and acknowledged norms of a society and if radicalism's intensity be gaged by the operating power of that aberration, then the issue is industrial autocracy and the corporate state. This is the real struggle of the consumer.

Senator Morse. I turn now to the subject of FTC's secret advance briefing of manufacturers on FTC findings.

Mr. Nader, your statement, taken as a whole, suggests that the automobile manufacturers, especially the biggest ones, get some kind of politically favored, special treatment from the Government's antitrust agencies. I must say that that thesis gets some support from a recent incident at the Federal Trade Commission.

The July 15 issue of *Automotive News* has an indignant editorial about it. A very short editorial, and I will read it. It is entitled "On Warranty Problem: Why Secret Meetings by FTC —Makers?"

[Exhibit 110]

On July 1, Federal Trade Commission gave auto makers a summary of its long investigation into auto warranties.

Auto dealers, who perform the warranty work and who, many dealers contend, are subsidizing the warranty program, tell us that they have not been advised of FTC findings. And neither has the public press, which represents the millions affected by the auto warranty program.

The industry and the public has too vital an interest in warranty work to be satisfied with secret meetings.

Is the FTC planning equivalent meetings with representative auto dealers or their association?

In this case, auto makers can hardly speak for their franchised dealers, since nothing in recent years has so upset auto dealers as has the factory handling of the warranty situation.

Until it is revealed what happened at the July 1 meetings, the public cannot know whether the discussions were limited to warranty advertising, chiefly a manufacturer problem.

Or whether it spilled over into public misunderstanding and repair problems, clearly a dealer concern.

Because the dealer image is intimately tied to consumer complaints, any meaningful discussion must include at some point dealers who are partners with the manufacturers in warranty work.

Mr. Nader, the FTC conducted a long investigation of automakers' warranty policies and problems, and the warranty system complaints of dealers and car owners. On July 1, they called in the automobile manufacturers and gave them an advance, secret summary of their findings.

The auto dealers were not invited. Consumers groups were not invited. The Senate Small Business Committee was not invited. The press was not invited.

Why do you think the automobile manufacturers were told what the FTC is eventually going to tell the rest of the country about warranties, before anyone else was told?

Mr. Nader. I think that is a good instance but by no means the only example of the uses of secrecy by the Federal Trade Commission.

First of all, the chief use of secrecy in a situation like this is to make sure that the situation does not get out of hand as far as the Federal Trade Commission is concerned.

In order to determine what I mean more clearly, assume hypothetically that the auto warranty report was made public. Here is a long awaited report, it affects millions of motorcar purchasers; if it was made public it is quite clear that it would be the subject of a good many opinions around the country as to what should be done, there would be criticism, there would be revelations of abuses in the press, and in effect it would tend to bring other forces into the calculus of the overall inquiry that the FTC may not be able to control.

Whereupon, on the other hand, where there is a secrecy theme operating here, the public cannot evaluate the Federal Trade Commission's performance, and so it not only serves the interests of the auto industry to keep these facts, and I understand it is a very critical report in the raw, to keep these facts from the public, but it also serves the bureaucratic needs of the FTC to protect its flanks, and I think this is not an isolated incident, and it can be seen as a heritage going back many years before the present incumbent commissioners.

I recall when I was looking into the problem of the odometer, which is a unit in the automobile that measures how many miles a car has traveled. For many years, the odometer was rigged so that the motorist would think he was traveling, say, 103 miles but actually he was only traveling 100 miles. It was rigged or calibrated to have a percentile of 3 percent over. This has consequences, car turnover in the aggregate is faster, mileage warranties run out sooner, for example, but the point is that the FTC for 30 years was looking into this, for some 30 years and had not done anything about it.

Now this would have been impossible if it wasn't for the secrecy of the Federal Trade Commission. You cannot launch an inquiry into something that involves a real deception of that scope and not do something about it one way or the other unless you engage in this type of secret communication with the industry, which went for over 30 years.

THE NEW INDUSTRIAL STATE?

One of the problems here, particularly in an age of inflation, and statements from the White House about the need for price and wage restraint, is again the secret negotiation between industry and Government. I think this again is a very serious problem. It was revealed a few months ago that since 1964 General Motors has been having secret negotiations with the Council of Economic Advisers before it announced its price increases.

And what has happened obviously, as a good horse trader, General Motors has come in with a higher bid than it was willing to settle for, and then it scaled down its bid and the Government thought it was getting a good deal, it was saving the consumer money, and General Motors of course got its price rise.

But perhaps the most deceptive part of this practice is when the auto companies have increased their prices, one looks for reaction from the White House and the Council of Economic Advisers, and wonder why they are not saying anything, why they are not speaking out, why they are not taking action.

The reason why they were not taking action is because they had already made a deal in private sessions prior to the announcement of the price increase.

I think that is fudamentally deceiving the public, and should be eliminated forthwith.

Senator Nelson. May I?

Senator Morse. Yes.

Senator Nelson. You say that General Motors has been having secret negotiations with the Government. Did it ever occur to you that it might be the Government that is having secret negotiations with General Motors?

Mr. Nader. It probably might be, just as well. They both have interests to protect.

Senator Morse. Mr. Nader, in your testimony you stated that General Motors has deposited funds in some 300 banks throughout the country, and that this was not entirely economically motivated by banking needs.

Would you explain to the committee what other motivations you think might be operating in this practice by General Motors?

Mr. Nader. Well, it is difficult to outline what I am sure are a number of motivations, which is another reason why that question could well be directed to the company.

I can estimate, however, that these are two effects at least. One in a rather mundane area.

There are many inventors in this country with ideas, some of them far out, some of them not very economical, some of them brilliant and lifesaving, and once an idea is refined into hardware at a prototype level, it has to get financing, which means banks. And when banks entertain these requests, it helps the status quo to have relatively substantial resources deposited in these banks.

This kind of relationship, of client-bank relationship, also gets the banks to simply refer these ideas to the companies and say, "You know here is somebody who is coming to us for financing. What do you think of this idea?"

And it is almost invariably the case that cold water is thrown on it. The most recent illustration is the long inability of two inventors in Pennsylvania to find financing for their steam car, which was driven around the new Senate Office Building a few weeks ago and was the subject of a Senate hearing, and is a rather proficient car with less than 1 percent of the air pollution, much cheaper to construct and cheaper to operate, and reduces most of the noise of vehicle operation.

This is a very exciting development. But they were unable to get minimal financing to get underway.

What has finally happened apparently is that a few days ago the California Legislature passed a resolution asking the highway patrol to obtain six of these cars from this group in Pennsylvania for prototype testing.

But what does this mean?

This means that a critical access to an industry, that is financing, can be blocked off by this concentrated financial power, and when, for example, the problem of air pollution and efficiency of operation is at stake, we are not talking about small issues.

Another motivation would be to solidify the interlocks between financial and manufacturing institutions. We got an idea of these interlocks in a recent House report that was made public about 2 weeks ago. I looked into the situation in General Motors, and have a memorandum on GM directors and their interlocks for submission in the record.

READING 38
Eco-Catastrophe
Paul Ehrlich

Science fiction or fact? In the following paper, Dr. Paul Ehrlich, professor of biology at Stanford University, presents a horror story designed to bias any reader against the manipulations of money-hungry corporations and self-seeking politicians. Whether or not this story comes true depends on what individual citizens such as you and I do to stop the deceptive practices followed by hucksters of goods which provide short-run satisfactions and long-run oblivion.

Guideposts for Thought While Reading

In what ways does this story bring out the limitations of a laissez-faire market economy? By spending public funds on social goods, how does government sometimes help perpetuate and extend the harmful, self-destructive actions of mankind?

THE END OF THE OCEAN

The end of the ocean came late in the summer of 1979, and it came even more rapidly than the biologists had expected. There had been signs for more than a decade, commencing with the discovery in 1968 that DDT slows down photosynthesis in marine plant life. It was announced in a short paper in the technical journal, Science, but to ecologists it smacked of doomsday. They knew that all life in the sea depends on photosynthesis, the chemical process by which green plants bind the sun's energy and make it available to living things. And they knew that DDT and similar chlorinated hydrocarbons had polluted the entire surface of the earth, including the sea.

But that was only the first of many signs. There had been the final gasp of the whaling industry in 1973, and the end of the Peruvian anchovy fishery in 1975. Indeed, a score of other fisheries had disappeared quietly from over-exploitation and various eco-catastrophes by 1977. The term "eco-catastrophe" was coined by a California ecologist in 1969 to describe the

Reprinted with the permission of Paul R. Ehrlich and the Editors of *Ramparts*.

most spectacular of man's attacks on the systems which sustain his life. He drew his inspiration from the Santa Barbara offshore oil disaster of that year, and from the news which spread among naturalists that virtually all of the Golden State's seashore bird life was doomed because of chlorinated hydrocarbon interference with its reproduction. Eco-catastrophes in the sea became increasingly common in the early 1970's. Mysterious "blooms" of previously rare micro-organisms began to appear in offshore waters. Red tides—killer outbreaks of a minute single-celled plant—returned to the Florida Gulf coast and were sometimes accompanied by tides of other exotic hues.

It was clear by 1975 that the entire ecology of the ocean was changing. A few types of phytoplankton were becoming resistant to chlorinated hydrocarbons and were gaining the upper hand. Changes in the phytoplankton community led inevitably to changes in the community of zooplankton, the tiny animals which eat the phytoplankton. These changes were passed on up the chains of life in the ocean to the herring, plaice, cod and tuna. As the diversity of life in the ocean diminished, its stability also decreased.

Other changes had taken place by 1975. Most ocean fishes that returned to fresh water to breed, like the salmon, had become extinct, their breeding streams so dammed up and polluted that their powerful homing instinct only resulted in suicide. Many fishes and shellfishes that bred in restricted areas along the coasts followed them as onshore pollution escalated.

By 1977 the annual yield of fish from the sea was down to 30 million metric tons, less than one-half the per capita catch of a decade earlier. This helped malnutrition to escalate sharply in a world where an estimated 50 million people per year were already dying of starvation. The United Nations attempted to get all chlorinated hydrocarbon insecticides banned on a worldwide basis, but the move was defeated by the United States. This opposition was generated primarily by the American petrochemical industry, operating hand in glove with its subsidiary, the United States Department of Agriculture. Together they persuaded the government to oppose the U.N. move—which was not difficult since most Americans believed that Russia and China were more in need of fish products than was the United States. The United Nations also attempted to get fishing nations to adopt strict and enforced catch limits to preserve dwindling stocks. This move was blocked by Russia, who, with the most modern electronic equipment, was in the best position to glean what was left in the sea. It was, curiously, on the very day in 1977 when the Soviet Union announced its refusal that another ominous article appeared in Science. It announced that incident solar radiation had been so reduced by worldwide air pollution that serious effects on the world's vegetation could be expected.

THE GREEN REVOLUTION

Apparently it was a combination of ecosystem destabilization, sunlight reduction, and a rapid escalation in chlorinated hydrocarbon pollution from massive Thanodrin applications which triggered the ultimate catastrophe. Seventeen huge Soviet-financed Thanodrin plants were operating in underdeveloped countries by 1978. They had been part of a massive Russian "aid offensive" designed to fill the gap caused by the collapse of America's ballyhooed "Green Revolution."

It became apparent in the early '70s that the "Green Revolution" was more talk than substance. Distribution of high yield "miracle" grain seeds had caused temporary local spurts in agricultural production. Simultaneously, excellent weather had produced record harvests. The combination permitted bureaucrats, especially in the United States Department of Agriculture and the Agency for International Development (AID), to reverse their previous pessimism and indulge in an outburst of optimistic propaganda about staving off famine. They raved about the approaching transformation of agriculture in the underdeveloped countries (UDCs). The reason for the propaganda reversal was never made clear. Most historians agree that a combination of utter ignorance of ecology, a desire to justify past errors, and pressure from agroindustry (which was eager to sell pesticides, fertilizers, and farm machinery to the UDCs and agencies helping the UDCs) was behind the campaign. Whatever the motivation, the results were clear. Many concerned people, lacking the expertise to see through the Green Revolution drivel, relaxed. The population-food crisis was "solved."

But reality was not long in showing itself. Local famine persisted in northern India even after good weather brought an end to the ghastly Bihar famine of the mid-'60s. East Pakistan was next, followed by a resurgence of general famine in northern India. Other foci of famine rapidly developed in Indonesia, the Philippines, Malawi, the Congo, Egypt, Colombia, Ecuador, Honduras, the Dominican Republic, and Mexico.

Everywhere hard realities destroyed the illusion of the Green

Revolution. Yields dropped as the progressive farmers who had first accepted the new seeds found that their higher yields brought lower prices—effective demand (hunger plus cash) was not sufficient in poor countries to keep prices up. Less progressive farmers, observing this, refused to make the extra effort required to cultivate the "miracle" grains. Transport systems proved inadequate to bring the necessary fertilizer to the fields where the new and extremely fertilizer-sensitive grains were being grown. The same systems were also inadequate to move produce to markets. Fertilizer plants were not built fast enough, and most of the underdeveloped countries could not scrape together funds to purchase supplies, even on concessional terms. Finally, the inevitable happened, and pests began to reduce yields in even the most carefully cultivated fields. Among the first were the famous "miracle rats" which invaded Philippine "miracle rice" fields early in 1969. They were quickly followed by many insects and viruses, thriving on the relatively pest-susceptible new grains, encouraged by the vast and dense plantings, and rapidly acquiring resistance to the chemicals used against them. As chaos spread until even the most obtuse agriculturists and economists realized that the Green Revolution had turned brown, the Russians stepped in.

In retrospect it seems incredible that the Russians, with the American mistakes known to them, could launch an even more incompetent program of aid to the underdeveloped world. Indeed, in the early 1970's there were cynics in the United States who claimed that outdoing the stupidity of American foreign aid would be physically impossible. Those critics were, however, obviously unaware that the Russians had been busily destroying their own environment for many years. The virtual disappearance of sturgeon from Russian rivers caused a great shortage of caviar by 1970. A standard joke among Russian scientists at that time was that they had created an artificial caviar which was indistinguishable from the real thing—except by taste. At any rate the Soviet Union, observing with interest the progressive deterioration of relations between the UDCs and the United States, came up with a solution. It had recently developed what it claimed was the ideal insecticide, a highly lethal chlorinated hydrocarbon complexed with a special agent for penetrating the external skeletal armor of insects. Announcing that the new pesticide, called Thanodrin, would truly produce a Green Revolution, the Soviets entered into negotiations with various UDCs for the construction of massive Thanodrin factories. The USSR would bear all the costs; all it wanted in return were certain trade and military concessions.

It is interesting now, with the perspective of years, to examine in some detail the reasons why the UDCs welcomed the Thanodrin plan with such open arms. Government officials in these countries ignored the protests of their own scientists that Thanodrin would not solve the problems which plagued them. The governments now knew that the basic cause of their problems was overpopulation, and that these problems had been exacerbated by the dullness, daydreaming, and cupidity endemic to all governments. They knew that only population control and limited development aimed primarily at agriculture could have spared them the horrors they now faced. They knew it, but they were not about to admit it. How much easier it was simply to accuse the Americans of failing to give them proper aid; how much simpler to accept the Russian panacea.

And then there was the general worsening of relations between the United States and the UDCs. Many things had contributed to this. The situation in America in the first half of the 1970's deserves our close scrutiny. Being more dependent on imports for raw materials than the Soviet Union, the United States had, in the early 1970's, adopted more and more heavy-handed policies in order to insure continuing supplies. Military adventures in Asia and Latin America had further lessened the international credibility of the United States as a great defender of freedom—an image which had begun to deteriorate rapidly during the pointless and fruitless Viet-Nam conflict. At home, acceptance of the carefully manufactured image lessened dramatically, as even the more romantic and chauvinistic citizens began to understand the role of the military and the industrial system in what John Kenneth Galbraith had aptly named "The New Industrial State."

At home in the USA the early '70s were traumatic times. Racial violence grew and the habitability of the cities diminished, as nothing substantial was done to ameliorate either racial inequities or urban blight. Welfare rolls grew as automation and general technological progress forced more and more people into the category of "unemployable." Simultaneously a taxpayers' revolt occurred. Although there was not enough money to build the schools, roads, water systems, sewage systems, jails, hospitals, urban transit lines, and all the other amenities needed to support a burgeoning population, Americans refused to tax themselves more heavily. Starting in Youngstown, Ohio in 1969 and followed closely by Richmond, California, community after community was forced to close its schools or curtail educational operations for lack of funds. Water supplies, already marginal in quality and quantity in many places by 1970, deteriorated quickly. Water rationing occurred in 1723 municipalities in the summer of 1974, and hepatitis and epidemic dysentery rates climbed about 500 per cent between 1970-1974.

THE EFFECTS OF AIR POLLUTION

Air pollution continued to be the most obvious manifestation of environmental deterioration. It was, by 1972, quite literally in the eyes of all Americans. The year 1973 saw not only the New York and Los Angeles smog disasters, but also the publication of the Surgeon General's massive report on air pollution and health. The public had been partially prepared for the worst by the publicity given to the U.N. pollution conference held in 1972. Deaths in the late '60s caused by smog were well known to scientists, but the public had ignored them because they mostly involved the early demise of the old and sick rather than people dropping dead on the freeways. But suddenly our citizens were faced with nearly 200,000 corpses and massive documentation that they could be the next to die from respiratory disease. They were not ready for that scale of disaster. After all, the U.N. conference had not predicted that accumulated air pollution would make the planet uninhabitable until almost 1990. The population was terrorized as TV screens became filled with scenes of horror from the disaster areas. Especially vivid was NBC's coverage of hundreds of unattended people choking out their lives outside of New York's hospitals. Terms like nitrogen oxide, acute bronchitis and cardiac arrest began to have real meaning for most Americans.

The ultimate horror was the announcement that chlorinated hydrocarbons were now a major constituent of air pollution in all American cities. Autopsies of smog disaster victims revealed an average chlorinated hydrocarbon load in fatty tissue equivalent to 26 parts per million of DDT. In October, 1973, the Department of Health, Education and Welfare announced studies which showed unequivocally that increasing death rates from hypertension, cirrhosis of the liver, liver cancer and a series of other diseases had resulted from the chlorinated hydrocarbon load. They estimated that Americans born since 1946 (when

DDT usage began) now had a life expectancy of only 49 years, and predicted that if current patterns continued, this expectancy would reach 42 years by 1980, when it might level out. Plunging insurance stocks triggered a stock market panic. The president of a major pesticide producer went on television to "publicly eat a teaspoonful of DDT" (it was really powdered milk) and announce that HEW had been infiltrated by Communists. Other giants of the petrochemical industry, attempting to dispute the indisputable evidence, launched a massive pressure campaign on Congress to force HEW to "get out of agriculture's business." They were aided by the agro-chemical journals, which had decades of experience in misleading the public about the benefits and dangers of pesticides. But by now the public realized that it had been duped. The Nobel Prize for medicine and physiology was given to Drs. J. L. Radomski and W. B. Deichmann, who in the late 1960's had pioneered in the documentation of the long-term lethal effects of chlorinated hydrocarbons. A Presidential Commission with unimpeachable credentials directly accused the agro-chemical complex of "condemning many millions of Americans to an early death." The year 1973 was the year in which Americans finally came to understand the direct threat to their existence posed by environmental deterioration.

And 1973 was also the year in which most people finally comprehended the indirect threat. Even the president of Union Oil Company and several other industrialists publicly stated their concern over the reduction of bird populations which had resulted from pollution by DDT and other chlorinated hydrocarbons. Insect populations boomed because they were resistant to most pesticides and had been freed, by the incompetent use of those pesticides, from most of their natural enemies. Rodents swarmed over crops, multiplying rapidly in the absence of predatory birds. The effect of pests on the wheat crop was especially disastrous in the summer of 1973, since that was also the year of the great drought. Most of us can remember the shock which greeted the announcement by atmospheric physicists that the shift of the jet stream which had caused the drought was probably permanent. It signalled the birth of the Midwestern desert. Man's air-polluting activities had by then caused gross changes in climatic patterns. The news, of course, played hell with commodity and stock markets. Food prices skyrocketed, as savings were poured into hoarded canned goods. Official assurances that food supplies would remain ample fell on deaf ears, and even the government showed signs of nervousness when California migrant field workers went out on strike again in protest against the continued use of pesticides by growers. The strike burgeoned into farm burning and riots. The workers, calling themselves "The Walking Dead," demanded immediate compensation for their shortened lives, and crash research programs to attempt to lengthen them.

It was in the same speech in which President Edward Kennedy, after much delay, finally declared a national emergency and called out the National Guard to harvest California's crops, that the first mention of population control was made. Kennedy pointed out that the United States would no longer be able to offer any food aid to other nations and was likely to suffer food shortages herself. He suggested that, in view of the manifest failure of the Green Revolution, the only hope of the UDCs lay in population control. His statement, you will recall, created an uproar in the underdeveloped countries. Newspaper editorials accused the United States of wishing to prevent small countries from becoming large nations and thus threatening American hegemony. Politicians asserted that President Kennedy was a "creature of the giant drug combine" that wished to shove its pills down every woman's throat.

Among Americans, religious opposition to population control was very slight. Industry in general also backed the idea. Increasing poverty in the UDCs was both destroying markets and threatening supplies of raw materials. The seriousness of the raw material situation had been brought home during the Congressional Hard Resources hearings in 1971. The exposure of the ignorance of the cornucopian economists had been quite a spectacle—a spectacle brought into virtually every American's home in living color. Few would forget the distinguished geologist from the University of California who suggested that economists be legally required to learn at least the most elementary facts of geology. Fewer still would forget that an equally distinguished Harvard economist added that they might be required to learn some economics, too. The overall message was clear: America's resource situation was bad and bound to get worse. The hearings had led to a bill requiring the Departments of State, Interior, and Commerce to set up a joint resource procurement council with the express purpose of "insuring that proper consideration of American resource needs be an integral part of American foreign policy."

POPULATION CONTROL NEEDED

Suddenly the United States discovered that it had a national consensus: population control was the only possible salvation of the underdeveloped world. But that same consensus led to heated debate. How could the UDCs be persuaded to limit their populations, and should not the United States lead the way by limiting its own? Members of the intellectual community wanted America to set an example. They pointed out that the United States was in the midst of a new baby boom: her birth rate, well over 20 per thousand per year, and her growth rate of over one per cent per annum were among the very highest of the developed countries. They detailed the deterioration of the American physical and psychic environments, the growing health threats, the impending food shortages, and the insufficiency of funds for desperately needed public works. They contended that the nation was clearly unable or unwilling to properly care for the people it already had. What possible reason could there be, they queried, for adding any more? Besides, who would listen to requests by the United States for population control when that nation did not control her own profligate reproduction?

Those who opposed population controls for the U.S. were equally vociferous. The military-industrial complex, with its all-too-human mixture of ignorance and avarice, still saw strength and prosperity in numbers. Baby food magnates, already worried by the growing nitrate pollution of their products, saw their market disappearing. Steel manufacturers saw a decrease in aggregate demand and slippage for that holy of holies, the Gross National Product. And military men saw, in the growing population-food-environment crisis, a serious threat to their carefully nurtured Cold War. In the end, of course, economic arguments held sway, and the "inalienable right of every American couple to determine the size of its family," a freedom invented for the occasion in the early '70s, was not compromised.

The population control bill, which was passed by Congress early in 1974, was quite a document, nevertheless. On the domestic front, it authorized an increase from 100 to 150 million dollars in funds for "family planning" activities. This was made possible by a general feeling in the country that the growing army on welfare needed family planning. But the gist of the bill was a series of measures designed to impress the need for population control on the UDCs. All American aid to countries with overpopulation problems was required by law to consist in part of population control assistance. In order to receive any assistance each nation was required not only to accept the population control aid, but also to match it according to a complex formula. "Overpopulation" itself was defined by a formula based on U.N. statistics, and the UDCs were required not only to accept aid, but also to show progress in reducing birth rates. Every five years the status of the aid program for each nation was to be re-evaluated.

The reaction to the announcement of this program dwarfed the response to President Kennedy's speech. A coalition of UDCs attempted to get the U.N. General Assembly to condemn the United States as a "genetic aggressor." Most damaging of all to the American cause was the famous "25 Indians and a dog" speech by Mr. Shankarnarayan, Indian Ambassador to the U.N. Shankarnarayan pointed out that for several decades the United States, with less than six percent of the people of the world had consumed roughly 50 per cent of the raw materials used every year. He described vividly America's contribution to worldwide environmental deterioration, and he scathingly denounced the miserly record of United States foreign aid as "unworthy of a fourth-rate power, let alone the most powerful nation on earth."

It was the climax of his speech, however, which most historians claim once and for all destroyed the image of the United States. Shankarnarayan informed the assembly that the average American family dog was fed more animal protein per week than the average Indian got in a month. "How do you justify taking fish from protein-starved Peruvians and feeding them to your animals?" he asked. "I contend," he concluded, "that the birth of an American baby is a greater disaster for the world than that of 25 Indian babies." When the applause had died away, Mr. Sorensen, the American representative, made a speech which said essentially that "other countries look after their own self-interest, too." When the vote came, the United States was condemned.

This condemnation set the tone of U.S.-UDC relations at the time the Russian Thanodrin proposal was made. The proposal seemed to offer the masses in the UDCs an opportunity to save themselves and humiliate the United States at the same time; and in human affairs, as we all know, biological realities could never interfere with such an opportunity. The scientists were silenced, the politicians said yes, the Thanodrin plants were built, and the results were what any beginning ecology student could have predicted. At first Thanodrin seemed to offer excellent control of many pests. True, there was a rash of human fatalities from improper use of the lethal chemical, but, as Russian technical advisors were prone to note, these were more than compensated for by increased yields. Thanodrin use skyrocketed throughout the underdeveloped world. The Mikoyan design group developed a dependable, cheap agricultural aircraft which the Soviets donated to the effort in large numbers. MIG sprayers became even more common in UDCs than MIG interceptors.

Then the troubles began. Insect strains with cuticles resistant to Thanodrin penetration began to appear. And as streams, rivers, fish culture ponds and onshore waters became rich in Thanodrin, more fisheries began to disappear. Bird populations were decimated. The sequence of events was standard for broadcast use of a synthetic pesticide: great success at first, followed by removal of natural enemies and development of resistance by the pest. Populations of crop-eating insects in areas treated with Thanodrin made steady comebacks and soon became more abundant than ever. Yields plunged, while farmers in their desperation increased the Thanodrin dose and shortened the time between treatments. Death from Thanodrin poisoning became common. The first violent incident occurred in the Canete Valley of Peru, where farmers had suffered a similar chlorinated hydrocarbon disaster in the mid-'50s. A Russian advisor serving as an agricultural pilot was assaulted and killed by a mob of enraged farmers in January, 1978. Trouble spread rapidly during 1978, especially after the word got out that two years earlier Russia herself had banned the use of Thanodrin at home because of its serious effects on ecological systems. Suddenly Russia, and not the United States, was the *bête noire* in the UDCs. "Thanodrin parties" became epidemic, with farmers, in their ignorance, dumping carloads of Thanodrin concentrate into the sea. Russian advisors fled, and four of the Thanodrin plants were leveled to the ground. Destruction of the plants in Rio and Calcutta led to hundreds of thousands of gallons of Thanodrin concentrate being dumped directly into the sea.

Mr. Shankarnarayan again rose to address the U.N., but this time it was Mr. Potemkin, representative of the Soviet Union, who was on the hot seat. Mr. Potemkin heard his nation described as the greatest mass killer of all time as Shankarnarayan predicted at least 30 million deaths from crop failures due to overdependence on Thanodrin. Russia was accused of "chemical aggression," and the General Assembly, after a weak reply by Potemkin, passed a vote of censure.

It was in January, 1979, that huge blooms of a previously unknown variety of diatom were reported off the coast of Peru. The blooms were accompanied by a massive die-off of sea life and of the pathetic remainder of the birds which had once feasted on the anchovies of the area. Almost immediately another huge bloom was reported in the Indian ocean, centering around the Seychelles, and then a third in the South Atlantic off the African coast. Both of these were accompanied by spectacular die-offs of marine animals. Even more ominous were growing reports of fish and bird kills at oceanic points where there were no spectacular blooms. Biologists were soon able to explain the phenomena: the diatom had evolved an enzyme which broke down Thanodrin; that enzyme also produced a breakdown product which interfered with the transmission of nerve impulses, and was therefore lethal to animals. Unfortunately, the biologists could suggest no way of repressing the poisonous diatom bloom in time. By September, 1979, all important animal life in the sea was extinct. Large areas of coastline had to be evacuated, as windrows of dead fish created a monumental stench.

But stench was the least of man's problems. Japan and China were faced with almost instant starvation from a total loss of the seafood on which they were so dependent. Both blamed Russia for their situation and demanded immediate mass shipments of food. Russia had none to send. On October 13, Chinese armies attacked Russia on a broad front.

NATURE BATS LAST

A pretty grim scenario. Unfortunately, we're a long way into it already. Everything mentioned as happening before 1970 has actually occurred; much of the rest is based on projections of trends already appearing. Evidence that pesticides have long-term lethal effects on human beings has started to accumulate, and recently Robert Finch, Secretary of the Department of Health, Education and Welfare expressed his extreme apprehension about the pesticide situation. Simultaneously the petrochemical industry continues its unconscionable poison-peddling. For instance, Shell Chemical has been carrying on a high-pressure campaign to sell the insecticide Azodrin to farmers as a killer of cotton pests. They continue their program even though they know that Azodrin is not only ineffective, but often *increases* the pest density. They've covered themselves nicely in an advertisement which states, "Even if an overpowering migration [sic] develops, the flexibility of Azodrin lets you regain control fast. Just increase the dosage according to label recommendations." It's a great game—get people to apply the poison and kill the natural enemies of the pests. Then blame the increased pests on "migration" and sell even more pesticide!

Right now fisheries are being wiped out by over-exploitation, made easy by modern electronic equipment. The companies producing the equipment know this. They even boast in advertising that only their equipment will keep fishermen in business until the final kill. Profits must obviously be maximixed in the short run. Indeed, Western society is in the process of completing the rape and murder of the planet for economic gain. And, sadly, most of the rest of the world is eager for the opportunity to emulate our behavior. But the underdeveloped peoples will be denied that opportunity—the days of plunder are drawing inexorably to a close.

Most of the people who are going to die in the greatest cataclysm in the history of man have already been born. More than three and a half billion people already populate our moribund globe, and about half of them are hungry. Some 10 to 20 million will starve to death *this year.* In spite of this, the population of the earth will increase by 70 million souls in 1969. For mankind has artificially lowered the death rate of the human population, while in general birth rates have remained high. With the input side of the population system in high gear and the output side slowed down, our fragile planet has filled with people at an incredible rate. It took several million years for the population to reach a total of two billion people in 1930, while a *second two billion will have been added by 1975!* By that time some experts feel that food shortages will have escalated the present level of world hunger and starvation into famines of unbelievable proportions. Other experts, more optimistic, think the ultimate food-population collision will not occur until the decade of the 1980's. Of course more massive famine may be avoided if other events cause a prior rise in the human death rate.

Both worldwide plague and thermonuclear war are made more probable as population growth continues. These, along with famine, make up the trio of potential "death rate solutions" to the population problem—solutions in which the birth rate-death rate imbalance is redressed by a rise in the death rate rather than by a lowering of the birth rate. Make no mistake about it, *the imbalance will be redressed.* The shape of the population growth curve is one familiar to the biologist. It is the outbreak part of an outbreak-crash sequence. A population grows rapidly in the presence of abundant resources, finally runs out of food or some other necessity, and crashes to a low level or extinction. Man is not only running out of food, he is also destroying the life support systems of the Spaceship Earth. The situation was recently summarized very succinctly: "It is the top of the ninth inning. Man, always a threat at the plate, has been hitting Nature hard. It is important to remember, however, that NATURE BATS LAST."

READING 39
Private Ownership Inconsistent with the Best Use of Land
Henry George

The right to own private property is one of the institutions often listed as a prerequisite to a market economy. Henry George argues that profit maximization in combination with private ownership of land can result in either underutilization or overutilization of the land resource from the standpoint of long-run social welfare. According to George, security to the returns from land, not legal title, is enough to encourage private initiative in a market economy. Hence, he argues for public ownership of land.

Guideposts for Thought While Reading
What other cases can you think of as examples of the misuse of the land resource due to private ownership? What alternatives to public ownership might be used to correct the misuse of land? Do you agree that ownership is not required to induce private entrepreneurs to fully develop the land resource?

Reprinted from Henry George, "Private Property in Land Inconsistent with the Best Use of Land; The True Remedy," *Progress and Poverty,* Robert Schalkenbach Foundation, 1960, pp. 328–330 and 397–402.

There is a delusion resulting from the tendency to confound the accidental with the essential—a delusion which the law writers have done their best to extend, and political economists generally have acquiesced in, rather than endeavored to expose—that private property in land is necessary to the proper use of land, and that again to make land common property would be to destroy civilization and revert to barbarism.

This delusion may be likened to the idea which, according to Charles Lamb, so long prevailed among the Chinese after the savor of roast pork had been accidentally discovered by the burning down of Ho-ti's hut—that to cook a pig it was necessary to set fire to a house. But, though in Lamb's charming dissertation it was required that a sage should arise to teach people that they might roast pigs without burning down houses, it does not take a sage to see that what is required for the improvement of land is not absolute ownership of the land, but security for the improvements. This will be obvious to whoever will look around him. While there is no more necessity for making a man the absolute and exclusive owner of land, in order to induce him to improve it, than there is of burning down a house in order to cook a pig; while the making of land private property is as rude, wasteful, and uncertain a device for securing improvement, as the burning down of a house is a rude, wasteful, and uncertain device for roasting a pig, we have not the excuse for persisting in the one that Lamb's Chinamen had for persisting in the other. Until the sage arose who invented the rude gridiron, which, according to Lamb, preceded the spit and oven, no one had known or heard of a pig being roasted, except by a house being burned. But, among us, nothing is more common than for land to be improved by those who do not own it. The greater part of the land of Great Britain is cultivated by tenants, the greater part of the buildings of London are built upon leased ground, and even in the United States the same system prevails everywhere to a greater or less extent. Thus it is a common matter for use to be separated from ownership.

SECURITY TO LABOR IS THE TRUE INCENTIVE

Would not all this land be cultivated and improved just as well if the rent went to the State or municipality, as now, when it goes to private individuals? If no private ownership in land were acknowledged, but all land were held in this way, the occupier or user paying rent to the State, would not land be used and improved as well and as securely as now? There can be but one answer: Of course it would. Then would the resumption of land as common property in nowise interfere with the proper use and improvement of land.

What is necessary for the use of land is not its private ownership, but the security of improvements. It is not necessary to say to a man, "this land is yours," in order to induce him to cultivate or improve it. It is only necessary to say to him, "whatever your labor or capital produces on this land shall be yours." Give a man security that he may reap, and he will sow; assure him of the possession of the house he wants to build, and he will build it. These are the natural rewards of labor. It is for the sake of the reaping that men sow; it is for the sake of possessing houses that men build. The ownership of land has nothing to do with it.

It was for the sake of obtaining this security, that in the beginning of the feudal period so many of the smaller landholders surrendered the ownership of their lands to a military chieftain, receiving back the use of them in fief or trust, and kneeling bareheaded before the lord, with their hands between his hands, swore to serve him with life, and limb, and worldly honor. Similar instances of the giving up of ownership in land for the sake of security in its enjoyment are to be seen in Turkey, where a peculiar exemption from taxation and extortion attaches to *vakouf*, or church lands, and where it is a common thing for a landowner to sell his land to a mosque for a nominal price, with the understanding that he may remain as tenant upon it at a fixed rent.

It is not the magic of property, as Arthur Young said, that has turned Flemish sands into fruitful fields. It is the magic of security to labor. This can be secured in other ways than making land private property, just as the heat necessary to roast a pig can be secured in other ways than by burning down houses. The mere pledge of an Irish landlord that for twenty years he would not claim in rent any share in their cultivation induced Irish peasants to turn a barren mountain into gardens; on the mere security of a fixed ground rent for a term of years the most costly buildings of such cities as London and New York are erected on leased ground. If we give improvers such security, we may safely abolish private property in land.

The complete recognition of common rights to land need in no way interfere with the complete recognition of individual right to improvements or produce. Two men may own a ship without sawing her in half. The ownership of a railway may be divided into a hundred thousand shares, and yet trains be run with as much system and precision as if there were but a single owner. In London, joint-stock companies have been formed to hold and manage real estate. Everything could go on as now, and yet the common right to land be fully recognized by appropriating rent to the common benefit. There is a lot in the center of San Francisco to which the common rights of the people of that city are yet legally recognized. This lot is not cut up into infinitesimal pieces nor yet is it an unused waste. It is covered with fine buildings, the property of private individuals, that stand there in perfect security. The only difference between this lot and those around it, is that the rent of the one goes into the common school fund, the rent of the others into private pockets. What is to prevent the land of a whole country being held by the people of the country in this way?

It would be difficult to select any portion of the territory of the United States in which the conditions commonly taken to necessitate the reduction of land to private ownership exist in higher degree than on the little islets of St. Peter and St. Paul, in the Aleutian Archipelago, acquired by the Alaska purchase from Russia. These islands are the breeding places of the fur seal, an animal so timid and wary that the slightest fright causes it to abandon its accustomed resort, never to return. To prevent the utter destruction of this fishery, without which the islands are of no use to man, it is not only necessary to avoid killing the females and young cubs, but even such noises as the discharge of a pistol or the barking of a dog. The men who do the killing must be in no hurry, but quietly walk around among the seals who line the rocky beaches, until the timid animals, so clumsy on land but so graceful in water, show no more sign of fear than lazily to waddle out of the way. Then those who can be killed without diminution of future increase are carefully separated and gently driven inland, out of sight and hearing of the herds, where they are dispatched with clubs. To throw such a fishery as this open to whoever chose to go and kill—which would make it to the interest of each party to kill as many as they could at the time without reference to the future—would be utterly to destroy it in a few seasons, as similar fisheries in other oceans have been destroyed. But it is not necessary, therefore, to make these islands private property. Though for reasons greatly less cogent, the great public domain of the American people has been made over to private ownership as fast as anybody could be got to take it, these islands have been leased at a rent of $317,500 per year, probably not very much less than they could have been sold for at the time of the Alaska purchase. They have already yielded two millions and a half to the national treasury, and they are still, in unimpaired value (for under the careful management of the Alaska Fur Company the seals increase rather than diminish), the common property of the people of the United States.

THE SOCIAL COSTS OF PRIVATE LANDHOLDING

So far from the recognition of private property in land being necessary to the proper use of land, the contrary is the case. Treating land as private property stands in the way of its proper use. Were land treated as public property it would be used and improved as soon as there was need for its use or improvement, but being treated as private property, the individual owner is permitted to prevent others from using or improving what he cannot or will not use or improve himself. When the title is in dispute, the most valuable land lies unimproved for years; in many parts of England improvement is stopped because, the estates being entailed, no security to improvers can be given; and large tracts of ground which, were they treated as public property, would be covered with buildings and crops, are kept idle to gratify the caprice of the owner. In the thickly settled parts of the United States there is enough land to maintain three or four times our present population, lying unused, because its owners are holding it for higher prices, and immigrants are forced past this unused land to seek homes where their labor will be far less productive. In every city valuable lots may be seen lying vacant for the same reason. If the best use of land be the test, then private property in land is condemned, as it is condemned by every other consideration. It is as wasteful and uncertain a mode of securing the proper use of land as the burning down of houses is of roasting pigs.

READING 40
The Economics of Minimum Wage Legislation
George J. Stigler

In this article, Dr. George J. Stigler, Charles R. Walgren distinguished service professor at the University of Chicago, attacks minimum-wage legislation as an ineffective way to deal with poverty. Stigler prefers a negative income tax to the disruptive effects of wage manipulation on the grounds that market efficiency and equity for the poverty-stricken are greater with the tax scheme.

Guideposts for Thought While Reading

What effects does Stigler predict the minimum-wage law will have on the welfare of the poverty-stricken? Why, according to Stigler, should the negative income tax be of greater benefit to the persons whom the minimum-wage law was designed to help?

The popular objective of minimum wage legislation—the elimination of extreme poverty—is not seriously debatable. The important questions are rather (1) Does such legislation diminish poverty? (2) Are there efficient alternatives? The answers are, if I am not mistaken, unusually definite for questions of economic policy. If this is so, these answers should be given.

Some readers will probably know my answers already ("no" and "yes," respectively); it is distressing how often one can guess the answer given to an economic question merely by knowing who asks it. But my personal answers are unimportant; the arguments on which they rest, which are important, will be presented under four heads:

1. Effects of a legal minimum wage on the allocation of resources.
2. Effects on aggregate employment.
3. Effects on family income.
4. Alternative policies to combat poverty.

Reprinted by permission of the publisher from George J. Stigler, "The Economics of Minimum Wage Legislation," *American Economic Review*, June 1946, pp. 358–365.

THE ALLOCATION OF RESOURCES

The effects of minimum wages may in principle differ between industries in which employers do and do not have control over the wage rates they pay for labor of given skill and application. The two possibilities will be discussed in turn.

Competitive Wage Determination

Each worker receives the value of his marginal product under competition. If a minimum wage is effective, it must therefore have one of two effects: first, workers whose services are worth less than the minimum wage are discharged (and thus forced into unregulated fields of employment, or into unemployment or retirement from the labor force); or, second, the productivity of low-efficiency workers is increased.

The former result, discharge of less efficient workers, will be larger the more the value of their services falls short of the legal minimum, the more elastic the demand for the product, and the greater the possibility of substituting other productive services (including efficient labor) for the inefficient workers' services. The discharged workers will, at best, move to unregulated jobs where they will secure lower returns. Unless inefficient workers' productivity rises, therefore, the minimum wage reduces aggregate output, perhaps raises the earnings of those previously a trifle below the minimum, and reduces the earnings of those substantially below the minimum. These are undoubtedly the main allocational effects of a minimum wage in a competitive industry.

The second and offsetting result, the increase of labor productivity, might come about in one of two ways: the laborers may work harder; or the entrepreneurs may use different production techniques. The threat of unemployment may force the inefficient laborers to work harder (the inducement of higher earnings had previously been available, and failed), but this is not very probable. These workers were already driven by the sharp spurs of poverty, and for many the intensity of effort must be increased beyond hope (up to 50 or more per cent) to avoid discharge.

The introduction of new techniques by the entrepreneurs is the more common source of increased labor productivity. Here again there are two possibilities.

First, techniques which were previously unprofitable are now rendered profitable by the increased cost of labor. Costs of production rise because of the minimum wage, but they rise by less than they would if other resources could not be substituted for the labor. Employment will fall for two reasons: output falls; and a given output is secured with less labor. Commonly the new techniques require different (and hence superior) labor, so many inefficient workers are discharged. This process is only a spelling-out of the main competitive effect.

Second, entrepreneurs may be shocked out of lethargy to adopt techniques which were previously profitable or to discover new techniques. This "shock" theory is at present lacking in empirical evidence but not in popularity.

Employer Wage Determination

If an employer has a significant degree of control over the wage rate he pays for a given quality of labor, a skillfully-set minimum wage may increase his employment and wage rate and, because the wage is brought closer to the value of the marginal product, at the same time increase aggregate output. The effect may be elucidated with the hypothetical data in Table I. If the entrepreneur is left alone, he will set a wage of $20 and employ 50 men; a minimum wage of $24 will increase employment to 70 men.

This arithmetic is quite valid, but it is not very relevant to the question of a national minimum wage. The minimum wage which achieves these desirable ends has several requisites:

1. It must be chosen correctly: too high a wage (over $28 in our example) will decrease employment. The accounting records describe, very imperfectly, existing employment and wages; the optimum minimum wage can be set only if the demand and supply schedules are known over a considerable range. At present there is no tolerably accurate method of deriving these schedules, and one is entitled to doubt that a legislative mandate is all that is necessary to bring forth such a method.
2. The optimum wage varies with occupation (and, within an occupation, with the quality of worker).
3. The optimum wage varies among firms (and plants).
4. The optimum wage varies, often rapidly, through time.

A uniform national minimum wage, infrequently changed, is wholly unsuited to these diversities of conditions.

We may sum up: the legal minimum wage will reduce aggregate output, and it will decrease the earnings of workers who had previously been receiving materially less than the minimum.

TABLE I Hypothetical Data Illustrating Employer Wage Determination

Number of workers	Wage rate	Marginal cost of a worker	Value of the marginal product[a]
10	$12		$36
20	14	$16	34
30	16	20	32
40	18	24	30
50	20	28	28
60	22	32	26
70	24	36	24

[a] Or marginal value product, if this is less.

WAGE RATES AND FAMILY INCOME

The manipulation of individual prices is neither an efficient nor an equitable device for changing the distribution of personal income. This is a well-known dictum that has received much documentation in analyses of our agricultural programs. The relevance of the dictum to minimum wage legislation is easily demonstrated.

One cannot expect a close relationship between the level of hourly wage rates and the amount of family income. Yet family income and needs are the fundamental factors in the problem of poverty. The major sources of discrepancy may be catalogued.

First, the hourly rates are effective only for those who receive them, and it was shown in Section 1 that the least productive workers are forced into uncovered occupations or into unemployment.

Second, hourly earnings and annual earnings are not closely related. The seasonality of the industry, the extent of overtime, the amount of absenteeism, and the shift of workers among industries, are obvious examples of factors which reduce the correlation between hourly earnings and annual earnings.

Third, family earnings are the sum of earnings of all workers in the family, and the dispersion of number of workers is considerable.

Fourth, although wages are, of course, the chief component of the income of low-wage families, they are by no means the only component.

The connection between hourly wages and the standard of

living of the family is thus remote and fuzzy. Unless the minimum wage varies with the amount of employment, number of earners, non-wage income, family size, and many other factors, it will be an inept device for combatting poverty even for those who succeed in retaining employment. And if the minimum wage varies with all of these factors, it will be an insane device.

THE PROBLEM OF POVERTY

Minimum wage legislation commonly has two stated objectives: the reduction of employer control of wages; and the abolition of poverty. The former and much lesser purpose may better be achieved by removing the condition of labor immobility which gives rise to employer control. Labor immobility would be reduced substantially by public provision of comprehensive information on employment conditions in various areas and industries. The immobility would be further reduced by supplying vocational training and loans to cover moving costs. But employer wage control is not the important problem; let us turn to the elimination of poverty.

Incomes of the poor cannot be increased without impairing incentives. Skillful policies will, for a given increase in the incomes of the poor, impair incentives less than clumsy policies. But the more completely poverty is eliminated, given the level of intelligence with which this is done, the greater will be the impairment of incentives. This is a price we must pay, just as impairment of incentives is a price we have willingly paid to reduce the inequality of income by progressive income and estate taxes. Society must determine, through its legislators, what minimum income (or addition to income) should be guaranteed to each family. We shall assume that this difficult decision has been made.

One principle is fundamental in the amelioration of poverty: those who are equally in need should be helped equally. If this principle is to be achieved, there must be an objective criterion of need; equality can never be achieved when many cases are judged (by many people) "on their merits." We are driven almost inexorably to family size and composition as this criterion of need. It is obviously imperfect; the sickly require more medical care than the healthy. But it is vastly easier to accord special treatment to certain families for a few items like medical care than to accord special treatment to every family for the sum of all items of expenditure.

It is a corollary of this position that assistance should not be based upon occupation. The poor farmer, the poor shopkeeper, and the poor miner are on an equal footing. There may be administrative justification (although I doubt it) for treating the farmer separately from the urban dweller, but there is no defense in equity for helping the one and neglecting the other. To render the assistance by manipulating prices is in any case objectionable: we help the rich farmer more than the poor, and give widely differing amounts of help to the poor farmer from year to year.

The principle of equity thus involves the granting of assistance to the poor with regard to their need (measured by family composition) but without regard to their occupation. There is a possible choice between grants in kind and in money. The latter commends itself strongly: it gives full play to the enormous variety of tastes and it is administratively much simpler.

Even if these general observations be accepted, the structure of administration is of grave importance, and I do not pretend to have explored this field. There is great attractiveness in the proposal that we extend the personal income tax to the lowest income brackets with negative rates in these brackets. Such a scheme could achieve equality of treatment with what appears to be a (large) minimum of administrative machinery. If the negative rates are appropriately graduated, we may still retain some measure of incentive for a family to increase its income. We should no doubt encounter many perplexing difficulties in carrying out this plan, but they are problems which could not be avoided, even though they might be ignored, by a less direct attack on poverty.

READING 41
The Real Costs of a Volunteer Military
Walter Y. Oi

It might be argued that it is morally wrong for some to serve in the armed forces while others do not. However, due to an increasing population relative to manpower requirements it is not feasible to require service from all eligible males (not to mention females). A scheme must be devised to provide the least cost to society to maintain the armed forces. Unfortunately, the common practice is to measure only the budgetary costs of the military. True economic costs should consider not only the direct outlay by the government, but also the costs to society of reducing the civilian manpower pool by allocating men to military service. Although the underlying social implications are unclear, it is possible to argue that monetary compensation may be used to provide equity among men of draft age in the United States. The amount of extra compensation required to induce civilians to enter the military is a measure of the private costs of the draft. From his experience as a consultant for the Department of Defense, Professor Walter Oi of the University of Rochester provides us with a strong argument for replacement of the draft with a market-oriented recruitment system for the armed forces.

Guideposts for Thought While Reading
How do true economic costs differ from budgetary costs? Why are budgetary costs insufficient from society's standpoint? How does imposition of the draft incur opportunity costs?

One of several proposed alternatives to the current draft is the establishment of an all-volunteer force. To say that a particular alternative such as an all-volunteer force is preferable to the current draft implies that the cost of this alternative is, in some

Reprinted by permission of the publisher from Walter Y. Oi, "The Real Costs of a Volunteer Military," *New Individualist Review,* Spring 1967, pp. 13–16.

sense, lower than the cost of procuring military personnel with the current draft system. Yet in his statement before the House Armed Services subcommittee, T. D. Morris, Assistant Secretary of Defense, indicated that an all-volunteer force of 2.65 million men would increase military payroll budgets by $4 to $17 billion per year.

DEFENSE BUDGET IS NOT A TRUE RESOURCE COST

The budgetary payroll of the Department of Defense is *not*, however, the economic cost of labor resources allocated to the uniformed services. The presence of a draft has surely affected both the level and structure of military pay; moreover, the men who actually entered active military service were recruited or conscripted through manpower procurement programs which rely in differing degrees on the coercive influence of a draft liability. A change to a purely voluntary force would have to be accompanied by increases in military pay, and substantial changes in the procurement channels through which men are recruited into the Armed Forces. The composition and structure of an all-volunteer force would thus differ significantly from that of the present force, which contains many men who were enlisted under the pressure of a draft liability.

There are at least three senses in which the maintenance of a defense establishment entails a financial cost: (1) budgetary cost, (2) cost to the economy, and (3) cost to the individual military service participants.

BUDGETARY COST WITH AND WITHOUT THE DRAFT

According to the defense budget for fiscal year 1965, the cost for active-duty military personnel was $12.7 billion while retirement benefits accounted for another $1.4 billion. If the higher levels of military pay which are required to attract sufficient volunteers were applied to the probable age structure of a voluntary force, this writer obtains an estimate of the budgetary cost that is $4 billion greater than that of a mixed conscript and volunteer force.[1]

[1] The reader is directed to the author's "The Costs of an All-Volunteer Defense Force," published in the volume of papers from the University of Chicago Conference on the Draft by the University of Chicago Press.

OTHER COSTS THAT HAVE NOT BEEN MEASURED

The financial cost of military personnel provides a measure of the value of the civilian outputs that could have been produced by the labor which was allocated instead to the Armed Forces; but this concept of cost completely ignores the welfare loss due to the occupational preferences of the individuals themselves for military versus civilian employments. In a sense, it is just a measure of technical efficiency, indicating the alternative cost in terms of foregone civilian output that was required to achieve given goals of military preparedness. The concept of full economic cost, on the other hand, acknowledges the occupational preferences of prospective recruits. If an individual has an aversion for service life, he could, in principle, be compensated enough to induce him to volunteer. Presently, individuals who would require such compensation are involuntarily inducted, while others reluctantly volunteer before they are drafted. These imputed compensations to overcome aversions for military service would be included in any computation of the full economic cost of acquiring military personnel; but our task here is merely to arrive at an estimate of financial costs. Finally, it must be remembered that the mechanics of the current draft law impose costs in the form of uncertainties on youths in the draftable ages. The incidence of inductions (who will be drafted) and the time of induction are not known in advance.

COST-ESTIMATION PROCEDURE FOR AN ALL-VOLUNTEER FORCE

To evaluate the comparative costs of an all-volunteer force and of the force which has evolved under current law, this writer first examined the implications of a continued draft which produced a mixed force of conscripts, true volunteers, and draft-motivated, reluctant volunteers. It was assumed for this paper that active duty force strengths in the years ahead (1970–75) would return to their pre-Viet Nam levels of 2.65 million men, in order to utilize available Department of Defense data.

The manpower procurement channels which have evolved under the current draft are reflected in the patterns of active military service which were observed in the six years prior to Viet Nam, 1960–65. An analysis of these patterns indicates the probable characteristics of a mixed force under a continued draft. In order to maintain a force strength of 2.65 million men, annual accessions of 507,700 men must be recruited or conscripted from civilian life. With a smaller male population in the period prior to Viet Nam, roughly 50 per cent of males who were physically and mentally qualified for military service entered the active duty forces. By 1970–75, it is projected that only 38.5 per cent of qualified males of military age will be demanded by the Armed Services.

To estimate the cost of an entirely voluntary force, it is necessary first to consider the case assuming that the draft would be abolished with no accompanying changes in pay or other recruitment incentives. Under this assumption, the services would obviously lose the draftees who had accounted for 21 per cent of the accessions to enlisted ranks in 1960–65. In addition, a significant fraction of regular enlistees could properly be called reluctant volunteers who enlisted in preference to being drafted. The incidence of reluctant volunteers was inferred from a survey of responses to the question:

> If there had been no draft, and you had no military obligation, do you think you would have volunteered for active military service?

If the draft were eliminated, reluctant volunteers would also likely be lost from the Armed Forces. Voluntary enlistments in all Services could be expected to fall by 38.1 per cent, and to the regular Army alone by 43.2 per cent. Moreover, these surveys indicate that 41.3 per cent of newly commissioned officers were motivated to enter military service because of the threat of being drafted.

The fall in initial accessions due to the loss of conscripts and reluctant volunteers would result in a decline in the sustainable force strength. Since a voluntary force, however, would enjoy a greater rate of re-enlistment, the decline in strength would be smaller than the fall in accessions. The annual turnover rate of Army enlisted men is around 25 per cent when over half of accessions are draftees and reluctant volunteers. If all enlistments were true volunteers, it is estimated that the turnover rate could be lowered to 17 per cent. The improved retention patterns which can be expected to apply to an all-volunteer force were then used to estimate the gross flow demand for accessions to achieve the assumed strength objective of 2.65 million men. The deficit between requirements (gross flow demand for assumed strengths) and voluntary enlistments could be eliminated by attracting more volunteers with higher military pay. To maintain the required enlistments in the Army, it was estimated that first term military pay would have to be increased by 68 per cent, from $2,500 to $4,200 per year. As a result, the pay of career men in the Army would have to increase by 17 per cent also. In addition to higher levels of military pay, the move to a voluntary force would imply a change in the composition of the Armed Services—the age structure would move to a larger fraction of older men in the career force. It would also be anticipated that a smaller fraction of officers would be college graduates.

OPPORTUNITY COST OF THE ARMY TO SOCIETY

In both the mixed and voluntary type of military force, 2.65 million men, it is assumed, would be required to maintain the defense of the nation, and thereby would be kept out of the civilian labor force. The financial cost to the economy can thus be defined as the opportunity cost equal to the value of goods and services that could have been produced by these servicemen. If servicemen were paid the same incomes as civilians of comparable ages and educational attainments, the men in the mixed force would earn $13 billion per year. The corresponding figure for the voluntary force would be $14.2 billion, or some 9.1 per cent higher than the mixed force, reflecting a preservation within the Armed Forces of the acquired military skills and experience of the older men, while in the mixed force many of the men do not remain in the Services beyond their initial term—thus losing this experience. Although the voluntary force has a lower average educational attainment, it also contains older men who usually earn higher salaries than younger men, and on balance the age effect outweighs the smaller average education. To the extent that military service is not a perfect substitute for civilian job experience, the financial cost to the economy of the present type of mixed force contains a downward bias: civilian employment experience provides a man with skills he can take directly to a new job, while military experience is only partially useful in later employment.

IMPLICIT TAX ON RELUCTANT MILITARY SERVICE PARTICIPANTS

The financial cost to individual military-service participants is restricted to their monetary losses, suffered by those men who were coerced into active military service by the draft liability. By 1970–75, it is projected that only 55,300 men would need to be involuntarily drafted; but another 153,700 men per year would be expected to volunteer for enlisted ranks because of their draft liabilities. By using data for 1963–64, this writer was able to arrive at estimates of annual civilian and first-term military incomes for these reluctant service participants. The differentials between alternative civilian and military incomes represents an implicit tax that is placed on those who were forced to serve. If each draftee serves 1.9 years, and each reluctant volunteer for 3.5 years, the aggregate implicit tax which is borne by members in an age group is estimated to be $691 million. If reluctant participants were also compensated for their aversion to military service life, it is estimated that the military pay budget would have to be increased by $826 million a year. This is the amount of the implicit tax, or cost, that is imposed on men who are coerced into military service by the draft.

ECONOMIC COST OF THE DRAFT EXCEEDS THE MILITARY BUDGET FOR AN ALL-VOLUNTEER FORCE

If the true volunteers were awarded the same pay as the reluctant service participants, the economic cost of the draft then easily exceeds the budgetary cost of moving to an all-volunteer force. It should be noted again that these financial costs altogether disregard the welfare loss through the occupational preferences of individuals for military versus civilian jobs.

To sum up, a force strength of 2.65 million men could be achieved on a purely voluntary basis by 1970–75 if the military pay budget were increased by approximately four billion dollars. Because of its higher retention rates, only 27.5 per cent of qualified males in each age class would be needed to sustain this voluntary force. On the other hand, if the draft is continued, the higher personnel turnover in a mixed force would mean that 38.5 per cent of all qualified males will have to enter military service each year. Some men will be involuntarily inducted, while others reluctantly volunteer because they might be drafted.

READING 42
Suburban Jobs and Black Workers
Richard W. Epps

This article from the *Business Review* of the Federal Reserve Bank of Philadelphia provides evidence on the changing structure and location of job opportunities and the employment and spendable income of the black community. Although the problem is a study of Philadelphia, it is indicative of major changes occurring in many urban centers. The author, Richard Epps, also describes some of the current experimental efforts to overcome obstacles to an improved job market for blacks.

Guideposts for Thought While Reading
What accounts for the high participation of black workers in city jobs? How is the changing industrial structure of the city affecting job opportunities for blacks? What programs does Epps suggest might have the greatest chance of success in aiding the urban black worker?

In the summer of 1968 when a "Jobmobile" searched along the streets of North and West Philadelphia offering jobs to the residents of ghetto neighborhoods, three thousand applicants filed through the trailer housing the roving employment agency. The "Jobmobile" canvassed areas employers seldom tread, and found that a tip about a job was all that was needed by many of the unemployed.

With city-wide unemployment then at a historically low 3.2 per cent, the influx of new workers was welcomed by employers suffering from the tight labor market. But there were problems. Many of the newly recruited workers needed basic training. Moreover, some employers with the greatest number of job openings were too far away from North and West Philadelphia to benefit from the newly tapped labor pool. As one businessman

Reprinted by permission of the Federal Reserve Bank of Philadelphia from Richard W. Epps, "Suburban Jobs and Black Workers," *Business Review*, October 1969, pp. 3–11.

who signed up a hundred workers from North Philadelphia complained, the expense and inconvenience of the two-hour bus and trolley ride to his suburban electronics plant caused most of the new employees to quit within a few weeks.

Although a problem for this suburban manager, the incident also is indicative of substantial problems for residents of older sections in Philadelphia. Because virtually all growth in employment is going on in the suburbs, the increasing number of black workers in older, less accessible areas of the city may have difficulty in finding jobs.

This part of the economic problem of the Negro community is receiving increasing notice, and programs are being designed to eliminate the impact of inaccessibility on employment. Proponents of black capitalism, for example, urge creation of new factories in Negro communities in part to give black workers a better chance of finding a job close to home. Also, some people have suggested that government subsidies be devoted to mass transit to help ghetto residents get to suburban plants. How important a problem is the inaccessibility these programs are designed to correct? Are Negroes closer or further from jobs, on average, than are white workers? Although these questions have been widely discussed, there have been few attempts to give quantitative answers. This article reports upon a measurement of the problem for Philadelphia.

THE CHANGING DISTRIBUTION OF JOBS AND PEOPLE

As have firms in other areas, many Philadelphia employers have found suburban locations to be more suitable than city industrial areas. Consequently, employment has been expanding rapidly in suburban areas of Philadelphia, while the City of Philadelphia, at least since the early fifties, has suffered an absolute decline in employment.

The worst loss for the City of Philadelphia has been in manufacturing activities where employment has plummeted nearly 20 per cent. The story in manufacturing has been repeated to a lesser extent in all industries except finance and services. Growth in these two areas has offset most of the decline in other industries.

The profile of population is similar to that of employment. City population declined slightly during the fifties, but recovered much of the loss during the early sixties. Suburban population expanded rapidly throughout the period.

While the city population has remained roughly constant in size, its racial composition has shifted sharply. Since 1950, the Negro proportion of the population of Philadelphia has nearly doubled—jumping from 18 to 32 per cent.

The apparent similarity of the shifts in employment and population disguises an important feature. Industries in which the city has done most poorly—manufacturing, transportation and public utilities, and construction—are the biggest employers of blue-collar workers. Replacing these firms are ones offering jobs to paper-shuffling and meeting-going white-collar workers. But the population of the city has become increasingly characterized by blue-collar workers such as truck drivers, carpenters, and janitors. Consequently, the city has a smaller number of appropriate jobs to offer to its citizens. Because Negro workers are especially concentrated in manual trades, the shift in structure of jobs probably affects them the most severely.

SPACE AND JOBS

High participation of Negro workers in city jobs adds to the importance of this shift in employment structure. In 1960, 92 per cent of the city's Negro workers found their jobs within the city limits, with a proportionately greater number of Negroes working in each occupation in the city than in the suburbs. One can attribute this greater concentration of Negro workers in the city to two principal factors: (1) the effect of distance to jobs on the *supply* of workers; and (2) the effect of discrimination by employers and consumers on the *demand* for workers.

Supply Side

The supply of Negro workers available to employers distant from Negro residential areas is less than that available to employers close to these areas. For one thing, commuting costs tend to discourage workers from taking employment in distant locations. Also, imperfect flows of knowledge about jobs and hesitancy of Negroes to work in all-white areas may reduce the supply available to employers located some distance from the ghettos.

The average worker in the Philadelphia area spent more than fifty cents a day getting to and from work in 1960, and covered about two and one-half miles each way. More lengthy trips of workers cost up to four dollars a day, and amount to more than fifteen miles each way. These expenditures make a big dent in paychecks of low-income workers, and may act as a powerful incentive for workers to attempt to find a job close to home, or to take no job at all if there are none close to home.

If housing markets functioned better, the cost of commuting would be less of a barrier to choosing a job. Workers could survey the whole metropolitan area for the best job, and move their residence if that best job were far away. But, moving the residence is not easy for black workers. Segregation in housing markets severely limits the number of places where black workers can live. And for workers with meager incomes, the necessity of finding cheap housing reduces the alternatives even more. If the best job is in a white community in the suburbs, a black worker may be effectively shut off from the local housing market.

Unable to reduce any or all of the cost of commuting by moving, black workers must subtract transportation costs from each week's paycheck, significantly reducing their income from distant jobs. Less regular or lower-paying jobs in the neighborhood become more attractive. If no jobs are available close to home, temporary withdrawal from the labor force may seem justified.

If job openings are far away from the job seeker's neighborhood, chances are he will not find out about them. Most workers depend upon advice and information from friends and acquaintances for guidance in their search for a job. With few Negroes living in suburban areas, there is little opportunity for the word about these outlying job openings to filter through to black workers. Employment agencies, public and private, aid the flow of information, but they play a role secondary to that of the more casual process of verbal communication.

Racial composition of the area in which jobs are located also has an impact upon the supply of workers in a subtle way. Negro workers may be hesitant to venture into all-white areas for jobs. The work force of plants in these areas is often predominantly white, and may appear non-receptive to black workers.

Demand Side

For some black workers, distance to jobs is not a constraint—there simply may be few jobs for them outside of black areas. Prejudice by employers or residents in white areas may largely eliminate demand for black workers. The problem is two-dimensional. First, there may be a tendency for employers to hire workers similar in race to their customers. For example, retail merchants in predominantly white areas, suspecting that their customers would like to trade with members of their own race, may hire mostly white workers. Conversely, stores in mostly Negro areas may hire black workers in the belief that it will help boost sales. Negro physicians and lawyers are concentrated in Negro residential areas; black teachers have usually been predominant in schools with largely black student bodies.

Second, Negroes in traditionally white occupations may have a difficult time finding employment except in Negro areas. Employers have tended to open only certain kinds of employment to Negro workers, typically in manual or menial jobs. Although managers increasingly look to Negroes to fill more responsible and skill-oriented positions, the transition has by no means been completed. Thus, Negro workers seeking non-manual jobs may often have a difficult time finding employment. Their best opportunities may be in Negro-owned firms or in firms where most of the work force is Negro. Since these firms are concentrated in areas of Negro residents, demand for these workers may be low in most white areas.

THE BALANCE OF SUPPLY AND DEMAND

The impact of distance from job opportunities differs by occupation. In general, employment of Negroes in blue-collar trades is most strongly affected by the supply side—the combination of commuter costs and information flow. White-collar workers, on the other hand, are most strongly affected by characteristics of demand—the low level of demand for black workers in predominantly white areas.

The importance of supply and demand considerations in employment of Negro workers was determined by comparing relative Negro employment in each part of the region with accessibility to black workers and the racial balance of local neighborhoods. Accessibility compares the closeness of an area to Negro workers with the closeness of that same area to white workers. And it represents the relative supply of black workers available to employers in an area. An accessibility of 20 per cent, for example, means that four times more white workers live within commuting distance of an area than do black workers. The index of racial balance measures the proportion of the residents of each area of the city that are Negro, and it is a proxy for the effect of demand upon employment opportunities of Negroes.

Cost of travel and flaws in the flow of information, both proxied for by accessibility, are of some importance for each occupation. Racial composition of the local market, a proxy for discrimination by employers, is an important consideration only for white-collar trades.

Perhaps because of the importance of discrimination, Negroes in white-collar occupations travel less far to work than do their white counterparts. Negro sales workers and managers travel less than half as far to their jobs as their white counterparts do; black professional and clerical workers travel only 80 per cent as far. This shorter distance suggests that jobs at a distance from Negro residential areas are not open to black workers in these occupations. This situation contrasts with that of Negroes in blue-collar pursuits who generally travel as far or further to work than their white counterparts.

DISTRIBUTION OF JOBS AND RESIDENCES

In 1960, the last year for which small-area employment figures are available, there were relatively few white-collar jobs in Negro areas, but Negro communities were close to large concentrations of blue-collar employment. Thus, the distribution of jobs was favorable for blue-collar workers, but unfavorable for white-collar workers.

This line-up of employment is changing because of the shifting structure of the city. Most blue-collar jobs are concentrated in manufacturing, construction, and public utilities, with a sprinkling of employment through other kinds of businesses. Manufacturing, the largest single employer, is currently involved in a search for space which is leading many firms engaged in that pursuit to the outer perimeter of the metropolis. As a hold-over from the pre-automobile days when transportation facilities were concentrated within the city, a large number of plants still ring the center city. Close to neighborhoods of Negro residents, these hold-overs form much of the employment market for Negro workers in blue-collar trades. The current movement of these firms out of the city will reduce this market.

In contrast to the story for manual workers, industries employing large numbers of white-collar workers—service industries and financial institutions—have grown rapidly within the city. The greater accessibility to Negro workers is less important for this group of employers, however. Composition of the product market served by firms and the attitudes of employers are the major determinants of employment opportunities for black workers. It is not clear that the growth of these firms in the city near Negro neighborhoods has led to any change in the composition of markets for their products. Many of the institutions that have grown most rapidly serve regional or national markets from a central city location. Those that locate in and serve Negro neighborhoods—the retail and local service shops—probably have not sustained the same growth. Thus, growth of white-collar employment in the city probably has not given black workers special advantages in competing for jobs. Still, black workers have made considerable progress in the white-collar occupations. Employment of black workers has grown more rapidly in white-collar than blue-collar jobs during the sixties, with Negroes filling an increasing proportion of the white-collar opportunities. This gain can be attributed to changes in attitudes of employers and to a rapidly growing demand for office workers in general.

IN AID OF NEGRO WORKERS

The apparent improvement in the outlook for jobs in white-collar occupations affects only one-fourth of the Negro labor force, however. For the larger segment of the black work force, the outlook is dimmer.

Accessibility is a growing problem for black workers in the blue-collar trades. The negative impact of distance from job opportunities, combined with the movement of blue-collar jobs to the suburbs and the concentration of Negroes in the city casts a threatening shadow on the outlook for employment of Negroes in blue-collar occupations. Efforts to counteract the effect of distance, therefore, will become important as suburbanization of employment continues.

In the abstract, there are three different kinds of solutions to the problem of inaccessibility:

a. increase employment in Negro areas,
b. integrate Negro homes throughout the region,
c. improve transportation and communication channels between Negro and suburban areas.

The first approach, advocated by backers of black capitalism and by many business and government leaders, would make a dent in the problem of inaccessibility. However, it may also have harmful social effects in the long-run. In part, the growing separation between the Negro community and major segments of employment in the metropolitan area is increasing the breach between black and white communities. Increased job opportunities within Negro communities for primarily black workers might accelerate this trend. In addition, government subsidies would be required to help firms locating in ghetto areas defray the high costs of operation that have led many firms to leave ghetto areas.

Integration of housing is a long-term solution. Efforts in this direction over the last decade have shown little substantial progress for two reasons. First, open-housing laws are enforced on a case-by-case basis. With limited manpower available for enforcement, there is a long lag between occurrence of alleged discrimination and correction of the abuse. Second, segregation may be partly voluntary. Given freedom of choice, many black workers may choose to live in black communities, although possibly not in the city.

Improvements in transportation and channels of communication are perhaps the more practical ways of counteracting the problems of inaccessibility in the near term. The flow of job information and transportation of workers is more amenable to alteration by public policy than are housing patterns. Also, the consequent increase in contact between black and white workers would be beneficial on social grounds.

Urban transportation systems typically are composed of public or quasi-public facilities, subject to substantial government control, if not to direct public ownership. The kinds and locations of facilities provided, therefore, can be guided by government to serve objectives such as providing adequate transportation to ghetto residents. But, two problems complicate the provision of transportation services to ghetto residents. First, because of the cost of auto-ownership, most residents of poor neighborhoods must rely on mass transit. While fees on users of highways support the construction and maintenance of highways, fees on users of mass transit have generally not been sufficient to support their construction and maintenance. Thus, government must decide to subsidize the transportation of poor workers if it is to provide a suitable system of mass transit for their use. Second, suburban locations of employment are widely dispersed; they are laid out according to an auto-oriented transportation system. Mass transit is most efficient for concentrated centers of employment and housing. Consequently, if mass transit can provide adequate transportation to dispersed centers of employment in the suburbs, the cost of so doing will be high.

Government and industry are currently involved in communicating information on job openings. As evidenced by Philadelphia's "Jobmobile," government is experimenting with new ways of getting information on jobs to residents of poor, inaccessible neighborhoods. In addition, special efforts by industry, such as the "Jobs" campaign of the National Alliance of Businessmen, an effort to recruit the hard-core unemployed, are helping improve communication on employment opportunities. But, improved communications alone will not be sufficient to eliminate the effect of suburbanization of employment upon black workers in blue-collar trades. A combination of subsidized transportation to reduce commuting cost and improved communications would seem to have the greatest chance of success.

READING 43
Negative Income Tax—Better Than Welfare?
James Daniel

Several issues are bound up in the problem of the alleviation of poverty. First, there is the question of administrative efficiency. How can government handle the distribution of relief money with the least budgetary cost? True economic efficiency demands that the consideration of benefits received by relief recipients include more than simple budget accounts. Second, degrading or demoralizing bureaucratic procedures may cause severe disutility to recipients and bring about external effects which tend to perpetuate the need for welfare. Finally, the basis for allotting the payments may have severe repercussions upon work incentives as well as upon other social behavior. The "negative income tax" is one solution. It was suggested some time ago by Professor George Stigler of the University of Chicago, and has recently been popularized by Professor Milton Friedman. In this article James Daniel, roving editor for *The Reader's Digest*, discusses the negative-income tax scheme as proposed by Professor Friedman.

Guideposts for Thought While Reading

From the standpoint of welfare recipients, what would be the advantages of a negative income tax in place of existing welfare programs? How would society benefit from the replacement of the present welfare programs with a negative income tax?

Sometime in the future, if an idea called the "negative income tax"—some of whose features are even now being adopted in Washington thinking—becomes law, the federal income-tax system is likely to become a two-way street. Going one way will be tax dollars—from more than 72 million family heads or single persons who will owe taxes to the government because their incomes *exceed* their exemptions and deductions. Going the other way will be government dollars—to an estimated four million family heads or single persons to whom the government will owe money because their incomes *fall short of* their exemptions and deductions.

At first hearing, the idea of using the federal tax machinery to aid the nation's poorest citizens appears to fly in the face of common sense and sound public policy. But a growing number of conservative and liberal economists and policy-makers are swinging toward the view that, at this stage in U.S. history, a negative income tax makes a lot of sense. It offers, they feel, a way out of our most serious domestic problem—the persistence of stubborn pockets of poverty in an ever-more-affluent society, and the failure of present public-assistance programs to eliminate this want. Along the way, the negative income tax promises a bonus benefit: for the first time *all* American adults would file an income-tax return, quite likely uncovering considerable income which now escapes taxation. Finally, the automated federal tax system would reduce administrative costs compared with the present welfare system, which has 110,000 employes handing out the checks.

The hard fact is that more than 26 million Americans today

have annual incomes below the official poverty line of $3335[1] for a nonfarm family of four. Eighteen million of these are "working poor" who get no direct government aid. As a group of the nation's leaders reported to Gov. Nelson Rockefeller's Arden House Conference on Public Welfare, another eight million are beneficiaries of federal, state and local welfare programs, such as those which aid the blind, the elderly, the permanently disabled and mothers with dependent children. Less than one percent are able-bodied men. All but a handful, then, are too young, too old, too sick or too tied-down minding children to become fully self-supporting, although there is evidence that many mothers would become at least partly self-supporting if the present welfare system were to offer them incentive.

Consider also that half of these 26 million poor are under 18. Put it another way: impoverished Americans make up only 13 percent of our total population of 202 million, but they include *one fourth* of our youth! Clearly, anything that might help poor children in their formative years would mean better, more productive taxpaying citizens later on.

WHERE THE MONEY IS

Most current government relief programs were started in the Depression, and were expected to last only until prosperity reappeared. Today they still survive, costing taxpayers close to $9 billion a year—which sounds like a generous sum until you realize that half of the money is concentrated in just four states: New York, California, Illinois and Pennsylvania. Outside of these few large, comparatively rich states, welfare payments vary wildly. Monthly aid-to-dependent-children payments, for example, range from $8.50 per child in Mississippi to $65.55 in New York. And, even after getting welfare checks, more than half of the families on relief are still below the poverty line.

Looking at the twin problems of poverty and welfare, critics of differing political persuasions have long sought a fundamental remedy. Whatever their starting point, they all seem to end up recommending some form of guaranteed annual income.

The simplest, most utopian proposal has been to declare that anyone who does not earn a certain income will receive the difference as a grant from Uncle Sam. Like most utopian schemes,

[1] Arrived at by multiplying the price of a minimal diet for four people by three, to allow for shelter, clothing and other living costs.

this one has serious flaws. One is the astronomical cost. If the working poor were to quit their jobs—and why wouldn't they, if they could achieve the same income without lifting a finger? —the yearly cost would be $22 billion to bring 26 million people up to the present $3335 poverty-line income.

Moreover, any guaranteed-flat-income welfare program usually has a built-in 100-percent "tax" on all job earnings up to that amount, just as families on welfare lose a dollar of their welfare check for each dollar earned. (Congress relented slightly in a law passed last year: by July 1969, states must permit families on relief to keep the first $30 of monthly earned income and one third of the remainder.) Thus a family has to be assured of an earned income substantially higher than the welfare check even to consider going to work. And, since the jobs open to the poor are of uncertain duration and there may be a long wait before being able to get back on relief, many fear giving up the security of a welfare check. The utopian guaranteed-income plan would extend these welfare-system defects to *all* of the nation's poor.

As an alternative, some Americans advocate the European plan of giving parents of young children "family allowances" without regard to income. One version studied by Congress would repeal the present $600-a-year exemption for each child, and just give every family head $50 a month per child, whether the parent is rich or poor. But estimates of what this would cost range beyond $28 billion per year, and most of the benefits would accrue to families above the poverty line.

FRIEDMAN FRONT & CENTER

Far more practicable is the negative income tax, a plan that keeps costs within bounds and preserves incentives for poor families to work their way off relief. Its leading exponent is Milton Friedman, a distinguished University of Chicago economist of a conservative but original turn of mind. His most popular book, *Capitalism and Freedom*, shows a strong sense of humanity and commitment to the free-enterprise system. His criticisms of our present welfare system are trenchant.

Friedman faults the system for "degrading" the persons helped and those helping. He thinks it is humiliating, for example, for social workers, despite rulings forbidding such visits, to stage midnight raids on the homes of mothers of dependent children to make sure that there is not a man in the house who ought to be supporting the children. He finds it ridiculous to have a system in which a man may believe his wife and children are better off without him in the house. He believes that requiring welfare families to report every dollar earned "penalizes industry or honesty or both." And he asks how the poor on welfare can ever learn to manage their own affairs if a social worker dictates how they shall spend their welfare checks, down to how many pencils a school child should buy.

It was to help the poor learn to take on responsibility that Friedman first developed his idea of a negative income tax in the 1940s and published it in 1962. His ideas moved to front and center stage among American economists last January when a pre-Inauguration task force appointed by President Nixon to give advice on welfare policies recommended, as one alternative, shifting the elderly, the blind and the disabled off welfare into the automatic Social Security program. A second task force on urban affairs suggested adopting the negative income tax as the ultimate replacement for other programs.

The basic outlines of Friedman's plan are relatively simple. A wage earner entitled to negative-income-tax pay would receive payment from the government with his wage check, just as a higher-income wage earner now has his taxes withheld. Others would file a statement of anticipated income once a quarter with the IRS, and if IRS computers found that the low-income family was eligible for a negative-tax payment, the family would get a quarterly, monthly or possibly weekly check. Once a year, before April 15, there would be a final adjustment for under- or over-payment.

In order to encourage the family to lift itself up, a household head would be entitled to receive only *half* of his or her unused exemptions and deductions. Thus a four-member family with no earned income would be entitled to $1500 a year from the government—50 percent of the difference between nothing and $3000.[2] One with $1000 of earnings would get back half of its unused exemptions-deductions, or $1000. At $3000 of earned income, the family would cross the break-even point into the positive-income-tax system.

[2] A taxpayer now is entitled to a $600 exemption for himself and each of his dependents, plus certain standard un-itemized deductions for contributions, etc. For a family of four at the bottom of the income scale, this adds up to $3000—surprisingly close to the present poverty-line level of $3335.

INCENTIVE TO SELF-RELIANCE

Friedman readily concedes two things to his critics. To conservatives, he admits that his plan is a version of the guaranteed-annual-income plan. But, he points out, in effect so is our present welfare system. His version is better, he maintains, because it is out in the open where the public can see it and identify its costs. To liberals, Friedman concedes that his level of support is well below that now paid to welfare recipients in the richer states. But he says that the richer states can, if they choose, enact supplementary negative-income-tax laws, and that his plan would give the poor more help than they now receive in most states.

One of the biggest gainers from his system, Friedman points out, would be professional social workers disillusioned with a system in which they must spend 90 percent of their time acting as policemen and paymasters. By divorcing them from control of relief families' purse strings, the negative income tax would permit the social worker to give advice when it is asked for, and thus is more likely to be taken.

Friedman says he is "deeply sympathetic" to taxpayers' instinctive feeling that people receiving relief should be told how to spend the money. "Those who pay the bill have the right to see that the money is spent for designated purposes. But it seems to me neither prudent nor noble to exercise the right. The major effect is to weaken the self-reliance of the recipients, diminish their humanity and make them wise in the stratagems for evading the spirit of the restrictions placed upon them." He appeals strongly to the fundamental American belief that whatever help government gives to people should encourage them to help themselves, so that eventually they will help support the government—not vice versa.

What about the cost of the negative income tax? Friedman estimates that his plan could be financed with the present $9 billion spent on direct welfare, plus $3 billion reallocated by Congress from such other long-standing anti-poverty programs as urban renewal, farm price supports, and the many new poverty programs enacted in the 1960s. He estimates that, all told, the federal government now spends more than $50 billion on programs allegedly helping the poor. (Many of these, he says, actually help the well-to-do more.)

Every human society has had some way of taking care of the poor, whether by the tribe, the church, the county poor farm or the settlement house. The argument isn't whether to have a welfare system, but what kind. Friedman believes that the simplest, fairest, least expensive and most effective way today is through the income-tax system. According to Friedman, the United States might assimilate the principle of the negative income tax without actively using that expression. Congressional legislation adopting work incentives and pressure for a national welfare minimum illustrate this. The separate elements of his negative-income-tax proposal may very well be incorporated within or grafted upon the present system, and eventually change it. Friedman says, "I don't care what they call it as long as they accept the proposals. Unfortunately, if it is accepted piecemeal, too many of our costly and unproductive programs will linger."

Americans refuse to face the problem at their own risk, he says. "The dilemma our nation faces in the welfare area is how to halt the proliferation of bad programs and ultimately dismantle them. But can we in good conscience attack existing welfare programs, whatever their shortcomings, unless we have something to put in their place?"

PART 5

The International Economy

READING 44
Restraints on Foreign Imports
Adam Smith

In this passage from his famous book, *The Wealth of Nations*, Adam Smith makes his classic argument for free trade. Smith's "Invisible Hand" in which individuals working in the interests of their own welfare promote the welfare of society under competition provides a powerful underpinning for the free-market ideology. Smith extends the argument to attack government restriction of commerce between countries as well as restraints on domestic trade.

Guideposts for Thought While Reading
What is the "Invisible Hand"? Why does Smith distrust those merchants who claim to labor for the common good? What is his basis for supporting free trade between nations?

OF RESTRAINTS UPON THE IMPORTATION FROM FOREIGN COUNTRIES OF SUCH GOODS AS CAN BE PRODUCED AT HOME

By restraining, either by high duties, or by absolute prohibitions, the importation of such goods from foreign countries as can be produced at home, the monopoly of the home market is more or less secured to the domestic industry employed in producing them. Thus the prohibition of importing either live cattle or salt provisions from foreign countries secures to the graziers of Great Britain the monopoly of the home market for butcher's meat. The high duties upon the importation of corn, which in times of moderate plenty amount to a prohibition, give a like advantage to the growers of that commodity. The prohibition of the importation of foreign woollens is equally favourable to the woollen manufacturers. The silk manufacture, though altogether employed upon foreign materials, has lately obtained the same advantage. The linen manufacture has not yet obtained it, but is making great strides towards it. Many other sorts of manufacturers have, in the same manner, obtained in Great Britain,

From the book *The Wealth of Nations*, Vol. I., by Adam Smith with an introduction by Prof. Edwin R. A. Seligman, Everyman's Library Edition. Published by E. P. Dutton & Co., Inc., and reprinted with their permission. Permission from J. M. Dent & Sons, Ltd.

either altogether, or very nearly a monopoly against their countrymen. The variety of goods of which the importation into Great Britain is prohibited either absolutely, or under certain circumstances, greatly exceeds what can easily be suspected by those who are not well acquainted with the laws of the customs.

That this monopoly of the home market frequently gives great encouragement to that particular species of industry which enjoys it, and frequently turns towards that employment a greater share of both the labour and stock of the society than would otherwise have gone to it, cannot be doubted. But whether it tends either to increase the general industry of the society, or to give it the most advantageous direction, is not, perhaps, altogether so evident.

THE INVISIBLE HAND

Every individual who employs his capital in the support of domestic industry, necessarily endeavours so to direct that industry, that its produce may be of the greatest possible value.

The produce of industry is what it adds to the subject or materials upon which it is employed. In proportion as the value of this produce is great or small, so will likewise be the profits of the employer. But it is only for the sake of profit that any man employs a capital in the support of industry, and he will always, therefore, endeavour to employ it in the support of that industry of which the produce is likely to be of the greatest value, or to exchange for the greatest quantity either of money or of other goods.

But the annual revenue of every society is always precisely equal to the exchangeable value of the whole annual produce of its industry, or rather is precisely the same thing with that exchangeable value. As every individual, therefore, endeavors as much as he can both to employ his capital in the support of domestic industry, and so to direct that industry that its produce may be of the greatest value, every individual necessarily labours to render the annual revenue of the society as great as he can. He generally, indeed, neither intends to promote the public interest, nor knows how much he is promoting it. By preferring the support of domestic to that of foreign industry, he intends only his own security; and by directing that industry in such a manner as its produce may be of the greatest value, he intends only his own gain, and he is in this, as in many other cases, led by an *invisible hand* to promote an end which was no part of his intention. Nor is it always the worse for the society that it was no part of it. By pursuing his own interest he frequently promotes that of the society more effectually than when he really intends to promote it. I have never known much good done by those who affected to trade for the public good. It is an affectation, indeed, not very common among merchants, and very few words need be employed in dissuading them from it.

GOVERNMENT INTERVENTION REDUCES WELFARE

What is the species of domestic industry which his capital can employ, and of which the produce is likely to be of the greatest value, every individual, it is evident, can, in this local situation, judge much better than any statesman or lawgiver can do for him. The statesman, who should attempt to direct private people in what manner they ought to employ their capitals, would not only load himself with a most unnecessary attention, but assume an authority which could safely be trusted to no single person, to no council or senate whatever, and would nowhere be so dangerous as in the hands of a man who had folly and presumption enough to fancy himself fit to exercise it.

To give the monopoly of the home market to the produce of domestic industry, in any particular art or manufacture, is in some measure to direct private people in what manner they ought to employ their capitals, and must, in almost all cases, be either a useless or a hurtful regulation. If the produce of domestic can be brought there as cheap as that of foreign industry, the regulation is evidently useless. If it cannot, it must generally be hurtful. It is the maxim of every prudent master of a family, never to attempt to make at home what it will cost him more to make than to buy. The tailor does not attempt to make his own shoes, but buys them of the shoemaker. The shoemaker does not attempt to make his own clothes, but employs a tailor. The farmer attempts to make neither the one nor the other, but employs those different artificers. All of them find it for their interest to employ their whole industry in a way in which they have some advantage over their neighbours, and to purchase with a part of its produce, or with the price of a part of it, whatever else they have occasion for.

What is prudence in the conduct of every private family, can scarce be folly in that of a great kingdom. If a foreign country can supply us with a commodity cheaper than we ourselves can make it, better buy it of them with some part of the produce of our own industry, employed in a way in which we have some advantage. The general industry of the country, being always in proportion to the capital which employs it, will not thereby be diminished, no more than that of the above-mentioned artificers; but only left to find out the way in which it can be employed with the greatest advantage. It is certainly not employed with the greatest advantage when it is thus directed towards an object which it can buy cheaper than it can make. The value of its annual produce is certainly more or less diminished, when it is thus turned away from producing commodities evidently of more value than the commodity which it is directed to produce. According to the supposition, that commodity could be purchased from foreign countries cheaper than it can be made at home. It could, therefore, have been purchased with a part only of the commodities, or, what is the same thing, with a part only of the price of the commodities, which the industry employed by an equal capital would have produced at home, had it been left to follow its natural course. The industry of the country, therefore, is thus turned away from a more, to a less advantageous employment, and the exchangeable value of its annual produce, instead of being increased, according to the intention of the lawgiver, must necessarily be diminished by every such regulation.

READING 45
Sophisms of Protection
Fredric Bastiat

Protectionism is an insidious and ever growing form of monopolization. Its proponents can show it to be of great benefit to every facet of the economy. Arguments against it depend upon generalities such as social costs which do not appeal to any special interest group or economic power block. Although this satirical attack is based upon a

Reprinted by permission of the publisher from Fredric Bastiat, *Sophisms of Protection*, G. P. Putnam's Sons, New York, 1874, pp. 73–80.

fanciful argument for protection of the lighting industry in France in the nineteenth century, the same half truths and subversion of economic principles are seen almost daily in the lobbying of special interest groups in the United States today.

Guideposts for Thought While Reading
What is the distinction made early in the paper between theory or doctrine versus practice? What is the error in logic in the arguments presented in favor of shutting out the sun? Does this suggest similar logical errors in the arguments commonly presented in favor of protectionism?

PETITION FROM THE MANUFACTURERS OF CANDLES, WAX-LIGHTS, LAMPS, CHANDELIERS, REFLECTORS, SNUFFERS, EXTINGUISHERS; AND FROM THE PRODUCERS OF TALLOW, OIL, RESIN, ALCOHOL, AND GENERALLY OF EVERYTHING USED FOR LIGHTS.

"*To the Honorable the Members of the Chamber of Deputies.*

"Gentlemen: You are in the right way: you reject abstract theories; abundance, cheapness, concerns you little. You are entirely occupied with the interest of the producer, whom you are anxious to free from foreign competition. In a word, you wish to secure the *national market* to *national labor*.

"We come now to offer you an admirable opportunity for the application of your—what shall we say? your theory? no, nothing is more deceiving than theory;—your doctrine? your system? your principle? But you do not like doctrines; you hold systems in horror; and, as for principles, you declare that there are no such things in political economy. We will say then, your practice; your practice without theory, and without principle.

"We are subjected to the intolerable competition of a foreign rival, who enjoys, it would seem, such superior facilities for the production of light, that he is enabled to *inundate* our *national market* at so exceedingly reduced a price, that, the moment he makes his appearance, he draws off all custom from us; and thus an important branch of French industry, with all its innumerable ramifications, is suddenly reduced to a state of complete stagnation. This rival, who is no other than the sun, carries on so bitter a war against us, that we have every reason to believe that he has been excited to this course by our perfidious neighbor England. (Good diplomacy this, for the present time!) In this belief we are confirmed by the fact that in all his transactions with this proud island, he is much more moderate and careful than with us.

"Our petition is, that it would please your honorable body to pass a law whereby shall be directed the shutting up of all windows, dormers, skylights, shutters, curtains, vasistas, œil-de-bœufs, in a word, all openings, holes, chinks, and fissures through which the light of the sun is used to penetrate into our dwellings, to the prejudice of the profitable manufacturers which we flatter ourselves we have been enabled to bestow upon the country; which country cannot, therefore, without ingratitude, leave us now to struggle unprotected through so unequal a contest.

"We pray your honorable body not to mistake our petition for a satire, nor to repulse us without at least hearing the reasons which we have to advance in its favor.

"And first, if, by shutting out as much as possible all access to natural light, you thus create the necessity for artificial light, is there in France an industrial pursuit which will not, through some connection with this important object, be benefited by it?

"If more tallow be consumed, there will arise a necessity for an increase of cattle and sheep. Thus artificial meadows must be in greater demand; and meat, wool, leather, and above all, manure, this basis of agricultural riches, must become more abundant.

"If more oil be consumed, it will cause an increase in the cultivation of the olive tree. This plant, luxuriant and exhausting to the soil, will come in good time to profit by the increased fertility which the raising of cattle will have communicated to our fields.

"Our heaths will become covered with resinous trees. Numerous swarms of bees will gather upon our mountains the perfumed treasures, which are now cast upon the winds, useless as the blossoms from which they emanate. There is, in short, no branch of agriculture which would not be greatly developed by the granting of our petition.

"Navigation would equally profit. Thousands of vessels would soon be employed in the whale fisheries, and thence would arise a navy capable of sustaining the honor of France, and of responding to the patriotic sentiments of the undersigned petitioners, candle merchants, etc.

"But what words can express the magnificence which *Paris* will then exhibit! Cast an eye upon the future and behold the gildings, the bronzes, the magnificent crystal chandeliers, lamps, reflectors, and candelabras, which will glitter in the spacious stores, compared with which the splendor of the present day will appear trifling and insignificant.

"There is none, not even the poor manufacturer of resin in the midst of his pine forests, nor the miserable miner in his dark dwelling, but who would enjoy an increase of salary and of comforts.

"Gentlemen, if you will be pleased to reflect, you cannot fail to be convinced that there is perhaps not one Frenchman, from the opulent stockholder of Anzin down to the poorest vender of matches, who is not interested in the success of our petition.

"We foresee your objections, gentlemen; but there is not one that you can oppose to us which you will not be obliged to gather from the works of the partisans of free trade. We dare challenge you to pronounce one word against our petition, which is not equally opposed to your own practice and the principle which guides your policy.

"Do you tell us, that if we gain by this protection, France will not gain, because the consumer must pay the price of it?

"We answer you:

"You have no longer any right to cite the interest of the consumer. For whenever this has been found to compete with that of the producer, you have invariably sacrificed the first. You have done this to *encourage labor*, to *increase the demand for labor*. The same reason should now induce you to act in the same manner.

"You have yourselves already answered the objection. When you were told: The consumer is interested in the free introduction of iron, coal, corn, wheat, cloths, etc., your answer was: Yes, but the producer is interested in their exclusion. Thus, also, if the consumer is interested in the admission of light, we, the producers, pray for its interdiction.

"You have also said, the producer and the consumer are one. If the manufacturer gains by protection, he will cause the agriculturist to gain also; if agriculture prospers, it opens a market for manufactured goods. Thus we, if you confer upon us the monopoly of furnishing light during the day, will as a first consequence buy large quantities of tallow, coals, oil, resin, wax, alcohol, silver, iron, bronze, crystal, for the supply of our business; and then we and our numerous contractors, having become rich, our consumption will be great, and will become a means of contributing to the comfort and competency of the workers in every branch of national labor.

"Will you say that the light of the sun is a gratuitous gift, and that to repulse gratuitous gifts is to repulse riches under pretence of encouraging the means of obtaining them?

"Take care,—you carry the death-blow to your own policy. Remember that hitherto you have always repulsed foreign produce, *because* it was an approach to a gratuitous gift, and *the more in proportion* as this approach was more close. You have, in obeying the wishes of other monopolists, acted only from a *half-motive;* to grant our petition there is a much *fuller inducement.* To repulse us, precisely for the reason that our case is a more complete one than any which have preceded it, would be to lay down the following equation: $+ \times + = -$; in other words, it would be to accumulate absurdity upon absurdity.

"Labor and Nature concur in different proportions, according to country and climate, in every article of production. The portion of Nature is always gratuitous; that of labor alone regulates the price.

"If a Lisbon orange can be sold at half the price of a Parisian one, it is because a natural and gratuitous heat does for the one, what the other only obtains from an artificial and consequently expensive one.

"When, therefore, we purchase a Portuguese orange, we may say that we obtain it half gratuitously and half by the right of labor, in other words, at *half price* compared to those of Paris.

"Now it is precisely on account of this *demi-gratuity* (excuse the word) that you argue in favor of exclusion. How, you say, could national labor sustain the competition of foreign labor, when the first has everything to do, and the last is rid of half the trouble, the sun taking the rest of the business upon himself? If then the *demi-gratuity* can determine you to check competition, on what principle can the *entire gratuity* be alleged as a reason for admitting it? You are no logicians if, refusing the demi-gratuity as hurtful to human labor, you do not *a fortiori,* and with double zeal, reject the full gratuity.

"Again, when any article, as coal, iron, cheese, or cloth, comes to us from foreign countries with less labor than if we produce it ourselves, the difference in price is a *gratuitous gift* conferred upon us; and the gift is more or less considerable, according as the difference is greater or less. It is the quarter, the half, or the three quarters of the value of the produce, in proportion as the foreign merchant requires the three quarters, the half, or the quarter of the price. It is as complete as possible when the producer offers, as the sun does with light, the whole in free gift. The question is, and we put it formally, whether you wish for France the benefit of gratuitous consumption, or the supposed advantages of laborious production. Choose, but be consistent. And does it not argue the greatest inconsistency to check as you do the importation of coal, iron, cheese, and goods of foreign manufacture, merely because and even in proportion as their price approaches *zero,* while at the same time you freely admit, and without limitation, the light of the sun, whose price is during the whole day at *zero?*"

READING 46
A Defense of Fixed Exchange Rates

Henry C. Wallich

Flexible exchange rates do not provide the necessary discipline to encourage economic authorities in each country to maintain sound monetary and fiscal policies, so argues Dr. Henry C. Wallich, professor of economics at Yale University. According to Wallich, most countries do not have the forbearance to stabilize their economy at a noninflationary level unless forced to by trade deficits. Dr. Wallich sees retaliatory currency depreciation building into full-scale "price wars" if the exchange rate is left to the forces of the free market.

Guideposts for Thought While Reading
What undesirable consequences does Professor Wallich see arising from the adoption of flexible exchange rates? How valid is his comparison of the states of the union and nations of the world vis-à-vis a single currency?

Reprinted from "The United States Balance of Payments, Exchange Rates—How Flexible Should They Be?," Hearings before the Joint Economic Committee, 88th Congress, 1st Session, pp. 495–499.

Let me say at the outset that I conceive of my paper as a defense of fixed rates. The title indicates that I would like to see the pros and cons weighed because there are pros and cons, of course.

Flexible rates have achieved a high measure of acceptance in academic circles, but very little among public officials. This raises the question whether we have a parallel to the famous case of free trade: almost all economists favor it in principle, but no major country ever has adopted it. Does the logic of economics point equally irrefutably to flexible rates, while the logic of politics points in another direction?

The nature of the case, I believe, is fundamentally different. Most countries do practice free trade within their borders, although they reject it outside. But economists do not propose flexible rates for the States of the Union, among which men, money, and goods can move freely, and which are governed by uniform monetary, fiscal, and other policies. Flexible rates are to apply only to relations among countries that do not permit free factor movements across their borders and that follow, or may follow, substantially different monetary and fiscal policies. It is the imperfections of the world that seem to suggest that flexible rates, which would be harmful if applied to different parts of a single country, would do more good than harm internationally.

It is quite arguable that the Appalachian area would benefit if it could issue a dollar of its own, an Appalachian dollar which in that case would sell, probably, at 60 or 90 cents. Exports from that region would increase, and unemployment would diminish. A great many good things would happen, but we are also aware of what it would do to the economy of the United States—and, therefore, we do not propose that solution. The question is, Do we want to look upon the world as quite different from the United States, as hopelessly divided into self-contained units where cooperation and efforts to coordinate policies are doomed to frustration? In that case, flexible rates may be the best way to avoid a very bad situation. But should we not try to establish within the world something that begins to approximate the conditions that prevail within a country, in the way of coordination of policies, freer flow of capital and of goods and so try to achieve the benefits of one large economic area within the world? That is what we should try for.

Now to resume: The proponents of flexible rates argue, in effect, that flexible rates can help a country get out of almost any of the typical difficulties that economies experience. This is perfectly true. If the United States has a balance-of-payments deficit, a flexible exchange rate allows the dollar to decline until receipts have risen and payments fallen enough to restore balance. If the United States has unemployment, flexible rates can protect it against the balance-of-payments consequences of a policy of expansion. We would then have less unemployment. If the United States has suffered inflation and fears that it will be undersold internationally, flexible rates can remove the danger.

All of these advantages are quite clear.

Other countries have analogous advantages. If Chile experiences a decline in copper prices, flexible rates can ease the inevitable adjustment. If Germany finds that other countries have inflated while German prices have remained more nearly stable, flexible rates could help to avoid importing inflation. If Canada has a large capital inflow, a flexible rate will remove the need for price and income increases that would otherwise be needed to facilitate the transfer of real resources.

There are other adjustments, however, that must be made in all of these cases. If a country allows its exchange rate to go down, some price adjustments still remain to be made. Furthermore, each time a country makes this kind of adjustment, allowing its exchange rate to decline, other countries suffer. If the U.S. dollar depreciates, we undersell the Europeans. It could be argued that if the U.S. price levels go down instead of the exchange rate, we also undersell the Europeans, and if because of a declining price level we have unemployment we would be buying still less from them. Nevertheless, there is a difference. A price adjustment tends to be slow and is likely to be no greater than it need be and tends to be selective for particular commodities. In contrast, an exchange rate movement is unpredictable. It can be large—we could easily have a drop of 10 or 20 percent in an exchange rate. It comes suddenly. And it compels other countries to be on their guard.

Why, given the attractions of flexible rates, should one advise policymakers to stay away from them? Since the dollar problem is the concrete situation in which flexible rates are being urged today, it is in terms of the dollar that they must be discussed. In broadest terms, the reason why flexible rates are inadvisable is that their successful functioning would require more self-discipline and mutual forbearance than countries today are likely to muster. Exchange rates are two sided—depreciation for the dollar means appreciation for the European currencies. To work successfully, a flexible dollar, for instance, must not depreciate to the point where the Europeans would feel compelled to take counteraction. I believe that the limits of tolerance, before counteraction begins today are narrow and that a flexible dollar would invite retaliation almost immediately.

In the abstract, the European countries perhaps ought to consider that if the United States allows the dollar to go down, it is doing so in the interests of all-round equilibrium. They ought perhaps to consider that with a stable dollar rate the same adjustment might have to take place through a decline in prices here and a rise in prices there. In practice, they are likely to be alive principally to the danger of being undersold by American producers if the dollar goes down, in their own and third markets. The changing competitive pressure would fall unevenly upon particular industries, and those who are hurt would demand protection.

The most likely counteraction might take one of two forms. The Europeans could impose countervailing duties, such as the United States also has employed at times. They could alternately also depreciate European currencies along with the dollar or, what would amount to almost the same thing, prevent the dollar from depreciating. This might involve the European countries in the purchase of large amounts of dollars. If they are to peg the dollar, they could minimize their commitment by imposing a simple form of exchange control that the Swiss practiced during the last war. The Swiss purchased dollars only from their exporters, also requiring their importers to buy these dollars thereby stabilizing the trade dollar, while allowing dollars from capital movements—finance dollars—to find their own level in the market.

The large volume of not very predictable short-term capital movements in the world today makes such reactions under flexible rates particularly likely.

Chairman Douglas. Is that not what has been done for the last 2 years or so by Great Britain and the Netherlands?

Mr. Wallich. Yes, in mild form for securities; that is correct, sir.

A sudden outflow of funds from the United States, for instance (because of the fear of budget deficits or many other things that could happen), would tend to drive the dollar down. As a result, American exporters could undersell producers everywhere else in the world. It seems unlikely that foreign countries would allow a fortuitous short-term capital movement to have such far-reaching consequences. It would not even be economically appropriate to allow a transitory fluctuation in the capital account of the balance of payments to have a major influence on the current account. Such a fluctuation should not alter the pattern of trade, because the situation is likely to be reversed. Other countries therefore would probably take defensive action to make sure that no industry is destroyed and after several years may have to be rebuilt because of the ups and downs of short-term capital movements.

It can be argued that under flexible rates the effects of such a movement would be forestalled by stabilizing speculation on a future recovery of the dollar. This is possible. It is possible also, however, that speculation would seek a quick profit from the initial drop in the dollar, instead of a longer run one from its eventual recovery. Then short-run speculation would drive the dollar down farther at first. In any case there is not enough assurance that speculators will not make mistakes to permit basing the world's monetary system upon the stabilizing effects of speculation.

In the case of countries which import much of what they consume, such as England, a temporary decline in the local currency may even be self-validating. If the cost of living rises as the currency declines, wages will rise. Thereafter, the currency may never recover to its original level.

This points up one probable consequence of flexible exchange rates: A worldwide acceleration of inflation. In some countries the indicated ratchet effect of wages will be at work. If exchange rates go down, wages will rise, and exchange rates cannot recover. In the United States the rise in the cost of imports would not be very important. But the removal of balance-of-payments restraints may well lead to policies that could lead to price increases. The American inflation of the 1950's was never defeated until the payments deficit became serious. Elsewhere, the removal of balance-of-payments disciplines might have the same effect. Rapid inflation in turn would probably compel governments to intervene drastically in foreign trade and finance.

Chairman Douglas. The payment deficit as a means of checking price advances—are you welcoming that?

Mr. Wallich. No, I do not, but I am aware, Mr. Chairman, that there is a choice to be made here—more employment or more stable prices. If we pursued more sensible policies and exerted a little more self-restraint, this choice would not be upon us. But if we insist on raising costs and raising prices in the presence of unemployment then this unpleasant choice must be made. As Mr. Friedman has said, it is quite clear that the discipline of the balance of payments has made for a more restrictive policy in this country than would have been followed in the absence of this discipline. It is quite conceivable that the absence of balance-of-payments disciplines would have strong inflationary effects in some countries. In that case governments would be compelled immediately to intervene drastically in foreign trade and finance; in other words, flexible exchange rates would contribute to their own extinction or to exchange control.

The prospect that flexible rates would greatly increase uncertainty for foreign traders and investors has been cited many times. It should be noted that this uncertainty extends also to domestic investment decisions that might be affected by changing import competition or changing export prospects. It has been argued that uncertainties about future exchange rates can be removed by hedging in the future market. This, however, involves a cost even where cover is readily available. The history of future markets does not suggest that it will be possible to get cover for long-term positions. To hedge domestic investment decisions that might be affected by flexible rates is in the nature of things impracticable.

The picture that emerges of the international economy under flexible rates is one of increasing disintegration. Independent national policies and unpredictable changes in each country's competitive position will compel governments to shield their producers and markets. The argument that such shielding would also automatically be accomplished by movements in the affected country's exchange rate underrates the impact of fluctuations upon particular industries, if not upon the entire economy. That international integration and flexible rates are incompatible seems to be the view also of the European Common Market countries, who have left no doubt that they want stable rates within the EEC. The same applies if we visualize the "Kennedy round" under the Trade Expansion Act. I think if we told the Europeans that, after lowering our tariffs, we were going to cast the dollar loose and let it fluctuate, we would get very little tariff reduction. They would want to keep up their guard.

If the disintegrating effects of flexible rates are to be overcome, a great deal of policy coordination, combined with self-discipline and mutual forbearance, would be required. The desired independence of national economic policy would in fact have to be foregone—interest rates, budgets, wage and price policies would have to be harmonized. If the world were ready for such cooperation, it would be capable also of making a fixed exchange rate system work. In that case, flexible rates would accomplish nothing that could not more cheaply and simply be done with fixed rates. It seems to follow that flexible rates have no unique capacity for good, whereas they possess great capacity to do damage.

A modified version of the flexible rates proposal has been suggested. This version would allow the dollar and other currencies to fluctuate within a given range, say 5 percent up and down. This "widening of the gold points" is believed to reduce the danger of destabilizing speculation. It might perhaps enlist speculation on the side of stabilization, for if the dollar, say, had dropped to its lower limit, and if the public had confidence that that limit would not be broken, the only movement on which to speculate would be a rise. The spectacle of a currency falling below par may induce, according to the proponents, a strong political effort to bring it back.

This proposal likewise strikes me as unworkable. For one thing, I doubt that people would have a great deal of confidence in a limit of 5 percent below par, if par itself has been given up. Political support for holding this second line would probably be less than the support that can be mustered to hold the first. For another, the execution of the plan would still require the maintenance of international reserves, to protect the upper and lower limits. But with fluctuating rates, dollar and sterling would cease to be desirable media for monetary reserves. International liquidity would become seriously impaired. A third objection is that under today's conditions, the complex negotiations and legislation required, in the unlikely event that the plan could be negotiated at all, could not go forward without immediate speculation against the dollar before the plan goes into effect.

It remains only to point out that, even in the absence of a high degree of international cooperativeness, a system of fixed exchange rates can be made to work. It can be made to work mainly because it imposes a discipline upon all participants, and because within this discipline there is nevertheless some room for adjustment. The principal sources of flexibility are productivity gains and the degree to which they are absorbed by wage increases. Wages cannot be expected to decline. But their rise can be slowed in relation to the rate of productivity growth, in which case prices would become more competitive relative to other countries. With annual productivity gains of 2 to 3 percent in the United States and more abroad, it would not take many years to remove a temporary imbalance.

READING 47
Exchange Rates—How Flexible Should They Be?
Milton Friedman

This testimony by Professor Milton Friedman before the Joint Economic Committee is an example of the viewpoint held by many market-oriented economists. Friedman, perhaps the foremost advocate of flexible exchange rates, believes that the balance-of-payments difficulties currently troubling the United States could be eliminated if the rate of exchange of dollars for other currencies was left to the forces of supply and demand. According to Friedman, it is absurd to allow our national policies to be modified to the extent that they have been in recent years simply due to foreign payments which amount to only 5 percent of our total national income.

Guideposts for Thought While Reading
What arguments does Friedman put forth to support flexible exchange rates? What other methods does he list for overcoming a balance-of-payments deficit? Why does Friedman rate these other methods inferior to flexible exchange rates?

OVERCOMING A BALANCE-OF-PAYMENTS DEFICIT

Many people concerned with our payments deficits hope that since we are operating further from full capacity than Europe,

Reprinted from "The United States Balance of Payments: Exchange Rates—How Flexible Should They Be?" Hearings before the Joint Economic Committee, 88th Congress, 1st Session, 1963, pp. 451–456.

we could supply a substantial increase in exports whereas they could not. Implicitly, this assumes that European countries are prepared to see their surplus turned into a deficit, thereby contributing to the reduction of the deficits we have recently been experiencing in our balance of payments. Perhaps this would be the initial effect of tariff changes. But if the achievement of such a result is to be sine qua non of tariff agreement, we cannot hope for any significant reduction in barriers. We could be confident that exports would expand more than imports only if the tariff changes were one sided indeed, with our trading partners making much greater reductions in tariffs than we make. Our major means of inducing other countries to reduce tariffs is to offer corresponding reductions in our tariff. More generally, there is little hope of continued and sizable liberalization of trade if liberalization is to be viewed simply as a device for correcting balance-of-payments difficulties. That way lies only backing and filling.

Suppose then that the initial effect is to increase our expenditures on imports more than our receipts from exports. How could we adjust to this outcome?

One method of adjustment is to draw on reserves or borrow from abroad to finance the excess increase in imports. The obvious objection to this method is that it is only a temporary device, and hence can be relied on only when the disturbance is temporary. But that is not the major objection. Even if we had very large reserves or could borrow large amounts from abroad, so that we could continue this expedient for many years, it is a most undesirable one. We can see why if we look at physical rather than financial magnitudes.

The physical counterpart to the financial deficit is a reduction of employment in industries competing with imports that is larger than the concurrent expansion of employment in export industries. So long as the financial deficit continues, the assumed tariff reductions create employment problems. But it is no part of the aim of tariff reductions to create unemployment at home or to promote employment abroad. The aim is a balanced expansion of trade, with exports rising along with imports and thereby providing employment opportunities to offset any reduction in employment resulting from increased imports.

Hence, simply drawing on reserves or borrowing abroad is a most unsatisfactory method of adjustment.

Another method of adjustment is to lower U.S. prices relative to foreign prices, since this would stimulate exports and discourage imports. If foreign countries are accommodating enough to engage in inflation, such a change in relative prices might require merely that the United States keep prices stable or even, that it simply keep them from rising as fast as foreign prices. But there is no necessity for foreign countries to be so accommodating, and we could hardly count on their being so accommodating. The use of this technique therefore involves a willingness to produce a decline in U.S. prices by tight monetary policy or tight fiscal policy or both. Given time, this method of adjustment would work. But in the interim, it would exact a heavy toll. It would be difficult or impossible to force down prices appreciably without producing a recession and considerable unemployment. To eliminate in the long run the unemployment resulting from the tariff changes, we should in the short run be creating cyclical unemployment. The cure might for a time be far worse than the disease.

This second method is therefore also most unsatisfactory. Yet these two methods—drawing on reserves and forcing down prices—are the only two methods available to us under our present international payment arrangements, which involve fixed exchange rates between the U.S. dollar and other currencies. Little wonder that we have so far made such disappointing progress toward the reduction of trade barriers, that our practice has differed so much from our preaching.

There is one other way and only one other way to adjust and that is by allowing (or forcing) the price of the U.S. dollar to fall in terms of other currencies. To a foreigner, U.S. goods can become cheaper in either of two ways—either because their prices in the United States fall in terms of dollars or because the foreigner has to give up fewer units of his own currency to acquire a dollar, which is to say, the price of the dollar falls. For example, suppose a particular U.S. car sells for $2,800 when a dollar costs 7 shillings, tuppence in British money (i.e., roughly £1=$2.80). The price of the car is then £1,000 in British money. It is all the same to an Englishman—or even a Scotsman—whether the price of the car falls to $2,500 while the price of a dollar remains 7 shillings, tuppence, or, alternatively, the price of the car remains $2,800, while the price of a dollar falls to 6 shillings, 5 pence (i.e., roughly £1=$3.11). In either case, the car costs the Englishman £900 rather than £1,000, which is what matters to him. Similarly, foreign goods can become more expensive to an American in either of two ways—either because the price in terms of foreign currency rises or because he has to give up more dollars to acquire a given amount of foreign currency.

Changes in exchange rates can therefore alter the relative price of U.S. and foreign goods in precisely the same way as can changes in internal prices in the United States and in foreign countries. And they can do so without requiring anything like the same internal adjustments. If the initial effect of the tariff reductions would be to create a deficit at the former exchange rate (or enlarge an existing deficit or reduce an existing surplus) and thereby increase unemployment, this effect can be entirely avoided by a change in exchange rates which will produce a balanced expansion in imports and exports without interfering with domestic employment, domestic prices, or domestic monetary and fiscal policy. The pig can be roasted without burning down the house.

The situation is, of course, entirely symmetrical if the tariff changes should initially happen to expand our exports more than our imports. Under present circumstances, we would welcome such a result, and conceivably, if the matching deficit were experienced by countries currently running a surplus, they might permit it to occur without seeking to offset it. In that case, they and we would be using the first method of adjustment—changes in reserves or borrowing. But again, if we had started off from an even keel, this would be an undesirable method of adjustment. On our side, we should be sending out useful goods and receiving only foreign currencies in return. On the side of our partners, they would be using up reserves and tolerating the creation of unemployment.

The second method of adjusting to a surplus is to permit or force domestic prices to rise—which is of course what we did in part in the early postwar years when we were running large surpluses. Again, we should be forcing maladjustments on the whole economy to solve a problem arising from a small part of it—the 5 percent accounted for by foreign trade.

Again, these two methods are the only ones available under our present international payments arrangements, and neither is satisfactory.

The final method is to permit or force exchange rates to change—in this case, a rise in the price of the dollar in terms of foreign currencies. This solution is again specifically adapted to the specific problem of the balance of payments.

Changes in exchange rates can be produced in either of two general ways. One way is by a change in an official exchange rate; an official devaluation or appreciation from one fixed level which the Government is committed to support to another fixed level. This is the method used by Britain in its postwar devaluation and by Germany in 1961 when the mark was appreciated. This is also the main method contemplated by the IMF which permits member nations to change their exchange rates by 10 percent without approval by the Fund and by a larger amount after approval by the Fund. But this method has serious disadvantages. It makes a change in rates a matter of major moment, and hence there is a tendency to postpone any change as long as possible. Difficulties cumulate and a larger change is finally needed than would have been required if it could have been made promptly. By the time the change is made, everyone is aware that a change is pending and is certain about the direction of change. The result is to encourage flight from a currency, if it is going to be devalued, or to a currency, if it is going to be appreciated.

There is in any event little basis for determining precisely what the new rate should be. Speculative movements increase the difficulty of judging what the new rate should be, and introduce a systematic bias, making the change needed appear larger than it actually is. The result, particularly when devaluation occurs, is generally to lead officials to "play safe" by making an even larger change than the large change needed. The country is then left after the devaluation with a maladjustment precisely the opposite of that with which it started, and is thereby encouraged to follow policies it cannot sustain in the long run.

Even if all these difficulties could be avoided, this method of changing from one fixed rate to another has the disadvantage that it is necessarily discontinuous. Even if the new exchange rates are precisely correct when first established, they will not long remain correct.

A second and much better way in which changes in exchange rates can be produced is by permitting exchange rates to float, by allowing them to be determined from day to day in the market. This is the method which the United States used from 1862 to 1879, and again, in effect, from 1917 or so to about 1925, and again from 1933 to 1934. It is the method which Britain used from 1918 to 1925 and again from 1931 to 1939, and which Canada used for most of the interwar period and again from 1950 to May 1962. Under this method, exchange rates adjust themselves continuously, and market forces determine the magnitude of each change. There is no need for any official to decide by how much the rate should rise or fall. This is the method of the free market, the method that we adopt unquestioningly in a private enterprise economy for the bulk of goods and services. It is no less available for the price of one money in terms of another.

With a floating exchange rate, it is possible for Governments to intervene and try to affect the rate by buying or selling, as the British exchange equalization fund did rather successfully in the 1930's, or by combining buying and selling with public announcements of intentions, as Canada did so disastrously in early 1962. On the whole, it seems to me undesirable to have government intervene, because there is a strong tendency for government agencies to try to peg the rate rather than to stabilize it, because they have no special advantage over private speculators in stabilizing it, because they can make far bigger mistakes than private speculators risking their own money, and because there is a tendency for them to cover up their mistakes by changing the rules—as the Canadian case so strikingly illustrates—rather than by reversing course. But this is an issue on which there is much difference of opinion among economists who agree in favoring floating rates. Clearly, it is possible to have a successful floating rate along with governmental speculation.

The great objective of tearing down trade barriers, of promoting a worldwide expansion of trade, of giving citizens of all countries, and especially the underdeveloped countries, every opportunity to sell their products in open markets under equal terms and thereby every incentive to use their resources efficiently, of giving countries an alternative through free world trade to autarchy and central planning—this great objective can, I believe, be achieved best under a regime of floating rates. All countries, and not just the United States, can proceed to liberalize boldly and confidently only if they can have reasonable assurance that the resulting trade expansion will be balanced and will not interfere with major domestic objectives. Floating exchange rates, and so far as I can see, only floating exchange rates, provide this assurance. They do so because they are an automatic mechanism for protecting the domestic economy from the possibility that liberalization will produce a serious imbalance in international payments.

WHY AREN'T FLOATING EXCHANGE RATES MORE POPULAR?

Despite their advantages, floating exchange rates have a bad press. Why is this so?

One reason is because a consequence of our present system that I have been citing as a serious disadvantage is often regarded as an advantage, namely, the extent to which the small foreign trade sector dominates national policy. Those who regard this as an advantage refer to it as the discipline of the gold standard. I would have much sympathy for this view if we had a real gold standard, so the discipline was imposed by impersonal forces which in turn reflected the realities of resources, tastes, and technology. But in fact we have today only a pseudo gold standard and the so-called discipline is imposed by governmental officials of other countries who are determining their own internal monetary policies and are either being forced to dance to our tune or calling the tune for us, depending primarily on accidental political developments. This is a discipline we can well do without. See my article entitled "Real and Pseudo Gold Standards."

A possibly more important reason why floating exchange rates have a bad press, I believe, is a mistaken interpretation of experience with floating rates, arising out of a statistical fallacy that can be seen easily in a standard example. Arizona is clearly the worst place in the United States for a person with tuberculosis to go because the death rate from tuberculosis is higher in Arizona than in any other State. The fallacy in this case is obvious. It is less obvious in connection with exchange rates. Countries that have gotten into severe financial difficulties, for whatever reason, have had ultimately to change their exchange rates or let them change. No amount of exchange control and other restrictions on trade have enabled them to peg an exchange rate that was far out of line with economic realities. In consequence, floating rates have frequently been associated with financial and economic instability. It is easy to conclude, as many have, that floating exchange rates produce such instability.

This misreading of experience is reinforced by the general prejudice against speculation; which has led to the frequent assertion, typically on the basis of no evidence whatsoever, that speculation in exchange can be expected to be destabilizing and thereby to increase the instability in rates. Few who make this assertion even recognize that it is equivalent to asserting that speculators generally lose money.

Floating exchange rates need not be unstable exchange rates

—any more than the prices of automobiles or of Government bonds, of coffee or of meals need gyrate wildly just because they are free to change from day to day. The Canadian exchange rate was free to change during more than a decade, yet it varied within narrow limits. The ultimate objective is a world in which exchange rates, while free to vary, are in fact highly stable because basic economic policies and conditions are stable. Instability of exchange rates is a symptom of instability in the underlying economic structure. Elimination of this symptom by administrative pegging of exchange rates cures none of the underlying difficulties and only makes adjustment to them more painful.

The confusion between stable exchange rates and pegged exchange rates helps to explain the frequent comment that floating exchange rates would introduce an additional element of uncertainty into foreign trade and thereby discourage its expansion. They introduce no additional element of uncertainty. If a floating rate would, for example, decline, then a pegged rate would be subject to pressure that the authorities would have to meet by internal deflation or exchange control in some form. The uncertainty about the rate would simply be replaced by uncertainty about internal prices or about the availability of exchange; and the latter uncertainties, being subject to administrative rather than market control, are likely to be the more erratic and unpredictable. Moreover, the trader can far more readily and cheaply protect himself against the danger of changes in exchange rates, through hedging operations in a forward market, than he can against the danger of changes in internal prices or exchange availability. Floating rates are therefore more favorable to private international trade than pegged rates.

THE CONSEQUENCES OF MAINTAINING FIXED EXCHANGE RATES

Though I have discussed the problem of international payments in the context of trade liberalization, the discussion is directly applicable to the more general problem of adapting to any forces that make for balance-of-payments difficulties. Consider our present problem, of a deficit in the balance of trade plus long-term capital movements. How can we adjust to it? By one of the three methods outlined: first, drawing on reserves or borrowing; second, keeping U.S. prices from rising as rapidly as foreign prices or forcing them down; third, permitting or forcing exchange rates to alter. And, this time, by one more method: by imposing additional trade barriers or their equivalent, whether in the form of higher tariffs, or smaller import quotas, or extracting from other countries tighter "voluntary" quotas on their exports, or "tieing" foreign aid, or buying higher priced domestic goods or services to meet military needs, or imposing taxes on foreign borrowing, or imposing direct controls on investments by U.S. citizens abroad, or any one of the host of other devices for interfering with the private business of private individuals that have become so familiar to us since Hjalmar Schacht perfected the modern techniques of exchange control in 1934 to strengthen the Nazis for war and to despoil a large class of his fellow citizens.

Fortunately or unfortunately, even Congress cannot repeal the laws of arithmetic. Books must balance. We must use one of these four methods. Because we have been unwilling to select the only one that is currently fully consistent with both economic and political needs—namely, floating exchange rates—we have been driven, as if by an invisible hand, to employ all the others, and even then may not escape the need for explicit changes in exchange rates.

We affirm in loud and clear voices that we will not and must not erect trade barriers—yet is there any doubt about how far we have gone down the fourth route? After the host of measures already taken, the Secretary of the Treasury has openly stated to the Senate Finance Committee that if the so-called interest equalization tax—itself a concealed exchange control and concealed devaluation—is not passed, we shall have to resort to direct controls over foreign investment.

We affirm that we cannot drain our reserves further, yet short-term liabilities mount and our gold stock continues to decline.

We affirm that we cannot let balance-of-payments problems interfere with domestic prosperity, yet for at least some 4 years now we have followed a less expansive monetary policy than would have been healthy for our economy.

Chairman Douglas. We thank you for that, Professor Friedman.

Mr. Friedman. Even all together, these measures may only serve to postpone but not prevent open devaluation—if the experience of other countries is any guide. Whether they do, depends not on us but on others. For our best hope of escaping our present difficulties is that foreign countries will inflate.

In the meantime, we adopt one expedient after another, borrowing here, making swap arrangements there, changing the form of loans to make the figures look good. Entirely aside from the ineffectiveness of most of these measures, they are politically degrading and demeaning. We are a great and wealthy Nation. We should be directing our own course, setting an example to the world, living up to our destiny. Instead, we send our officials hat in hand to make the rounds of foreign governments and central banks; we put foreign central banks in a position to determine whether or not we can meet our obligations and thus enable them to exert great influence on our policies; we are driven to niggling negotiations with Hong Kong and with Japan and for all I know, Monaco, to get them to limit voluntarily their exports. Is this posture suitable for the leader of the free world?

Chairman Douglas. I do not wish to interrupt you, but I would like to say that I think many visits to Monaco are for a different purpose. [Laughter.]

Go ahead.

Mr. Friedman. It is not the least of the virtues of floating exchange rates that we would again become masters in our own house. We could decide important issues on the proper ground. The military could concentrate on military effectiveness and not on saving foreign exchange; recipients of foreign aid could concentrate on how to get the most out of what we give them and not on how to spend it all in the United States; Congress could decide how much to spend on foreign aid on the basis of what we get for our money and what else we could use it for and not how it will affect the gold stock; the monetary authorities could concentrate on domestic prices and employment, not on how to induce foreigners to hold dollar balances in this country; the Treasury and the tax committees of Congress could devote their attention to the equity of the tax system and its effects on our efficiency, rather than on how to use tax gimmicks to discourage imports, subsidize exports, and discriminate against outflows of capital.

A system of floating exchange rates would render the problem of making outflows equal inflows unto the market where it belongs and not leave it to the clumsy and heavy hand of Government. It would leave Government free to concentrate on its proper functions.

In conclusion, a word about gold. Our commitment to buy and sell gold for monetary use at a fixed price of $35 an ounce is, in practice, the mechanism whereby we maintain fixed rates of exchange between the dollar and other currencies—or, more precisely, whereby we leave all initiative for changes in such rates to other countries. This commitment should be terminated. The price of gold should be determined in the free market, with the U.S. Government committed neither to buying gold nor to selling gold at any fixed price. This is the appropriate counterpart of a policy of floating exchange rates. With respect to our existing stock of gold, we could simply keep it fixed, neither adding to it nor reducing it; alternatively, we could sell it off gradually at the market price or add to it gradually, thereby reducing or increasing our governmental stockpiles of this particular metal. In any event, we should simultaneously remove all present limitations on the ownership of gold and the trading in gold by American citizens. There is no reason why gold, like other commodities, should not be freely traded on a free market.

READING 48
Gold and the International Monetary System

Thomas E. Davis

This article explains the development of a system of international exchange in which gold is playing a role of diminishing importance. Concern is felt that as gold becomes a smaller part of the total international reserve assets, a preference for gold over other reserve assets may destabilize international trade. The author concludes that, given the strong desire on the part of most nations to maintain their national sovereignty, the immediate development of an international agency to act as a central bank for the world is unlikely. Given existing institutions, it is clear that many *ad hoc* adjustments and close international cooperation will be necessary to prevent monetary chaos and harmful restraint of trade.

Reprinted by permission of the publisher from Thomas E. Davis, "Gold and the International Monetary System," *Monthly Review*, Federal Reserve Bank of Kansas City, March 1970, pp. 11–20.

Guideposts for Thought While Reading

What are the weaknesses of the gold-exchange standard which is currently used for international trade? What is the two-tier price system for gold? What might explain the desire of central banks throughout the world to prefer gold over other reserve assets? What might happen if the United States stopped pegging the dollar to gold, and the dollar effectively became the principal international reserve asset?

Substantial progress has been made during the past few years toward assuring the future viability of the international monetary system. It is of considerable importance that national authorities have demonstrated increased awareness of the need and advisability to correct balance of payments disequilibria through prompt application of domestic economic policies and, when necessary, through timely and moderate changes in exchange rate parities. Also, concrete steps have been taken to cope with the international liquidity problem through the creation of a new international reserve asset in the form of special drawing rights (SDR's), which are designed to assure a desirable long-run growth in reserve assets consistent with the needs of a growing world economy. The SDR agreement is thought to be of special significance because it has made it possible for the world economy to move to a deliberate and considered management of international reserves, and concomitantly away from its previous dependence on gold as a primary international reserve asset. For this reason, the SDR agreement has been hailed in many quarters as a fundamental reform of the international monetary system.

While the problem of adjusting external disequilibria is now being given increased attention, and the problem of providing for an increase in total liquidity apparently has been met by the SDR arrangement, a number of observers feel that there is still a third problem that confronts the future viability of the system. This problem is related to the composition of international reserve assets. In brief, it is felt that given the present and foreseeable composition of reserve assets—consisting of gold, SDR's, and foreign exchange—varying preferences for one asset vis-à-vis another may give rise to large and destabilizing movements in reserve assets. Interest in the coexistence problem of different types of reserve assets has grown recently because, with the advent of the SDR agreement, gold is expected to play a diminishing role in the international monetary system, while SDR's are expected to play an increasingly larger role. Accordingly, some observers are concerned whether the envisioned monetary role of gold will prove to be a workable and stable arrangement given traditional institutional practices with respect to gold. In view of these developments, this article discusses the rationale for some of the recent changes in the international monetary system, explains the grounds advanced by those observers concerned about the future role of gold, and briefly examines some alternative plans and proposals that have been suggested to deal with the future monetary role of gold.

RECENT EVOLUTION OF THE GOLD EXCHANGE STANDARD

The international monetary system in force since the end of World War II evolved out of the financial experiences of the 1930's and was largely incorporated into The Articles of Agreement of the International Monetary Fund (IMF) in 1944. A fundamental feature of this system is the agreed aim of member countries to adhere to a regime of fixed exchange rates among national currencies. Under the provisions of the system, each member country of the IMF is required to declare to the Fund the par value of its currency in terms of gold or the gold content of the present U.S. dollar, and is obligated to maintain the exchange rate of its currency within one per cent either side of the declared par value. A country may elect to change the par value of its currency if its balance of international payments is in fundamental disequilibrium and if the change meets with the approval of the Fund.

To maintain exchange rates within one per cent of parity, most member countries stand ready to intervene when necessary in their foreign exchange markets through the purchase or sale of acceptable international reserve assets against their own currency. For example, most countries other than the United States fulfill their parity obligation by supporting their currencies through the purchase or sale of U.S. dollars. The United States, unlike other countries, has elected to fulfill its parity obligation by freely buying and selling gold—only with foreign official institutions and only for legitimate monetary purposes—at the fixed price of $35 an ounce. Thus, the present system of fixed exchange rates rests basically on the convertibility of the U.S. dollar into gold at the established price of $35 an ounce, and on other countries' currencies being convertible into the U.S. dollar within the legal limits of their declared par values.

For any system of fixed foreign exchange rates to function properly it is necessary for countries to have an adequate supply of international reserve assets. Under the traditional gold standard, which was the fixed rate system existing in the years prior to World War I, gold served as the principal reserve asset. Under this system, countries made their domestic currencies and gold freely interconvertible at a fixed price, so that exchange rates were stabilized between their gold import and export points through the actions of private gold arbitrageurs. However, with the collapse of the gold standard in the interwar period—brought about partly by the inadequate supply of gold relative to needs and the desire of countries to break the monetary constraint that the gold standard imposed upon domestic economic policies—national monetary authorities resorted to the growing practice of using national currencies, primarily the pound and the U.S. dollar, as a useful reserve supplement to gold. The gold standard thus evolved between 1919 and 1939 into a system in which countries held their reserve assets partly in gold and partly in national currencies. After World War II, this type of system continued to evolve in the direction of countries holding a greater proportion of their international reserve assets in the form of national currencies, primarily U.S. dollars. For this reason, the present international monetary system—in which reserve assets consist mainly of official holdings of gold and convertible national currencies—is generally referred to as a gold exchange standard.

While the gold exchange standard has grown in importance since World War II, it has been criticized by some economists as having certain inherent weaknesses. To provide some insight into the recent changes that have been made in the system, it is useful to examine the nature of these weaknesses. In general terms, they are thought to derive from the very process of the gold exchange standard itself, i.e., the process by which countries increasingly resort to holding national currencies as a substitute for gold. This process, it is claimed, will eventually prevent the system from generating reserve assets in an amount and quality necessary to be both internationally acceptable and consistent with the needs of an expanding world economy. More precisely, these weaknesses are said to be as follows: (1) the gold exchange standard tends to create a shortage of gold relative to the monetary demand for gold, and (2) the gold exchange standard tends to progressively undermine confidence in the reserve currency used as a substitute for gold.

The contention that a shortage of gold for monetary purposes will develop under the gold exchange standard is related basically to the forces which affect the supply and demand for gold. On the demand side, it is assumed that in the context of a growing world economy experiencing constant money prices, the nonmonetary or private demand for gold will grow along with world output and income. However, it is then maintained that the assumption of constant money prices is not likely to be realized because the substitution of a credit form of money for gold permits countries to adopt more inflationary monetary policies than would otherwise be the case. Thus, given a general upward trend in prices and a fixed monetary price for gold, the private demand for gold will accelerate as gold becomes relatively cheaper than other metals for industrial, artistic, and other purposes. Also, under the same conditions, the supply or production of gold will be discouraged as the profitability of gold production is diminished due to a rise in the cost of production relative to the fixed price of gold. For these reasons, it is believed that the nonmonetary demand for gold will eventually surpass the production of new gold. Therefore, to maintain a single market price of gold, monetary authorities inevitably must become net suppliers of gold to the market. In this event, it is argued, some alteration in the gold exchange standard becomes necessary to prevent its collapse because the sale of monetary gold to meet nonmonetary demands causes a decline in the stock of gold reserve assets.

The second weakness of the gold exchange standard is said to develop when a reserve currency is accumulated to satisfy the growing demand for reserve assets not met by an inflow of gold. When this occurs, the reserve currency country not only will experience an increase in its liquid liabilities, but also is likely to experience a drop in its gold assets. A decline in the gold assets of the reserve currency country is likely to develop, it is pointed out, because if other countries act to maintain a traditional ratio between their gold holdings and their growing holdings of the reserve currency, they will have to absorb not only new gold production but also gold from the reserve currency country. In consequence, the net liquidity position of the reserve currency country will deteriorate, as its liabilities increase relative to its gold holdings, and confidence in the gold convertibility of the reserve currency will progressively diminish. Thus, it is held, the process inherent in the gold exchange standard eventually will lead to a crisis with respect to the gold convertibility of the national currency used as a substitute for gold.

These weaknesses are characteristic of some of the difficulties encountered by the gold exchange standard in recent years. While U.S. dollars were willingly accumulated as a reserve asset by foreign countries in the 1950's, sizable deficits in the U.S. balance of payments in the 1960's led to increasing concern over the U.S. net liquidity position and to growing reluctance by foreign countries to rely on further acquisitions of dollars as a reserve asset. Also, from 1960 on, the market price of gold came under occasional upward pressure as the normal nonmonetary demand for gold was supplemented by a speculative demand motivated by expectations that the monetary price might have to be raised. In recognition of these and other developments, national authorities began a series of studies in 1964 to explore the adequacy of the international reserve structure. From these studies a consensus arose that the existing sources of reserve growth might prove inadequate in the future due to a possible shortfall in monetary gold relative to total reserve needs and the likelihood that this shortfall would not be met by increased holdings of U.S. dollars. Out of this consensus emerged the Rio Agreement of 1967 to establish a new special drawing rights facility at the IMF.

Prior to the final acceptance of the SDR facility, however, the foreign exchange markets became alarmingly unsettled with the devaluation of the British pound, and the speculative demand for gold increased substantially to culminate in the gold crisis of late 1967 and early 1968. To meet this crisis the seven active member countries of the "London gold pool" supplied about $3 billion of gold to the private market in an effort to stabilize the price at $35 an ounce. However, as the speculative demand for gold did not abate, the members of the pool decided to terminate their operations in March 1968. Specifically, they announced that "henceforth officially-held gold should be used only to effect transfers among monetary authorities," and therefore they decided "no longer to supply gold to the London market or any other market." They also announced that "as the existing stock of gold is sufficient in view of the prospective establishment of the facility for Special Drawing Rights, they no longer (felt) it necessary to buy gold from the market." These decisions, of course, established what has come to be called the two-tier price system for gold.

Following this action designed to insulate monetary gold stocks from speculative demands in the private market, final acceptance was accorded the SDR facility in 1969. Moreover, at the annual meeting of the IMF in the fall of 1969, a decision was made to begin the actual allocations of SDR's effective January 1, 1970. Specifically, it was decided to allocate $9.5 billion of SDR's to participating members of the facility on the following schedule: $3.5 billion on January 1, 1970; $3 billion on January 1, 1971; and $3 billion on January 1, 1972. By virtue of this decision, the long-sought goal to create a new international reserve asset that was not subject to the vicissitudes of the supply and private demand for gold as well as the external payments position of reserve currency countries was finally realized.

The cumulative effect of these two recent changes in the gold exchange standard—the establishment of the two-tier price system for gold and the implementation of the SDR facility—has generally been interpreted to have the following implications. The gold exchange standard has substantially evolved into a system that no longer will be dependent on increases in monetary gold or reserve currencies as the principal sources of reserve assets. To meet the future need for an adequate growth of reserves, the system will rely instead upon a multilateral and considered decision to create SDR's. Thus, it is believed that, while gold will continue to play a role in the international monetary system, its importance relative to other reserve assets will steadily diminish over time.

CONCERN ABOUT THE FUTURE ROLE OF GOLD

The future viability of the system now in place has been questioned by a number of observers because of concern over the prospective monetary role of gold. This concern has arisen for essentially two reasons. First, some observers feel that it may not be desirable to establish a system that allows for little or no increase in the value of monetary gold stocks, given traditional institutional practices regarding gold. Second, others feel that it may not be practical to operate a multiple reserve asset system under existing arrangements when the reserves consist of such widely different assets as gold, reserve currencies, and SDR's. Although these two reasons focus on separate aspects of the gold problem and imply quite different remedies, an underlying feature common to both is the belief that the system could be vulnerable to destabilizing movements in reserve assets arising mainly out of the traditional preference of central banks for gold as a reserve asset.

The preference of central banks for gold is thought by many to be an anachronistic practice not keyed to the historical trend of nations toward a manmade credit form of money and away from a commodity form of money. As intellectually appealing as this view is, it should be recognized that the attractiveness of gold to central banks does not stem from the commodity value of gold alone. Monetary authorities have long known that to generate a supply of gold for monetary purposes—a supply in excess of private demand—it is necessary that the monetary value be set higher than the commodity value. Hence, the monetary value of gold established by monetary authorities has long served to determine the commodity value of gold.

The attractiveness of gold to monetary authorities has rested instead on other attributes of gold. One such attribute is that gold is a unique asset in that it does not constitute somebody else's liability, which is in marked contrast to national currencies used as a reserve asset. By virtue of this unique property, which puts gold beyond the direct and decisive control of any one country, gold is considered a prime international reserve asset that is universally acceptable as a means of payment. Also because of this unique property, gold is said to convey to its national holder a degree of autonomy in international economic relations, and thereby it is considered a means by which a country can protect its national sovereignty. Another attribute of gold attractive to monetary authorities is that it serves as a store of value. This is especially true for countries which are concerned about the exchange risk of their reserve assets and which do not attach much weight to earning interest on their reserve assets, since gold is a sterile asset that yields no interest. The precautionary motive for holding gold as a store of value appears realistic from the standpoint of many central banks, especially in a world marked by inflationary pressures, external disequilibria among countries, and occasional changes in the gold value of important national currencies.

In cognizance of the pragmatic reasons underlying the preference of central banks for gold, some observers are concerned that the new system may not work successfully without any increase in the value of monetary gold stocks. In their view, the main source of trouble in the past has been that a shortage of gold in the system has caused a drain on U.S. gold reserves and created an element of uncertainty regarding the gold convertibility of the U.S. dollar. This uncertainty has been a major factor undermining the smooth functioning of the system. While proponents of this view recognize that it is useful to develop other types of reserve facilities to supplement gold, such as SDR's, they also believe that central banks will continue to want an increase in their gold reserves in some reasonable proportion to the increase in their other reserve assets. Implicit in this view is the belief that due to the preference for gold by central banks, SDR's are not likely to be considered a perfect or near perfect substitute for gold until such time in the future when they have proven their strength and usefulness—which, it is contended, is by no means assured. Thus, it is held that, without an increase in the value of monetary gold stocks, confidence in the gold convertibility of the U.S. dollar may continue to present a problem and cause further disturbances and instability to the system.

The second cause for concern over the future role of gold is related to the expected difficulties of managing a multiple reserve asset system when differences exist in the attributes of, and the preferences for, reserve assets. More precisely, it is felt that in a system in which reserve assets are to be held in such widely different forms as gold, reserve currencies, and SDR's, there is a clear danger of massive shifts from one type of reserve asset into another. In recognition of this problem, the designers of the SDR facility agreed on specific rules to put the coexistence of SDR's and other reserve assets on a safe footing. In general terms, these rules specify that SDR's are not to be used by member countries for the sole purpose of changing the composition of their total reserves, and that SDR's are to be used by both deficit and surplus countries in an appropriate relationship with other reserve assets. However, even though these rules may help meet the problem of coexistence between SDR's and other reserve assets, there remains unsolved the problem of coexistence between gold and dollars.

The reason for concern over the problem of coexistence between gold and dollars is that in a system in which gold plays a diminishing role due to little or no increase in monetary gold stocks, the problem may become acute. This is because the traditional preference for gold under such a system is likely to increase, if for no other reason than gold will constitute a steadily smaller proportion of total reserves. Moreover, if the demand for gold as a reserve asset did increase, countries might very likely satisfy this demand at the expense of the gold stocks of the reserve currency country—the United States. Another aspect of the same problem is the belief that the preference for gold by monetary authorities is likely to be heightened by the emergence of a substantial premium price for gold in the private market.

In this event, it is contended, the preference for gold would heighten and the likelihood would increase that a large shift out of dollars and into gold would occur. Such a shift would clearly inhibit the growth of total reserves and would put considerable strain on the gold convertibility of the dollar and the parity relationships of all other currencies.

SOME PLANS AND PROPOSALS

A number of plans have been advanced recently to cope with the difficulties expected to arise under a system in which monetary gold is to play a diminishing role while the preference for gold by central banks may remain strong. In broad terms, these plans break down into three distinct alternative proposals. One would restore gold to its previous position of preeminence, another would dethrone gold completely by establishing a reserve currency as the principal reserve asset, and the third would centralize all reserve assets into one common unit of account.

The first proposal would restore gold to a dominant position as a reserve asset by increasing the official price of gold. This would have the effect of raising the value of existing gold holdings, both official and private, and the value of new gold production. Also, provided that the price rise was substantial enough so that speculation about a future increase was ruled out for some time, the value of official stocks would be further augmented by an inflow from private hoards. In this manner, the reserve position of the United States and some other countries would be greatly enhanced since the value of their reserve assets would increase while the value of their liabilities to foreigners would remain unchanged. This effect on reserves, it is believed, would not only alleviate the present constraint imposed upon the system due to a relative shortage of gold, but would also meet the expected inconsistency between the future demand for gold as a reserve asset and its future supply.

There are several principal economic arguments against this proposal. First, an increase in the price of gold, sizable enough to be creditable and to prevent expectations of a further price rise for some time, inevitably would create a large inflationary potential. This potential would exist because of the large paper profits realized by both official and private holders of gold. While some of these private profits might be safely sterilized through offsetting domestic monetary policies, it is felt that an inflationary potential would still exist because the large increase in official reserves would have an adverse bearing on balance of payments discipline. Second, the distributional effects of an increase in the price of gold would be arbitrary and inequitable, benefiting those countries which now hold or produce a large portion of the world's gold supply. The benefits of future reserve growth, it is felt, should be distributed on a less capricious basis. Finally, the possibility would exist that some time in the future another increase in the official price of gold would be necessary, thus setting the stage for another crisis involving the coexistence of gold as a reserve asset and gold as a speculative commodity. For these and other reasons, an increase in the official price of gold is generally not considered a satisfactory solution to the gold problem.

The second proposal would demonetize gold by having the United States terminate the present gold convertibility of the dollar. This move would have the effect, it is thought, of reducing the monetary preference for gold and eliminating the means by which a potentially massive and destabilizing shift out of dollars and into gold could occur. It would also have the effect, it is believed, of moving the world onto a formal dollar standard, because the intrinsic strength of the dollar in international trade and finance would dictate the establishment of the dollar as the principal international reserve asset. Some proponents of a formal dollar standard contend that under such a system, in which the supply of foreign held dollars would effectively serve to determine the foreign money supply, the United States theoretically would be able to conduct its domestic monetary policies in a manner free of balance of payments constraints and toward a goal of achieving monetary stability in the entire world economy.

The principal objection to this proposal is that many countries probably do not want a dollar standard imposed on them by the unilateral action of the United States. If countries were to accept a formal dollar standard, they would effectively be abandoning autonomy and independence in the conduct of their own domestic monetary affairs. In other words, many countries probably would object to giving the United States the freedom to conduct its monetary policy without regard to balance of payments considerations for fear that the United States might pursue policies inappropriate to their own individual needs. Because some countries probably would not join a formal dollar standard, it is thought that they would form a coalition against the dollar by pegging their currencies individually to gold and by allowing their currencies to float as a bloc against the dollar. In this event, restrictions undoubtedly would have to be imposed on trade and payments to maintain such a system. Therefore, it is claimed, the end result of suspending the gold convertibility of the dollar would be an undesirable and serious fragmentation of the international monetary structure and a stifling of world trade.

The third proposal would centralize all existing reserve assets—gold, reserve currencies, and SDR's—into a common pool by requiring countries to deposit or earmark their holdings of these assets with a designated international agency. These deposits would be denominated in a common unit of account and would be used to make official settlements between deficit and surplus countries according to an agreed formula related to the composition of their respective deposits. Future increases in world reserves would come about principally through the issuance of SDR's, which would be deposited with the pool and used in the same fashion as existing reserves. Countries would be allowed to retain working balances in reserve currencies, but the amount of reserve currencies initially deposited with the pool would become funded as a fixed fiduciary reserve not eligible to be increased in the future. Some variants of this basic proposal—of which there are many—would allow the international agency accepting reserve deposits to buy and sell gold in the private market in order to impart a degree of stability to the commodity value of gold. Advocates of the proposal to pool international reserve assets into one common unit of account believe that it would successfully meet the two interrelated problems regarding gold: an expected shortage of gold relative to monetary demands and a potential disruptive shift out of dollars and into gold by official holders.

While many observers feel that centralizing reserve assets into a common pool would be a logical solution to the problems posed by gold, the near-term implementation of such a proposal remains doubtful. One reason is that some minor technical problems are involved, such as defining and limiting the amount of working balances in foreign exchange that countries would retain. However, such problems conceivably could be resolved without too much difficulty. A more basic obstacle is that a sufficient number of countries apparently are not willing to relinquish their freedom of choice over the composition of their reserve assets, particularly in exchange for a unitary claim against an international agency. Historically, countries have had the freedom to apportion their reserve assets in various forms according to their assessed needs and economic policies. Loss of this freedom might be considered by many countries to be an infringement upon their national sovereignty.

CONCLUSION

None of the proposals discussed above to deal with the potential compositional problem posed by gold have been acceptable to most countries. The objections to these proposals essentially derive from two conflicting national goals. One is the desire of countries to establish a rational international monetary system designed to minimize disturbances to international trade and payments and to maximize economic welfare. The second is the desire of countries to protect their own economic autonomy and sovereignty in a world characterized by economic uncertainties and political conflict. Thus, countries are unwilling to restore gold to its previous position of preeminence through an increase in the official price of gold because experience has shown that such a system is not a viable or a rational one. On the other hand, most countries are not yet willing to establish a formal dollar standard or to centralize all existing reserve assets into a common pool to be administered by an international agency because both proposals would entail a surrender of national sovereignty in the monetary sphere.

In view of the unacceptability of these proposals, the most likely outcome over the near future is that countries will continue the present arrangements, making *ad hoc* changes when necessary to preserve the international monetary system. One possible change in the future might be that the attributes of a particular reserve asset, perhaps SDR's, would be altered through international negotiations in an attempt to equalize the attractiveness of all reserve assets. Another possibility might be that monetary authorities would voluntarily alter their reserve-asset preferences to prevent harmful strains in the monetary system. In any event, it seems reasonable to conclude that, until a greater measure of orderliness and security prevails in international monetary and political affairs, gold will continue to play an important role in the international monetary system. For this reason, it would appear vitally necessary from the standpoint of preserving the stability of the reserve asset structure and the monetary system in general that international financial consultation and cooperation be continued and strengthened in the years to come.

READING 49
An Essay on the Principle of Population
Thomas R. Malthus

The Malthusian doctrine is perhaps the best known of all economic ideas. The apparent implications of the gentle clergyman's theory are reason enough to call the discipline of economics "the dismal science." His contemporaries of the 1780s found the essay disturbing; current evidence provided by population and production statistics is even more disturbing. Unless a solution is found soon, Malthus' prediction that the world population would live at the subsistance level may be verified.

Guideposts for Thought While Reading

What possible policies might be developed to overcome the population problem with minimum restriction on individual freedoms?

I think I may fairly make two postulata.

First, That food is necessary to the existence of man.

Secondly, That the passion between the sexes is necessary, and will remain nearly in its present state.

Reprinted from Thomas R. Malthus, *An Essay on the Principle of Population*, Reeves and Turner, London, 8th edition, 1878, pp. 1–38.

These two laws ever since we have had any knowledge of mankind, appear to have been fixed laws of our nature; and, as we have not hitherto seen any alteration in them, we have no right to conclude that they will ever cease to be what they now are, without an immediate act of power in that Being who first arranged the system of the universe; and for the advantage of his creatures, still executes, according to fixed laws, all its various operations.

Assuming then, my postulata as granted, I say, that the power of population is indefinitely greater than the power in the earth to produce subsistence for man.

Population, when unchecked, increases in a geometrical ratio. Subsistence increases only in an arithmetical ratio. A slight acquaintance with numbers will shew the immensity of the first power in comparison of the second.

By that law of our nature which makes food necessary to the life of man, the effects of these two unequal powers must be kept equal.

This implies a strong and constantly operating check on population from the difficulty of subsistence. This difficulty must fall some where; and must necessarily be severely felt by a large portion of mankind.

Through the animal and vegetable kingdoms, nature has scattered the seeds of life abroad with the most profuse and liberal hand. She has been comparatively sparing in the room, and the nourishment necessary to rear them. The germs of existence contained in this spot of earth, with ample food, and ample room to expand in, would fill millions of worlds in the course of a few thousand years. Necessity, that imperious all pervading law of nature, restrains them within the prescribed bounds. The race of plants, and the race of animals shrink under this great restrictive law. And the race of man cannot, by any efforts of reason, escape from it. Among plants and animals its effects are waste of seed, sickness, and premature death. Among mankind, misery and vice.

AN EXAMPLE OF POPULATION INCREASE

I said that population, when unchecked, increased in a geometrical ratio; and subsistence for man in an arithmetical ratio.

Let us examine whether this position be just.

In the United States of America, where the means of subsistence have been more ample, the manners of the people more pure, and consequently the checks to early marriages fewer, than in any of the modern states of Europe, the population has been found to double itself in twenty-five years.

This ratio of increase, though short of the utmost power of population, yet as the result of actual experience, we will take as our rule; and say,

That population, when unchecked, goes on doubling itself every twenty-five years, or increases in a geometrical ratio.

IMPLICATIONS FOR THE WORLD

Taking the population of the world at any number, a thousand millions, for instance, the human species would increase in the ratio of—1, 2, 4, 8, 16, 32, 64, 128, 256, 512, &c. and subsistence as—1, 2, 3, 4, 5, 6, 7, 8, 9, 10, &c. In two centuries and a quarter, the population would be to the means of subsistence as 512 to 10: in three centuries as 4096 to 13; and in two thousand years the difference would be almost incalculable, though the produce in that time would have increased to an immense extent.

No limits whatever are placed to the productions of the earth; they may increase for ever and be greater than any assignable quantity; yet still the power of population being a power of a superior order, the increase of the human species can only be kept commensurate to the increase of the means of subsistence, by the constant operation of the strong law of necessity acting as a check upon the greater power.

READING 50
The French Galbraith
Paul A. Samuelson

Professor Paul A. Samuelson, the noted economist, comments in this article on the writings of Servan-Schreiber which warns Europeans against the invasion of American corporations. Samuelson notes that although the United States has gained prominence for its intellectual and scientific advances, the countries of western Europe, Japan, and other less-than-most-affluent nations have made unprecedented gains in productivity in the last decade, leading to balance-of-payments problems for the United States.

Guideposts for Thought While Reading
How does Samuelson account for the progress made by European countries? How might Servan-Schreiber's writing have similar effects in Europe to the writing of Thomas Paine in the United States?

"Fifteen years from now it is quite possible that the world's third greatest industrial power, just after the United States and Russia, will not be Europe, but *American industry in Europe.*"

With this blast of trumpets, J.-J. Servan-Schreiber begins his book, "The American Challenge," recently the best seller in France of any book, fiction or nonfiction. (Indeed, as will presently become clear, I am not sure in which category it belongs.) Its thesis is simple.

Military warfare has been succeeded by economic warfare, and the Americans are occupying Europe. Wellington's belief that Waterloo was won on the playing fields of Eton gives way to the new view that victory emerges from the seminars in management at the Harvard Business School. Were Stalin appraising the power of the Pope today, he would ask: "How many computers does he have?"

Europe is not given much more time. For "by extrapolating present trends, it seems clear we Europeans . . . [though] we will

Reprinted by permission of the publisher from "The French Galbraith," *Newsweek*, July 22, 1968, p. 73. Copyright Newsweek Inc., July 22, 1968.

grow even richer . . . will be overtaken and dominated, for the first time in our history, by a more advanced civilization."

THE TECHNOLOGICAL GAP

Who is Servan-Schreiber? Only 44, he served with the Free French Air Force; wrote an exposé of French atrocities in Algeria based on personal experience; and is editor of L'Express, the popular French newsweekly. He is one of Europe's "new men." According to Arthur Schlesinger Jr.'s foreword, " 'The American Challenge' may do for European unity very much what Thomas Paine's 'Common Sense' did for American independence." (Fortunately, as Samuel Johnson observed, in writing introductions one is "not under oath.")

The student riots and general strikes that have recently hit France postdate the writing of the book, posing new problems undreamed of in the author's philosophy. The American corporation invader may wish to bypass French soil as high-cost scorched earth, unreceptive to his industrial seed. Hence, it is well that the author has addressed himself to all of Europe—Germany and the Common Market countries generally—and not just to France.

All of Europe has become obsessed in recent years with the concept of "the technological gap." Nobel prizes go these days to Berkeley and not Berlin. The supersonic planes that only a fool would think to build are built here better. Industrious Americans edit the letters of Horace Walpole more elegantly than proper Englishmen can afford to do.

Worst of all is the "brain drain." Hitler's push of intellectuals to our shore has been succeeded by the pull of American paychecks. Now a Fermi or a Segrè can hope to coax Nobel prizes out of Berkeley equipment. The roads that lead to Rome also lead away from it.

THE BIG BONER

One hates to spoil a pretty story, but talk of the ruin of Europe is tommyrot. The amateur who shuns the conventional wisdom must take care lest he swallow the novel nonsense.

Assertion

"From the end of the cold war and the launching of the first sputnik, American power has made an unprecedented leap forward. It has undergone a violent and productive internal revolution."

Fact

From 1950 to 1968, Europe and Japan have *narrowed* the productivity gap between America and themselves at a rate unprecedented in all history. Theirs has truly been a "miracle sprint." Since sputnik, America's balance of international payments has chronically weakened. Effete Europe has run chronic surpluses, outselling us at home and abroad.

The miraculous progress of the less-than-most-affluent nations has been the big story of our times. No one predicted it. Not Marx. Not Spengler. Not Toynbee. Not even my old teacher Joseph Schumpeter.

That Japan outgrows Russia is perhaps not surprising. But who could have expected this of Austria and Italy? Even Britain, whom we all pity, has averaged faster growth in the postwar era than ever she did in Victoria's glorious days of free enterprise.

Servan-Schreiber correctly perceives that American workers have ceased to possess monopoly access to modern managerial methods and equipment. That Europe's living standards can grow faster than ours merely by imitating our technology is the corollary he misses. It is Europe's vanity, not her pocketbook, that is hurt by America's new supremacy in pure science.

Can 500,000 French book buyers be wrong? *Mais, oui.*

READING 51
Economic Revolution in the Soviet Union
Marshall I. Goldman

In this reading, Dr. Goldman, professor of economics at Wellesley College, analyzes the capitalistic economic reforms in Russia, which are often attributed to the efforts of Professor Evsei Liberman. The "revolutionary" introduction of the profits, interest, and rent concepts has revealed some surprising problems which the Russians had not known existed. Dr. Goldman concludes that Russian entrepreneurial creativity still will not match that of economies which allow private ownership of capital.

Guideposts for Thought While Reading

Why did the Russians decide to introduce the economic reforms? How did the computer fail to solve the Russian economic problems? How does the computer tend to "boss" the Russian economy? Why isn't the reform a move to full capitalism?

On the eve of the Fiftieth Anniversary of the Communist Revolution, the Russians have embarked on yet another economic revolution. With hardly a word about ideological purity, Premier Alexei Kosygin has announced that profits, sales and rate of return on investment will replace fulfillment of quotas as the main standards of success for every Soviet firm Moreover, Soviet managers will have to pay interest or capital charges for the capital they use. Profits will be divided up in a form of profit-sharing, and some enterprises will even have to pay rent. The economic reforms are matched in their significance, according to one Russian economist, A. Birman, only by the transition to N.E.P. in 1921 and the launching of the Five Year Plans in 1929-32. Clearly what the Soviets are currently attempting amounts to a repudiation of formerly sacred doctrines.

PROBLEMS IN THE RUSSIAN ECONOMY

Why have the Russians picked this juncture to make such basic structural changes? It is not an impetuous action. The call for reform originated with Professor Evsei Liberman in September 1962.[1] This was followed by more than three to four years of active debate and about two years of actual experimentation. During this period the majority of Russian economists came to acknowledge that there was a need for a drastic overhaul. They were obviously shocked when they saw their rate of economic growth fall badly during their Seven Year Plan from 1959 to '65. Most observers came to realize that a long-run upturn in the growth rate would depend on the resolution of some basic underlying problems. What was needed was improvement of day-to-day operating procedures as well as reform of the process by which longer-run changes were made. All of this would require a more productive use of the country's capital and the stimulation of innovation.

By the early 1960s, the Soviet economy had become a very complicated mechanism and was in serious danger of self-strangulation. The central planners were finding it harder and harder to make efficient decisions without help from factory managers. There were simply too many eventualities for Moscow to be able to plan for them. Yet the central planners continued to insist on detailed control over day-to-day operations. The factory managers were given little authority to deviate from quantitative plans, frequently drawn up a year or more in advance. Moreover, plant managers were often led to produce completely inappropriate items by a misdirected incentive system. The system contained no mechanism for responding to error. Often there was more concern about the bureaucrats than about the factory's customers. It was true that these methods had brought growth in the past, but increasingly output was unrelated to needs.

Growth and change had been obtained in the past largely by pressure and prodding. Because managers and planners were almost always submerged in their daily operating problems and had very short-term goals, the government had to launch campaign after campaign to shake the economy out of its deeply furrowed ruts. This was the only way to move industry to Siberia or force the growth of the chemical industry or the use of

[1] Many Westerners have come to refer to all that has followed as Libermanism.

natural gas. While such campaigns often accomplished their stated purpose, Soviet observers began to point out that they also involved considerable waste. Invariably all other activities would be halted in order to devote exclusive efforts to the campaign goal. Occasionally a second campaign would then be necessary to right the balance.

The Russians also discovered that their capital productivity had fallen badly. Capital was less productive because of the inefficient operating methods just described. The problem was intensified because capital was treated as a free good. There was no interest or repayment. Consequently, factory managers would try whenever possible to hoard capital, especially raw materials, for their productive needs. In this way they could insulate themselves from the transportation tie-ups and supply bottlenecks that were a hallmark of centralized planning. But in addition to input accumulations, many factories and stores have begun recently to find themselves with stocks of their output which have accumulated unexpectedly because of unsuitability or poor quality.

Partially as an effect and partially as a cause of all these factors, little innovation arose from within the factory itself. When the priorities were high enough, as on military and space projects, there could be impressive innovation. But lesser projects produced none of the instant innovation which seemed to characterize Western industry. When innovation came it was often too costly and too late. For instance, Russian officials now admit that during the five years required to work out the production problems of the Ural 4 computer and the Zaporozhets automobile, both had been made obsolete by production advances in the West.

What the Russians needed was some system that would provide them with self-generated flexibility and growth. Only with such a reform could they hope to improve their rate of economic growth, compete more effectively in foreign markets, improve the supply of consumer goods and ameliorate their inventory problem. It would not suffice just to know when to introduce new products; there also had to be some way of knowing when to drop old ones.

THE SEARCH FOR A SOLUTION

For a time many economists thought that the computer would solve all these problems. It was expected that advances in planning and computing technology would eventually make it possible to determine centrally all production, price investment and consumption decisions. The various unknowns would be thrown in and the necessary answers would come parading out in neat formation. Soon, however, even some of the computer specialists came to realize the impracticality of relying on the computer alone. There were simply too many unknowns for everything to be determined centrally.

Looking around, the Russians saw that in the Western countries, and even in a country like Jugoslavia, the market economy handled day-to-day transactions with a maximum of efficiency and a minimum or regulation. The Russians also saw that the problems of learning and responding were solved when the market economy was combined with something like the American system of competitive enterprise. Whatever shortcomings it may have, business enterprise in the United States responds to "feedback." In such a system, failure to so respond can lead to financial loss for some identifiable group or person. Consequently, managers have a great incentive to respond. The Russians realized that if their problems were to be solved, they would need similar responsive effort and flexibility in their economy.

In September 1965, Premier Kosygin announced that the reorganization would gradually be extended to the whole economy. He ordered the adoption of a slightly revised set of gauges which in addition to profits included rate of return on capital, interest, capital charges and rent. Market research and advertising were also to be more used. To say the least, such economic forms are highly unorthodox by Soviet standards. None the less, as of January 1966, Soviet managers in 43 major factories were to be judged on the fulfillment of sales or profits targets and the rate of return on capital (profits as a percent of capital). These factory managers will have to deduct interest at a rate of .5 to 2 percent on any bank loans they may have. No longer will sums of capital be allocated to them as a gift from the budget for capital already borrowed. These capital charges are to average 6 percent of the enterprise's fixed and working capital. The interest charge and capital charge are to be supplemented by a rent charge, to vary so that firms and mines more favorably located than others will not earn undue profits. All of these charges must be deducted from profits before premiums can be paid or the rate of return calculated.

In a further effort to increase flexibility, Soviet authorities are introducing new supply procedures. Wherever possible, enterprises are authorized to work out their own purchase and sale agreements without the interference of ministerial authorities. This will ultimately mean the increased use of salesmen, trade fairs, marketing research and advertising. If stocks of merchandise are made readily available in local warehouses, managers should have less reason to hoard supplies in their own private warehouses. Ultimately, it is thought, this could lead to the end of centralized allocations for all but the highest priority goods.

The rate of return is to be used in conjunction with either profits or sales as the second criterion of success. Rate of return is now defined as profit in relation to capital, as Liberman had suggested. Previously when rate of return was discussed, it referred to profit as a percent of cost.

With the new criteria the manager has a strong incentive to cut back on his capital stock. Anything the manager does to reduce the denominator in the profit-to-capital ratio will presumably lead to a more efficient use of capital and a reduction of inventories. But by reducing his capital, the rate of return is further improved because interest and capital deductions will be lower, and therefore profit (the numerator) will be higher. If this curbs the squandering of capital, then capital productivity will be increased and an important goal of the reform will have been achieved.

The net profit that remains after the deduction of interest, capital charge and rent determines not only the rate of return but also the amount that is available for the discretionary use of the factory manager. The manager is entitled to put a specified portion of net profit into three funds—the Incentive Fund, the Cultural and Housing Fund and the Development Fund, all three of them designed to promote the firm's productivity.

Since the size of these funds depends on the enterprise's profitability, they are expected to stimulate the workers' interest in holding down costs more than in the past when extra pay and bonuses ("premiums") depended on the quantities produced. In the new system, fulfillment of targets remains an important factor in calculating the amounts that can be put into the fund, but over-fulfillment is rewarded at a lower rate. This is the reverse of former procedures. According to Liberman, this will stimulate plant directors to seek higher targets in the beginning and not hold back on their efforts.

Managers, engineers and the like will get all their bonuses from the incentive fund, but for the blue-collar workers there will also be some payments from the old wage fund, so that the worker is not penalized if his performance is good but the enterprise fails to be profitable for reasons beyond his control. The size of the bonuses varies from industry to industry and differs according to the situation of the enterprise, but there is a formula that puts a limit on the amount of profits that can be spent this way, in order to be sure that wages do not increase faster than productivity.

The Development Fund is a particularly important one, designed to encourage innovation and investment by the firm itself. The share of profits that can be put into this fund is related to the size of the capital of the enterprise; yearly amortization charges are added to it and also proceeds from the sale of old or surplus capital equipment. Ultimately as much as one-fifth of all the capital investments made in the Soviet Union may come out of the Development Funds of individual enterprises. Liberman sees a connection between this kind of decentralization of investment and the direct incentive payments to workers and managers, because the Development Fund, by increasing the importance of self-financing for each enterprise, gives managers much more control than they had in the past. Moreover, the use of bonuses from the other funds and cultural and housing benefits are also to a considerable extent under their control.

IMPLICATIONS OF THE REFORM

No one among Soviet officials pretends that implementation of the Reform will be easy. As Kosygin remarked to the Supreme Soviet, there are two immediate problems: poor pricing and bureaucratic resistance. Existing Soviet prices do not adequately reflect the true value of the product. Wholesale prices have not been thoroughly revised since 1955. Supply-and-demand relationships among different commodities have changed markedly since then. By producing those items which have unduly high prices, factory managers will be able to make unintended profits on an undesired assortment of goods. This could easily provoke the reintroduction of detailed controls.

Kosygin also mentioned that there has been resistance to the Reform by those who fear it will undermine their own positions. "A certain conservatism and lack of initiative," he asserted, "are sometimes displayed in trying to solve a number of matters connected with the operation of the economic reforms." There has been foot-dragging by the ministries of the industries affected. Kosygin declared: "The ministries should not demand an excessive amount of reference notes and information of various kinds from the enterprises." To the extent that ministerial intervention limits a firm's ability to deal through direct contracts, it eliminates the possibility of feedback.

Of course it is not just the bureaucrats who oppose the change. Like their counterparts all over the world, many Soviet managers fear the effects of competition and are reluctant to abandon the relatively tranquil climate of fixed markets and stable production quotas in which they have operated. Finally, like the workers in the movie "The Man in the White Suit," there are many Soviet workers who recognize that increased efficiency will mean layoffs and unemployment.

Some Soviet officials feel that the new interest rate and capital charge will hold back the introduction of new capital. This indicates a misunderstanding of the function of capital charges. A charge for capital should not frustrate investment if the proposed equipment is productive enough to make possible repayment of the capital charge. If it is not productive enough, then the investment should not be made in the first place. It was just because of the absence of such a restraint that capital has been consumed so wastefully in the past. However, just in case the managers do hold back too much on investment, senior officials have the power to exempt new capital from the capital charge until the new equipment is operating at full capacity.

To the surprise of some, the Reform is also creating problems where it was thought none existed. The introduction of economic guides like interest and rent has created a schizophrenic split between Russia's domestic and foreign-trade interests. With their new economic methods, the Russians have begun to reevaluate their production possibilities. They have discovered that they have not engaged in the most productive kind of foreign trade. Now that they are beginning to recognize the impact of rent and interest, they find that they have seriously underestimated the substantial costs of the capital and land resources involved in expanding the production of their raw materials. As a result they have complained publicly and repeatedly that they have been *subsidizing* their East European allies with such items as oil, iron ore and coal. Naturally this comes as a shock to the East Europeans who have long complained above Soviet *overpricing* of raw materials.

THE COMPUTER IS BOSS

However, the Russians will have to face the uncertainty of whether the Reform will be basic enough to make it possible for the risk-taking manager to coexist with the computer. In the United States, the computer and the methods which it makes possible such as input-output and linear programing are like any other business tools. Their main function is to provide additional information for the ultimate decision-maker. But in private competitive enterprise, the manager generally decides to accept or reject the findings of such devices in light of his own independent judgment.

Because all industry in the U.S.S.R. is state-owned, the computer is often viewed in a different light there. State managers must always stand ready to make a public accounting of their actions. Therefore they in turn want someone or something to provide them with authority to act. If there is written authorization to do something, then the person is free to act because he knows that he will be able to point the finger at someone or something else. In such an environment, the use of the computer is considered particularly desirable since it can provide justification or authorization for managerial action.

But there is the danger that the solutions offered by the computer will be viewed not as possibilities but as binding solutions. Just because the answer is from the impersonal computer and just because it is in writing, the manager opens himself up to criticism if he takes another course of action. It will be interesting to see if the Reform will make Soviet managers independent enough so they will feel free to use the computer instead of being used by it. If not, it will be found that one form of inflexibility has been substituted for another.

Administrative efficiency, in the final analysis, is dependent on more than the availability of hardware; there must also be well-trained managers. Heretofore the Soviets have used production engineers who have been trained to produce in large quantities and to secure unavailable components. Will it be possible to revise the whole concept of managerial administration so that two generations of quantity-oriented production specialists can be converted into quality-conscious innovators? As the Minister of Education has acknowledged, such a change can hardly take place overnight. In recognition of the urgent need to develop a new breed of manager, open admiration is now expressed for such managerial hatcheries as the Harvard Business School. In fact, a Russian exchange student is now enrolled in

Cambridge learning the technique of teaching American business administration.

WILL INVENTION AND INNOVATION IMPROVE?

Assuming that managerial practices can be improved, will this also stimulate the flow of innovation? Theoretically, the Russian manager should be able to operate as efficiently and be as inventive as his counterpart in the large American corporation. The Reform, with its emphasis on sales, profit and rate of return, is much the same incentive system that is used by such large American corporations as DuPont and General Electric. Similarly, these American corporations permit decentralized investment within certain limits, just as will now be the case in the U.S.S.R. Consequently, like their American counterparts, the new Soviet enterprises should now be able to promote numerous important innovations and move the inventions from their laboratories to the production floor.

Innovation in the United States, however, does not originate solely in the larger corporations. In fact, there are many who argue that much of the American leadership in innovation comes not from the larger corporation, but from the small private enterprise. Despite the growth of large corporate research laboratories, a large proportion of the basic discoveries in the United States continue to come from small firms, which sometimes succeed so well that they turn into large corporations themselves —like Polaroid, Itek or Xerox. It is hard to see how the Russians even with the Reform will be able to avail themselves of this particular kind of innovation.

The phenomenon of the small and creative entrepreneur is possible only where there is private ownership of capital. The man with the idea must be able to solicit financial support for his project from a wide variety of financial sources. It is not enough to have inventors with ideas that are advanced for their day; there must also be a wide variety of financiers around to support them. The more sources of capital there are, the more likely it is that an investor will be found who can appreciate the worth of a particular investment. When the state controls all the society's capital, the sources of capital are sharply reduced. Normally there will be no more than one decision-maker and no court of appeal. If the state's capital controller happens to lack the vision to appreciate a particular invention, no matter how brilliant the discovery may be, it will not move past the idea stage. Innovation also requires a willingness to take a risk and lose. The stewardship of the state's funds, however, generates extreme conservatism, hardly a desirable environment for promoting innovation.

In partial recognition of the handicap associated with state control of capital, the Reform does permit some decentralized investment by the enterprise in the hope that inventors will be able to seek out alternative capital support. Yet even if the single government veto over capital is abolished, there may be a need for something more. To be successful, the Reform must touch off a competitive spark among the country's managers. Whatever its limitations, the phenomenon of competition in the West plays a basic role in stimulating the search for new and better processes and products. While the Soviets are trying to emulate this spirit, it is questionable whether they will be successful in generating it at the enterprise level. There have been some very dynamic nationalized enterprises like Volkswagen. But such firms have made their mark in competitive coexistence with private enterprises. So far it has been very difficult to ignite that inventive spark when all the enterprises in a country are owned by the state.

Radical as the Reform is, it does not herald the advent of capitalism. As the Chinese have been quick to note, however, the use of such tools of the marketplace as profit, interest and rent certainly is not a reaffirmation of Marxism. What is in progress seems to be a determined effort to improve the effectiveness of a form of state capitalism. The dynamic operation of a massive and complex industrial system dictates the use of certain universal techniques. The Russians do not have too much choice; it is like trying to go up the down escalator. As their economy becomes more complicated, it becomes harder and harder to move forward at a rapid rate. Without the Reform, their economy may well be carried backward. With the Reform, they hope it will be able to move forward—at the very least, hold its own.

71 72 73 74 7 6 5 4 3 2 1